The Early Church

THE I.B.TAURIS HISTORY OF THE CHRISTIAN CHURCH

GENERAL EDITOR: G.R. EVANS

The Early Church
Morwenna Ludlow, University of Exeter

The Church in the Early Middle Ages
G.R. Evans, University of Cambridge

The Church in the Later Middle Ages
Norman Tanner, Gregorian University, Rome

Early Modern Christianity
Patrick Provost-Smith, Harvard University

The Church in the Long Eighteenth Century
David Hempton, Harvard University

The Church in the Nineteenth Century
Frances Knight, University of Wales, Lampeter

The Church in the Modern Age
Jeremy Morris, University of Cambridge

THE I.B.TAURIS HISTORY OF THE CHRISTIAN CHURCH

The Early Church

Morwenna Ludlow

I.B. TAURIS
LONDON · NEW YORK

Published in 2009 by I.B.Tauris & Co. Ltd
6 Salem Road, London W2 4BU
175 Fifth Avenue, New York, NY 10010
www.ibtauris.com

Distributed in the United States and Canada Exclusively by Palgrave Macmillan
175 Fifth Avenue, New York, NY 10010

Vol 1: *The Early Church*   978 1 84511 366 7
Vol 2: *The Church in the Early Middle Ages*   978 1 84511 150 2
Vol 3: *The Church in the Later Middle Ages*   978 1 84511 438 1
Vol 4: *Early Modern Christianity*   978 1 84511 439 8
Vol 5: *The Church in the Long Eighteenth Century*   978 1 84511 440 4
Vol 6: *The Church in the Nineteenth Century*   978 1 85043 899 1
Vol 7: *The Church in the Modern Age*   978 1 84511 317 9

A full CIP record for this book is available from the British Library

Typeset in Adobe Caslon Pro by A. & D. Worthington, Newmarket, Suffolk
Printed and bound in Great Britain by CPI Antony Rowe, Chippenham

THE I.B.TAURIS HISTORY OF THE CHRISTIAN CHURCH

Since the first disciples were sent out by Jesus, Christianity has been of its essence a missionary religion. That religion has proved to be an ideology and a subversive one. Profoundly though it became 'inculturated' in the societies it converted, it was never syncretistic. It had, by the twentieth century, brought its own view of things to the ends of the earth. The Christian Church, first defined as a religion of love, has interacted with Judaism, Islam and other world religions in ways in which there has been as much warfare as charity. Some of the results are seen in the tensions of the modern world, tensions which are proving very hard to resolve – not least because of a lack of awareness of the history behind the thinking which has brought the Church to where it is now.

In the light of that lack, a new history of the Christian Church is badly needed. There is much to be said for restoring to the general reader a familiarity with the network of ideas about what the Church 'is' and what it should be 'doing' as a vessel of Christian life and thought. This series aims to be both fresh and traditional. It will be organized so that the boundary-dates between volumes fall in some unexpected places. It will attempt to look at its conventional subject matter from the critical perspective of the early twenty-first century, where the Church has a confusing myriad of faces. Behind all these manifestations is a rich history of thinking, effort and struggle. And within it, at the heart of matters, is the Church. *The I.B.Tauris History of the Christian Church* seeks to discover that innermost self through the layers of its multiple manifestations over twenty centuries.

SERIES EDITOR'S PREFACE

Against the background of global conflict involving interfaith resentments and misunderstandings, threatening 'religious wars' on a scale possibly unprecedented in history, Christians and the Christian Church are locked in internal disputes. On 2 November 2003, a practising homosexual was made a bishop in the Episcopal Church in the United States, America's 'province' of the Anglican Communion. This was done in defiance of the strong opinion in other parts of the 'Communion' that if it happened Anglicanism would fall apart into schism. A few years earlier there had been similar rumblings over the ordination of women to ministry in the same Church. A century before that period, the Roman Catholic Church had pronounced all Anglican ordination to the priestly or episcopal ministry to be utterly null and void because of an alleged breach of communion and continuity in the sixteenth century. And the Orthodox Churches watched all this in the secure conviction that Roman Catholic, Anglican and all other Christian communities were not communions at all because they had departed from the truth as it had been defined in the ecumenical Councils of the first few centuries. Orthodoxy alone was orthodox. Even the baptism of other Christians was of dubious validity.

Those heated by the consecration of a 'gay' bishop spoke on the one side of faithfulness to the teaching of the Bible and on the other of the leading of the Holy Spirit into a new world which knew no discrimination. Yet both the notion of faithfulness to Scripture and the idea that Jesus particularly wanted to draw the outcasts and disadvantaged to himself have a long and complex history which makes it impossible to make either statement in simple black-and-white terms.

One of the most significant factors in the frightening failures of communication and goodwill which make daily headlines is a loss of contact with the past on the part of those taking a stand on one side or another of such disagreements. The study of 'history' is fashionable as this series is launched, but the colourful narrative of past lives and episodes does not necessarily make familiar the patterns of thought and assumption in the minds of those involved. A modern history of the Church must embody that awareness in every sinew. Those embattled in disputes within the Church and disputes involving Christian and other-faith communities have tended to take their stand on principles they claim to be of eternal validity, and to represent the will of God. But as they appear in front of television cameras or speak to journalists the accounts they give – on either side – frequently reflect a lack of knowledge of the tradition they seek to protect or to challenge.

The creation of a new history of the Church at the beginning of the third millennium is an ambitious project, but it is needed. The cultural, social and political dominance of Christendom in what we now call 'the West' during the first two millennia made the Christian Church a shaper of the modern world in respects which go far beyond its strictly religious influence. Since the first disciples were sent out to preach the Gospel by Jesus, Christianity has been of its essence a missionary religion. It took the faith across the world in a style which has rightly been criticized as 'imperialist'. Christianity has proved to be an ideology and a subversive one. Profoundly though it became 'inculturated' in the societies converted, it was never syncretistic. It had, by the twentieth century, brought its own view of things to the ends of the earth. The Christian Church, first defined as a religion of love, has interacted with Judaism, Islam and the other world religions in ways in which there has been as much warfare as charity. We see some of the results in tensions in the modern world which are now proving very hard to resolve, not least because of the sheer failure of awareness of the history of the thinking which has brought the Church to where it is now.

Such a history has of course purposes more fundamental, more positive, more universal, but no less timely. There may not be a danger of the loss of the full picture while the libraries of the world and its historic buildings and pictures and music preserve the evidence. But the connecting thread in living minds is easily broken. There is much to be said for restoring as familiar to the general reader, whether Christian or not, a command of the sequence and network of ideas about what the Church *is* and what it should be *doing* as a vessel of Christian thought and life.

This new series aims, then, to be both new and traditional. It is organized so that the boundary-dates between volumes come in some unexpected places. It attempts to look at the conventional subject matter of histories of the Church from the vantage-point of the early twenty-first century, where the Church has confusingly many faces: from Vatican strictures on the use of birth-control and the indissolubility of marriage, and the condemnation of outspoken German academic theologians who challenge the Churches' authority to tell them what to think and write, to the enthusiasm of Black Baptist congregations in the USA joyously affirming a faith with few defining parameters. Behind all these variations is a history of thought and effort and struggle. And within, at the heart of matters, is the Church. It is to be discovered in its innermost self through the layers of its multiple manifestations over twenty centuries. That is the subject of this series.

Contents

For Peter and Carole

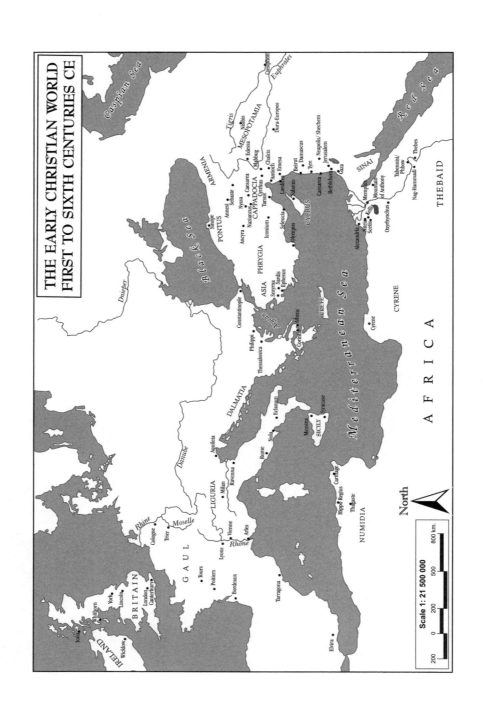

THE EARLY CHRISTIAN WORLD
FIRST TO SIXTH CENTURIES CE

Caspian Sea

Red Sea

Black Sea

Mediterranean Sea

AFRICA

North

Scale 1: 21 500 000

200   0   200   500   800 km.

IRELAND
Wicklow
Iona
Whithorn
York
Lincoln
London, Canterbury
BRITAIN

GAUL
Cologne
Trier
Moselle
Rhone
Vienne
Lyons
Arles
Rhone
Tours
Poitiers
Bordeaux

Tarragona

Elvira

LIGURIA
Milan
Aquileia
Ravenna
Rome
Nola
Eclanum

DALMATIA

SICILY
Messina
Syracuse

Carthage
Hippo Regius
Thagaste
NUMIDIA

Danube

Dnieper

Thessalonica
Philippi
Constantinople

Athens
Corinth
ACHAEA

CYRENE
Cyrene

Sinope
PONTUS
Amnes
Ancyra
PHRYGIA
Iconium
ASIA
Smyrna
Sardis
Ephesus
Olympus

ARMENIA
Sebaste
Caesarea
Nazianzus
Nyssa
CAPPADOCIA
Tarsus
Orrhus

Tigris
MESOPOTAMIA
Edessa
Nisibis
Ctesiphon
Euphrates
Dura-Europos
Mabbug
Chalcis
Antioch
Seleucia
Selucia
CYPRUS
Salamis

Laodicea
Beirut
Damascus
Tyre
Neapolis/Shechem
Jerusalem
Bethlehem
Caesarea
Gaza
Emesa

SINAI
Memphis
Nitria
Scetis
Alexandria
Nilly
Oxyrhynchus
Mountain of Anthony

Nag-Hammadi
Tabennisi/Phbow
Thebes
THEBAID

Preface

This book is an attempt to tell the story of the early Christian Church in a way which is clear and readable, whilst doing justice to the complexity and diversity of Christianity in the first six centuries CE. This is not an easy task. Frequently, histories of this period try to create a simple narrative of development, steering a direct path through the period despite all the awkward obstacles in the way. Sometimes the motive for such a narrative is pedagogical – to give a clear structure to the bewildering range of evidence. Often, an additional motive is to construct the history of the early Church in such a way as to validate ideas of what the Church is today: thus some histories will emphasize the role of bishops and the sacraments; others will stress the use of Scripture and the rule of faith; still others will point to the development of Christian asceticism. Whatever the motives, however, the effect of composing too simplistic a story of the early Church is that it flattens out the contours of what was a very bumpy and winding road. It can have the tendency to suggest that the end result was somehow inevitable and it can thus fail to take seriously other forms and expressions of Christianity which were held by minorities or which did not survive. More insidiously, it can obscure the way in which early Christianity was deeply indebted to its Jewish origins and continued to be influenced by the intellectual and cultural legacy of pagan Greece and Rome long after the Empire was officially Christian.

Of course, there are also dangers of trying to avoid too easy a narrative structure. The material can become difficult to understand or interpret. The reader can fail to see any connection between the Church of the past and that of the present. More subtly, the author can be accused – with some justification – of stressing the variety of early Christianity in order to defend a more inclusive and diverse understanding of the Church in the present day.

Aware of these difficulties, I have tried in this book to write good history: that is, I have tried to steer a path between the mere accumulation of evidence and the construction of an over-simplified narrative. I have assumed neither that the development of the Church was a purely secular process, nor that it can be explained entirely in theological terms. Finally the book has tried to do justice to the range of Christian beliefs and practices, whilst pointing to the factors which held them together as being distinctively Christian. At root, it does assume that the kaleidoscopic variety of early Christianity can be viewed through a single lens.

What *kind* of diversity characterized the early Church? Most obviously, perhaps, Christianity changed over time: the beliefs and practices of Christians in the sixth century were different from those in the first, perhaps most markedly in respect to Christianity's relationship to Judaism. But changes over a briefer time-scale can also be identified: for example, the increasing institutionalization of the Church in its first decades, or the changes that occurred with Constantine's adoption of Christianity in the fourth century. Besides temporal diversity, however, there was geographic diversity: although Christian communities were often remarkably well connected through letters and travel, nevertheless local traditions of belief and worship proved to be very important. For example, the second-century controversy over the date of Easter (the 'Quartodeciman' controversy) and the fifth-century debates about the relation between Christ's humanity and divinity were each fuelled by strong regional theological loyalties. Thirdly, there was often a variety of opinions and habits apparent even within local communities. This is evident, for example, in the tensions caused by the followers of Marcion and Valentinus in Rome in the second century and the effect of the Arian controversies in Milan and Antioch in the fourth.

There were, then, different expressions of Christianity, yet believers recognized that those who identified themselves as 'Christian' should be part of the same Church. The disagreement over the date of Easter was painful precisely because it was felt to be wrong that Christians in different parts of the Mediterranean world were celebrating Easter at different times: there should be one feast for the one community. Varieties of practice and belief within cities or individual congregations caused even more tension: if Valentinus and Marcion had not regarded themselves as Christians alongside others in Rome they would not have presented such a threat to those who argued against them. It was through such arguments that Christians in this period developed the idea that there had to be limits to the variety of belief within Christianity. Out of reasoned controversy came, for example, the systematic exposition of the doctrines of the Trinity and the nature of Christ.

The 'definitions' of the Church councils on these matters can perhaps be best understood not as defining the *doctrines as such*, but as defining the *boundaries* of acceptable Christian belief. Although Christians within the mainstream Church were agreed that it was necessary to have unity on some matters (for example, that Jesus Christ was both human and divine), it was often unclear how much flexibility there could be about the meaning of such terms as 'human' and 'divine'. Furthermore, there were many theological topics on which disagreement was either willingly accepted or at least tolerated. Although the Church Fathers often wrote about unity of belief, the reality was more like an acceptable variety of belief.

The identity of the early Church was by no means exclusively bound up with questions of belief – practice was also hugely important. For this reason, this book has tried to give due weight to aspects of Christian life such as liturgy (especially baptism and Eucharist), the use of Scripture, the response to persecution, the veneration of saints and martyrs, and asceticism. Often, faith and practice influenced each other. For example, the very widespread early use of a three-fold formula in baptism – 'in the name of the Father and of the Son and of the Holy Spirit' – influenced the development of the doctrine of the Trinity; conversely, arguments against the Arians about the doctrine of the Trinity had an impact on liturgy, since they condemned those who did not use the three-fold formula in baptism. Similarly, the question of Christ's relationship to the Father was intertwined with the question of whether one could properly pray to Christ, or whether one should pray to the Father through the mediation of Christ. Just as with beliefs, there were variations in Christian practice over time and space, but also sometimes differences within communities. Congregations at the beginning of this period were divided about the extent to which Jewish traditional practices should be continued; later on, churches were divided over the propriety of venerating Mary as the 'mother of God'.[1] Nevertheless, one can say that all Christian communities in this period depended to a greater or lesser extent on these kinds of practice for their identity as Christian.

For the historian, who must examine those Christians whom many other Christians thought to be beyond the pale, 'early Christianity' as a historical phenomenon should also of course include these 'unacceptable' or heretical varieties of practice and belief. For this reason, my account has tried to take seriously the claim of people like Marcion, Arius and Nestorius to represent Christian truth – whilst also explaining why the mainstream Christian Church rejected them. Despite the great diversity of faith and practice amongst those who called themselves Christians, it still makes sense to talk of 'Christianity' as one phenomenon. Even though there was not a clear set of identical practices or beliefs which all Christian congregations shared (there was no one creed, no one liturgy, not even the same Bible), nevertheless there were enough overlapping resemblances between them to enable one to identify them as Christian.[2] Wittgenstein famously observed that one could not isolate a list of properties which define a particular game as a game, but one could recognize a set of overlapping characteristics or family resemblances which enable us to use the same word 'game' for a wide variety of practices.[3] Similarly, one can use the term 'Christian' for a surprisingly diverse collection of people.

The idea of 'family resemblances' is particularly appropriate for early Christian communities who traced their inheritance of the Gospel back to the original eyewitnesses of Christ's life, death and resurrection. Despite their often radically different interpretations of the Gospel the Gnostics and Valentinians, for example, claimed to trace their faith back to the Apostles, just as other Christians did. Their opponents, of course, denied that such groups were the true 'descendants' of the Apostles and in effect accused them of being illegitimate offspring. The concept of 'family resemblances' also helps us understand the way in which the fiercest arguments can be between those who share a common origin, but who dispute the true ownership of their inheritance, or challenge the way the inheritance has been used. Thus, much of the heat generated by the Trinitarian and Christological controversies was due to the sincere conviction of each side that they were the true inheritors and interpreters of the Christian tradition ('tradition' here including Scripture).

In the earlier chapters of the book I often refer to Christian 'churches' or 'congregations' in order to emphasize the lack of institutional unity. Towards the end of the period, it makes more sense to talk about 'the Christian Church', since successive Christian councils had made decisions about matters of Church organization, practice and doctrine and had declared various individuals or groups to be outside 'the Church'. In this period, the councils considered to be 'ecumenical', i.e. applying to all Christians, were those of Nicaea (325), Constantinople (381), Ephesus (431), Chalcedon (451) and Constantinople (553). But even the Church as defined by adherence to these councils was not as unified as one might expect; furthermore, those 'outside' the Church according to the definition of these councils were not necessarily as different as one might expect. There is still, for example, controversy about who was being accused in the condemnations of 'Origenism' in 553 and whether they were rightly condemned. Furthermore, there is a strong feeling amongst many Christians today that there should be more consideration in the west towards those Oriental churches who, for various complicated reasons, did not accept the Council of Chalcedon in 451.

In steering my path through the first five to six centuries of Christianity, I have chosen a basic chronological structure. But within this I have stressed different themes and places. The reader should not imagine that I

think that Rome ceased to be important after the second century, nor that
Antioch only began to be a significant Christian centre in the fifth. Similarly, Christian asceticism was important throughout this period, not just
in the fourth century. I have aimed to highlight such cities and themes at
points in the narrative where they will illuminate my account. In particular,
I hope that I have given some sense of place and cultural context, which is
often missing from accounts of the early Church, particularly those which
focus on the development of doctrine.

I have quoted early Christian writers quite frequently in an effort to
convey the vitality of their style, but I have tried to use translations which
are both quite recent and as accessible as possible. A chapter-by-chapter
bibliography of the sources of these primary texts is included at the end of
the book. I have otherwise kept notes and references relatively minimal,
giving references to ideas which are controversial or of particular interest, rather than giving evidence for every point. In order to encourage as
wide a readership as possible I have tried to refer to those books which will
be most accessible and I have therefore chosen to restrict my references to
literature in English. I am very aware that any book of this kind stands on
the shoulders of previous scholarship and I here gratefully acknowledge the
work of those many scholars in my field from whose work I have benefited
and whose ideas have filtered into my own teaching and writing.

In Chapter 1 I discuss the character of the early Christian communities
in the first few decades after the death of Christ. The chapter examines
the factors which were common to the early Christians, for example their
fundamental monotheism, their beliefs about Jesus, their use of baptism
and community meals. It also deals with the development of leadership in
the Church and the gradual formation of the Christian canon of Scripture.
The issue of Christianity's relationship to Judaism is also considered.

Chapter 2 begins by assessing the Christian experience of persecution
in the second century, using as evidence some first-person accounts (both
Christian and pagan) and some third-person Christian accounts of early
martyrs. The rest of Chapter 2 together with Chapter 3 contains an account
of three kinds of early Christian writing which need to be understood in the
light of the Christian experience of persecution: that is, apology (defences
of Christianity against pagans), works written against Jews or 'Judaizers',
and works written against Christian heretics. Here I focus in particular on
the thought of Justin Martyr, Marcion, Valentinus, Irenaeus and Melito.

In Chapters 2 and 3 the geographical focus is on Rome; in Chapter 4
this moves east to Alexandria and south to Carthage. With Antioch, these
were the great cities of the early Roman Empire. Two sketches of Alexandria and Carthage form the backdrop to a more detailed discussion of two

great theologians, Origen and Tertullian. The emphasis in this chapter is
partly on understanding their theology and explaining how they tried to
solve various problems. But attention is also paid to the kinds of works
they wrote, in order to emphasize how, even at this relatively early stage,
educated Christians were beginning to develop a self-confident and distinct
Christian literary culture.

Chapter 5 deals with one of the important turning-points in the relationship between 'Church and Empire': the final phases of persecution and the
rise to power of Constantine. It concludes with an account of the controversy surrounding Arius and his doctrine of Christ, including a discussion
of the first ecumenical council, called by Constantine at Nicaea in 325.

The fourth century was an extraordinarily fertile time for Christian
theology, particularly in the east. Chapter 6 looks at this period from the
perspective of doctrinal theology, with a particular focus on Athanasius
(from Alexandria), the Cappadocian theologians Basil of Caesarea, Gregory
of Nazianzus and Gregory of Nyssa, and finally Ephrem, who worked in
Nisibis and Edessa at the eastern borders of the Roman Empire and who
wrote in Syriac. Prompted by the idea that all the theologians in Chapter 6 thought that beliefs about Christ were intimately connected with the
practice of discipleship and the imitation of Christ, Chapter 7 deals with
early Christian asceticism. The distinction between doctrinal theology and
devotional or 'spiritual' writing is an artificial one in this period and is
particularly thin in a writer like Ephrem. Chapter 7 looks at the motivations
behind the Christian ascetic life and its development in individual (hermit)
and community-based forms in various parts of the Empire. Again there is
an emphasis on the idea that although there were many family resemblances
between different Christian ascetic traditions, there were also huge variations in practice. For example, the chapter discusses the dramatic privations
of the Syrian pillar ascetics and the more moderate, although undoubtedly
still rigorous, Cappadocian monasticism. There were very different degrees
of ascetic seclusion, ranging from almost complete isolation in the desert,
through semi-organized groups of hermits, to monastic communities. There
were even married men and women who stayed at home and fitted ascetic
discipline into the warp and weft of their daily lives. The chapter concludes
with an assessment of some bishops who combined a profound commitment
to ascetic practice with a very public and city-based life in the service of the
Church.

Chapter 8 begins with setting one of those bishops – Ambrose – in
context in the city of Milan. This brief study forms the basis for a more
detailed examination of Augustine, who identified his time in and around
Milan while Ambrose was bishop as the pivotal moment in his life. Augus-

tine's theology is studied from several different perspectives, with the aim of trying to clarify his main themes and identifying his most important texts. Chapter 9 has a similar structure, moving from a sketch of Antioch at the time of John Chrysostom to a historical and theological study of the controversies over the nature of Christ which dominated debate in the churches of Antioch, Alexandria and Constantinople in the middle decades of the fifth century. It concludes with a discussion of the Council of Chalcedon and the Christology of Leo, Bishop of Rome.

In the fifth century, the stability of the Roman Empire suffered greatly from the growing strength of 'barbarian' tribes (many of whom were Christian, albeit Arian). The very varied impact of these incursions on different parts of the Empire and the very uneven acceptance of the decisions of Chalcedon among Christian congregations, means that it is very difficult – indeed undesirable – to draw a neat and tidy conclusion to this period of Christian history. The final chapter therefore assesses the state of the Empire and the state of Christianity in the sixth century, returning to the theme with which the book began: the 'contained diversity' of Christianity, impossible to define by a set of clearly defined doctrines or rituals, but possible to identify through a series of closely intertwined family resemblances. By the end of the sixth century, although there were marked differences and many painful separations, the Christian family existed as the many communities ultimately gathered together by their faith in and their commitment to follow Jesus Christ.

This book represents a step away from most of my previous writing and in its preparation I have had a great deal of help, for which I am most grateful. First, I should particularly like to thank the series editor, Gillian Evans, who persuaded me to write the book and who encouraged me, with a great deal of patience, through my various hesitations on the way. My editor at I.B.Tauris, Alex Wright, has also been a source of much enthusiasm and energy.

I am grateful to Andrew Gregory and David Taylor for advice on general themes and bibliography at a very early stage of the project. Over the past years, I have benefited immensely from the wisdom of John Barton and Christopher Tuckett on matters biblical, although I have not consulted them on any specific aspect of this book. Several of my colleagues at Exeter have read various chapters and commented very helpfully on them: many thanks to David Horrell, Alastair Logan and Mike Higton (who attempted to teach me to write shorter sentences). Siam Bhayro and Louise Lawrence have provided very helpful bibliographic advice and ideas. Any idiosyncrasies that remain are my own responsibility. Collectively, my department at Exeter has been both a willing sounding-board for various interpretations and explanations and a seemingly endless fount of encouragement, enthusiasm and cups of coffee (thank you especially to Francesca Stavrakopoulou).

Many thanks are due to my husband Piers, my children Lydia and Eva, and my parents for putting up patiently with a book which should have been finished by Christmas but lasted past Easter. Piers, as always, has valiantly read every word and I have benefited immensely from his historian's sensitivity to the balance between narrative and evidence.

Finally, this book is dedicated with much love and respect to my parents-in-law, Peter and Carole. I hope you enjoy my attempt at *un peu d'histoire*.

From Jesus Christ to the Church
(MID-FIRST TO MID-SECOND CENTURIES)

> Those who welcomed [Peter's] message were baptized. ... They devoted
> themselves to the apostles' teaching and fellowship, to the breaking of bread
> and the prayers. ... All who believed were together and had all things in
> common; they would sell their possessions and goods and distribute the
> proceeds to all, as any had need. Day by day, as they spent much time together
> in the temple, they broke bread at home and ate their food with glad and
> generous hearts, praising God and having the goodwill of all the people. And
> day by day the Lord added to their number those who were being saved.
> (Acts 2.41–7)

So Luke describes the reaction to Peter's preaching on the day of Pente-
cost. Although many particular aspects of Luke's narrative have been challenged, the words above are probably a reasonable description of the general
character of the earliest Christian community.[1] It was based in Jerusalem
and centred around the teaching and leadership of those who had been
closest to Jesus before his death. Despite Jesus' crucifixion, his followers
shared a strong belief that his death was not the end; some of them had had
vivid experiences of the living Jesus, and many felt that they were posses-
sors of the special gift of God's Spirit or power. The followers of Jesus were
full of optimism and hope for a divinely given new life, and the community
was growing. The group was marked not only by its beliefs about Jesus but
by common worship, prayer and a shared community meal. Its members
also shared their possessions in order to help fellow-believers who were in
need. They believed that their community signified a new departure for its
members – each believer's new beginning was marked by baptism – yet they
continued to worship in the Temple.

The undivided fellowship depicted in this account appears not to have
lasted long. Perhaps it never exhibited the Paradise-like state that Luke

appears to evoke in his narrative. To some, the 500 years that followed
might seem to be characterized more by fracture, schism and disagreement than the spirit of loving fellowship. Nevertheless, throughout the
period covered by this book Christian communities continued to be united
– however loosely – by the same elements: by their hope in what God had
worked for them through Jesus Christ; by gathering around certain individuals who were seen as continuing the work of the Apostles; by baptism,
the sharing of bread and wine, and the offering of prayers and hymns; by
the aspiration to an ethic that supported the poor and needy, both in their
communities and beyond. The earliest evidence for all these factors will be
examined in this chapter.

There were, however, obvious differences between the earliest Christian
community in Jerusalem and the communities of later centuries. Jesus' earliest followers were all Jews: they unquestioningly accepted a monotheistic
belief in the God of Abraham, Isaac and Jacob, and they would have considered their faith in Jesus' teaching to be largely continuous with that.[2] The
degree of continuity between the beliefs of the first Christians and contemporary Judaism is highly contested by New Testament scholars. It certainly
differed somewhat from person to person, not least because the Judaism of
the first century was not a monolithic or uniform religion. Jews differed,
for example, in their interpretations of the Law, and in the degree to which
they were affected by Hellenic culture. Nevertheless, one can assume that
for many Christians, baptism probably marked a renewed commitment to
God or a new understanding of God's relationship to Israel, rather than a
'conversion' in the modern sense. Even the descriptions of Paul's 'conversion
experience', which seem to indicate a dramatic break with his past, may best
be understood as an experience of a new, albeit life-changing, calling rather
than a conversion from one set of religious beliefs to another.[3]

The relationship between Christianity and Judaism became increasingly
more complex, however, as Jesus' followers began to accept Gentiles into
their fellowship without demanding the usual markers which determined
one as a Jew (notably circumcision and the following of certain food laws).
For this reason, the question of the continuity of belief in Jesus with Judaism became a point of debate for the early Christians themselves: to what
extent was Christianity a reinterpretation of Judaism and to what extent
should Christians define themselves against it? Precisely these questions
emerge from a reading of the earliest Christian writings. For the earliest
followers of Jesus, as for other Jews, 'the Scriptures' meant the Hebrew
Bible – essentially the Law, the Prophets, the Psalms and sometimes the
books of Wisdom. The earliest Christian writings vividly show the tension
between ancient tradition and the new witness of the Apostles, as the

authors reinterpreted the Hebrew Scriptures in the light of their convictions about Jesus and, indeed, interpreted the meaning of Jesus in the light of the teachings of the Hebrew Scriptures.

Some of these Christian writings were later accepted by Christians as together forming a new 'testament' or witness to complement the 'old' testament of the Hebrew Bible. The formal 'canon' of the New Testament came about only as a result of a long and gradual process of acceptance over several hundred years, not being definitively fixed until the mid- to late fourth century. The earliest written evidence of Christian communities is in the letters of Paul (written in the 50s CE), but the first anthology of Paul's letters was apparently not in circulation until around 100CE. Collections of Jesus' sayings circulated first in oral, then in written form. One such collection, known today as 'Q', was incorporated into the Gospels of Matthew and Luke (both written towards the end of the first century CE). Another collection underlay the second-century *Gospel of Thomas*, which did not become part of the eventual Christian canon. Other sayings of Jesus seem to have been preserved through early Christian liturgy – for example, the *Didache*'s quotation of the Lord's Prayer – or the teaching of those about to be baptized, recorded in *1 Clement*:

> For he said: 'Show mercy, that you may be shown mercy; forgive that it may be forgiven you. As you do, so it will be done to you; as you give, so it will be given to you; as you judge, so you will be judged; as you show kindness, so will kindness be shown to you; the amount you dispense will be the amount you receive.' [4]

The similarity between some of these words and those of the Gospels is evident and it is sometimes difficult to know whether an author was quoting words from a collection of sayings or whether he was alluding to one of the Gospels (authors often quoted text from memory and were often rather relaxed about the accuracy of their quotation).

It seems likely, then, that from about the 50s CE there were various, rather fluid, written collections of Jesus' sayings, which formed the basis for the Gospels as we know them and which existed for a while alongside them.[5] They seem to have faded out of use as the Gospels became transmitted beyond the communities in which they were originally written. This seems to have happened around the turn of the first and second centuries. The story is slightly different for each of the four Gospels which are now canonical. Mark, written around 70CE, was the earliest Gospel and, with Q, was one of the sources of the Gospels of Luke and Matthew (towards the end of the first century CE). These latter two Gospels began to circulate among Christian communities in Asia Minor and Greece: for example, they were both known to Polycarp, Bishop of Smyrna, whereas Ignatius of

Antioch, writing a generation earlier, seems to rely mostly on oral traditions for his material about Jesus.[6] The Gospel of Mark was known to Marcion and to Justin writing in Rome in the mid-second century and probably circulated in Egypt around the same time, but it was not as widely used in this period as Matthew and Luke. The Gospel of John was written around 90–100CE in Ephesus; it was apparently not known by Polycarp, but was accepted by Irenaeus as one of the four Gospels a generation later and was also used in Egypt during the second half of the second century.

Until Irenaeus' forthright arguments for a four-fold Gospel around a hundred years later, there seems to have been a fair degree of uncertainty in the Christian communities about the idea of a plurality of Gospel texts. Famously, Marcion argued for the acceptance of Luke alone (and an severely edited version at that); Justin may have used or compiled a synopsis of Matthew, Mark and Luke.[7] Justin's pupil Tatian made a fusion of the four Gospels, the *Diatessaron*, which was used by Syriac-speaking Christians as their standard Gospel text for many years. Marcion's version enjoyed popularity among his own followers, but on the whole these unified Gospel synopses were rejected by Christians from the end of the second century onwards. One of the more remarkable aspects of early Christianity is the choice of a multiplicity of Gospel witnesses, despite the availability of amalgamated editions.[8]

The reasons for this choice perhaps lie in the nature of the Gospel texts themselves. Neither in the writings of the New Testament nor in those of the Apostolic Fathers can one find an absolutely exhaustive history or biography of Jesus (although perhaps Luke comes closest in this respect). Nor can one find a systematically worked-out theological doctrine of who Jesus was and what he did. To think that somehow there *should* be is to impose our modern assumptions about the nature and purpose of religious texts on to these works. On the other hand, to assume that there *could not* be relatively complex reflection in those kinds of text simply because they were early (and thus 'primitive') is to misunderstand their purpose and to underestimate their authors. Many of the earliest Christian writings (both in the canon and outside it) were letters written to specific individuals or communities for a specific reason. The Gospels, even if written as a more general kind of witness to the life and teachings of Jesus, were not intended to be exhaustive historical or theological accounts. Their narrative form draws their audience in, invites one to engage and become involved with the story; the story was assumed to be in a profound sense truthful, but was not intended to be a blow-by-blow history. This is because the Gospels – like Paul's letters – were generally intended to be read or heard by people who *already* knew something about Jesus Christ. The impact of differences of theological emphasis or contradictions between the narratives was thus considerably lessened by the fact that the texts were being read in communities which were already associated together by certain core beliefs and practices. This explains the otherwise odd fact that the most reliable texts of the Gospel of Mark end not with resurrection appearances (as the other Gospels do), but with the empty tomb.[9]

Even the texts that bear a closer relation to theological treatises, like Hebrews, assume a readership familiar with the basic themes of Christ's life, death and resurrection. Because Jesus' followers first spread their faith in him by word of mouth, these earliest texts represent a further stage of reflection on what the *significance* of that faith was. They are therefore reflective, sometimes argumentative or defensive, but very rarely present a summary basis of Christian faith. As suits their various purposes, their language is often highly figurative, not least because the Christian writers were seeking to express belief in Jesus in terms they had inherited from their culture, both Jewish and Hellenic. Most importantly, they used the Hebrew Bible, which was itself a very complex collection of images and ideas. Christian texts of the first and early second centuries pick up on these images, develop and adapt them in a variety of imaginative ways. (See the use of Jewish titles for Christ and the adaptation of concepts such as sacrifice, discussed below.) Indeed, it is helpful to view these early Christian writings, at least in some respects, as works of Scriptural interpretation – that is, of course, interpretations of the Hebrew Bible.[10]

These early Christian texts, therefore, are a difficult source for the historian. They emerged from different communities and individual texts circulated in various parts of the Mediterranean region at different times. Their relationship to each other and to the Hebrew Bible is not at all straightforward. Their genre and style are complex: the most appropriate description of the earliest written thought about Jesus Christ is that it is more a 'kaleidoscope of imagery' than a carefully worked-out theology.[11] However, there is an extreme lack of archaeological evidence and very little literary evidence from sources outside the Christian community for what they believed and how they lived. For all their complexities, then, the early Christian writings are our best evidence. For all their failings, they do reveal an inter-linked family of Christian communities which shared certain common beliefs about Jesus and common ways of representing those beliefs in their rituals and their moral codes.

What, then, did the first Christian communities believe about Jesus Christ? Although the very earliest Christian texts, especially Paul's letters,[12] are more interested in Christ's death and resurrection than in other circumstances of his life, there is general agreement in them on the basic facts of his biography. Jesus was born of a human mother and grew up in a Jewish family in Palestine.[13] The Gospels of Matthew and Luke added birth narratives to this basic account, perhaps to emphasize Jesus' real humanity. The Gospels view Jesus' baptism by John as the beginning of his ministry and describe him travelling to preach, teach and heal. Even Paul, who has little biographical detail about Jesus, clearly felt that it was important that Jesus was a teacher and exemplar of a holy life, for he quotes some of Jesus' teachings and regards it as the duty of the Christian to imitate Jesus' way of living, especially Jesus' obedience to the Father, his meekness, gentleness and concern for the weak and the poor.[14] This is also an important theme in the Apostolic Fathers: for example, readers were urged to imitate 'the pattern' of Jesus' humility and his goodness.[15] As Christians became more susceptible to arrest and persecution by the Roman authorities, this imitation could stretch even to imitating Jesus' death. This theme is particularly prominent in Ignatius and Polycarp: 'Let us then be imitators of his endurance, and if we suffer for his name's sake let us glorify him. For this is the example which he gave us in himself.'[16] It is likely that Paul became a hero figure – and himself an example to imitate – precisely because he was thought to have imitated Christ even to the point of a violent death.[17]

In addition to portraying Jesus the teacher as a model to be imitated, the Gospel writers also emphasized the *content* of his preaching – especially the theme of the Kingdom of God which was expressed most strikingly perhaps in the parables. For Jesus, the Kingdom of God indicated not a place (not even a heavenly place) but rather God's rule. His teachings about the Kingdom of God not only showed the goodness, justice and loving kindness of divine kingship but also demonstrated its stark contrast with the current condition of the world. Jesus thought that something was going to happen soon which would bring about God's kingdom – that is, his preaching was marked by a strong focus on eschatology, or teachings about the 'end' (*eschaton*, in Greek). Furthermore, he thought that he was participating in that event in some way.[18] There is much debate about what exactly Jesus himself thought about his involvement (for example, whether it would necessarily involve his death, or whether he anticipated his resurrection). In any case, the authors of the New Testament and the Apostolic Fathers were writing from the perspective of their belief in Christ's resurrection. Therefore, they depicted Jesus' death and resurrection as the events which brought about the kingdom which he preached – or, more accurately, which initiated the events which would eventually bring it about in all its fullness. Some of the earliest Christian writers – notably Paul, especially in his earliest writings – shared Jesus' eschatological outlook: that is, they looked forward to the imminent arrival of the end of the world (the *eschaton*). They developed this by connecting it to an expectation of Jesus' imminent return to earth from heaven:

> For since we believe that Jesus died and rose again, even so, through Jesus, God will bring with him those who have died. For this we declare to you by the word of the Lord, that we who are alive, who are left until the coming of the Lord, will by no means precede those who have died. For the Lord himself, with a cry of command, with the archangel's call and with the sound of God's trumpet, will descend from heaven, and the dead in Christ will rise first. Then we who are alive, who are left, will be caught up in the clouds together with them to meet the Lord in the air; and so we will be with the Lord for ever. (I Thessalonians 4.14–18)

This hope is expressed in perhaps its most vivid form in the Book of Revelation. It is also found, for example, in other works like the *Didache*:

> Be watchful over your life; never let your lamps go out or your loins be ungirt, but keep yourselves always in readiness, for you can never be sure of the hour when our Lord may be coming.[19]

Other writers interpreted the coming of the kingdom more in terms of the new spiritual life which they felt they enjoyed since Jesus' death and resurrection.[20] This was often connected with a strong belief that Jesus' resurrection was a guarantee of their own. In this period, the exact nature of that resurrection after death was not specified. Most important was the belief that one's present life was not all that there was; that the new spiritual life which had been granted in baptism would be perfected after death and that the journey of coming to know God the Father through Jesus Christ and his Holy Spirit would end in a homecoming in which the believer would see God 'face to face'.[21]

Virtually all the early Christian texts explicitly mentioned Christ's death and resurrection, but they did so with widely varying degrees of detail.[22] Clearly, the Gospels offered the fullest narrative accounts and they interpret the significance of Jesus' death in various ways. For example, they depicted Christ as speaking from the Cross the words of the Psalmist and saw the crucifixion as the fulfilment of various prophecies or symbolic passages in the Hebrew Bible:

> At three o'clock Jesus cried out with a loud voice, 'Eloi, Eloi, lema sabachthani?' which means, 'My God, my God, why have you forsaken me?' (Mark 15.34, quoting Psalms 22.1 in Aramaic; cf. Matthew 27.46)

> Then Jesus, crying with a loud voice, said, 'Father, into your hands I commend my spirit.' Having said this, he breathed his last. (Luke 23.46, quoting Psalm 31.5)

> After this, when Jesus knew that all was now finished, he said (in order to
> fulfil the scripture), 'I am thirsty.' (John 19.28, quoting Psalm 69.21)

Another method is to explain the significance of Jesus' death through
concepts with resonances in Jewish theology, such as sacrifice or the defeat
of death (see below).

Much debate about the theology of the writings of this period has focused
on the so-called 'titles' of Christ – expressions such as 'Messiah', 'Son of
Man', 'Son of God' and so on, which can tell us something about who the
authors thought Jesus was and in what his importance lay. Although there
are drawbacks to an exclusive focus on these words, they do provide a useful
way into early conceptions about Jesus. In particular, they highlight the
interplay of Jewish and other cultural backgrounds and they draw attention to the fact that the questions which modern theologians and historians
most want to ask about Jesus (for example, was he God?, did he think he
was God?) are not necessarily the questions which preoccupied the earliest
Christians.[23]

It seems probable that Jesus referred to himself as the 'Son of Man', but
what he meant by this is rather more unclear. It seems to have been connected
with Jesus' recognition that his preaching would lead to his rejection, but it
was also possibly linked to his hope that he would eventually be vindicated
by God.[24] It was therefore an eschatological concept, which might explain
why the title only appears in the Gospel traditions, which also emphasize
Jesus' preaching about the Kingdom of God. Similarly, the title 'Lord' does
not tell us very much. It was probably used by some first-century Greek-
speaking Jews as an alternative to the divine name in Hebrew, YHWH,
which they were forbidden to pronounce. It was also used by Greek pagans
to refer to certain deities. However, its use for Jesus did not necessarily
imply that the writer thought Jesus was God (or a god), for it could also
be used as a polite form of address, particularly for a man to whom one
owed obedience. So, like Mary's term for the risen Jesus, 'Rabbouni', the
term 'Lord' tells us about the *respect* in which Jesus was held but not very
much about what early Christians thought his life, death and resurrection
achieved for humankind, and nothing about how they conceptualized his
actual nature (was he human or divine?).[25]

More helpful is the term 'Messiah', for which the Greek term *Christos*
is a translation. This is the most common title applied to Jesus by Paul, for
example, and it clearly stems from a Jewish tradition. In Hebrew a *mashiah*,
a messiah, was someone who had been anointed. Traditionally, anointing was the mark of kings, priests and prophets. Imagery relating to all
these categories was used by New Testament writers to explain who Jesus
was (not always, however, in connection with the actual term 'messiah').

In forms of Judaism with a particular eschatological expectation, 'messiah' was often used to refer to a hoped-for king who would come to rule Israel as a successor to King David. Did Jesus therefore think that he was this messiah? Possibly. At any rate, very early on his followers assigned to him this role, almost certainly with eschatological hopes in mind. However, this conclusion must be qualified in several important ways. First, the Gospel writers (and possibly Jesus himself) sought systematically to *undermine* several assumptions about such a messiah: Jesus was portrayed as rejecting all normal forms of earthly political power, as contrasting the Kingdom of God with human kingship, as subverting the imagery of human kingship. Secondly, not all Jews had Messianic expectations – so any sense that Jesus as messiah (even a reinterpreted messiah) was the 'obvious' fulfilment of a uniform Jewish expectation must be rejected. (When later Christians attacked Jews for not spotting that Jesus was the messiah, they were falsely assuming that all first-century Judaism was awaiting such a person.) Finally, although the title *Christos* was used very early for Christ, it rapidly lost the association with specifically Jewish eschatological expectation and became a kind of further proper name, almost as if to specify which Jesus was being spoken about. In his writings Paul never, for example, tries to argue that Jesus *was* 'the Messiah'.[26]

It might be thought that the term 'Son of God' would present a cut-and-dried case that Jesus was thought to be divine, but even here the evidence is rather ambiguous: in itself the term did *not* imply divinity, although it usually denoted someone who was an agent of God. It may well have been connected by early Christians to Jesus' resurrection – the idea being that Jesus was 'made' Son of God at that point; it almost certainly reflected the fact that Jesus addressed God as 'Abba, Father' and invited other Christians to do so too.[27] Thus early Christians seemed to have believed that through Jesus they too could be counted as 'sons of God'.[28] In Paul, this idea is extended with another metaphor: Christ is the true Son of the Father, but through him all who believe in him are made sons by adoption:

> For all who are led by the Spirit of God are children of God. For you did not receive a spirit of slavery to fall back into fear, but you have received a spirit of adoption. When we cry, 'Abba! Father!' it is that very Spirit bearing witness with our spirit that we are children of God, and if children, then heirs, heirs of God and joint heirs with Christ – if, in fact, we suffer with him so that we may also be glorified with him. (Romans 8.14–17)

This was a particularly powerful image in a society in which it was common for men without sons to adopt a boy or young man to be their legitimate heir: it expresses a sense of being *uniquely* chosen that is missing from the English concept. It also creates a deliberate paradox with another central theme in Paul's theology: the *universal* nature of God's offer of sonship. That idea was strongly connected with the parallel which Paul drew between Jesus and Adam. For Paul, Jesus and Adam were in different ways representative of all human nature. Just as Adam represented the failings of human nature, so Jesus Christ represented the possibility that all could return to a proper relationship with God again: 'for as all die in Adam, so all will be made alive in Christ'.[29]

A further range of language used by the New Testament writers for Jesus harks back to the 'Wisdom' traditions of the Hebrew Bible. In these, God's 'Wisdom' and God's 'Word' are described in ways that almost suggest that they are independent beings alongside the one God. Wisdom in particular is vividly personified in Proverbs and the Wisdom of Solomon. What these terms meant exactly to the Jewish writers is not clear – they may just have been powerfully imaginative ways of depicting God's wise ordering of the world (both through creation and his providential action thereafter) and his ability to act powerfully in the world whilst remaining transcendent (a development of Genesis 1's idea that God could create merely by speaking). Yet the ambiguous position which the authors gave to Wisdom and the Word – as being supremely expressive of God's nature yet not identical to God – was undoubtedly exploited by Christian writers who wanted to say something similar of Jesus. What was different was the way in which the New Testament use of this language saw God's Wisdom and Word as definitively embodied in one particular human being. The most famous passage to do this was, of course, the opening of John's Gospel, which deliberately harked back to Genesis 1: 'In the beginning was the Word, and the Word was with God, and the Word was God.' This passage, together with the Colossians' 'hymn'[30] and the opening of the Book of Hebrews, expressed the belief that not only did Jesus reveal or embody the wisdom and power of God, but that he was so close to God that he was involved even in God's creative activity:

> He is the image of the invisible God, the firstborn of all creation; for in him all things in heaven and on earth were created. (Colossians 1.15–16)

> In these last days he has spoken to us by a Son, through whom he created the worlds. He is the reflection of God's glory and the exact imprint of God's very being, and he sustains all things by his powerful word. (Hebrews 1.2–3)

Such language naturally suggested that in some sense the Word which was in Jesus existed before Jesus' birth, indeed before the beginning of the world. John's Gospel expressed this belief vividly in narrative form, beginning with the idea that the Word who was 'with God ... came to dwell among us' and constantly reinforcing the idea that Jesus would ascend to heaven where he was before.[31] Similar passages pointing to the idea of a pre-existent Son can be found in the non-canonical writings of the period: they suggested, for example, that Christ was the inspiration of the Prophets and was sent from or by God.[32] Ignatius wrote of 'Jesus Christ who before the ages was with the Father and who was manifested at the end'.[33] It is clear that this kind of language exalted Jesus more than the other titles we have considered; it seems to have made more definite claims about Jesus' divinity. Nevertheless, even here one should be cautious. The authors were developing the concepts of Wisdom and Word in order to apply them to a specific historical person, Jesus. Nevertheless the language remained ambiguous: faith in the one God was still central and the *precise* nature of the relationship between the Son, Jesus, to his Father was not defined. Of course, later Church Fathers used these texts to prove their own interpretations of this relationship, as we shall see; but this does not justify reading back into the New Testament a fully developed Christology.

As well as studying the titles of Jesus, it is useful to look at what the earliest Christians thought Jesus would or could *do* for them, rather than what he *was*. Their ideas were focused around several closely interconnected themes: Christ's crucifixion, resurrection and ascension into heaven, and the gift of the Holy Spirit. Although there is no formal theology of the atonement either in the New Testament or in the Apostolic Fathers, there are clear indications that the writers thought *that* Christ's death and resurrection effected salvation, even if they were unsure *how*. This is most evident in Paul, whose writings emphasize the saving power of the Cross. Paul sometimes explained salvation in terms of *sacrifice*: the holy one, Jesus, was offered on behalf of sinful humanity and this opened up forgiveness, and a new life for those who believe in him. He also suggested that the believer could *participate* in Jesus' death and resurrected life through baptism, which was interpreted specifically as the death to sin (or an old way of life) and initiating new life.[34]

> How can we who died to sin go on living in it? Do you not know that all of us who have been baptized into Christ Jesus were baptized into his death? Therefore we have been buried with him by baptism into death, so that, just as Christ was raised from the dead by the glory of the Father, so we too might walk in newness of life. For if we have been united with him in a death like his, we will certainly be united with him in a resurrection like his. (Romans 6.2–5)

These two ideas – sacrifice and participation – did not fit together in a neat or systematic way in Paul's theology. Paul (like other Christian writers in the first and later centuries) employed a range of figurative language to get as close as he could to expressing what he thought was ultimately an inexpressible mystery.

In the Apostolic Fathers the belief in Jesus' death as a holy sacrifice was often expressed in the idea that Christ's flesh and blood effected salvation: for example, the *Epistle of Barnabas* asserted that Christians were 'sanctified by the remission of sins, that is, by his sprinkled blood'.[35] By extension, Christ's flesh and blood were something believers must believe in, even venerate, in order for that salvation to become effective in them:

> Let us fix our gaze on the Blood of Christ, and let us know that it is precious to his Father, because it was poured out for our salvation, and brought the grace of repentance to all the world. (*1 Clement* 7.4)[36]

Thus Christ's flesh and/or blood became in itself symbolic of the new life of salvation or some specific quality associated with it and Ignatius even went so far as to salute his addressees 'in the blood of Jesus Christ, which is eternal and lasting joy'.[37] This language clearly also alluded to the Eucharist – a theme to which we will return below. The idea of Jesus' ascension into heaven, which was alluded to throughout John's Gospel and narrated in an apparently more straightforward fashion in Luke and Acts, was accompanied by belief that Jesus' power would remain with his followers in the form of the Holy Spirit:

> 'But you will receive power when the Holy Spirit has come upon you; and you will be my witnesses in Jerusalem, in all Judea and Samaria, and to the ends of the earth.' When he had said this, as they were watching, he was lifted up, and a cloud took him out of their sight. (Acts 1.8–9)[38]

The theme of the pouring out of God's Spirit is an important one in Peter's preaching (as it is described in Acts) and Paul's letters.[39] Both in his sacrificial death and in his gift of the Spirit, Jesus Christ was seen as a mediator. The language of mediation was particularly strong in the Letter to the Hebrews, where it accompanied the idea of Jesus Christ as a unique and final High Priest, mediating between God and humankind.[40] The little we know about early Christian liturgies and rituals also reveals the hope that even when ascended to heaven Jesus Christ would remain a mediator between the community and the Father. A typical prayer which implies that the Christian can call on God *because* of the work he has done through Jesus Christ appears in *1 Clement*:

> We will entreat the Creator of all things with heartfelt prayer and supplication that the full sum of his elect … may ever be preserved intact through his beloved Son Jesus Christ, by whom he has called us out of darkness to light, and from ignorance to the clear knowledge of the glory of his name.[41]

The idea of prayer to God through the mediation of Christ is also evident in early Christian eucharistic prayers. As the quotation from Acts at the beginning of this chapter makes clear, early Christian communities met to break bread together. These community meals were accompanied by meal-time prayers, as would have been traditional Jewish practice. Such prayers were adapted by Christians in ways that expressed their specific beliefs and hopes in Christ:

> We give you thanks, our Father, for the holy vine of David, your child, which you made known to us through Jesus your child.
>
> *To you be the glory forever.*
>
> We give you thanks, our Father, for the life and knowledge that you made known to us through Jesus your child.
>
> *To you be the glory forever.*
>
> As this fragment of bread was dispersed upon the mountains and was gathered to become one, so may your church be gathered together from the ends of the earth into your kingdom.[42]

In this liturgy from the *Didache*, the worship of the community was conceived of as a sacrifice in which the whole community participated. This concept of sacrifice was often, although not always, connected with the interpretation of Christ's death as sacrifice. The words from the *Didache* above also expressed a strong hope for the eschatological salvation of the whole Church – a hope that is set in the context of a vivid expectation of the imminent and traumatic end of the world.[43] Eucharistic themes in John's Gospel – such as the identification of Christ with the bread of life – also suggested a close association of the Eucharist with Christ's resurrection and the promise of new life.[44] The idea seems to be that in sharing the bread, which was symbolically identified with Jesus Christ, the community felt that they were sharing in (or would share in) Jesus' resurrection. (This idea is similar to the second strand in Pauline theology identified above, but with a focus more on the Eucharist than baptism as the means of participation in Christ's saving work.)

While some early eucharistic traditions stressed Jesus' resurrection, others put more emphasis on Jesus' crucifixion and on the breaking of bread as a memorial of his death. These traditions are reflected in the synoptic Gospels and I Corinthians. In these texts, the meal-time prayer which had already become traditional in some Christian communities was taken to echo the very words which Jesus spoke at the last meal before his death.

> For I received from the Lord what I also handed on to you, that the Lord Jesus on the night when he was betrayed took a loaf of bread, and when he had given thanks, he broke it and said, 'This is my body that is for you. Do this in remembrance of me.' In the same way he took the cup also, after

supper, saying, 'This cup is the new covenant in my blood. Do this, as often as you drink it, in remembrance of me.' For as often as you eat this bread and drink the cup, you proclaim the Lord's death until he comes. (I Corinthians 11.23–6) [45]

Such a formulation puts a strong emphasis on commemoration – in particular, remembering God's saving actions. Such commemoration was an important aspect of the prayers at Passover meals which Jesus' words were meant to evoke (regardless of whether the Last Supper was the Passover meal or not).[46] The ideas of commemoration and participation were not clearly distinguished in these early prayers; in both it can be argued that there was a sense that through the shared meal Christ was somehow being made present.[47] The story of the disciples on the road to Emmaus (Luke 24.13–35) is a dramatic evocation of the combined elements of memory, sharing bread and Christ's presence. The fact that Christ is only 'somehow' present is conveyed by the disciples' initial lack of recognition and Christ's vanishing. The story also points to the interesting combination of a meal with the exposition of the Hebrew Scriptures. The difference between the *Didache* tradition and the synoptic tradition suggests that different communities developed their own ritual meal-time prayers in the early decades of Christianity. What united all such early prayers, however, was the connection with an actual meal,[48] their role in uniting the community and the implicit sense of unity with other communities taking part in the same kind of meal elsewhere.

Baptism performed the same role of symbolizing the unity of the community and giving the baptized person a strong sense of belonging. Early Christian baptism carried with it a clear idea of initiation: the believer through baptism was identifying himself or herself with a specific group. It may be that baptism became for Christians the once-and-for-all rite of initiation for converts that circumcision was for Jews[49] – with the obvious difference that baptism applied to women as well as men. Just as some pagans became 'Godfearers' – attending synagogue and worshipping the one God of Abraham, but not receiving circumcision – it is likely that some people were associated with the earliest Christian communities without being baptized. (This situation was later formalized into the concept of the catechumenate, according to which believers signalled their intention to be baptized and received Christian teaching with that aim in mind.) It seems that baptism was necessary for full participation in the special community meals.[50]

Besides the idea of initiation, early Christians associated baptism with purification and the forgiveness of sins. Christian baptism seems to have been similar in some respects to Jewish purificatory washings, particularly those of converts. However, the association of baptism with repentance and forgiveness and the application of it to everyone, Jews as well as proselytes, was apparently new.[51] The connection of baptism with a call to repentance is evident in the Gospel accounts of both John the Baptist's and Jesus' preaching. The connection of baptism with forgiveness led to it being understood as salvific: 'Your life has been saved by water'.[52] Another aspect of the understanding of baptism was its interpretation as dying to sin and rising with Christ (discussed in relation to Paul's theology above).

Since baptisms were closely associated with the community meals which the earliest Christians took in each others' houses, baptisms probably took place in private baths or in local springs or rivers (after which the community would move inside).[53] A three-fold formula for baptism – 'in the name of the Father, and of the Son and of the Holy Spirit' – seems to have become established very early, but baptism 'in the name of Jesus' was probably also very common.[54] Paul seems to have associated baptism with the declaration that 'Jesus is Lord!'[55] The use of the metaphor of being clothed 'with Christ', or 'with a new self', suggests that the candidates removed some or all of their clothes in order to be baptized and perhaps put on new garments afterwards.[56] Frequent references to anointing and being 'sealed' indicate that the candidates were anointed with oil at some point.[57] For obvious reasons, the only explicit mentions of baptism in the very early Church refer to the baptism of adult candidates: it is possible that when whole households were converted to Christianity infants were baptized as well, but this is very uncertain. (Clarity over the issue has not been helped by the fact that those who supported infant baptism and those who rejected it have both sought to validate their views by reference to the New Testament.)[58]

Both the eucharistic prayers and the rite of baptism adapted certain aspects of Jewish tradition to a new Christian context. The same applied to the other aspects of community worship. Early Christians probably met to sing psalms, and possibly other, newly composed, hymns. They also set aside one day a week as a particular day for worship. Originally this was the Jewish Sabbath on the seventh day of the week, but as time progressed it became for increasing numbers of Christians the first day of the week, the Sunday on which they believed the resurrection had taken place. The veneration of this day of the week also connected with a traditionally held Jewish association of the 'eighth day' with eschatological perfection.[59] Arguments over whether one should venerate the seventh-day Sabbath or the first-/eighth-day 'Lord's day' were one source of tension in early Christian communities.[60] The setting aside of the Sunday following the Passover as a special celebration of the resurrection was not established until the second century. The first Jewish Christians presumably celebrated Passover in the traditional manner. It is unclear what communities of Gentile converts did. The first evidence of a specifically new and Christian celebration of the Passover is found in the *Letter of the Apostles* (*c.*150CE); for several decades after that Christians argued about whether the celebration of the resurrection should be on the 14th day of the Jewish month Nisan (whatever the day of the week) or on the Sunday following. Underlying these arguments were not only regional variations in practice but fraught questions about how close to traditional Jewish practice Christian communities should remain.

Leadership in early Christian communities was provided by those who preached the new message about Jesus Christ, who led the rites of baptism and the Eucharist, who owned the houses in which the early Christian groups met or who had a moral authority owing to their own way of life. (These roles were not necessarily filled by the same people: Paul, for example, seems only rarely to have baptized.[61]) We can assume that most of those who wrote the earliest Christian texts – especially the letters – were leaders of their own communities. Some of the early Christian writings appear to be from the leader of one group giving advice to other leaders.[62] Early Christians often viewed their leaders as heirs of the tasks given by Jesus to the Apostles, either literally, because they had been taught or appointed by Apostles, or in a figurative sense:

> Now the Gospel was given to the Apostles for us by the Lord Jesus Christ; and Jesus the Christ was sent from God. That is to say, Christ received his commission from God, and the Apostles theirs from Christ. ... So thereafter, when the Apostles had been given their instructions, and all their doubts had been set at rest by the resurrection of our Lord Jesus Christ from the dead, they set out in the full assurance of the Holy Spirit to proclaim the coming of God's kingdom. And as they went through the territories and townships preaching, they appointed their first converts – after testing them by the Spirit – to be bishops and deacons for the believers of the future.[63]

Not content with tracing bishops back to the Apostles and thus to Christ, the author even claims the institution was foretold in the Book of Isaiah![64] Later churches in the great cities of the Empire often claimed to have been founded by an Apostle, and churchmen tried to trace back a succession of Church leaders to one of the Apostles (see, for example, the lists in the fourth-century Eusebius of Caesarea's *Ecclesiastical History*).

In the first decades of the Christian movement, various terms began to be applied to the leaders, especially *diakonos* (minister, 'one who serves'), *presbyter* (elder) and *episkopos* (literally, 'overseer', but usually translated as 'bishop'). These words were originally probably very fluid or even interchangeable, especially the terms *presbyter* and *episkopos*. Paul refers to himself as the minister (*diakonos*) of Christ. As communities developed a more formal structure they probably usually had one main leader, assisted by deacons (*diakonoi*) who seem often to have helped with practical matters like communications with other churches and the distribution of assistance to the needy. Philippians, *1 Clement* and the *Didache* mention 'bishops' and 'deacons'; Polycarp has 'presbyters' and 'deacons'; but bishops and presbyters seem to play the same role in all these texts and the role of deacons is not clear.[65] Although there is mention of all three terms in the pastoral epistles, one should be very cautious about assuming that there was a fully formed 'three-fold ministry' so early: in I Timothy, for example, the terms *presbyter* and *episkopos* could be read as synonyms.[66] Only by the beginning of the second century can one see, in the letters of Ignatius of Antioch for example, an argument for a quite firmly hierarchical system in which bishops oversaw the work of presbyters who were assisted by deacons. Only bishops, or someone appointed by them, could celebrate the Eucharist. Even then, we cannot be sure that this practice was common outside Asia Minor (or even inside Asia Minor – Ignatius is arguing for it, not assuming it was everywhere in place).

There is uncertainty about the precise roles of women in early Christian communities. It is fairly clear that women were very important in the development of early Christianity, for example in giving financial assistance, providing a house for groups to meet and worship in and being hospitable to travelling preachers. Clearly certain women were important converts in that they brought their whole household with them. Paul mentions several such women in his letters. But whether women had a more formal position in their communities is much more controversial (and, like the issue of infant baptism, is especially so because modern debates about women's ministry have reached back to prove their cases from the ancient texts).[67] Phoebe is described as a *diakonos* and Paul's *prostatis* ('patron') in Romans 16.1–2. Although *diakonos* has often been translated 'deaconess', there is no verbal distinction made between Phoebe and male deacons: the existence of a specific office of deaconess, as opposed to deacon, was not known until much later and its application to Romans is anachronistic. Having said that, it is not clear what her role was, beyond the fact that she was a financial supporter of the community and that she was travelling on the community's behalf, perhaps by carrying Paul's letter. I Timothy – a later text – gives advice for ministers in the Christian community:

> Now a bishop must be above reproach, married only once, temperate, sensible, respectable, hospitable, an apt teacher, not a drunkard, not violent but gentle, not quarrelsome, and not a lover of money. He must manage his own household well, keeping his children submissive and respectful in every way – for if someone does not know how to manage his own household, how

> can he take care of God's church? ... Deacons likewise must be serious, not double-tongued, not indulging in much wine, not greedy for money; they must hold fast to the mystery of the faith with a clear conscience. And let them first be tested; then, if they prove themselves blameless, let them serve as deacons. Women likewise must be serious, not slanderers, but temperate, faithful in all things. Let deacons be married only once, and let them manage their children and their households well; for those who serve well as deacons gain a good standing for themselves and great boldness in the faith that is in Christ Jesus. (I Timothy 3.2–5, 8–13)

Given the structure of this passage, it seems very likely that the 'women' referred to are women deacons, although it is possible that they are the wives of deacons. (The fact that I Timothy 2.11–15 rejected the teaching authority of women reflects the fact that 'deacon' does not appear to be used at this date for someone with a teaching function.)

If this evidence hints at a change in the role of women as deacons, is the same true of them as presbyters or *episkopoi*? A case has been made that Evodia and Syntyche in Philippians 4.2 are leaders of local house churches, i.e. *episkopoi*, rather than deacons, in the terminology of that letter.[68] Paul's letter to the Romans suggests that some husbands and wives were joint leaders of house churches: Prisca and her husband Aquila (Romans 16.3), and Andronicus and Junia, who are apparently assumed to be Apostles (Romans 16.7).[69] It would be very surprising indeed if no early Christian woman led a baptism ceremony or a eucharistic meal, given that Christianity was in general welcoming to women and that some later groups (albeit marginal ones) used women in these roles.[70] The question is how common such women were. The lack of positive evidence and the relative scarcity of arguments *against* women leading baptisms or Eucharists suggests that such women were very few and/or very early. We know for certain that some women sought to speak authoritatively in their communities, for they are criticized in the pastoral epistles. Whatever the precise role of women in the earliest days of the Church, as the Church became increasingly institutionalized it reflected the social attitudes of the time towards women's leadership, whether that leadership was thought of as being primary intellectual, spiritual or political. The difference between texts like the undisputed Pauline epistles and the pastoral epistles, and again between late first-century works and those written at the beginning of the second century, reflects the increasingly formal organization of the Church communities. As they became more institutionalized it seems that the role of women became more restricted.

Another way in which Christian communities were associated by common practice was in their ethics. We saw above the importance given to charity towards the needy and this seems to have been a very common concern (even if it did not often lead to the actual possession of all things in common, as the writer of Acts claimed for the first Jerusalem community):

> The strong are not to ignore the weak, and the weak are to respect the strong. Rich men should provide for the poor and the poor should thank God for giving them somebody to supply their wants.[71]

Clement even encouraged his readers by reminding them that earlier members of the congregation even sold themselves into slavery to provide for other Christians who were destitute.[72] Believers were instructed to care for widows and orphans, and indeed widows were held in especial esteem, eventually gaining in some communities a formal liturgical role and a position among the clergy.[73]

There were strict sexual mores in the early Christian groups: marriage was seen as the only correct or holy context for sexual activity. This would not have set Christians apart from contemporary Jewish or Roman moralists; what was more unusual was a strong current in early Christian ethics which advocated the rejection of marriage and seemed to see holiness in chastity. This is evident, for example, in some of Paul's writings. Much of this current seems to have been connected with the expectation of an imminent end to the world – although it was to resurface again in later Christianity in very different circumstances. It should be noted that although Paul is cautious about marriage he did not condemn it outright and seems to have had a more moderate position than some of the Corinthians to whom he was writing.

Food is a sensitive issue in all cultures, but in first-century Judaism food laws were a particularly potent religious and ethnic marker. Fairly early on, Christians seem to have welcomed into their common meals Gentiles with different food customs: the basis of the move is depicted in narrative fashion in Acts 10.9–16 (Peter's vision of the sheet carrying different types of food).[74] Once this bridge had been crossed, Christians had to deal with the issue of whether they could eat food which came from the carcasses of animals sacrificed in pagan temples.[75]

Far more controversial, however, was the issue of circumcision. This was the marker above all markers of Jewishness, and the decision of some Christians to welcome Gentiles without demanding that the men be circumcised clearly caused great tension. It may have been one of the factors which eventually caused Christian communities to develop from being groups *within* Judaism to being groups which defined themselves in contrast to Judaism. That is, it was not the inclusion of Gentiles in itself that separated the Christians from Judaism, but the way in which Christians welcomed Gentiles as Christians without requiring them also to be circumcised.

Early Christian communities, then, can be seen as sharing a set of common practices. Few of these practices were *absolutely* unique to Christianity – they were to greater or lesser extents adaptations of rituals and moral codes found in Judaism or the wider Mediterranean context. But it was the particular way in which these rituals and moral codes were adapted by Christians that united the communities. Even then, one must allow for a certain amount of variation from community to community, some more closely influenced by Judaism than others, some taking a stricter stance on marriage than others, different communities varying in the words used for the eucharistic meals and baptism ceremonies.

Modern scholars have sought to explain the nature of these Christian groups by associating them with other groupings in late antique society, such as religious cults, philosophical schools, synagogue communities and city guilds or fraternities (*collegia*). There are some striking similarities with all these types: for example, the performing of various rituals which bound the community together; the important role of charismatic teachers and their succession of pupils; shared practices and texts; community meals and a shared responsibility for poor members. Nevertheless, none of these categories quite matches how the Christian groups viewed themselves. In the early Christian writings, a mixture of themes was used flexibly and imaginatively to explain what the new communities were. For example, Christians described themselves as a kind of extended family or household (Roman households included servants and slaves) united under God or Christ as the *paterfamilias*.[76] These households of God were envisaged as – ideally – being united in their members' love and respect for one another. Such attitudes transcended the ties of blood, obligation or convenience which held normal human households together. One also finds in the New Testament a striking theme of bodily unity, which reinforced the language of unity in love: this is most famously expressed perhaps in I Corinthians 12–13.[77]

Another way of extending the family motif in a more universal direction was to refer to Christian groups collectively as Israel (or the new Israel). This term was – and is – deeply problematic in that it could be taken to claim that God had transferred his promises from the old, literal, ethnic Israel to a new, figurative or spiritual Israel. However, in some earliest Christian writings it was used merely to express the idea that God had *extended* his promises beyond the ethnic family of Israel to include the Gentiles too, without the implication that God had rejected the original people of the covenant. It was especially the theologians of the next generations who used the concept of the new Israel to argue that God had rejected the Jews.

One idea that the concept of Israel conveyed effectively – particularly in an era when Jews were already spread in a diaspora beyond Palestine – was that one could simultaneously be part of a small local community (a tribe, a family, a synagogue) *and* part of a wider nation. It was this concept which seems also to have been expressed by the Greek term *ekklesia*. Now most usually translated 'church', the term originally meant 'meeting' or 'council' and was used of secular or religious meetings. Although use of the term varied from writer to writer in this period it is notable that it could bear both a universal meaning – the whole Christian community – and a more particular one – an individual congregation. Paul tended to use it in the latter sense, but in later letters in the Pauline tradition, 'church' was used in the universalistic sense and expressed with the imagery of the body of Christ.[78] Furthermore, 'the church' could refer both to the present particular historical situation of Christian groups and to the Christian community's ideal existence. Some authors wrote, for example, of a pre-existent or fore-ordained 'church'[79] and others anticipated the eschatological perfection of the Church with images such as the heavenly feast and the new Jerusalem.[80]

The use of terms like 'Israel' and 'the church' both to denote specific, divided, historical realities and to refer to ideal, unified, communities raises two fundamental questions about the development of the Christian Church in this period: first, to what extent were Christians 'one' with the Judaism from which they had emerged and, secondly, to what extent were they 'one' with each other?

Until fairly recently, it was conventional for Church historians to write of the 'parting of the ways': an irrevocable splitting away of Christians from Jewish congregations. This was assumed by many scholars to have happened at some point around the destruction of the Temple at the hands of the Romans in 70CE (although the timing of the split was much disputed). However, the current consensus is that the reality was much more complex and that the dividing lines between Christianity and Judaism were very fluid for many years – not least because both Christianity and Judaism were themselves not rigidly unified phenomena (many scholars prefer to refer to early 'Christianities' and early 'Judaisms'). There were Jewish households who accepted Jesus Christ and who were baptized, and who continued to worship in their synagogue, to celebrate the seventh-day Sabbath and to keep the Passover. There were Gentile Godfearers who belonged both to the synagogue and to a house church. There were some converts from paganism who had much less familiarity with Jewish customs and whose communities probably exhibited more of a 'break' with Judaism, but who, for example, accepted the Hebrew Scriptures. Eventually, some Christian communities rejected even these.[81] Some important historical judgements have challenged the earlier view. For example, scholars point out that the diaspora of Jews from Palestine began *before* the fall of the Temple in 70CE, and that, therefore, many Christian churches outside Palestine grew out of Jewish communities. Furthermore, the evidence surrounding the supposed ban of Christians from synagogues issued by Jewish leaders meeting at Jamnia is much more difficult to interpret than was once thought: there appears not to have been a clear policy of expelling Christians, although there were undoubtedly tensions. The friction in this period between Christians and the vast majority of Jews who did not accept Christ should not be underestimated. While some communities coexisted well, others undoubtedly had painful and bitter arguments and these are reflected in the pages of the New Testament and other early Christian texts.[82] In this period, one can say that Christianity and Judaism were increasingly distinct and were certainly endeavouring to define themselves against each other, even if there was no clear split. But, yet again, one must also note that the situation differed from Christian community to Christian community.

Were early Christian groups one with each other? This chapter has painted a picture of what might be called 'contained diversity'.[83] What one finds in the evidence of the earliest Christian writings is not one clearly defined institution with a fully defined creed or a clear set of community rules, but rather a constellation of groups which are associated with one another by a series of close family resemblances in what they believed, which texts they used, how they worshipped and how they organized their community life. They were also linked by a network of personal associations, which are witnessed to by the large number of early Christian texts which are letters. What is remarkable about these early Christian communities is that they were simultaneously preoccupied with their own disagreements *and* hopeful that somehow these troubles would be overcome in God's plan for the followers of Jesus Christ. This explains why some can read the history of the beginnings of the Church and see discord and schism right from the start, while others can read it and find an ideal primeval unity: both are there, although if one looks carefully, it may be that the earliest Christians were fully aware that one existed in reality while the other persisted as their eschatological hope.

CHAPTER 2

Hopes and Fears
(SECOND CENTURY)

By 100CE Christianity had spread widely throughout the main cities of the eastern Mediterranean and beyond.[1] Nevertheless, there was a common feeling that Christianity was still very much a religion of Palestine, Asia Minor, some cities in Greece and Macedonia, and Rome. By contrast, a hundred years later authors felt able to claim that Christianity had spread to the very ends of the earth, even though they were simultaneously aware of their position as a rather precarious minority. One might suspect the later historian Eusebius of retrospective hyperbole when he claimed, 'like dazzling light the churches were now shining all over the world and to the limits of the human race faith in our saviour and Lord Jesus Christ was at its peak',[2] but his language reflected that of writers of the time. Irenaeus – himself a native of Asia Minor who had travelled to Gaul – wrote of 'the church, dispersed throughout the world to the ends of the earth' and he argued that 'the churches founded in Germany believe and hand [the faith] down no differently, nor do those among the Iberians, among the Celts, in the Orient, in Egypt or in Libya, or those established in the middle of the world'.[3]

While Irenaeus was referring largely to provinces of the Roman Empire the author of a contemporary North African treatise *Against the Jews* boasted that whilst the Romans could only rule within the limits of their empire, Christianity had spread beyond those fortified boundaries to the far west of North Africa (the regions known in Latin as Gaetulia and Mauretania), throughout the Iberian peninsula and 'the diverse nations of the Gauls and the haunts of the Britons – inaccessible to the Romans, but subjugated to Christ'.[4] Further east, the writer includes the German tribes and the peoples of Dacia (approximating to modern Romania and Moldova) and of Sarmatia and Scythia (a region stretching from the southern reaches of modern Russia, through Ukraine, Belarus, Bulgaria and the lands of the northern Caucasus). Even if one allows for exaggeration, it must be the case that Christianity had spread beyond the boundaries of the Roman Empire (boundaries which were in any case notoriously fragile and prone to shifting). As in the earliest days of the Church, it had continued to spread via trade routes which themselves followed the Roman imperial armies. Consequently, Christianity in and beyond the furthest reaches of the Empire was probably only known in certain key cities or camps. Problems are caused for the historian by the lack of textual or archaeological evidence in these regions; however, one can sometimes track the growth of Christianity through the lists of bishops preserved by various communities. Thus, for example, by 235CE the community of Christians in the Sassanid Empire of Persia was big enough to sustain about 20 bishops.[5]

Despite their increasing geographical spread, many churches kept in contact with each other remarkably well, utilizing the trade routes (both land and sea) and the letter-writing culture of the Roman Empire. So, as mentioned in the previous chapter, many early Christian texts were letters which were originally sent to one specific individual or church community and which were later copied and circulated more widely – a process not dissimilar to, for example, the 'publication' of the letters of the younger Pliny after his death. Of course, communication was somewhat haphazard, and depended a great deal on the strength of personal relationships as well as the feasibility of travel. But news about the spread of new churches filled the Christian communities with a clear sense of excitement and confidence in the truth of their faith.

At the same time, however, life for these Christians was undoubtedly insecure. The spread of Christianity was uneven, and even the larger Christian groups were a small minority in the places in which they lived. This often caused friction not only with pagans but also with Jews. To make matters worse (and despite what the quotation from Irenaeus above seems to imply) Christians were far from being unified in their own beliefs. This period sees a multiplicity of interpretations of Christian faith and the first systematic and detailed attempts to describe and counter opposing viewpoints. As part of this process, it also saw the development of Christian doctrine, as lay teachers and bishops attempted to make clear what made them different not only from their pagan and Jewish neighbours but also from those Christians with whom they disagreed. All three kinds of tension (with pagans, with Jews, with each other) were connected with the early Christians' experience of persecution in this period: it seems likely that many outbreaks of persecution occurred when frictions brought Christians to the attention of Roman governors and when governors thought that executing Christians would bring an end to the unrest. Moreover, the threat of death seems to have strengthened the resolve of many of these early Christians and, in particular, made them more determined to defend and define their own interpretation of what it meant to call oneself 'a Christian'.

This period, then, was characterized by a potent mix of Christians' high self-confidence and an acute awareness of their uncertain circumstances. This mixture is reflected in Christian theology, particularly in eschatology – Christian beliefs about death, heaven and hell. Most Christians of this period expressed a fervent hope for the perfection of their salvation in a future life, often accompanied by a heightened expectation of the imminent end of the world and the punishment of their persecutors. Much of their language can seem florid, extreme, even fanatical, to a modern reader, but it can only be understood in its context, and in particular in the light of that paradoxical combination of utter certainty that God's plan was being fulfilled through the spread of the Church together with a conviction of the transience of the present age. On the other hand, in this same period we find the first systematic attempts to set out the beliefs of Christianity in a reasoned form, often using contemporary philosophy. Although the tone of such writings has usually been contrasted with the high emotional pitch of Christian texts about martyrdom or against heretics, they need to be understood as arising from the same context and are in fact no less impassioned.

The early Christians' experience of persecution is a vexed issue, coloured not only by modern anxieties about the notion of martyrdom (particularly in the current context, in which martyrdom is often coupled with the concept of religious extremism, if not terrorism), but also by early accounts of the history of the Church. The experience of martyrdom was so intense and the Christians' response to it so extraordinary that it is easy to conclude on a hasty reading that persecution was a near-universal phenomenon during the second and third centuries and until the accession of Constantine. However, modern scholars have stressed the fact that although persecution in this period was acute, it was also sporadic. In this respect, it is to be distinguished from the rather different persecutions under Decius and Valerian in the mid-third century and from the so-called 'Great Persecution' of Diocletian in the fourth, which was different again.[6] Consequently, it is important to be clear about what the primary texts show about the nature and extent of persecution from 100 to 250, and what they reveal about Christians' experience of and response to their trials.

There are a variety of texts attesting to persecution in this period, both pagan (for example, a letter of Pliny the Younger) and Christian (notably the numerous 'acts of the martyrs', narratives written to commemorate the deaths of particular Christians). The letters of Ignatius, Bishop of Antioch, anticipate his own martyrdom with brilliant – if shocking – turns of phrase. In the vivid *Passion of Saints Perpetua and Felicity* we have an apparently autobiographical account of Perpetua's trial and stay in prison, to which is appended another author's account of the martyrdom of Perpetua and her companions. Some texts focus mostly on a trial in which Christians confront their accusers and confess their faith; others concentrate mainly on the martyrs' deaths. In some cases, there is evidence that later hands edited the texts according to the sensibilities of a later age; nevertheless, most scholars now seem to agree that there is enough evidence in the texts that is reliable, not least because it mostly fits with accounts by pagan authors. Rather than reading them in order to find out concrete facts about particular persecutions in particular places, it is perhaps more illuminating to read them as pointing to a number of themes, both historical and theological.

Despite the obvious ideological slant of the texts, there is a great deal that one can learn historically about persecution in the second to early third centuries. Firstly, there is much evidence to support the view that persecution in this period was not only sporadic and often due to tensions between Christians and the rest of the local community, but that these tensions were usually dependent on particular local circumstances. For example, the *Acts of the Martyrs of Lyons and Vienne* deals with a spate of persecution around 177, in towns whose Christian congregations were largely formed from the population of immigrants from Asia Minor who had settled in Gaul, following the trade route of the Rhône Valley. The text suggests that the tensions which might have arisen in any case between the local and the immigrant populations were focused in particular on the alien practices of the Christians, as people who 'brought in new and foreign religions'.[7] It is likely that such tensions between insiders and outsiders were sometimes exacerbated by the occurrence of natural disasters, such as the vicious onset of disease or famine: thus the persecutions along the Rhône may have been precipitated by the waves of contagious disease which spread throughout the Empire from 165 onwards. In the previous century, Nero's persecution of Christians in Rome was attributed to his desire to find someone to blame for the devastating fire of 65CE.[8] Nearly a century and a half later, this kind of complaint seems to have become a typical one, expressed perhaps most famously by Tertullian:

> they think the Christians the cause of every public disaster, of every affliction with which the people are visited. If the Tiber rises as high as the city walls, if the Nile does not send its waters up over the fields, if the heavens give no rain, if there is an earthquake, if there is a famine or pestilence, straightway the cry is 'Away with the Christians to the lion!'[9]

Despite Tertullian's poetic expression and his sarcastic reply ('– What! Shall you give such multitudes to a single beast?') there is no reason to doubt his basic claim. Although many gods could be venerated in Greco-

Roman polytheistic religion, individuals typically focused on a selection of gods. Some were worshipped for various specific reasons (for example, for a good harvest, for protection during childbirth or in storms at sea), but many people grew up with a special loyalty to the local god, who was often envisaged as the protector of the local town from such disasters as Tertullian describes. If Christians failed to do honour to their local town's deity, therefore, they were failing not only to fit in with local custom but failing to participate in rituals which were designed to preserve the welfare of the whole community. The common accusation that Christians were 'atheists',[10] which seems odd to modern readers, can be understood in this context: Christians were acknowledged to worship a god, but in their refusal to take part in local cults, their irresponsibility was thought to be on a par with that of those who denied the existence of deities altogether.

In addition to the accusation of atheism, the other typical charge against Christians in this period was that they were immoral. Sometimes this charge was left undefined, sometimes it was developed along the lines that Christians indulged in infanticide and cannibalism (the accusation of 'Thyestean feasts' refers to Thyestes who ate his own children) or incest ('Oedipan couplings').[11] It seems that these were partly standardized accusations meant to evoke the extremes of immorality; they may also have been provoked by a (perhaps wilful) misunderstanding of the Christian rituals of the Eucharist, and the *agape* meal and, perhaps, the kiss of peace.[12]

Despite such evidence of popular distrust of Christians, it is clear that the Roman authorities were not in this period pursuing a consistent policy of persecution – far less of eradication. When Pliny wrote to Trajan, there was some *precedent* for executing Christians (which Pliny was already following). But there seems not to have been a clear or formal imperial *policy*, because Pliny wanted to find out what the emperor's preferred procedure was, provoked by the large numbers of local people bringing to him lists of those accused of being Christian. Two things perplexed him: is being a Christian in itself a legitimate charge? and how rigorously should Christians be prosecuted? He makes it clear that he thinks the Christians are foolish, even insane (a common view among pagans), but he explained that his current policy was to provide ample means for waverers to repent and escape. For those who did not, the punishment was harsh: execution. Nevertheless, the conclusion of his letter suggested very strongly that the aim of the exercise was not the extermination of Christians but rather their return to the ways of civic religion: 'there is no doubt that people have begun to throng the temples which had been almost entirely deserted for a long time. ... It is easy to infer from this that a great many people could be reformed if they were given an opportunity to repent.'[13]

Evidence such as the correspondence between Pliny and Trajan suggests, then, that the Roman authorities were not concerned to seek Christians out, and they claimed they were happy to give Christians every opportunity to mend the error of their ways. However, it is also clear that the experience of some Christians at least was that once one person was caught the rest of his or her family and associates were likely to become involved, even if they were not actually arrested. According to the moving account of Perpetua's trial, her father (who might have been a Christian himself) begged her to deny her faith: 'Lay aside your pride; do not destroy all of us. None of us will ever be able to speak freely again if you suffer any of this.'[14] The persecution of Christians in Lyons and Vienne seemed to involve a particularly proactive search on the part of the authorities: 'all the zealous ones (especially those through whom things have been established here) were collected from out of the two Christian communities. ... Even some of our gentile household slaves were being seized, since the governor ordered publicly that all of us be investigated.'[15] In general, martyrdom accounts suggest that the variety of those Christians who were arrested reflected the variety of the Christian community as a whole: men and women, the wealthy and local tradesmen, freedmen and slaves.[16]

The genre of many martyrdom accounts, the *Acta*, was based largely on reports of their trials. The *Acta* purposely contrasted the uncontrolled behaviour of the crowd with the Roman authorities' judicial process, in order to emphasize that it was the state which had ultimate responsibility for the martyrs' deaths; moreover, while the populace used violence in the heat of the moment, the governors imposed terrible violent deaths after careful consideration and due process:

> First of all, they nobly endured all that was brought on them in heaps by the populace: jeers, blows, draggings, plunder, stoning, confinement, and all such things that are apt to occur when an enraged mob acts as though against enemies and foes. They were brought up into the market-place and, after being questioned by the military tribune and the foremost authorities of the city in the presence of the whole mob, they confessed and were confined to prison until the arrival of the governor.[17]

The fact that the governor of a province alone had the authority to impose a death penalty, and that Roman citizens could be sent to Rome for trial, meant that the Christians had often to endure several stages of an extended judicial process.

The question of a trial raises the questions: with what crime were the Christians charged? and how did their trials proceed? The 'legal procedure' which Pliny settled on, and which indeed seems to have been common in the Empire as a whole, was in effect a test of the Christians' sincerity.

He first asked the captives whether they were Christians, as if recognizing that Christians were unwilling to deny that they bore the name of Christ. He also knew that genuine Christians would not blaspheme by swearing an oath nor pray to another god, nor curse Christ, nor 'make an offering to [Trajan's] statue'. Thus he gave anyone accused of being a Christian an opportunity to do these things, in order to exculpate himself or herself. The fundamental crime was not the prisoners' failure to sacrifice to the gods, or for the good of the emperor; rather, this was a test of the more basic issue: were they Christians or not? Trajan's reply implicitly accepted Pliny's suggestion that 'it is the mere name of "Christian" which is punishable, even if innocent of crime'.[18] Furthermore, in the accounts of Christians brought to trial, their constant willing reiteration of the phrase 'I am a Christian' seems to underline this point, as does the equally constant declaration that they were not being executed for their immoral or criminal behaviour.[19]

But why should being a Christian be a crime? Although this question is much debated by historians, it seems that the exercise devised by the Romans to test the Christians' sincerity was in effect also a test of their loyalty to the emperor and the Empire. While Christians appeared to have angered people at a local level by their neglect of community cults, they also angered the Roman authorities at another level by their refusal to honour the imperial cult – that is, by their refusal to sacrifice for the good of the emperor, or to his genius (guardian deity). It was not so much that intellectual assent to some quasi-divine status of the emperor was being required, but that all inhabitants of the Empire (and especially its citizens) were expected to participate in the imperial cult in order to secure the well being of the Empire. Refusal to participate was an act of disloyalty, not just a religious error.[20] To the Roman authorities, the sacrifice was a symbol of good faith, whose religious and political elements could not be disentangled. On the other hand, they saw the name 'Christian' as a symbol of a fundamental faithlessness, both to the Empire and its gods. Both Christians and their persecutors agreed, then, that loyalty was the fundamental issue: the sacrifice and the name 'Christian' became crucial because they were potent symbols of (dis)loyalty, which could not be disentangled from the question of a person's basic allegiance.

The Christian accounts of martyrdoms imply that Christians were sentenced to execution if they confessed and refused to recant (although historically speaking this appears not always to have been the case). Some were tortured before they were killed and others died as a result of torture or imprisonment in appalling conditions. One method of executing Christians was to throw them to the beasts in the arena – that is, they shared the fate of many other criminals and military/political prisoners in the

Roman Empire, by being forced to fight against wild beasts in the arena for the entertainment of the crowds. Unlike the professional gladiators who fought against wilds beasts or each other, they had no armour or weapons. The *Passion of Saints Perpetua and Felicity* gruesomely implies that the governor planned a special show for the emperor's birthday, as if to make a particularly public spectacle of the Christians' disloyalty.[21] It has even been suggested that the local governor's over-enthusiastic pursuit of Christians in Lyons and Vienne can be explained by his need to provide more victims for the games: a move which would satisfy the people's desire for this kind of entertainment and make him popular with wealthy citizens who would normally have to pay for gladiators.

Other Christians were burnt at the stake or executed by the sword. Although the latter was in theory reserved for Roman citizens, in practice this custom was sometimes ignored.[22] Throwing Christians to the lions thus symbolized their perceived position as outsiders in the Empire. The martyr texts' emphasis on wild beasts also encapsulated the early Christians' opinion of the violence and irrationality of imperial power. Ignatius' *Letter to the Romans*, for example, anticipated his death by beasts in Rome and described his captors themselves as beasts: 'From Syria to Rome I have been fighting the wild beasts, through land and sea, night and day, bound to ten leopards, which is a company of soldiers, who become worse when treated well.'[23] (Those from an arrested Christian's community would often bribe the captors either in order to obtain better conditions or to gain access to provide the prisoner with food and spiritual comfort.)

These texts, therefore, reveal something about how Christians *experienced* and *interpreted* the phenomenon of martyrdom, besides yielding the kind of factual information discussed above. One important aspect of this process of interpretation was Christian reflection on the question of martyrdom and suicide. The former was lauded, the latter condemned; but there was increasing awareness that the boundary between the two was not very clear. The *Martyrdom of Polycarp* stressed that when it became clear that Polycarp was in danger of arrest, he allowed himself to be persuaded to leave the city, and that he changed location at least once more before he was arrested. The text protected Polycarp against the charge of cowardice[24] and condemned voluntary martyrdom, not least by deliberately contrasting Polycarp with Quintus, about whom there is a salutary tale:

> Now someone called Quintus ... became afraid when he saw the wild beasts. This was the man who forced himself and some others to present themselves voluntarily [for trial]. The proconsul ... persuaded him to swear and to offer sacrifice. For this reason ... we do not commend those who give themselves up [to suffering], seeing the Gospel does not teach so to do.[25]

Justin Martyr, although he expected 'to be plotted against and fixed to the stake', nevertheless made it clear that no one should seek death.[26] Against the claim that suicide would bring Christians instantly closer to God, he argued that it would be against the divine will, hindering the birth and education of future Christians. He was, perhaps, defending Christians against the implicit charge that they sought martyrdom too quickly: 'when we are examined, we make no denial, because we are not conscious of any evil, but count it impious not to speak the truth in all things, which also we know is pleasing to God, and because we are also now very desirous to deliver you from an unjust prejudice'.[27]

Other texts were more ambivalent. Tertullian impressed on his readers that they should not avoid persecution. In effect he argued that the whole structure of military life (perhaps implicitly the whole structure of life under Roman imperial rule) continually confronted Christians with a decision between 'two masters', God and Caesar: the 'test' was not so much facing up to the consequences of arrest when informed against by someone else but being brave enough to follow out the consequences of one's loyalty to Christ. In this ethic, martyrdom seemed all but inevitable – for soldiers at least.[28] Other texts even demonstrated an enthusiasm for martyrdom. The martyrs of Lyons and Vienne, for example, apparently prayed for their witness to Christ to be 'perfected' by a martyr's death.[29] Most strikingly, Ignatius appealed to Christians in Rome not to act with misguided generosity to prevent his death:

> I am writing to all the churches and giving instruction to all, that I am willingly dying for God, unless you hinder me. I urge you, do not become an untimely kindness to me. Allow me to become bread for the wild beasts; through them I am able to attain to God. I am the wheat of God, and am ground by the teeth of the wild beasts, that I may be found to be the pure bread of Christ. Rather, coax the wild beasts, that they may become a tomb for me to leave no part of my body behind, that I may burden no one once I have died. Then I will truly be a disciple of Jesus Christ, when the world does not see even my body. Petition Christ on my behalf, that I may be found a sacrifice through these instruments of God.[30]

It is perhaps not surprising that a tradition arose that Ignatius gave himself up to Trajan, 'being in fear for the church of the Antiochians'.[31] Perhaps some Christians felt that by handing themselves over they could selflessly forestall or prevent the arrest of others in their community. Nevertheless, even if Ignatius' gruesome desire to 'enjoy the wild beasts that are prepared for me … if they be unwilling to assail me, I will compel them to do so' does not strictly amount to suicide, a sympathetic reading of his words is particularly hard in comparison to other texts which explicitly distance their heroes from all trace of suicide or self-glorification. When Perpetua, for example, guided the executioner's sword to her throat, her action was described as being motivated from empathy with the novice gladiator who was too nervous or overwhelmed to give the killing blow.[32]

The idea that martyrdom 'perfected' the martyr points to some more directly theological themes. First is the idea of martyrdom as witness.[33] Martyrs were portrayed as witnesses to God and especially to Jesus Christ, both through the confession 'I am a Christian' and through their deaths. A frequent feature of the *Acta* is the conversion of bystanders by the witness of the martyrs in word and deed: 'So the people all went away bewildered and many of them came to believe.'[34] This act of witness was never portrayed as the work of the martyrs themselves but as the work of God working through them: indeed, their witness is a participation in the witness of Christ, 'the faithful and true witness' to God the Father.[35] For this reason, some martyrdom accounts deliberately drew parallels between the arrest, trial and death of the martyr and those of Jesus Christ.[36] The participation in Christ's witness included a participation in his death and resurrection and this seems to be primarily what the martyrs meant by their perfection: 'But if I suffer, I will become a freed person who belongs to Jesus Christ, and I will rise up, free, in him. ... That is the one I seek, who died on our behalf: that is the one I desire, who arose for us.'[37]

The connection between Christ and the martyr was depicted by various symbols. Ignatius' bold claim that 'I am the wheat of God, and am ground by the teeth of the wild beasts, that I may be found the pure bread of God' alluded to the biblical identification of Christ as the 'bread of God' and the 'bread of life' (the bread which Ignatius later said he himself desired).[38] The materiality of bread indicated that Ignatius believed that his participation in Christ went beyond a mere moral identification with or imitation of Christ.[39] Participation in Christ's resurrection through sharing his death was also sometimes described in terms reminiscent of the baptismal liturgy (which itself was often seen as a symbolic descent into death and rising again): a purificatory washing, a 'second baptism' and a symbolic rebirth.[40] The martyrs were said to share Christ's victory over death, their persecutors and the devil.[41] As if to heighten the paradox of a victory through death, the victory was often described in terms of a military or gladiatorial triumph, or the Christian was compared to a victorious athlete.[42] The martyrs were portrayed as turning the world upside down: their death was life; they overcame not with power but with love.[43] The texts about martyrs also revealed an eschatological hope which was heightened by a confidence in their own destinies: Ignatius and Perpetua, for example, were certain that they would soon join the risen Christ in heaven. Sometimes the martyrs' hopes for themselves were coupled with the authors' predictions of the fate of their persecutors: when Perpetua and her companions meet Hilarianus, the procurator conducting their trial, they 'began to say to him. ... "What you do to us, God will do to you"'.[44]

Without understanding the early Christian experience of persecution it is very difficult to understand the other important kind of Christian literature in this period, that is, defences of the Christian faith. These defences were typically directed against three different kinds of challenge to the Christian faith: the type of writing known as apology dealt with pagan culture, especially its religion and philosophy; heresiology was directed against groups which claimed to be Christian but whose claims were disputed by other Christians; and, finally, various kinds of Christian texts distinguished Christianity from Jewish faith and practice. In most of these texts one finds direct verbal attacks on the people or beliefs which are perceived as threatening Christianity; when reading them in a modern context, this is particularly noticeable in the case of Christian condemnations of Jews. In arguing that such attacks can only be understood in the context of Christian experience of martyrdom and Christians' equally bitter attacks on other groups, this book is of course not claiming that such Christian attitudes were defensible, merely that they need to be seen as one part of a rather complex process of self-definition and – as the Christians at the time saw it – of self-defence.

Although scholars have conventionally separated apology, heresiology and writings against Jews, it is helpful to treat them as three examples of a wider kind of writing, all of which took place against a background of sporadic persecution. This is not least because we know that many of the so-called 'apologists' also wrote works against Jews and heretics. There is also no very clear dividing line between texts which were clearly addressed to actual pagans, supposed heretics and Jews on the one hand, and those which used an attack on such persons and their beliefs as a means of teaching the mainstream Christian community itself. Sometimes, indeed, there has been much argument whether a text like Justin's *Dialogue with Trypho* involves a real Jew, or whether it is simply using a Jewish character as a construct with which to think through the distinctions between Christian and Jewish faith. Thus defences of Christianity (or attacks on its opponents) are not necessarily distinguishable from the catechetical works – texts which were used for teaching new converts before their baptism (catechumens) – or from texts used to strengthen the faith of more established Christians. So although distinctions in literary genre often help us understand the purpose of different kinds of Christian writing, genres were often used fairly flexibly by early Christian writers: part of their process of self-definition in the face of both pagan culture and Jewish antecedents was precisely their borrowing, adaptation and subversion of various traditional literary forms. The remainder of this chapter will deal with defences of Christianity in the context of pagan culture – the form normally known as apology, while works which deal with the challenges presented by Judaism and marginal Christian groups will form the subject of the next.

What is important about the apologists is that they *argue*.[45] Instead of proclaiming the Gospel to new or potential converts, an apology was usually addressed to pagans in positions of high authority (sometimes the emperors themselves) with the aim of persuading them, through reasoned argument, that Christianity was not a threat to the Empire, since it was a noble, moral and ancient faith. The implicit or explicit corollary was that persecution should therefore cease.

We know very little about most of the apologists beyond what they tell us in their own texts and a few hints from the fourth-century historian Eusebius. They are often known as the 'Greek apologists', for like most Christian writers in this period (including those who lived in Rome), they wrote in Greek.[46] Some were laymen, pursuing careers as teachers: Aristides and Athenagoras, for example, were based in Athens, where the influence of the philosophical and rhetorical schools was still very strong, despite the increasing importance of Rome as an intellectual as well as a political centre.[47] Justin was born in Flavia Neapolis (ancient Shechem, modern Nablus) in Samaria, but travelled first to Ephesus and thence to Rome as a teacher of Christianity. His pupil Tatian was 'born in the land of the Assyrians',[48] travelled to Rome, where he remained until after Justin's martyrdom around 165, and finally returned to the east where he became a teacher, possibly founding his own school. The prominence of these lay teachers in this period of Christianity is very striking, as is their assumption that Christian belief is a suitable subject for the kind of teaching provided by the prominent pagan teachers and philosophers of the day. Justin and Aristides, indeed, still continued wearing the *pallium* or philosopher's cloak as a sign of their teaching profession. Other apologists, however, continued the tradition of the bishop-teacher/writer found in the Apostolic Fathers: Theophilus and Melito were bishops of the important cosmopolitan cities of Antioch (in the province of Syria) and Sardis (in Asia Minor) respectively. The apologists probably all wrote their main works in the latter half of the second century, during the reigns of Antoninus Pius and Marcus Aurelius. Aristides, Justin Martyr and Athenagoras addressed their apologies directly to the emperor of the time (plus, in some cases, his heir or heirs). Theophilus' *Apology* is a reasoned defence of Christianity addressed to the otherwise unknown pagan Autolycus. Tatian's *Discourse to the Greeks* is not strictly an apology, being a passionate attack on Greek culture with no specific addressees – the reasons for considering it alongside the other works will become clear below. For obvious reasons, apology as a literary form emerged at the heart of the Roman Empire.[49]

Several themes occurred with frequency in the apologists' works. Usually the writer made his case by assuming some kind of common ground between him and his addressees: they shared the same high estimate of reason, moral behaviour and religious piety, for example. The apologist's aim was to persuade his addressee that Christianity was as rational, pious and moral as contemporary Roman religion – or, indeed, that it was more so. As in the martyr accounts, one finds Christian authors rebutting the reported accusations of incest and cannibalism, often by drawing a contrast between the morality of their Christian communities and their pagan contemporaries.[50] Thus, for example, Justin argued that Christians became more not less moral after their conversion:

> We who formerly delighted in fornication ... now embrace chastity alone; we who formerly used magical arts, dedicate ourselves to the good and unbegotten God; we who valued above all things the acquisition of wealth and possessions, now bring what we have into a common stock, and communicate to every one in need; we who hated and destroyed one another, and on account of their different manners would not live with men of a different tribe, now, since the coming of Christ, live familiarly with them, and pray for our enemies, and endeavour to persuade those who hate us unjustly to live conformably to the good precepts of Christ, to the end that they may become partakers with us of the same joyful hope of a reward from God the ruler of all.[51]

A favourite theme in this kind of discourse is the immorality of the violent spectacles put on to entertain the Roman populace: emphasizing that Christians are commanded to be pure not only in deed but in thought too, Theophilus argued that even watching a gladiatorial combat would make Christians 'partakers and abettors of murders'.[52] Tatian was particularly concerned that in order to supply some people with entertainment, other people are bought and sold merely to be killed: 'you purchase men to supply a cannibal banquet for the soul, nourishing it by the most impious blood-shedding'.[53] Even the most erudite and supposedly most moral teachers were not beyond criticism: Justin and Tatian noted the way in which the philosophers constantly disagreed with one another and claimed that through their disputes these supposedly wise men were revealed as arrogant, fanciful, vain, greedy and petty.[54] Echoing Plato's criticisms of the earlier sophists, Athenagoras accused their more recent counterparts of 'searching out secrets ... making the art of words and not the exhibition of deeds their business and profession'.[55] By contrast, even the most lowly members of the Christian

communities ('uneducated persons, and artisans, and old women') demonstrated the benefit of Christianity through their deeds, even though they
were unable to prove it in words. Here Athenagoras referred in particular to
Christ's command to 'Love your enemies ... bless them that curse you; pray
for them that persecute you.'[56] Justin also backed up his claims to Christian
morality with words from Christ, whereas Theophilus put more emphasis on the Hebrew Bible, citing the Ten Commandments and other moral
instructions, assuming that the Gospel was in agreement, but quoting it
more rarely. These extracts give a useful snapshot of the ideals and values of
the Christian communities in the late second century.

In addition to denying pagan claims about immorality, the apologists
also defended themselves against charges of impiety. Indeed, they did not
take part in the worship of pagan gods, but this was because those gods
were neither truly divine nor worthy of worship. Attacks on the immoral
or ridiculous character of the myths about pagan gods are found in most of
the apologists, as are arguments against the worship of idols and demons.[57]
Athenagoras countered the charge of atheism with a reasoned argument:
Christians were not atheists, because they acknowledged one God, the
creator of the world and all that is in it. This Creator-God cannot be served
through the worship of the things he himself made (i.e. Christians cannot
use statues in worship); nevertheless Christians direct their piety towards
God, rather than rejecting it altogether as true atheists would.[58] Some of the
apologists, however, acknowledge more explicitly that one person's piety is
another's impiety: Justin Martyr nicely grasps the nettle, remarking 'Hence
are we called atheists. And we confess that we are atheists, so far as gods
of this sort are concerned, but not with respect to the most true God, the
Father of righteousness and temperance and the other virtues, who is free
from all impurity.'[59] In other words, there could be no question of simply
adding the Christian God to the Greco-Roman pantheon, alongside Jupiter and Juno, Minerva and Apollo.

Consequently, the apologists worked hard to defend the rationality of
monotheism, together with their belief in the divine and salvific power of
Jesus Christ. Most of the doctrinal issues that they cover – the doctrine of
creation, the nature of God, the relation of God the Father to Jesus Christ
– are focused on this. In their doctrine of creation, they argued against
Greco-Roman mythologies (which did not depict the gods as creators of
the world) and philosophies (which had various interpretations of the relationship between god(s) and the world).[60] By contrast with these views, the
apologists argued firmly for God's creation of all aspects of the world, both
visible and invisible, often with direct or indirect reference to the opening words of the Book of Genesis. One point which is drawn from such a

doctrine of creation was a clear distinction between God and the world, especially the material world. This was exploited by the apologists in order to condemn idol worship as something which confuses the two.[61] The strong distinction between God and matter was aided, in the case of Theophilus and Tatian, by the idea of the creation of the world from nothing – as opposed to the idea that God gave form to already existing matter (as in Athenagoras).[62] A second move the apologists made was to begin to discuss how the generation of the Son from the Father differed from the creation of the world by God. Whereas the world was created from nothing, or formed from some pre-existent matter, the Son came from God – and thus was God. Their language was not always very consistent in this respect, however, and the need for clarification was one of the issues lying behind the Arian controversy at the beginning of the fourth century.[63]

It was partly in order to elucidate this distinction between creation and generation that the apologists, particularly Justin, developed their idea of the Son as 'Logos'. Picking up on the use of 'Logos' (Greek for 'Word' or 'Reason') as a title of Jesus Christ in the New Testament and its use in Greek translations of the Hebrew Bible and later Jewish literature to express a power or agency of God, Justin developed it to explain the relation of God and Jesus Christ by analogy with a mind and its word:

> He ministers to the Father's will, and ... He was begotten of the Father by an act of will; just as we see happening among ourselves: for when we give out some word [*logos*], we beget the word; yet not by cutting away, so as to lessen the word [*logos*] in us, when we give it out. ... The Word of Wisdom, who is Himself this God, begotten of the Father of all things, and Word, and Wisdom, and Power, and the Glory of the Begetter, will bear evidence to me, when He speaks by Solomon the following ... 'The Lord made me the beginning of His ways for His works. From everlasting He established me in the beginning, before He had made the earth, and before He had made the deeps, before the springs of the waters had issued forth, before the mountains had been established. Before all the hills He begets me.'[64]

Besides the idea that a word is both separate from and one with the mind that expressed it, Justin worked from the double sense of Logos in Greek: it meant both word and thought (or reason). Thus he argued in the passage above that the Word is with God (as thought) and was expressed or given out by God (as Word). As the text suggests, crucial to the distinction between the Logos and the world is that he existed in and with God the Father before the world began – 'before the morning-star and the moon'.[65] Justin made a clear distinction between the world which is created or made (thus is not God), and the Logos who is generated or begotten (and thus *is* God). He also began the long Christian tradition of distinguishing between God the Son/Logos who is begotten and God the Father who is unbegotten.[66]

The Logos doctrine was used by Justin to express not only the relationship between God the Father and God the Son, but also the relationship between the Son and the world. Firstly, if the Word is both with God and can be expressed (or sent out) by God, it was easier to understand how one can 'believe of a crucified human that He is the first-born of the unbegotten God': because of the unique qualities of the Word he can be both (in) God and in the world.[67] Justin in particular emphasized that the Logos was present in the world before the Incarnation: he was the one who appeared to Abraham, Jacob and Moses; he inspired the Prophets.[68] Not only that but the best of the pagan philosophers such as Plato and Socrates had received the Word, although their reception of it was only partial: 'For whatever either lawgivers or philosophers uttered well, they elaborated by finding and contemplating some part of the Word [Logos]. But since they did not know the whole of the Word [Logos], which is Christ, they often contradicted themselves.'[69] Again Justin exploited the dual force of 'Logos' as meaning both word and reason, in effect asserting that the Son was the word that inspired the Prophets but also the reason that inspired the best philosophy of the Greeks, and could inspire the thoughts even of simpler people, 'for He was and is the Word/Reason who is in everyone'.[70] With this doctrine of the Logos, Justin also cleverly argued for the antiquity of Christianity: Christ as Logos was part of the history of both the Jews and the Gentiles before Christ, albeit in a partial sense. Justin also adapted another sense of 'Logos' as meaning a principle of order and rationality in the cosmos: thus as Word the Son was not only source of revelation to humanity but a force in creation which gave order and beauty to the world.

Some discussion of the Logos idea in Justin and other early Christian theologians appears to assume that it must be *either* a 'Christian' ('biblical') *or* a 'Greek' ('philosophical') idea. It is true that Justin was influenced by Stoic and Platonic sources: for example, the idea of divine Logos as a principle of rationality and good order pervading the whole of existence echoes a Stoic concept, and Justin also adapted both Stoic and Platonic concepts to express the idea that pagans and Christians could both share in the divine Logos, albeit to differing degrees.[71] Theophilus too adapted Stoic terminology to express the relation between God the Father and Son.[72] Equally, however, these writers could point to biblical sources of their ideas. As with most if not all writers in this period, the question of their sources is not 'either/or', but 'both … and': the success of their writing depended on their ability to borrow, adapt and meld different ideas and images together in order to express the truth which they believed was embodied by Jesus Christ.[73] Nor should the use of Greek philosophical terminology be thought to be aimed solely at converting pagans, or defending Christianity before them; of equal importance was the task of explaining and clarifying Christian beliefs for those who were already part of the Church.

Another way of contextualizing the role of philosophy in Justin is to note that his theology centres not on the quest for knowledge for its own sake but on the proclamation of God's salvation. It is true that this is often expressed in terms of the divine revelation of knowledge (as it is indeed in John's Gospel, for example), but Justin did not neglect the importance of the incarnation of the Logos in Jesus of Nazareth, through whom alone he believed humans could grasp the Logos fully. Besides this, Justin also expressed salvation in other terms, for example as God's victory, or as healing: 'we worship and love the Word who is from the unbegotten and ineffable God, since also he became human for our sakes, that, becoming a partaker of our sufferings, He might also bring us healing.'[74] This latter notion depended on faith in the historical person Jesus who healed the sick and whose death on the Cross brought about a new kind of healing for humankind.

It was particularly important for the apologists to stress that Christians believed that their current sufferings would be overcome, for one objection they faced from the Romans was that the God they preached appeared to be weak – dying on the Cross and being unable to prevent the deaths of many of his followers. In responding to this objection Christians appealed to the idea of resurrection: as we have seen, undoubtedly one reason why the Christians felt able to endure trials was their hope in the resurrection of the body and a dwelling place in God's kingdom. The idea of the resurrection was, however, clearly a big stumbling block for the apologists' pagan addressees. Pagan opinions on the possibility of life after death varied, but whether one was a Platonist or Aristotelian committed to the idea of the immortality of the soul, or an Epicurean or Stoic sceptic, the resurrection of the body would have seemed outlandish and difficult to comprehend. Nor could the issue easily be pushed aside: the resurrection of Christ was obviously central to Christian belief and liturgy and, as we have seen, it appears to have been asserted even more strongly in the context of persecution. Thus apologists felt obliged to explain the possibility of the resurrection of the body, even when faced with deliberately tasteless objections (for example, what happens to the body parts of humans which are consumed by animals?).[75] Athenagoras' argument in *The Resurrection* is remarkable for the fact that he quotes Scripture only once (I Corinthians 15.54), and for his apparently almost exclusive reliance on rational argument. Nevertheless this aspect can be exaggerated: the arguments clearly assume and indeed depend on the existence of a divine being (for example, Athenagoras argues that the resurrection is neither impossible nor improbable given that it is the work of the same being who created the world[76]) and several fairly specific ideas about future judgement and the co-dependence of the human soul and body are also crucial to his case. Although pagan readers might have been persuaded into such views, there is no reason to suppose that the ideas were self-evidently rational to his audience, as Athenagoras' arguments often appear to imply.

Although it has been argued that the apologists' eschatology was more moderate or less important than that of the martyr accounts, it is not clear that this is the case. Theophilus, Athenagoras and Justin, for example, all argue for the morality of Christian communities partly on the grounds that they await a final judgement in which God will separate the good (destined for heaven) from the sinners (destined for eternal punishment).[77] The use of the idea of punishment by fire is common, although it is difficult to know how literally it was intended. Justin did not emphasize the idea of an imminent end to the world (which might seem to imply Christian hopes for the imminent end of the Empire), but he appears to have thought that the world would end relatively soon.[78] He sought to reassure his Roman addressees that 'when you hear that we look for a kingdom, you suppose, without making any inquiry, that we speak of a human kingdom; whereas we speak of that which is with God'.[79] However, his view that the Christians hoped for Christ's thousand-year reign with the elect in the Holy Land might have kindled a fear that Christians had political ambitions (particularly since the Romans had put down a Jewish rebellion in Palestine only about 20 or so years before).[80] One can argue that the apologists' hopes were focused on the resurrection and Christ's future kingdom on earth, while martyr accounts tended to stress the martyr's immediate presence with Christ in heaven. But these views are not strictly contradictory and in fact the apologists and the authors of the martyrdom accounts shared similar *beliefs* – where they differed was how they expressed them, which varied according to their addressees.

In sum, apology was aimed at persuading the Roman authorities that 'the frequent local persecutions of Christians were unjust, unnecessary and unworthy of enlightened rulers'.[81] In order to prove it was unjust, the apologists stressed their moral virtue; in order to show it was unnecessary they emphasized that they presented no threat to the Empire; in order to show that it was unworthy they argued for their piety, and the antiquity and reasonableness of their faith. As a result, apology was the first Christian kind of writing to grapple in a focused and detailed way with the issues that were increasingly setting them apart from many features of contemporary pagan culture (a culture which was most Christians' own, given that most

Christians in this period were converts from within the Roman Empire). As such, it had undoubted strengths: it led Christians to think in a different way about their faith, to consider it from the perspective of rational argument. Although this led to many questions about the relation between faith and reason which remained unanswered (not least because the questions were usually only raised implicitly), it did cause writers such as Justin to make important advances in Christian doctrinal theology. In particular, the development of the concept of the Logos to express the relation between God the Father and God the Son was hugely significant for later theology.

Apology was also clearly important in the sense that it demonstrated that Christianity could appeal to philosophers and statesmen, as well as to slaves, tradesmen and women. Both Greek and Roman culture propagated intellectual snobbery and it is clear that underlying complaints about Christianity's novelty was a more fundamental belief that it was not sophisticated enough to warrant detailed attention. Clearly, Christianity had already begun to attract what one might call 'intellectual' converts, as the case of Justin himself shows; nevertheless, as one can see through the influence of his own writings, it accelerated even more through the development of apology as a form. Therefore, while apology may not have been successful in directly persuading emperors to stop persecuting Christians, its major success was in attracting an increasing number of increasingly clever, sophisticated and articulate men who did much to advance and defend Christian theology in the coming years and who also did much to develop a literary culture within Christianity. (The next two chapters will develop this theme.) Although the immediate appeals against persecution were not successful, then, one can argue that apology as a form did much to increase the social and cultural acceptability of Christianity as a religion, a factor which was necessary for its eventual adoption as the religion of the Empire.

But apology also had its weaknesses. As remarked above, there is very little evidence to suggest that its attempts at persuading those in power had direct results (Justin himself was martyred and Marcus Aurelius was no great admirer of the Christian faith). Apology also suffered from a fundamental tension or ambiguity: despite the fact that the apologists were trying to establish a common ground with their interlocutors, ultimately they were trying to prove their own religious superiority. Because he could not agree to simply adding his God to the Greco-Roman pantheon, even a writer like Justin (who did accept some fundamental common values between pagan and Christian religion) was forced into trying to show not just that his religion was *acceptable* to the Roman authorities, but that it was in fact *superior* – even on their own terms. This kind of argument might have been a good strategy for mission, but it had clear weaknesses when used to persuade rulers that Christians were no threat. (The problem was of course exacerbated by the fact that Justin thinks that what pagans have in common with Christians they in fact borrowed from Moses' writings, or had implanted in them by the Logos – so even these things are not truly their own, but Christ's.)

A related problem was that of establishing any significant common ground between Christianity and its pagan context. Although many Christians were converts from paganism, once they converted they saw it only through Christian eyes; this inevitably skewed their appreciation of what was important or significant in pagan culture. Neither ridiculing the worship of pagan gods and reading Homer and Hesiod in a very simplistic way nor cherry-picking the philosophy of the schools took seriously the ordinary piety of many Romans in the Empire, whether slaves or senators. Addressing queries about the *possibility* of resurrection seemed to miss the fundamental pagan concern: *why* should resurrection be a good thing to hope for? But to argue the case from a Christian perspective, to ground the general resurrection in Christ's resurrection, would have been to assume belief in precisely that which was under question. There was a sense in which it was impossible for apology to be a successful form of persuasion.

This is perhaps why one finds some writers who are described as apologists taking a stance which more determinedly opposes Christianity to its pagan context. Thus Aristides and the *Preaching of Peter* speak of Christians as a different race (*genos*) from pagans on the one hand and Jews on the other. The ease with which they were able to do this was undoubtedly helped by the fact that Jews had been distinguishing themselves from Gentiles for many generations. This distinction was based on an original racial difference, even though many Jews were culturally highly Hellenized and increasing numbers were converts (proselytes). The notion of being a separate race came to be associated more with a sense of religious identity – specifically the idea that the Law and its observance set them apart from the rest of society in a significant way. If the idea of being a 'distinct race' was ambiguous when applied by Jews to themselves, the Christians' adaptation of this language to those who had never been racially, culturally or historically distinct stretched the concept even more. If they felt a people apart, it was because Christians thought their beliefs and loyalties alone made them so.

But it was a moot issue whether they *should* see themselves as separate. In this period, the question perhaps received its most trenchant answer in Tatian's *Discourse to the Greeks*, in which he launches a vitriolic attack on the culture, myths and beliefs of the Greeks:

While inquiring what God is, you are ignorant of what is in yourselves; and, while staring all agape at the sky, you stumble into pits. The reading of your books is like walking through a labyrinth, and their readers resemble the cask of the Danaïds. ... [82] While you arrogate to yourselves the sole right of discussion, you discourse like the blind man with the deaf. Why do you handle the builder's tools [i.e. the tools of reason and language] without knowing how to build? Why do you busy yourselves with words, while you keep aloof from deeds, puffed up with praise, but cast down by misfortunes?[83]

Yet even this work demonstrates the inherent tensions of such a form of writing, for, as this quotation shows, Tatian's form of expression, his eloquence, the very fact that he alludes to classical mythology demonstrate that he is himself a product of the very culture he is trying to repudiate. One cannot help suspecting that the man who 'in his early years acquired considerable reputation by his lectures on Greek philosophy and science' enjoyed his former training too much to let go of it easily.[84]

This chapter has shown that the relationship between Christians and pagans in this period was fraught with tensions. On the one hand, however much some Christians (such as Ignatius, Tatian or the authors of the martyr acts) chose to define themselves over against what they saw as the inherently pagan culture of the Roman Empire, most Christians were simply unable to remove themselves from the social, literary and intellectual culture of the Roman Empire – it was still in many ways *their* culture, however much they felt at odds with it. On the other hand, those, like Justin and the other apologists, who tried to argue for the acceptability of the Christian faith by establishing common ground between it and some widely held contemporary beliefs, found themselves faced with a difficult dilemma: either to accept Christianity as one faith among others in a pluralist society, or to argue for the superiority of Christianity, which in effect undermined the common ground which they were working hard to establish. Furthermore, while arguing against pagan polytheism, they often used arguments from philosophical pagan monotheists. Even in the case of the relationship with paganism, then, boundaries which at first seem clear can soon be perceived to be complex and questionable. As the next chapter will show, the question of negotiating boundaries was even more complex when it came to Christianity's relationship with Judaism and the relationships between increasingly diverse Christian groups.

CHAPTER 3

Negotiating Boundaries: Varieties of Christianity in Rome and the West

(SECOND TO THIRD CENTURIES)

What was it like to be a Christian in Rome in the latter half of the second century? The traditional day for meeting was Sunday: on this day, Justin tells us, the 'memoirs of the apostles' (the Gospels) or 'the writings of the prophets' were read, followed by a homily in which the presiding member encouraged the congregation to imitate the good things they had heard about. The congregation next offered prayers for themselves and 'for all others in every place' and greeted each other with a kiss. There followed a celebration of the Eucharist. Justin's description of this tried to defend Christians' moral virtue against pagans confused about the nature of Christian practices:

> There is then brought to the president of the brethren bread and a cup of wine mixed with water; and he taking them, gives praise and glory to the Father of the universe, through the name of the Son and of the Holy Ghost, and offers thanks at considerable length for our being worthy to receive these things at his hands. And when he has concluded the prayers and thanksgivings, all the people present express their assent by saying Amen. This word Amen answers in the Hebrew tongue to [the Greek] *genoito* 'so be it'. And when the president has given thanks, and all the people have expressed their assent, those who are called by us deacons give to each of those present to partake of the bread and wine mixed with water over which the thanksgiving was pronounced, and to those who are absent they carry away a portion.[1]

Justin explained that only those who are baptized can share in this celebration and indicates that Eucharist follows the baptism of converts, as well as being the focus of each Sunday celebration.

In the late second century Roman Christians worshipped in private houses, just as the Christians named in Paul's Epistle to the Romans did.

In his greetings in Chapter 16, Paul characterizes some as being of the congregation associated with Aquila's and Prisca's household, and others as congregating around (probably at the house of) several different small groups of named individuals. This tradition of associating a congregation with the name or names of the householder seems to have continued into the following centuries in the way in which the most ancient Roman churches, even when they moved to grander premises, retained the name not of a saint or martyr but of a patron.[2] In these houses Christians met for the celebration of baptism and Eucharist, for instruction and sometimes perhaps for a community meal, more substantial than the Eucharist and probably supplied by the host (the so-called *agape* or love-feast).[3]

Christians also held ceremonies to remember and show respect for the dead, close to their place of burial. As with many early Christian practices, this custom showed both continuities and discontinuities with the surrounding Roman pagan culture (which was still for most Christians *their* culture, in many important ways). For Christians, as for other Romans, burial was a crucial matter for which family, household or wider community were responsible. (Tertullian suggests that Christian collections in this period were used partly to provide for the burial of the poorer members of the congregation.[4]) Christians may have rejected cremation on grounds of their belief in the resurrection, but it seems that in the second–third centuries the general Roman trend was away from cremation (not least because burial allowed the wealthy the opportunity for ostentatiously beautiful sarcophagi). Christians appeared to have followed the common Roman practice of celebrating funeral meals near the burial place, although instead of celebrating the birthday of the dead, they celebrated the day of death, that is, the day of the Christian's rebirth into new life. This anniversary became particularly important in the case of martyrs – hence the habit of referring to the anniversary of a martyrdom as the saint's *natalis*, or birthday. Later writers criticized some Christians for their over-enthusiastic celebration of such feasts and marring the holy places with drunkenness. Markedly more sedate are the meals depicted in some catacomb paintings: these probably show Christians' feasts for the dead, although it is difficult to be certain whether they depict a funeral feast, an *agape*-celebration, or a Eucharist – indeed, the distinctions between these three types of shared meal may not have been clear at this stage, for each was accompanied by prayers. What is, however, generally accepted now is that the catacombs were not places of regular Sunday worship.[5] Their location outside the city walls was inconvenient, and in the second century Christians were still being buried alongside pagans, making burial sites inappropriate, if not risky, places for worship. As the communities developed in the third century, richer members provided land specifically for Christian burials: some of these we now know as the famous Christian catacombs of Rome, often bearing the name of the person who provided them or the Christian leader who was in charge of them. Like the pattern of Sunday worship, this development suggests a picture of several individual communities, each bound together not only by common faith and ethos but also often by dependence on one or more patron households.

The Christian congregations included men, women and children, old people, slaves, freedmen and citizens. Women probably formed a majority in the congregations and performed important social roles, not least in the Christian education of their own children and often by their financial contributions. A particular group – widows – were often singled out for special respect. They were often given priority when alms were distributed and one text implies that they had a special duty of prayer.[6] There is little evidence, however, that women in Rome had leadership roles: although some women were Christian teachers in this period, they were either specifically teachers of orphaned children and widows, or leaders of groups marginal to and rejected by the mainstream congregations.[7] Although Christians affirmed the spiritual equality of women and men, the way in which early writers such as Clement echoed the injunction of I Timothy 2.11 that women should be silent in their meetings suggests a strong feeling (in Rome at least) against women's leadership.[8]

The congregations welcomed members with very different ethnic and religious backgrounds.[9] This mix reflected the highly cosmopolitan population of the city of Rome. Many residents of Rome came from the eastern part of the Empire and Greek was a very common language in the capital among the rich and poor alike, among both the highly educated and the illiterate. Christian mission to Rome came from the east and Greek speakers seem to have been even more predominant in the congregations than in the society at large: thus Greek was Christianity's *lingua franca* in Rome as in most places elsewhere.

Justin draws particular attention to the presence in his congregation of the needy, notably orphans, widows and the sick: 'Those who have, support those who have not, and we always stay together.'[10] Indeed, early Christian literature of this period shows such a marked concern for the care of the poor that there has been a lot of debate about the precise social composition of these early communities: the best guess is that they contained very few (if any) aristocratic Romans, but probably depended an increasing amount on those who were sufficiently well to do to provide a room large enough to worship in and who could help support the poorer members of the congregation. In a society which was used to very cramped living conditions, a Christian meeting would not have required a very big room, and such accommodation could sometimes have been rented, not owned. Similarly, in a community bound together very tightly by the experience of persecution and by a very strong ethos of supporting the weak, the sharing of resources need not necessarily imply that any of the members was very well off.[11] Nevertheless, as the Christian communities grew through the second and into the third centuries, there is increasing evidence of more wealthy members. We know, for example, that at least one largish villa on the outskirts of Rome was used for Christian worship[12] and there are accounts of specific Christians giving lavishly to their congregation. Less happily, Hermas reported that there was a danger of the wealthy members of a congregation becoming dangerously distracted, even obsessed, by their wealth, thus disrupting the harmony of the community.[13]

The existence of Christians like Justin shows that Christianity was increasingly reaching those who had money enough to be very well educated. Although Justin's intellect was exceptional, Christianity had in fact always relied on the literate because of the importance of texts in Christian worship and mission. Converts from Judaism came from a culture in which children (both boys and girls) were educated to a certain standard of literacy either at home or at a school run by the local Jewish community. By contrast, literacy among Gentile converts to Christianity was nearly always a sign of paid education, although the duration and the cost of that education varied massively from family to family. So when Justin wrote that some members of his congregation were illiterate and unable to express themselves well, this was an indication of income as well as literacy.

What is very striking about the social mix of the congregations in Rome is the number of men who presented themselves not primarily as priests or pastors but as teachers. In some cases, such as Justin's, this may have been partly to defend themselves against pagan suspicion, by portraying themselves as a known cultural type: the travelling philosopher-teacher who, like so many others, came to Rome to pursue his profession at the heart of the Empire. But there is no need to doubt that Justin sincerely saw himself as a philosophical teacher (he does not appear to be the 'presiding member' whom he describes as leading the Eucharist celebration). The group which met for instruction in the rooms above the bath of Myrtinus could well have been a reading group which met for further instruction outside the weekly services. Justin was far from being alone in being this kind of Christian lay teacher.

A Christian in Rome in the latter half of the second century, then, would have worshipped in one of several independent congregations, each of which was very varied, socially and ethnically. They depended on patrons to provide a place of worship and to take a lead in donating money for the provision of celebratory meals, alms for the poor and a burial place. Congregations had a presiding member who led the ceremonies of baptism and Eucharist. There were assistants (deacons) who helped particularly with the distribution of the bread and wine at the Eucharist and with the support of the poor and needy. There were also teachers like Justin who may have had a more informal and semi-detached relationship with their congregation.

The previous chapter described Christianity's relations with pagans – not only the experience of persecution and but also attempts to defend the validity and morality of Christianity in the face of such persecution. But there were an increasing number of disagreements between Christians themselves, and this chapter will trace the social context and the theological content of these disputes. It will also deal with Christians' relations with Jews in this period. In the process of defending their views, Christian theologians further developed and refined Christian doctrine; more negatively, the tensions in their relations with Jews and with each other produced a highly emotive rhetorical style. The bitterness of these attacks had long-lasting consequences for the history of the Church. As suggested in the last chapter, it is helpful to consider all three types of writing – that is, against pagans, alleged heretics and Jews – as attempts at Christian self-definition in a context in which Christians were a small and sporadically persecuted minority. Christian faith and practices overlapped in significant ways with those of pagans and Jews, and there were many variations between Christian groups. But the fact that second-century Christians *felt* they were a persecuted minority (whether or not that was an exaggerated fear) meant that they reacted to views which were 'similar but different' as if they were threats. This does not excuse the sometimes violent tone of the disagreements, but it does go some way towards explaining it.

In describing these relationships and arguments, the chapter will focus on Rome, the capital of the Empire, largest city of the known world. Although the number of tensions and disagreements was not necessarily typical of the rest of the Empire, they were well documented and serve as useful illustrations of problems elsewhere. Furthermore, as will be seen in the next chapter, the effects of arguments in Rome often spread like ripples to disturb Christian communities throughout the Empire.

A major reason for the multiplicity of congregations was the size of the city of Rome: with a population approaching a million it was by far the largest city in the Empire and received thousands of visitors every year.[14] As Christianity spread from the east, missionary teachers brought the Gospel to Rome and founded different co-existing house churches. Some of these pre-dated Paul's letter to the Romans, which was written around 55CE. The separate congregations were no doubt aware that there were other Christian communities in the city. They probably regarded themselves as being united in faith with these other communities – or at least with those they thought of sufficiently like mind. After all, Christians of this period were already happy to speak of a Church which was spiritually united, despite its geographic diversity throughout the Mediterranean.[15] However, it is very unclear how much contact there was between the Roman congregations in this period and there was no overall bishop at least until Victor in 189.

The situation of Christianity in Rome in the second century is still more complex though: not only were there multiple different congregations, but there was an increasing variety of Christian belief – a diversity which was already causing dispute and great anxiety. Many of the disputants are now known as heretics, but for the historian to label them as that from the outset is to make artificially sharp the very fuzzy and confused boundaries between different varieties of Christianity at this stage. For example, virtually everything that has been said so far about Christian groups in Rome applies to the followers of the 'heretics' Valentinus and Marcion. We know that they met in private houses to celebrate the Eucharist and baptism and their groups probably contained a similar social mix.[16] There were certainly Marcionite martyrs and there were probably some martyrs among the followers of Valentinus.[17] Both Marcion and Valentinus were members of mainstream Christian congregations, at least for a while. Most Marcionite and Valentinian teaching, even of the most basic kind, seems to have been directed at those who were already of the Christian faith. The Valentinians seemed to be focused on explaining or giving a deeper meaning to Christianity, the Marcionites on correcting misapprehensions about Christ. Tertullian complained that they pulled true Christians away from the fold, rather than converted pagans.[18] Although the Marcionites formed separate churches fairly early, it seems very likely that the original followers of Valentinus and other similar thinkers were 'normal Christians' who attended their usual congregations on Sunday, but who also met to be instructed by their teachers at other times. There appears to be little original intention to found separate churches. Later, when debate and hostility became entrenched, the different groups met separately for worship as well as for their teaching, and their rituals as well as their theology diverged from mainstream Christian practice.

One reason for the diversity of opinion within the Christian communities seems to have arisen precisely from the presence of men like Justin and Valentinus – highly educated teachers who travelled to Rome to follow their career. Valentinus is said to have been born in Egypt and was taught in

Alexandria. His eloquent and learned writing style (praised highly even by his enemies) certainly seems to be evidence of such an education. After teaching in Alexandria, he came to Rome some time between 136 and 140 and seems to have joined one of the Christian congregations there. Tertullian reports that Valentinus expected to become a bishop and left in pique when someone else succeeded. Whether or not Tertullian's typically acid comment can be believed in all respects, it does suggest that Valentinus did not set up his own church from the beginning, and, perhaps, that he did not leave his congregation because of his doctrinal views. Originally, then, the teaching role of someone like Valentinus was probably very similar to that of Justin, even though the content of their teaching differed. The presence of independent teachers with small groups of pupils was part of the culture in Rome. On the surface, Valentinus and Justin seem similar to pagans such as Galen (who travelled from Pergamum to teach medicine), Fronto (an orator from Africa) and perhaps Celsus.[19] Justin presents Christianity as a philosophy, Galen regards it as a philosophy, and the pagan philosopher Celsus sees it at least as a rival to philosophy. Although Justin says he taught for free, this does not necessarily distinguish all Christian teachers from their pagan counterparts: some pagan teachers of philosophy did not take a fee, and some Christian teachers probably charged (or at least tacitly expected a donation of money or material support such as food or accommodation). Perhaps inevitably at this stage when Christian doctrine was so little defined, the presence of such highly educated thinkers teaching in groups outside the main Sunday services meant that an increasing variety of opinion emerged.

This was not the only pattern, however. The figure who first caused great anxiety to Justin was Marcion, a ship owner from Sinope in Asia Minor who presumably originally arrived in Rome because of his trade. Like Justin and Valentinus, he was a Christian before he arrived. He is said by early Christian writers to have joined a normal Christian congregation – indeed Tertullian reports that he gave the congregation the considerable sum of 200,000 sesterces (enough to buy a house in Rome).[20] Marcion appears not to have been quite so highly educated as Justin and Valentinus, and his writings lack the same kind of teaching style. Instead of teaching semi-independently, Marcion set up his own congregation in 144, apparently causing an open and clean break with his former congregation (they gave his money back). At least some of Marcion's theological work must have already been written by then. Initially at least his movement had great success: he is said to have followers among 'all nations' already in the 150s.[21] 'As wasps make their nests, so the Marcionites make their congregations,' wrote Tertullian.[22] There must have been some who regretted the loss of

Marcion's entrepreneurial talents.

Had Marcion and the followers of teachers like Valentinus simply taught different views from other Christians that might not have been a problem. The difficulty lay in two related things. First, they were successful either in establishing separate congregations (Marcion) or in teaching Christians who attended the usual congregations (Valentinus). In both cases, Christian writers like Justin, Irenaeus and Tertullian were anxious that increasing numbers of Christians were being pulled away from the truth by those who also called themselves Christians. This, of course, was the second major cause of alarm. Marcionites and Valentinians believed in Christ, bore the name of Christ, celebrated his sacraments and read the holy books which foretold and described his coming to the world. The problem was that they interpreted the significance of these things differently. Christians' arguments with each other were thus very different from their arguments with pagans (even setting aside the issue of persecution). However much Christians borrowed from pagan philosophy, however much theologians like Justin argued for their faith in Greek philosophical terms, there was always a clear decision in view: for Christ or against him. Marcionites and Valentinians, however, sincerely believed that they were for Christ. Their views were far too close for comfort for the Christians represented by Justin, Irenaeus and Tertullian.

This points to the other obvious reason for the diversity of Christian views in Rome: although social factors were important – the existence of multiple congregations not fully in contact with one another, the presence of semi-autonomous teachers like Valentinus and Ptolemy offering extra tuition – the other extremely important factor was the character of Christian faith in itself. In essence it was very simple: faith in Jesus Christ, Son of God, Saviour. This faith had been transmitted by the first eyewitnesses of Christ – the Apostles. Christianity's use of the Hebrew Scriptures also located faith in Christ, i.e. the Messiah, in relation to an older Jewish tradition.[23] But the reality was rather more complex. For a start, although most Christian faith started from the Apostles' testimony about Christ, different communities used different traditions of this apostolic witness. In this period we see a move towards a consensus about the use of the four Gospels and the letters of Paul, but this was by no means universal among Christians and there was considerable disagreement about which other apostolic writings were useful (for example, *The Shepherd of Hermas* was sometimes included, and the Book of Revelation sometimes left out). Secondly, faith in Christ was often confirmed and explained by reference to the writings of what we now call the Old Testament, but from the beginning different authors drew this confirmation from the OT writings in different ways.

Various Christian groups also related to the traditions and practices of Judaism in very different ways, as we shall see. Thirdly, these writings – both old and new – contained much that was mysterious and puzzling. There were problems of coherence between the Hebrew Scriptures and the apostolic writings, and even between the apostolic writings themselves (the four Gospels being a case in point). It is not surprising – particularly in intellectual centres like Rome and Alexandria – that Christian adherents sought further explanation of their new faith and that those who sought to explain it came up with many diverse interpretations.

Specifically, controversy in Rome seemed to centre on two related sets of questions. The first set of questions articulated common personal religious responses to the Christians' declaration that 'Jesus Christ is Son of God and Saviour': Why is there evil in the world? Who is this Jesus and what does he have to do with me? What will happen to me? The second set of questions revolved around the resources that Christians used to answer the first set of questions: What is the witness of the Apostles? How can I gain access to it? How does it relate to the writings of the Jewish Prophets? How should I read them? This chapter will now look at the answers given to these questions by Valentinian and Marcionite Christians, before explaining why those answers were rejected by the wider Church. It will conclude by showing how the Christians' conflict with the Jews can also be seen to revolve around similar questions.

But first a caveat: the problem with dealing with those declared heretical is that their written works, however influential at the time, were not preserved like orthodox Christian writings. Many discussions of their views have had to rely on the accounts of their thought preserved by orthodox – and clearly very biased – Christian authors. In some cases scholars now have a means of cross-checking: for example, several texts from the Valentinian and other Gnostic traditions were preserved in the fourth-century papyrus books discovered at Nag Hammadi in Egypt in 1945. In the case of Marcion, scholarship has not been so lucky. What follows, then, is to be taken as a likely guess at their answers to the above questions, rather than assertions based on hard evidence.

Marcion appears to have been preoccupied by the evil condition of the world – not just the presence of human sin and death, but also what he saw as evidence of the evil character of the natural world. Tertullian caricatures him as complaining about things as trivial as bed bugs and stinging insects![24] Marcion also seems to have been disgusted by human physicality, particularly sex and childbirth, which he saw as messy, weak and inextricably connected with death.[25] Why was there such evil in the world? Bar Daisan's treatise *Book of the Laws of the Lands* (which was probably directed against

Marcionites, amongst others) puts the question directly:

> If God is one ... and he has created mankind intending you to do what you
> are charged to, why did he not create mankind in such wise that they could
> not sin but always did what is right?[26]

Marcion's answer to this kind of question was startlingly simple: the wretch-
edness of the world and of the human condition *was* the responsibility of its
Creator, but God was *not* 'one'. Marcion expressed faith in another, higher
God, who was the Father of Jesus Christ and through Jesus Christ the
redeemer of the world.

This was Marcion's famous doctrine of 'two Gods'.[27] It may have been
influenced by the distinction made by some Middle Platonist philosophers
between a supreme deity, removed from the world, and a secondary active
god (the Demiurge) who gave the matter of the world its present form.[28] The
modern term 'Middle Platonism' covers a very varied collection of philosophies, but Marcion's system differs markedly from them all. In his own eyes
at least, his thought arose from his reading of the Hebrew Scriptures and
from his reflection on Paul's theology (which was the only part of the apostolic tradition he accepted). In particular, Marcion seems to have taken his
starting point from Paul's antithesis of the Law (enslaving, associated with
sin and death, the mark of the old dispensation) and the Gospel (liberating, bringing life, the mark of the new dispensation). Totally unlike Paul,
however, Marcion associated the Law with a Creator-God and the Gospel
with a higher God, the father of Jesus Christ. Each God had its own plan
for the world and humanity. The two Gods of Marcion's system were *not*
two metaphysical principles (good vs evil, light vs dark, spirit vs evil) but
rather two dramatic agents whose characters Marcion read in the pages of
his sources.

The Creator-God was the God of the Law, which was imposed and
enforced in a legalistic and narrow way. The evil aspect of the world
sprang from its creation from evil matter: the Creator-God, however, was
responsible for that creation. Furthermore, he was responsible for creating
humanity weak and susceptible to temptation, responsible for casting
humans out of paradise, and responsible for subjecting them to law and
punishing their failures. His Law was designed to save, but only enslaved.
Hence, although one cannot say that Marcion's creator was evil personified,
and although from a philosophical point of view Marcion left the existence
of the original evil matter somewhat unexplained, he clearly depicted the
Creator-God as accountable for the wretched state of human kind. In this
theology, the Creator-God is not evil, but he did make an evil world; in the
Creator-God's dealings with it he is not evil, but 'petty and fickle, impatient
and jealous, warlike and wild'.[29]

Marcion expressed a profound faith in the redemption offered by the Higher God, newly revealed in Jesus Christ. Following through his belief about the evil character of the material world, Marcion asserted that Christ did not have a body of the kind humans have, for that would involve him too closely with evil matter (Tertullian accuses him of teaching that Jesus suddenly appeared on earth as an adult without a human birth 'in the fifteenth year of the reign of the emperor Tiberius').[30] Marcion did, however, believe that Christ truly suffered on the Cross. Through his death, Jesus purchased back those who were under the power of the Creator-God (Marcion made a lot of Paul's image of redemption: the Saviour 'buying back' those who legally speaking belonged to their Creator). This salvation was offered to all – even those who had lived before Christ – but Marcion did not think that all would accept it. Because the world and human bodies were seen as inextricably bound up with evil, Marcion's concept of salvation seems to have been focused on a future act of redemption in which the Saviour would rescue his followers from the world. In the meantime, Marcionites were bidden to a life of extreme asceticism, forgoing marriage and sex, eating a very limited diet, as if to spite the Creator-God and show him that they did not care for the things of this world.[31] Given the implications this would have for the growth of his Church (no children of converts) and given his selective reading of Paul, it is possible that Marcion had an expectation of an imminent end to the world; one can imagine him preaching on the following verses:

> Brothers and sisters, the appointed time has grown short; from now on, let even those who have wives be as though they had none … and those who deal with the world as though they had no dealings with it. For the present form of the world is passing away.[32]

Marcion's scriptures looked very different from those Christians use today. As we have already noted, the only apostolic witness he trusted was that of Paul, and even then he regarded the Pauline epistles as having being adulterated in places by believers in the Creator-God. He accepted the Gospel of Luke as being fundamentally Pauline, although again he suspected that others had added to it. One of Marcion's works was an edition of these apostolic writings, expurgated of their false elements. For this reason, he is often cited as the first creator of a New Testament canon, and the one who provoked the mainstream congregations into forming their own. But this is probably to envisage too sharp a distinction between the situations before and after Marcion: the reaction against his single Gospel from writers like Irenaeus suggests that many congregations had a tradition of using all four Gospels for teaching and in their Sunday assemblies. The four-fold Gospel seemed natural, almost inevitable to Irenaeus (at least, that was the impression that he was trying to convey to his readers):

> There cannot be either more or fewer gospels than there are. Since there are
> four regions of the world in which we exist, and four principal winds, and
> since the church, spread out over all the world has for a column and support
> the Gospel and the Spirit of life, consequently it has four columns, from all
> sides breathing imperishability and making men live.[33]

Even after Marcion and Irenaeus, however, there was uncertainty about
the contents of the New Testament canon beyond the core of the four
Gospels and the Pauline epistles. Marcion is also often characterized as
'rejecting' the Old Testament, on the grounds that these were the Scriptures of the Creator-God. Here again, the situation was more complex:
Marcion certainly did not revere or venerate these writings and they were
not read at Marcionite worship. On the other hand, Marcion thought that
the Hebrew Scriptures were *true*: it was just that they were true statements
about the God who should not be worshipped. Marcion's second known
work, the *Antitheses*, was a set of opposing propositions about the Creator-
God and the Higher God respectively. Possibly they were intended to aid
his followers to read the Hebrew Scriptures without falling into error.[34]

Marcion's theology appears at once both very alien and yet strangely
half-familiar. His theology of the two Gods is very odd, and his reading of
Paul is forced. But from what we can tell of his theology from the reports
of his opponents, there is much that is familiar: his strong sense of the
liberating power of the Gospel, of redemption through Christ's death and
resurrection, of faith in Christ as the key to salvation. Despite his somewhat extreme asceticism, he had a fairly conventional belief in the Church
and the sacraments. Trying to understand Marcion is like seeing a friend
through the security peep-hole in a front door: he seems recognizable, but
distorted, and very far away.

Trying to understand the thought of Valentinus and his followers,
by contrast, is more like entering a hall of mirrors: immediately one
is surrounded by a plethora of distorted and shifting images. Without
wanting to beg too many questions about the relationship of Valentinus to
the movement known as Gnosticism, the following account will first focus
on what is known about him, then turn to consider the evidence for his
sources and early followers.

Those Valentinian writings that exist in their entirety were written by
followers of Valentinus; from his own pen we have merely a few fragments,
or quotations, preserved in the writings of other Christian writers. From
these we can tell that Valentinus believed that 'death is the work of the
creator of the world'; some of the fragments suggest a division between this
God and a higher redeeming God.[35] The world's imperfection seems to arise

from its falling short from the divine perfection: 'However much a portrait is inferior to a living face, just so is the world worse than the living realm.'[36] Valentinus seems to associate the human Jesus with the 'Son' or 'Word' or 'name' of the redeeming God. This God can make up what is lacking in humans to save them,[37] and overcome death.[38] He 'visits the heart, makes it holy and fills it with light'.[39] He acts through his Son/Word/Name who is expressed in the person Jesus. Jesus is human in some respects, although it is very difficult to assess exactly what Valentinus thought of Jesus' nature: his opponents accused him (or his followers) of believing that he did not have a real human birth, therefore neither real human flesh, nor a true death.[40] The only clue we have from Valentinus himself is a bizarre comment that Jesus had an extraordinary digestive system, never excreting his food because nothing within him was subject to corruption. This seems to suggest that for Valentinus (as for Marcion) Jesus had a material body but that some of its physical functions were different from the human norm. As we have seen, Valentinus believed that people could be saved by the Son. In his writings there is a hint of the view for which later Valentinians became famous, that some people have been chosen for all time for salvation: 'From the beginning you have been immortal and you are children of eternal life', perhaps because of the deposit of a divine or spiritual 'seed' in some humans.[41]

Strikingly absent from these fragments is the famous 'Valentinian' myth of the 30 aeons, which Irenaeus recounted.[42] It postulated a realm of the divine – the *pleroma* ('fullness' in Greek) – composed of 30 *aeons* ('ages') or *archons* ('powers'), arranged in male–female pairs. The *pleroma* was a hierarchy in which pairs of aeons gave rise to others. Each aeon was given an enigmatic name, often taken from Scripture. The original pair, *Ineffable* and *Silence*, produced *Parent* and *Truth*. These four give rise to another four: *Word*, *Life*, *Human Being*, *Church*. The pair *Word* and *Life* then generated a set of ten powers, and *Human Being* and *Church* spawned a set of 12. This made the fullness or *pleroma* of 30 powers. According to this myth, evil in the world was explained not by the fall of humanity but by an original fall from the *pleroma* of one of the aeons: this aeon was usually named in Valentinian thought as *Sophia* – Wisdom. Her fall gave rise to the world, for the fallen *Sophia* generated not only matter ('shadow'), but also a craftsman (*demiourgos* in Greek) who gave it form. This craftsman or 'Demiurge' was associated with the Creator-God and Law-giver of the Hebrew Scriptures. (This is the point at which the otherwise rather different Marcionite and Valentinian systems are most close.) *Sophia* also gave birth to *Christ*, which in turn produced *Jesus*. Finally *Sophia* engendered a further 'left-handed' or evil power, who was sometimes known in a Pauline phrase as 'the ruler of this world'.[43] In sum, the *pleroma* gave rise to the fallen *Sophia*; through or from her come about not only matter, the creator of the world and the evil ruler of that world but also the agents of humanity's redemption.

Such myths may seem utterly outlandish and they lent themselves to easy parody by early Christian writers (Irenaeus has a particularly effective caricature of Valentinian language, constructing his own quartet of 'Gourd and Supervacuity and Cucumber and Melon').[44] But they were a vivid attempt to explain the existence of evil in the world, by suggesting that Adam and Eve's error merely reflected an earlier transcendent fall: *Sophia*, a bit like Eve, desired to know more than was permitted; her fall resulted in the generation of matter which was only a shadow of the original truth of the *pleroma*.[45] As part of the shadowy, less good realm, Adam and Eve's sin seems inevitable rather than a puzzle. The Valentinian myth was dependent on prior knowledge of the Bible: it was designed to explain things the Scriptures did not explain fully, and the strange multiple manifestations of the Son (Word, Christ, Jesus) reflect the multiple titles for Jesus Christ in the New Testament. Just as Marcion's *Antitheses* may have been a text enabling his followers to read the Hebrew Scriptures without error, so myths of this kind might have served as explanatory keys to reading both the Hebrew and apostolic writings. (In all likelihood, they were at least partly motivated by the anti-Marcionite desire to show how these texts could be read together.) Perhaps it was this kind of further explanation that Valentinus offered in his reading groups of Roman Christians.

According to Irenaeus, one important form of the myth was developed by Ptolemy (supposedly a pupil of Valentinus). In this, names were given to the unnamed individual powers in the sets of ten and 12 aeons and the story of *Sophia* was more complex. Most importantly, there was a clear doctrine of an elect, that is those people chosen from all time to be saved. Ptolemy suggested that all humans were divided into three categories, by analogy with the way each human was thought to comprise body, soul and spirit.[46] The elect were spiritual (people of the *pneuma*): these had the divine seed or knowledge or spirit within them which allowed them to be saved. Those who would be rejected were entirely bodily (people of the *soma*). In an intermediate category – which often seemed to refer to 'ordinary' Christians – were people of the soul (*psyche*). These were apparently eligible for a lesser kind of salvation. The existence of this curious half-way house seems to confirm the idea that followers of Valentinus envisaged themselves as special or élite Christians rather than opposed to their fellow Christians. This was not, of course, the way that people like Justin, Irenaeus and Tertullian saw the matter!

Scholars are very divided about the extent to which these myths were Valentinus' own conception, to what extent he adapted the material from earlier groups of 'Gnostics', and to what extent it was developed further by his followers. However one resolves those particular questions, it does seem clear that myths in the form described by Irenaeus developed in communities which were recognizably Christian but which sought answers which they felt were not provided by the usual Christian preaching.

Irenaeus' work, which we commonly call *Against Heresies*, was entitled by its author *The Refutation and Overthrowing of the So-Called 'Knowledge'* (*gnosis* in Greek). Later theologians up to the present day have tended to refer to Irenaeus' opponents collectively as the 'Gnostics', but this reflects neither Irenaeus' nor his opponents' use of the word. Marcion is now not usually thought of as a 'Gnostic'; the arguments regarding Valentinian Christians are more complex, but they bring an important issue to the foreground: how different were these writers from other Christians? At some points in his critique Irenaeus tried to show how different they were; at others he was clearly worried that their similarities might tempt his readers to join them, or lead outsiders to treat his Christianity and Valentinus' Christianity as the same.

Irenaeus reported that the followers of a certain Carpocrates call themselves 'Gnostics' and he himself extended the term to a few more groups.[47] He never called Valentinus and his pupils Gnostics, nor implied that they called themselves Gnostics, but merely asserted that Valentinus 'adapted the principles of the heresy called "gnostic" to the peculiar character of his own school'[48] – this can be taken to imply that Valentinian theology has been corrupted by 'Gnosticism', but that it is not itself Gnostic. On the one hand, both Valentianians and the Gnostics appear to have used myths about multiple aeons to explain the generation of the world; both identified salvation with the possession of a special knowledge (*gnosis*) by an elite few. On the other hand, in the Valentinian system everything derived from the one source (the *pleroma* was in a sense one, despite consisting of multiple aeons);[49] the Gnostics, however, seem to have believed that outside the *pleroma* there was a lower or darker realm into which *Sophia* fell, or by which she was attracted.[50] Furthermore, many Gnostics thought the Demiurge (Creator) was an evil being, while the Valentinians separated out the roles of the evil 'ruler of the world' (the 'left-handed aeon') and the Creator of the world (the 'Demiurge'), who had more of a neutral role.

It was dualism – the belief in a universe fundamentally divided between light and dark – that made one a Gnostic in the technical sense, according to Irenaeus. It is likely that Valentinus was influenced by Gnostic myths, which he adapted in two broad ways. First, he used contemporary Platonism to convert a dualist myth (light vs dark) into a basically monistic one (everything comes from the *pleroma*). Secondly, he used specifically

Christian ideas (especially those from Paul's epistles) in a more systematic way.

If the Marcionites and Valentinians had been more different, less identifiably Christian, Irenaeus would not have felt so threatened. Instead he saw all these groups as splintering the unity of the Christian Church, fracturing its essential truth and distorting its Scriptures. The theme of unity dominates Irenaeus' work. It was he who wrote of 'the church, dispersed throughout the world to the ends of the earth'.[51] His own biography gives a clue as to why this picture of a spiritually unified but geographically scattered Church was key to his understanding of Christianity. Irenaeus was born around 130–40CE and probably originated in Asia Minor, perhaps in Smyrna itself.[52] He was well educated, perhaps in Smyrna or in Rome. By the 170s he was a presbyter in either Lyons (the major city of Roman Gaul) or neighbouring Vienne, ministering to the sizeable number of Christians among the Greek-speaking migrants from Asia Minor. Irenaeus was on a journey to Rome during the Rhône valley persecutions (mentioned in the previous chapter). On his return, Irenaeus seems to have taken the martyr Pothinus' place as leader of the community. He kept a close eye on what was going on in Rome: he knew of the teachings of Marcion and Valentinus, and had read works by Justin Martyr, Theophilus and Tatian.[53] He also was involved in discussions about celebrating Easter – an issue which was dividing the mainstream Christian congregations in Asia Minor (who chose to celebrate the resurrection of Christ on the day of Passover, the 14th day of the Jewish month Nisan) and the Christian community in Rome (who, in order always to celebrate Easter on the same day of the week, marked it on the Sunday following Passover). Irenaeus wrote a letter to Victor, Bishop of Rome, defending the practice of those Christians in Asia Minor and urging both sides to agree to differ.[54]

Based in Lyons, but with strong links to the Christian communities in Rome and his native Asia Minor, Irenaeus was aware of the geographic spread of Christianity and the need for unity in faith, whilst being more flexible on some aspects of Church practice. The unity of the Church *per se* was not, however, the foundation of Irenaeus' faith; rather, it was a conclusion which he drew from his central belief in the unity of God. In *Against Heresies* and *On the Apostolic Preaching* (his two works which survive today) Irenaeus constantly reiterated this cornerstone of his faith:

> But we hold fast the rule of truth, that there is one almighty God who founded everything through his Word and arranged it and made everything out of the non-existent. ... He is the God of Abraham, the God of Isaac, the God of Jacob. There is no other God above him ... he [is] the Father of our Lord Jesus Christ, as we shall show.[55]

And this is the order of our faith, the foundation of the edifice and the support of our conduct: God, the Father, uncreated, uncontainable, invisible, one God, the Creator of all: this is the first article of our faith. And the second article: the Word of God, the Son of God, Christ Jesus our Lord, who was revealed by the prophets according to the character of their prophecy and according to the nature of the work of the Father, by whom all things were made, and who, in the last times, to recapitulate all things, became a man amongst men, visible and palpable, in order to abolish death, to demonstrate life and to effect communion between God and man. And the third article: the Holy Spirit, through whom the prophets prophesied and the patriarchs learnt the things of God and the righteous were led in the path of righteousness, and who, in the last times was poured out in a new fashion upon the human race renewing man, throughout the world, to God.[56]

Such statements show Irenaeus' faith in the complete dependence of everything on the One God. In these he clearly stated his beliefs that the world was created from nothing; that God created both the matter of the world and humankind; that God not only created the world but continues to support, nourish and save it. This made it harder for Irenaeus to explain the presence of evil in the world: there was no shadowy matter pulling heavenly beings away from the good, no heavenly being who fell of her own accord away from the good, no Creator separate from the Saviour God. Instead, Irenaeus stressed that God's creation was good and, like Paul, he stated that all evil stemmed from Adam because of Adam's disobedience (Romans 5.12, 19). Although Irenaeus put more emphasis than Paul on the devil tempting Adam and Eve to sin, he stressed that their sin – and the punishment of death – was their responsibility. But why would free, good humans living in a good creation want to sin? Irenaeus' answer was twofold. First, God prohibited Adam and Eve from eating from the tree of good and evil not because that fruit was in itself bad for them but that by having this duty to obey God's command they 'might know that [they] had as lord the Lord of all'.[57] Thus although they were in a paradise 'better than this earth, excelling in air, beauty, light, food, plants, fruit, waters, and every other thing needful for life', Adam and Eve were tempted by the only thing they did not have: the ability to be 'lords' over themselves – to be independent from God. Secondly, 'the man was a young child, not yet having a perfect deliberation, and because of this he was easily deceived by the seducer'.[58] Irenaeus seems to have thought that although the world was created good, God's plan was to draw Man into further future perfection and a closer relationship with him.[59] This combination of goodness with a potential to mature into something better is indicated by Adam and Eve's childlike state. The Fall in Irenaeus, then, was not so much a Fall from the pinnacle of created perfection but rather a deviation in God's plan to bring all creation to that perfection.[60] Specifically, the Fall brought into the world spiritual and physical death, error, ignorance and corruption.[61]

The brief summaries of faith quoted above affirm that the Creator-God is one and the same as the 'Father of our Lord Jesus Christ' and that he created the world 'through his Word'. Creation came about through the Son, the Word of God, but he is entirely one with God. So Irenaeus wrote that Christians followed 'as our teacher One only [i.e. Jesus Christ], and him the Only true God'. This Jesus was not another God besides the Creator, but 'he … who made all things can alone, together with his Word, properly be termed God and Lord'. This was confirmed by the Prophets and Apostles who confessed 'the Father and the Son, but [name] no other as God'.[62] In order to explain the paradoxical relationship of the Son and the Father, Irenaeus developed the 'Logos theology' of Justin Martyr, arguing that the 'Word' and the 'Spirit' of God both expressed something inherent in the notion of God itself: 'And as God is verbal [or 'rational'], therefore he made created things by the Word; and God is Spirit, so that he adorned all things by the Spirit, as the prophet also says, "By the Word of the Lord were the heavens established, and all their power by his Spirit"' (Psalms 32.6).[63] In places, Irenaeus used another vivid metaphor to express this relationship:

> God needed none of these [angels or aeons] to make whatever he had foreordained to make, as if he did not have hands of his own. For always with him are his Word and Wisdom, the Son and the Spirit, through whom and in whom he made everything freely and independently, to whom he also speaks, when he says, 'Let us make man after our image and likeness.' (Genesis 1.26)[64]

This concept of the Word and Spirit as the two hands of God was most evident in Irenaeus' theology of creation, but cropped up also in descriptions of divine providence ('For never at any time did Adam escape the hands of God'), and salvation ('And, therefore, throughout all time, man who was in the beginning moulded by the hands of God is made in the image and likeness of God').[65] Even apart from the explicit use of this metaphor, Son and Spirit were frequently depicted as working together in Irenaeus' theology, in creation, salvation and revelation ('the Scriptures are indeed perfect, since they were spoken by the Word of God and his Spirit').[66] Thus his theology can perhaps be seen as more Trinitarian than Justin's (which tends to focus on the Father and his Word), but there was still no attempt at a philosophical doctrine of the Trinity (which would need, for example, to distinguish between the Son's relationship to the Father and the Spirit's relationship to the Father).

Jesus Christ was truly human, as well as truly God: he was 'a man among men', both in body and soul.[67] Christ was not merely incarnate

in one individual, but there was a strong sense in Irenaeus' theology that
Christ 'summed up' all humans in himself: Irenaeus even suggested that
Jesus underwent every age of human development – 'infants, children, and
boys, and youths and old men' – to stress this point.[68] This idea is commonly
known by the Greek term *anakephalaiōsis* ('summing up', 'bringing to a
head'). The idea stemmed from the Pauline contrast: 'as all die *in Adam*,
so all will be made alive *in Christ*' (I Corinthians 15.22).[69] Just as Adam
'summed up' all humanity in the dual sense that all humanity descended
from him and all human death stemmed from him, so Christ 'sums up' all
humanity in the sense that he became incarnated in all humanity and in the
sense that he brings life to all humanity. The sense in which Jesus Christ
unites all persons in him was left vague by Irenaeus, but depended both on
the Pauline statement quoted above and on a common ancient belief that
human nature was in an important sense one 'thing'. As the true Word of
the Father, Christ revealed God to all humankind.[70] Through his death and
resurrection he conquered death.[71] He will come to judge those who do not
receive him;[72] to those who do, he will bring immortality, incorruption and
communion with God.[73]

In his assertion that through Christ salvation is made possible for all
humans, Irenaeus was clearly distancing himself from the Valentinian idea
that only one category of humans contain the divine 'spark' which allows
them to be saved. Irenaeus even stressed that knowledge of the *written*
Gospel (either by reading or hearing it) was not required for salvation in
Christ: all that was needed was assent to the 'ancient tradition of the apostles' of belief in 'One God, maker of heaven and earth and everything in
them, and in Christ Jesus the Son of God'.[74] However, although Irenaeus
thought that Christ's incarnation *in some sense* united all humanity, and
although he clearly thought that salvation was *offered* through Christ to all,
he did *not* think that ultimately all humans would be saved. Books IV and
V of *Against Heresies* make it clear that Irenaeus thought that Christ would
come to judge humanity, separating the 'wheat from the chaff', and that the
unjust were doomed to eternal separation from God, due to lacking God's
Spirit.[75]

> But God inflicts on those who willingly depart from him that separation from
> himself which they have chosen of their own accord. But separation from
> God is death, and separation from light is darkness; and separation from God
> consists in the loss of all the benefits which he has in store. Therefore, those
> who cast away by apostasy these things mentioned, being in fact destitute
> of all good, experience every kind of punishment. God, however, does not
> punish them immediately himself, but that punishment falls upon them
> because they are destitute of all that is good. Now, good things are eternal

and without end with God, and therefore the loss of these is also eternal and never-ending.[76]

While the Marcionites and Valentinians tended to think of salvation in terms of salvation of *part* of the human *from* the rest of the world, Irenaeus argued that Christian salvation was of the *whole* human, soul *and* body, and would take place *in* the world – albeit a newly perfected world. Inspired by the language and imagery of Revelation, Book V of Irenaeus' *Against Heresies* painted a vivid picture of the last times. First, there would be a time of tribulation in which the Roman Empire would fall apart and the Antichrist would come: 'And there is therefore in this beast, when he comes, a recapitulation made of all sorts of iniquity and of every deceit, in order that all apostate power, flowing into and being shut up in him, may be sent into the furnace of fire.'[77] This overthrow would be achieved by Christ whose return (*parousia*) Irenaeus seemed to expect relatively soon.[78] Crucially, Christ's return would also bring with it the resurrection of the just and God's thousand-year reign in a renewed creation. Following this would come the resurrection of the unjust, the Last Judgement and the final separation of humanity to their destinies. The unjust would go to Gehenna, and the just would dwell in a 'new heaven and a new earth' where they would be rewarded by an increasingly more perfect knowledge and love of God. Irenaeus was emphatic about the renewal of the material world, stressing that all God's creation was good, and thus would be renewed. This tradition of millennialism was particularly popular in Asia Minor, Irenaeus' spiritual homeland. It was in tension (but did not formally contradict) the idea that the souls of martyrs would be with Christ in heaven immediately after their death. Fearing that this popular view would undermine belief in the resurrection of the body, Irenaeus argued that souls of the just would await their resurrection in a kind of shadowy intermediate state.[79]

Irenaeus' writings lack the systematic nature of much modern theology and they display a bewildering range of argument and imagery. The key to understanding them lies in Irenaeus' tenacious grasp of the fundamental apostolic preaching – a belief in God the creator and Father of Jesus Christ – which Irenaeus often describes as his 'rule of faith'. This rule is sometimes linked to the confession made by converts before their baptism (the second version of the rule quoted above concludes: 'for this reason the baptism of our regeneration takes place through these three articles'). The rule was also Irenaeus' key to reading Scripture. If one read the writings of the Prophets and Apostles according to that rule, it would ensure that they were understood as a record of one united history of salvation – the history of the one God working for the good of his creation. Practical implications sprang from this: read according to the rule of faith, the old and new

Scriptures were kept together (against the Marcionite practice) and did not need to be supplemented by any extra writings (such as the Valentinian and Gnostic myths). The rule of faith also acted as a measure of orthodoxy, ruling out the heretics as much as it ruled in those whom Irenaeus regarded as belonging to the true faith. Unlike the secret doctrines boasted of by his opponents, it had been handed down openly from the first Apostles, to their followers, and thence to their followers right until Irenaeus' own day. Thus the 'rule of faith' was also the key to understanding Irenaeus' notion of the apostolic tradition: the successive appointment of Christian witnesses by the Apostles and their followers was not important in Irenaeus' eyes because of some sanctity of the appointment process in itself; rather it was important because of the deposit of truth which the Apostles passed from one to another.[80] In this way, Irenaeus succeeded in creating a remarkably unified vision of the Christian faith, from his reflections on Scriptures, his arguments against opponents and his reading of earlier writers like Justin and Ignatius. Although he was not based in Rome when he wrote them, his *Against Heresies* and *Demonstration of the Apostolic Preaching* provide both a useful perspective on the controversies emanating from Rome and an attempt to resolve them in a way which allowed for a unified faith amongst a scattered and diverse Church.

In Chapter 2, it was noted that the second century was a period characterized by Christian attempts to make sense of their own identity, in contrast to pagans, Jews and other Christians with whom they disagreed. Having addressed the issue of Christian–pagan relations in Chapter 2 and of inter-Christian debate in this chapter, it now remains to examine the complicated question of how Christians related to Jews in this period.

Most Christians acknowledged that they and the Jews worshipped the same God.[81] Indeed they typified Judaism as a religion of God's Law. But they also asserted that this Law had now been fulfilled or, to put it more negatively, rendered void by Jesus Christ. Thus Jews were those who not only failed to recognize Jesus as the prophesied Messiah but who mistakenly held on to outdated and pointless practices (circumcision was an example commonly cited).[82] In addition, most Christians thought that the Jews were also directly responsible for Christ's death: thus, for example, Justin Martyr accused Jews of supposing 'that [Christ] was crucified as hostile and cursed by God, which supposition is the product of your most irrational mind'.[83] The accusation that the Jews in effect 'killed God' is expressed with notoriously vivid language in Melito's work *On the Pascha*[84]:

It is [Christ] who has been murdered.
And where has he been murdered? In the middle of Jerusalem.

By whom? By Israel.
Why? Because he healed their lame,
and cleansed their lepers
    and brought light to their blind
    and raised their dead,
        that is why he died. ...
O lawless Israel, what is this unprecedented crime you committed, thrusting
your Lord among unprecedented sufferings,
    your Sovereign,
    who formed you,
    who made you,
    who honoured you,
    who called you 'Israel'?
But you did not turn out to be 'Israel';
    you did not 'see God'...[85]

Justin's expression was less violent, but when he reflected on the commands
to 'Love the LORD your God with all your heart and with all your soul
and with all your might ... and your neighbour as yourself',[86] he drew the
shocking conclusion that 'you [Jews] were *never* shown to be possessed
of friendship or love either towards God, or towards the prophets, or
towards yourselves, but as is evident, you are *always* found to be idolators
and murderers of righteous men, so that you laid hands even on Christ
himself'.[87] Thus the charge of deicide – killing God – was compounded by
the charge that the Jews had in fact never been faithful to the Law. While
the charge of deicide was in a sense nonsensical to those who rejected Jesus'
identity as Son of God, the accusation that Jews were faithless to the Law
was far more offensive, not least because it denied the validity of their way
of life as a response to God, both in the past and in the future.

Christians often interpreted the destruction of the Temple in 70CE and
the devastation of Judaea following the Bar Kokhba revolt in 135CE as divine
punishment for the alleged murder of Christ, or at the very least as signs that
the Jewish way of life was decaying. In fact, however, modern scholars of
late antique Judaism are keen to stress that it was vibrant and thriving – not
least because there was already a growing diaspora Jewish community *before*
the troubles of 70 and 135. In Rome the Jewish population ran into the tens
of thousands. The large and prosperous Jewish community in Alexandria
had its own administration and relative independence. There was also a
flourishing Jewish literary culture. At the end of the second century Rabbi
Judah ha-Nasi produced a compilation of oral interpretations of the Jewish
law, known as the Mishnah. It was a written and edited collection of material
from earlier rabbinic scholars which had been preserved in oral tradition.
The Mishnah was itself subject to extensive commentary in this period

– commentary which eventually took formal written form in the Palestinian and Babylonian Talmuds of later centuries.[88] Aquila, Symmachus and Theodotion produced their Greek translations of the Hebrew Scriptures between the mid-second and early third centuries. The Alexandrian Philo (c.30BCE–c.50CE) and Josephus (c.37/8–110/15CE), a Palestinian Jew who spent much of his time in Rome, demonstrated the way in which some writers integrated Jewish subject matter with Greco-Roman ideas or forms. Philo's work in the early first century used the thought of Platonic philosophers in his detailed and imaginative exegesis of the Hebrew Scriptures; Josephus wrote works which were influenced by the genres of Greek history and biography. Archaeological evidence (although limited) adds to this picture of thriving communities both in Palestine and beyond: the early third-century synagogue at Dura Europos on the Euphrates is the most striking example of Jewish art in this period and suggests a self-confident and relatively wealthy community.

Clearly, then, the Christians' claim that the Jewish way of life was decaying was a theological assertion rather than a historical one. It suited their purposes to declare that not only had the Law been superseded but that the people who followed the Law were weakened. The fact that they were able to make the latter claim might be thought to suggest that in this period Christian encounters with Jews were relatively minimal. The situation probably differed from place to place: Irenaeus' 'almost complete ignorance of contemporary Judaism'[89] seems to reflect his location in Gaul, where the Jewish community was small and probably very scattered. On the other hand, the structure and style of Melito's writing suggests that he knew of various Jewish literary forms, probably including the Jewish Passover recitation, the Haggadah,[90] and perhaps some forms of Jewish exposition and comment on Scripture, such as Targum (an expository translation in Aramaic) and Midrash (a freer commentary on the text).[91] Melito was writing in Sardis, a town in Asia Minor with a large and long-established population of Jews.[92] His violently antagonistic language might have arisen from local friction between church and synagogue, but that should not be taken to imply that such friction existed between all Christians and Jews in this period. Ordinary contacts between them in many towns may have continued to be frequent and close.

Justin's *Dialogue with Trypho* appears to be much less hostile than Melito's text. It purports to be an account of a historical conversation with a real Jew set in Ephesus shortly after the Bar Kokhba revolt, but several modern scholars have suggested that Justin was simply one of the first Christian authors to construct fictive Jewish characters 'to think with'. Whether that is the case or not, Justin clearly knew something of contemporary Jews: he emphasized their continuing obedience to the Law (even after the destruction of the Temple), including the commands concerning circumcision, the Sabbath and the festivals. He appeared to know about Jewish practices of reading and interpreting Scripture and about their style of prayer. He referred to the synagogue and to its 'rulers'.[93] These points suggest that Justin was in contact with Jews in Rome and/or Ephesus and perhaps that the *Dialogue* reflected actual debates he had had with scholarly Jews.

It is often asserted that Syrian Christianity was much more closely related to Judaism than Christian communities further west. Evidence for this is the influence of the Targum traditions (Aramaic interpretative translations of the Hebrew Bible) on the Syriac translation of the Hebrew Scriptures, known as the Peshitta.[94] Various other Jewish exegetical traditions also influenced Christian theology in Syriac. Some historians have concluded, therefore, that Syriac Christianity developed from the conversion of whole Jewish communities in, for example, Edessa, or even that it was the result of mission by the very early Jewish-Christians from Palestine.[95] (The later theory was encouraged by a Syriac account that the first-century King Abgar of Edessa and his family were converted soon after Christ's death by Addai, an Apostle sent personally by Christ. Unfortunately, this tradition seems to be not earlier than the fourth century CE.)

The assessment of these claims about the Jewish origins of Christianity in Syria is extremely problematic. The assertions are often propelled by prior beliefs about the nature of Syrian Christianity itself: either the view that it represented a purer, more genuine form of Christianity, in continuity with its Jewish roots and uncontaminated by Hellenistic philosophy, or the view that it was a more primitive form of Christianity, less philosophical, less interested in sophisticated doctrinal controversy, more focused on ritual. Such views have as much to do with the proponent's own view of the value of Greek philosophy to early Christianity as they do with the evidence. Secondly, while the influence of Jewish traditions on the Peshitta and Syriac theology is undeniable, scholars are very divided as to whether this dependence is merely literary or whether it demonstrates a more concrete continuity between the Jewish and Christian communities in Edessa: was the Peshitta, for example, translated by a Jewish community which then converted to Christianity, or was it translated by Christians as a rival to the Hebrew Scriptures and Aramaic Targum traditions used by their Jewish contemporaries? On balance, it seems likely that Syrian Christianity was the result not of mainly Jewish or Jewish-Christian roots, but of the conversion of individuals and families from a wide variety of religious backgrounds (including Judaism).[96] This is not to deny the Jewish influence on Syrian theology, nor to deny that Christians in Edessa ever met Jews from the large Jewish population there; rather, it *is* to say that the dependence is substantially a literary one.

Whether in Melito's harsh polemic or in Syrian theology's use of Jewish concepts and images, Christians borrowed, adapted or challenged Jewish literature. Even Justin, who has some concrete information about contemporary Judaism, mainly constructs the character and beliefs of his Jewish opponent around a picture of Judaism he finds in the Hebrew Scriptures (which, since they pre-date the fall of the Temple, cannot describe the post-Temple Jews known to Justin). The way in which early Christians *writers* seemed to interact with Jewish *texts*, more than with Jews themselves, skews our understanding of what contact and knowledge 'ordinary' Christians had of their Jewish contemporaries. For example, the Christians' focus on Jesus as their Christ and Messiah tended to lead them to assume that the expectation of a Messiah figure was central to all Judaism, a categorization which simply does not fit the evidence about the range of Jewish beliefs at the time. In addition, Christians increasingly viewed Jewish observance of the Law in a very one-dimensional way, often focusing on those prescriptions which they found alien or offensive to Greco-Roman culture, instead of those rites which were more similar to Christian celebrations.

One reason for this lack of deep engagement with Jewish concerns and beliefs may be that some of the early Christian literature concerning Judaism was not motivated so much by conflicts and encounters with Jews as it was motivated by disagreements *within* the Christian communities. Specifically, such works should probably be seen in the context of arguments against Marcion. His rejection of the Hebrew Scriptures in fact encouraged most Christian communities to continue to read them both privately and in the public liturgies. However, Marcion also forced Christians to think through the implications of reading texts which were also the Scriptures of the Jews, but which were obviously read differently by Jews. In order to be able to keep reading the Hebrew Scriptures with integrity, non-Marcionite Christians thought they ought to read them as referring to Jesus Christ throughout. They used methods like typology (in which figures and objects in the Old Testament were understood as *prefiguring* or pointing towards those in the New Testament) and a prophecy-fulfilment schema (in which all the events of Jesus' life were seen as *predicted* by the writers of the Old Testament, particularly the Prophets).[97] For example, Irenaeus structures his *Demonstration of the Apostolic Preaching* around a relation of the two testaments in terms of prophecy and fulfilment; in this work and in *Against Heresies* he used a systematic set of typological readings to show that figures and objects in the Old Testament (e.g. Adam, Eve, the tree of the knowledge of good and evil) prefigured those in the New (Christ, Mary, the Cross).

Similarly a long section of Justin's *First Apology* seeks to show that Christ's incarnation, death and resurrection were predicted by the Prophets; several chapters in the *Dialogue with Trypho* claim that the Mosaic laws are types of things concerning Christ.[98] All these are attempts to show how Christians can read the two testaments *together*. Melito's frank assumption that to say that Christ 'fulfilled' the Law is tantamount to saying he rendered it null and void may also have been the result of anti-Marcionism: whereas Marcion assumed two gods, one of Law and one of Gospel, Melito seemed determined to show one God, whose plan for salvation involved the replacement of Law by Gospel, and whose Passover in Egypt merely pointed to the sufferings and triumph of Christ.[99] Furthermore, Syrian theology's more positive use of Jewish influences can be interpreted as the result of 'a Christian urge to adapt and assimilate Old Testament and other Jewish sources to its own ideological concepts', precisely against the practice of Marcionites (who were very numerous in Syria, forming the majority of Christians in some areas).[100]

Because Christians believed that Christ was the summing-up of all humanity, the high-point of all human history, inevitably Christian techniques of reading the Hebrew Scriptures relativized their importance in comparison to the writings of the New Testament. (In fact, early Christianity tended to denigrate the importance of *writing* as such: originally the Old Testament alone was referred to as 'the Scriptures', or 'writings', in contrast with the Gospel, which was a preached truth to which the Gospels and epistles were mere witnesses.) Furthermore, a large portion of the Hebrew Scriptures described a Law which most Christians now thought was no longer necessary. The price for keeping the Hebrew Scriptures thus seemed to be their demotion to a secondary role as the 'Old' Testament.

There is a sense in which all Christian theology is liable to this tendency and there are ways in which all Christian theology is 'supercessionist'. However, early Christian attitudes to the Old Testament appear to have been characterized by two practices which many, if not most, twenty-first-century Christian traditions want to avoid. The first was such a thoroughgoing Christological reading of the Old Testament that virtually nothing had meaning unless it was read as predicting or prefiguring Christ, his life, death and resurrection. The second was an extremely dismissive attitude to the Jews' reading of their own Scriptures. The systematic relativizing of the Hebrew Scriptures as pointers to or predictive of the higher truth found in Christ meant that second-century Christians nearly always ended up accusing the Jews of not reading their own Scriptures properly.[101] By this, Christians often meant that Jews read it literally (allegedly 'over-literally'), in contrast with Christian typological and prophetic exegesis. Emerging from this accusation seems to be a Christian assumption that three things could not be consistently retained together: Christ, the Old Testament and a literal reading of the Old Testament. If one accepted Christ and accepted the Holy Scripture, the latter had to be read largely as typology and prophecy. If, on the other hand, one accepted Christ but insisted on a more literal reading of the Old Testament, as Marcion did, the apparently inevitable consequence was the rejection of those writings as Holy Scripture. Accordingly, Christians seemed to assume that if the Jews accepted their writings as Holy Scripture and rejected Christ, this rejection must have been impelled by their overly literal reading of the Old Testament. Unfortunately, this belief was a conclusion drawn from a particular line of theological reasoning and bore little relation to the reality of very varied Jewish exegetical traditions, including, for example, Midrash and the highly developed allegory used in Philo's exegesis.

The accusations that Jews failed to recognize Christ – and even killed him – were uppermost in Christians' minds, because their piety was focused on Christ. But in many ways the charges that the Jews had failed to keep their Law (or were falsely adhering to a meaningless Law), and that they could not read their own Scriptures properly were the most insidious charges of all. Not only did they strike at what Jews themselves held most dear but they imposed a stereotypical perception of contemporary Jewish practice and exegesis – a stereotype that was to be perpetuated by Christians for generations and generations.

CHAPTER 4

Alexandria and Carthage: The Development of Christian Culture

(SECOND TO THIRD CENTURIES)

For over two millennia, the city of Alexandria has been famous for two things: its library, symbol of Hellenistic literary culture, and its lighthouse, the Pharos, one of the seven wonders of the ancient world. The Pharos was built in the middle of the third century BCE to guide ships into the harbour. Vital for the economy of the eastern part of the Empire, Alexandria was the transit point for grain from the fertile Nile delta. Successive generations of powerful men (including, later on, Christian bishops) could control or even block this trade to the city's or their own advantage. The city itself had been founded by Alexander in the early 330s BCE. When his successors divided his empire between them, Alexandria became the capital of an Egyptian kingdom, ruled by the Ptolemaic dynasty. Kings Ptolemy I and II in particular were enthusiastic patrons of intellectual life, encouraging many scholars to travel to Alexandria. The Museum – a religious and intellectual institution dedicated to the Muses – and the Serapeum were founded at this time.

The Ptolemies expanded the collections of texts in these locations into the famed library, motivated not only by genuine scholarly interest but also by a competitive urge to see Alexandria excel Antioch (capital of the Seleucid Empire) and Pergamon (the Attalid capital) as an intellectual centre. By the second century CE the great library was in decline; nevertheless, there was still a strong intellectual life in Alexandria which attracted visitors to its schools of philosophy, medicine and other disciplines.[1] Many of these scholars and students were from Greece. Greek became the language of administration and education, and eventually the language of most of Alexandria's residents.[2] Ethnically and culturally, however, Alexandria

73

remained a heady mix of Egyptian, Hellenic and other influences. Ptolemy I took as the patron god of his new dynasty and city a Hellenized version of the Egyptian god Osorapis (Sarapis) to whom the magnificent Serapeum temple was dedicated.[3] The city had a large population of Egyptians and a significant community of Jews. This mix continued under Roman imperial rule.

Carthage had a similar double aspect: besides being the port which supplied the western part of the Empire with wheat, olive oil and wild beasts for the shows in Rome, Carthage also trained talented young men who worked in North Africa, Rome and further afield.[4] For example, Apuleius, the author of the second-century novel *The Golden Ass*, moved from Carthage to Athens, Rome and back to North Africa again. He later praised Carthage, 'where every citizen is a cultivated person and where all devote themselves to all fields of knowledge, children by learning them, young men by showing them off, and old men by teaching them'.[5] Carthage itself had its origins as a Phoenician trading colony, and echoes of the worship of Baal remained for centuries in local names, in cults (later Romanized as the worship of Saturn) and even, it is sometimes claimed, in the violence of the Roman gladiatorial shows. The region had a tumultuous history: after the Punic Wars (first century BCE) North Africa became a Roman province and there was a new influx of settlers from Italy, but there was continual friction between Roman imperial forces and local African tribes. Rome was only a short sea passage away and the cultural interchange between Carthage and Italy was strong. By the second century, the language of administration, education and of many of the population was Latin, although this *lingua franca* overlaid a complex variety of ethnic, linguistic and religious connections, Phoenician, African, and Italian. In size and importance, Carthage neared (or, to its inhabitants, rivalled) Alexandria. In the western part of the Roman Empire it was clearly second only to Rome.[6]

Given their size and their position on important trade routes, it is not surprising, therefore, that Alexandria and Carthage, like Antioch and Rome, were home to important communities of Christians. Owing to their strong intellectual traditions, they were to give rise to two of the most articulate and influential Christian writers of the second and third centuries: Origen and Tertullian. In many ways these two can be regarded as the great fathers of Greek and Latin theology, respectively.

We know little about the origins of Christianity in either city. Like many Mediterranean churches, Alexandria claimed an apostolic tradition: Mark, the author of the Gospel, was held to have founded the church there.[7] Eusebius reports that Philo (c.20BCE–c.50CE) 'welcomed with whole-hearted approval the apostolic men of his day, who it seems were of Hebrew stock and therefore, in the Jewish manner, still retained most of their ancient customs'.[8] The historian even claims that the ascetic community of *therapeutae* ('healers') which Philo describes in great detail and with great respect was in fact the community which Mark founded.[9]

There is no evidence for the Markan foundation and it is impossible to claim a Christian community was living there at the time of Philo (who was himself contemporary with Jesus of Nazareth). However, Eusebius does seem to have been correct in one assumption – that Alexandrian Christianity first took root in its already large and vigorous Jewish population. Jews had probably been settling in Alexandria almost since its foundation; by the middle of the second century BCE they may have constituted as much as a third of the population. Jews were granted a certain degree of self-government and the right to follow their religious laws and traditions, but few Jews (and indeed few native Egyptians) were citizens of the city. Relations between Jews and their fellow Alexandrians were not necessarily easy; in particular under Roman rule Jews became caught up in the tensions between the Egyptian-Greek population and the imperial forces. On some occasions, as in 38CE, the Roman provincial governor in effect allowed a pogrom against the Jews in order to try to maintain his good standing with the rest of the population. Philo was one of those who travelled to Rome to protest on behalf of his community. On a later occasion, in 115CE, Jews in Alexandria revolted against the Roman authorities. In both cases, tens of thousands are said to have died, and from then on Alexandrian Judaism was never as vigorous as it had been.

Philo himself was a highly educated Jew, devotedly loyal to the Hebrew Scriptures and Jewish customs, but keen to show that they were compatible with the Greek culture in which he had been educated. A Greek translation of the Hebrew Bible had been made in Alexandria in the third to second centuries BCE, and Philo, like many of his Jewish contemporaries, regarded this Septuagint translation as inspired and authoritative, and felt no need to consult the Hebrew. Philo clearly regarded himself more as an exegete than a philosopher, although equally clearly these terms for him were complementary not opposed.[10] In his desire to interpret his ancient religion in terms of Hellenism, he argued that Greek philosophers' ideas came to agree with those from the Pentateuch because they had copied or stolen them from Moses. He thus shared the dilemma of the Christian apologists (who borrowed some of his arguments): their particular argument for the harmony of Greek philosophical ideas and their religion implicitly asserted the priority and superiority of the latter.[11] Philo's own particular philosophical influence was Platonism – his writing on the creation is influenced, for example, by Plato's *Timaeus*. Because Clement of Alexandria and Origen broadly share this philosophical bias it has sometimes been assumed that Alexandria in the first three centuries CE was especially a seat of Platonic philosophy. The truth is that we know less than we would like to about the philosophical climate in this period of Alexandrian history, and that there is as much evidence for other philosophical influences as for Platonism.[12] Furthermore, Alexandria's intellectual history was coloured at least as much by literary criticism and by medicine and other branches of science as by philosophy.

Clement of Alexandria (c.150–c.215) was a highly cultured Christian of Alexandria who seems to have been a lay teacher of the Christian faith. It used to be said that he was the head teacher of a Christian 'catechetical school' in Alexandria and that Origen was his successor, but the existence of such a school as a formal institution (for instance, with buildings) is now doubted. Furthermore, although Origen was clearly influenced by Clement, it is not known whether they met. Clement opposed both pagan criticisms of Christianity and the superstitions and determinist exclusivity of Gnostic groups in Alexandria, while borrowing concepts from both pagan and Gnostic writings. Like Philo, he was concerned to show that his religion was both true, moral and intellectually defensible in terms familiar to contemporary well-educated students of philosophy. From the Gnostics, Clement took the idea of a true *gnosis*, a true knowledge which Christians possessed. Unlike them, however, he argued that it was offered universally to all people. One idea that seems to have had a particular influence on Origen is that of the Christian life as a progressive journey, which depended on both grace and human effort.[13] It may have been influenced by the Valentinian idea of three groups of Christians, Clement adapting this to suggest that all people could move up from the lowest rank to the highest.

Tracing Origen's biography is made difficult by the fact that in later centuries his reputation was fought over by fans and opponents: both groups had reason to embellish or edit his life story to suit their case. The longest account comes from Eusebius, a favourable commentator; the general structure of this is generally accepted, although some of the details are very uncertain. Origen was born around 185CE.[14] If he was born into a Christian family, as seems likely,[15] he would probably have been educated in the Christian Scriptures at home alongside his training in the Greek curriculum at school. When Origen was in his late teens, his father died as a result of the persecution of Emperor Septimius Severus. Thereafter, Origen seems to have earned his living as a teacher, first of Greek literature, and perhaps also of the other subjects on the advanced curriculum for young men: mathematics, astronomy and music. Around this time he also began to be sought out as a teacher of the basics of Christian faith. Some Christian teachers

had left Alexandria because of the persecutions; this, plus Origen's reputation for clarity, wisdom and his care of his students, meant that his teaching was much in demand. Eventually, Origen gave up his teaching of the
Greek literary curriculum and focused on teaching Christianity. To begin
with, his role may have been similar to that of Justin Martyr in Rome – he
certainly shared Justin's interest in using philosophy to explain the Christian faith and his emphasis on Christianity as a moral and rigorous way of
life. Later, he was given a more official role as teacher of catechumens (those
preparing for Christian baptism) by Demetrius, Bishop of Alexandria, and
he may have assumed leadership of the Alexandrian 'catechetical school'.

It was in this period that Origen began to write, composing, for example,
commentaries on the Book of Lamentations, on Psalms 1–25, on Genesis
and John's Gospel. He also began work on the *Hexapla*, or 'six-fold work'.
This was a six-column compendium of versions of the Old Testament: the
Hebrew, a Greek transliteration of the Hebrew and four Greek translations
including the Septuagint, which was the standard text of the Hebrew Bible
for Christians as well as Jews. Although it was perhaps Origen's greatest
achievement, the *Hexapla*'s vast size meant that it was apparently never
copied, and modern scholars can only reconstruct its context from traces
left in works by Origen and his successors. Besides these works, which were
directly focused on the task of reading Scripture, Origen also wrote *On
First Principles*, which is a more systematic account of Christian doctrine
and an explanation of the methods of reading Scripture. During this period
Origen benefited from the patronage of a wealthy Alexandrian, Ambrosius,
which allowed him to pay for secretaries, to whom he dictated his works,
and scribes – both boys and girls – who made multiple copies available to
his rapidly expanding audience, both in Alexandria and beyond.[16]

Unfortunately Origen's relationship with Bishop Demetrius was
made difficult by Origen's enquiring approach to the Christian faith and
his ambiguous role as a lay teacher with no formal ecclesiastical authority, but with increasing spiritual and intellectual influence. He began to
travel further afield to teach and on one of his journeys was ordained priest
in Caesarea in Palestine – which suggests that Demetrius had refused to
ordain him. In around 234 Origen left to live permanently in Caesarea,
taking his library with him. Here he continued to produce more commentaries and theological works, plus several series of sermons on biblical texts.
Besides preaching and teaching the basics of Christian faith, Origen also
took in students, both local and foreign, for a more specialized education
which involved a rigorous philosophical programme and the detailed study
of large amounts of pagan literature.[17] In Palestine he got caught up in a new
wave of persecutions under the Emperor Decius (249–51): although he was

not killed, as the bishops of Rome and Jerusalem were, he was imprisoned, probably tortured and died later of ill health around 254.

Origen was from first to last a teacher. The earliest surviving piece of writing to mention him thanked him precisely for his teaching and praised his method which combined discipline with an inspiring example of moral and pious behaviour.[18] It also pointed to Origen's use of a penetrating but sympathetic method of Socratic questioning. The author remembered above all Origen's sympathetic friendship and the enthusiasm which overcame his pupil's initial reluctance. The direction of his life in Caesarea suggests that Origen viewed the roles of priest and teacher as very closely interconnected. Even the most notorious report about Origen – that he castrated himself – is perhaps connected to his sense of vocation as a teacher: historians normally repeat Eusebius' explanation that Origen carried out this act from an overly eager ascetic urge to fulfil literally Jesus' words, 'there are eunuchs who have made themselves eunuchs for the kingdom of God' (Matthew 19.12); but Eusebius adds that a further motivation was Origen's desire to protect himself from accusations of improper behaviour, because his pupils included women as well as men.

It is tempting to connect the importance of teaching in Origen's life to his upbringing in Alexandria: the existence of a long-established tradition of textual scholarship and teaching of various kinds was probably a more important influence on Origen than the existence of any particular 'school', whether Christian or philosophical. But this influence did not just affect Origen's sense of vocation; it seeped into his theology itself. Although the following account organizes and tidies up what is a rather varied and amorphous body of work, the concept of teaching and teachers is a useful lens through which to view Origen's theology and one which can make sense of some ideas which otherwise seem alien, or even dangerous, to modern readers. The concept of education in play here is not that which applied to all school children, but a more specialized sense which would have applied to those (usually men) who chose to follow a master after their elementary schooling and professional training (e.g. in rhetoric) had been completed. The type of 'higher education' that most directly influenced Christianity was philosophical, but it was not the only sort: its essential characteristics would also have applied to the kind of specialist practical and conceptual training that a medic like Galen gave his pupils. This kind of specialized and elite education was understood as: the following of a specific teacher; as a movement from learning basic facts to asking more profound and probing questions; as a training in how to read texts; and finally as a life-changing experience.

Origen often characterized Jesus Christ as a teacher. For example, he began *On First Principles*:

> All who believe and are convinced that grace and truth came by Jesus Christ and that Christ is the truth ... derive the knowledge that calls men to lead a good and blessed life from no other source but the very words and teaching of Christ.

Origen shared with Justin the idea of the Logos (the divine Word or Son) as the expression or revelation of the truth of God. But he developed much more vividly than Justin the idea of the Incarnation as the means by which God enables humankind to receive this revelation. Against the arguments of the pagan Celsus, who assumed that if a divine being took on a human body and soul it would corrupt him, Origen argued that the Incarnation enabled the Word to 'come down to the level of him who is unable to look upon the radiance and brilliance of the deity'. Like a teacher, Christ anticipates his pupils' progress: he adapts himself to those who are beginners, 'until he who has accepted him in this form is gradually lifted up by the Word and can look even upon, so to speak, his absolute form'.[19] Like a teacher with pupils of different abilities, the Word allowed himself to appear to people in different ways according to their need. For example, some of the disciples saw the transfigured Christ, while others only his plain state. Origen thought that the Gospels showed that Jesus taught people in different ways, giving basic explanations of the parables to his wider audience, but deeper explanations to his close disciples.[20] Even the discrepancies between the four Gospels reflected the fact that 'Jesus is many things, according to the [various] understandings of him, of which it is quite likely that the Evangelists took up different notions'.[21] (Thus Origen, theologian and textual critic, deftly turns a textual problem to theological advantage!)

Origen explored Jesus' role as teacher from different perspectives. Sometimes he viewed it generally as moral cleansing or spiritual healing.[22] Sometimes he focused on one incident as if it demonstrated a specific teaching technique. For example, in interpreting the story of Jesus instructing the elders in the Temple, Origen attributes to the child Jesus a Socratic method of questioning! 'He asked the teachers questions ... not to learn something, but to instruct them by asking questions. Asking questions and answering wisely flow from the same source of teaching, and it belongs to the same knowledge to know what questions to ask and how to answer.'[23] According to Origen, the Christian was called to imitate Christ, morally and spiritually, even to the point of accepting martyrdom as Christ obediently accepted death on the Cross. Similarly, the Christian teacher was called to imitate Christ's pedagogy, leading by moral and spiritual example, matching his teaching to the abilities of his pupils and leading each on constantly to higher things.

Greek education of children relied on a notoriously hard and dull method of memory and repetition, first of basic word forms and then of texts. For many people, of course, this was as far as their education went. Even the teaching of rhetoric (the art of public speaking and persuasion) to young men could be rather mechanical. A philosophical education, which encouraged able pupils to think for themselves and promised to change their lives, must have seemed scarily liberating. Although Origen would never have described the teaching of the essentials of Christian faith as boring, he did seem to draw a distinction between learning the basics, which was necessary for all Christians, and a more speculative approach which was only appropriate for the more advanced. Thus in the preface to his work *On First Principles*, he set out 'a definite line and unmistakable rule' regarding those doctrines which the Apostles thought 'necessary' and therefore taught 'in the plainest terms to all believers, even to those who appeared to be somewhat dull in the investigation of divine knowledge'.[24] These doctrines were: that 'God is one, who created and set in order all things'; that this God gave both the Prophets and the Gospels; that this God was Father of Jesus Christ 'who was begotten of the Father before every created thing' and who came to earth, took flesh, truly died, rose from the dead and ascended into heaven; that the Holy Spirit, who is 'united in honour and dignity with the Father', 'inspired each one of the saints, both the prophets and the apostles'. In addition to this three-fold declaration (very similar to the kind of rule of faith asserted by Irenaeus[25]), Origen also thought that the Apostles clearly taught that the immortal soul was freely responsible for its deeds in this life and would be punished or rewarded for them after death; that there would be a resurrection of the body; that the world began to exist at a definite time and at some time would cease to exist; and, finally, that 'the scriptures were composed through the Spirit of God and that they have not only that meaning which is obvious, but also another which is hidden from the majority of readers'.[26]

Origen described these as 'elementary and foundation principles': they were the basis for, but did not make up, a 'connected/single body of doctrine'. Any student wanting to achieve that, and anyone who wanted answers for the uncertain questions which Origen also raised in the Preface, should proceed by 'clear and cogent arguments' and with 'illustrations and declarations … in the holy scriptures'.[27] It is generally agreed that this is what Origen attempted to do in the rest of *On First Principles* – although commentators differ greatly as to whether they put the emphasis on Origen's desire to *systematize* or on his desire to *speculate* on uncertain questions. Origen's language suggested that he thought the 'elementary and foundation principles' were points which needed to be connected up to form a definite shape or 'body of doctrine' (as mathematicians might construct a form), or foundations on which a doctrinal 'building' could be constructed. Elsewhere he wrote of sketching out a picture, before painting in the colour.[28] All these images suggest – against his critics – that Origen thought that even his more speculative thought was still *within* the framework created by the canon of faith.

Origen is also criticized for his elitist attitude to Christian education: the idea that while all can know the basics, some can know more. At one level there is no denying this hierarchical structure to his theology, but it is moderated in several ways. First, and most importantly, Origen thought that all deficiencies in human knowledge would be made up in the future life. Using the metaphor of sketching and painting, he wrote: 'It is clear, then, that to those who have now in this life a kind of outline of thought and knowledge there shall be added in the future the beauty of the perfect image.'[29] Origen explained the possibility of this future knowledge using the image of 'a lecture room or school for souls' in heaven.[30] He also quoted Paul's hope that although 'now we see in a mirror, dimly, but then we will see face to face' (I Corinthians 13.12): this implies a recognition that, despite Origen's enthusiasm for speculation, *all* human knowledge is dim by comparison with heavenly wisdom. This is the second way in which his elitism was moderated. Thirdly, he was countering an even more thorough-going elitism found in the theology of Valentinian Christians.[31] Whereas they thought that humans were divided into three distinct groups – the elect people of the spirit (*pneuma*), the rejected people of the body (*soma*) and the intermediate people of the soul (*psyche*) whose fate was not determined – Origen in effect taught that humans could move from one category up to another. In the end, he believed that *all* created beings would become 'spiritual'.

How did Origen explain and defend the 'first principles' of Christian theology? At the heart of his work was his belief that God is immaterial (not composed of matter) and invisible. God alone exists without a body.[32] This Origen asserted not only against those Christians and Jews who read some biblical statements anthropomorphically but also against those Stoic philosophers who thought that divinity was a kind of material element which underlay and gave order to the other elements in the universe.[33] It is against the latter that Origen particularly emphasized that the Spirit is immaterial and was not some substance to be divided up amongst those who shared in him.

Having established this, Origen then explained that God the Father is the source of all that is and that everything in a sense reflects back on him. However, the way in which the Father was the source of the Son and the Spirit was carefully distinguished in Origen's theology from the way in which the Father was the source of the created universe. Firstly, Origen asserted that the Son and the Spirit were – like the Father – immaterial, intellectual and spiritual. They share the nature of the Father. But, Origen insisted, this did not mean that the Father's substance was divided up to make the Son and Spirit, for that would imply that the Father was material (for only that which is material can be split and divided). Nor was it the case that the Son and Spirit were accidental overspillings from the divine origin. (Origen was deliberately opposing various versions of the Gnostic myth here.) Rather, the Son was 'begotten' by the Father[34]: the biological metaphor stressed that the Son shared the Father's nature and was begotten by his will, not by accident. But unlike any animal begetting, the Son was begotten timelessly and eternally by the Father, for it would be impossible to imagine that the Father was at any time without his Wisdom.[35]

Much debate has been generated by the emphasis which Origen put on the idea that the Son is the 'image of the Father': did this imply the Son's inferiority? For Origen 'image' was a biblical metaphor,[36] which was to be understood not in the sense in which a picture or a sculpture is an image of someone (an entirely material sense of imaging), but in the sense in which a son is the image of his father, sharing, for example, character traits and mental aptitudes:

> This image preserves the unity of nature and substance common to a father and son. For if 'all things that the Father does, these also does the Son likewise', then in this very fact that the Son does all things just as the Father does, the Father's image is reproduced in the Son, whose birth from the Father is as it were an act of his will proceeding from the mind.[37]

Even when Origen stated that the Son is the 'image of his [i.e. the Father's] goodness', again the metaphor is principally biblical (Wisdom 7.25) and intended to show that the Son's goodness is *derived* from the Father and that it is *one* with the Father's, i.e. that there are not two rival goodnesses, or that the Son's true goodness is opposed to the Father's merely apparent goodness (as Marcion claimed).

Critics of Origen, both in late antiquity and today, have claimed that he used 'image' language in a Platonic fashion, to suggest that the Son was *merely* an image of the Father, i.e. that he was merely an imprecise reflection, or an inferior copy of the Father's goodness. (Part of the difficulty here is the uncertainty over the exact original Greek of Origen's texts, some of which only survive in Latin versions which were translated either by followers – who may have ironed out some controversial features – or enemies – who may have heightened them).[38] On the whole, however, Origen guarded against this interpretation; his ontology (his understanding of what 'being' is) rested on a fundamental distinction between God the creator and that which is created. On this was superimposed another distinction between the immaterial (God and rational minds/souls) and the material. While Origen did think that immaterial things were superior to material ones, this distinction was not as important as the creator/created distinction: God is clearly superior to any created rational soul. Furthermore, in his theology there were to be no *ontological* distinctions between one uncreated person and another – that is, he did not think that any one of the three persons of the Trinity was more real than the others. Similarly, no created soul was more real than another, although, morally speaking, some were better and others were worse.

Origen thought that the Father was superior to the Son neither in the sense that he existed before the Son nor that he was more real or more good. Yet Origen did argue that the Son was begotten by the Father, or derived from him. In this sense there is an 'order' in the Trinity. This order is reflected in the roles of the three persons: the Son reveals the Father and this knowledge is made known to humankind by the Spirit. On this topic, Origen's language did suggest that there was something about the Son which enabled him (but not the Father) to 'empty himself' in the Incarnation, in order to reveal something of God in a way which is fitted to humanity's weak understanding. Conversely, in prayer there is an opposite 'movement' from Spirit, through Son, to Father. Origen suggested that people should pray 'mingled with the Spirit of the Lord', and partaking 'of the Word of God, who stands in the midst even of those who do not know him, who is never absent from prayer, and who prays to the Father with the person whose Mediator he is'.[39] Obviously, the language of mediation and of Christ being High Priest was biblical,[40] and Christ's mediatorial role was connected with his incarnation; nevertheless the paradox remained that for Origen the Word was not less than the Father, yet was somehow particularly fitted in some way to be the incarnate one who mediated between the world and God. It was in God's dealings with the world, and not apparently in God's eternal self, that the idea of God as source of the Son and the Spirit seemed most clearly to result in them being ordered beneath him in Origen's theology.

By contrast, Origen thought that God's role as source of the universe – as its creator – clearly set God not only above it but in a completely different order of reality from it. There appears to be no 'great chain of being' in Origen's theology in which God the Father is at the top and the material world is at the bottom. A better analogy might be that of a sphere: the world is that which exists within the sphere, God is that which lies outside and surrounding it.

Origen's cosmology is hugely controversial – again the unreliability of the texts is a problem. A central maxim for Origen was that 'the end will be like the beginning', but it is not at all clear what this meant.[41] In *On First Principles* Origen described first a state of original peace and unity with God, secondly a 'falling away' from this state, and finally the reconciliation of the world again to the Father, in Christ. Some have taken this to mean a movement from immateriality (a state where rational souls alone existed with God) to materiality (the material world was a punishment for the souls' fall) and then to an eschatologically perfected immateriality. But this account has been questioned on several counts.[42] For example, Origen repeatedly argued that God alone can exist without a body: surely this ruled out the existence of souls which pre-existed and then fell into bodies? Secondly, it is now generally recognized that the claim of Methodius (a fourth-century critic of Origen) that Origen denied the resurrection of the body was based on a fundamental misreading of Origen's work. Origen seems to have taken Paul at his word when he wrote of the resurrection of a 'spiritual body' and to have argued for a resurrection body composed in a different way from bodies in this life.[43] This may be rather different from the more literal defences of the resurrection of the body, atom by atom, found in the apologists before and the Cappadocians after Origen, but it does not amount to the denial of any resurrection body at all. Consequently, one might guess that if the 'end will be like the beginning' for Origen, souls did indeed exist with some kind of body.

As always, it is useful to bear in mind the theology that Origen was countering here: he opposed Gnostic and Valentinian denials of the resurrection of the body, but equally he opposed what he thought to be grotesquely materialistic predictions of the eschatological kingdom come to earth, in which the faithful would be rewarded with material goods for their perseverance.[44] Against both, Origen seems to have been trying to argue for the transformation and spiritualizing of the material world – including material bodies – however hard it was for him to articulate a way in which the material could be spiritualized without disappearing altogether. Underlying Origen's thought here seems to have been not only the accounts of Christ's resurrection but also those of his transfiguration, which suggested the possibility of humans' transformation: Christ in his resurrection *and* incarnation is the one who reveals the possibility of and actualizes the transformation of all people.

This brings us to the final controversial aspect of Origen's cosmology of salvation: his claim that all people would be saved. The question of whether he thought the devil himself would be saved is disputed (Origen appears to say so in one place and deny it in another – possibly indicating his aware-

ness that the idea was controversial). The overall direction of his theology, however, pointed to the eventual salvation of the whole world and all
humanity. The key term is 'eventual': Origen posited a system of purificatory
punishment after death.[45] It was in this sense, above all, that the end would
be like the beginning for Origen, when all creation – individually and as
a whole – would be peacefully united with God in its love, knowledge and
worship of the divine.[46] Typically for Origen, he often described this in
intellectual terms, and he often used Platonic terminology to write of the
rise of the soul towards God. But in Origen's theology this rise indicated
not the way in which the soul will eventually leave the body behind (as it
did for Plato), but the rise of each individual as he or she was transformed,
both in intellect and in body. It must be stressed, however, that unlike the
doctrine of the Trinity, the belief that humans have rational souls and that
there will be a resurrection of the body, Origen always expressed a reserve
about the *kind* of resurrection body and the *nature* of the end-times – a
reserve which indicates the distinction in his theology between the basic
principles of Christianity (as expressed in the Preface to *On First Principles*)
and the more speculative parts.

An important part of higher education in this period, whether one was
training to be a rhetor, a philosopher or a doctor, was a training in how to
read texts. This built on the more elementary stages of education which
were also very text-based. Origen seemed to have wanted Christians to
become trained in the reading of Scripture in the way that a philosopher
trained his pupils to read Plato or Aristotle and a doctor trained his how
to read Hippocrates. (A textual approach was not regarded as opposed to
more practical education.) It has been suggested that certain late antique
literary techniques can be traced in Origen's concern to teach his pupils to
establish the correct text (e.g. by using the *Hexapla* to find alternative translations when one is nonsensical); to *read* a text carefully (with particular
attention to identifying who is speaking: Greek had no quotation marks); to
interpret or *understand* a text (paying particular attention to obscure words,
the structure of a narrative and the use of rhetorical or literary devices);
and finally to judge or *evaluate* a text, bringing out a moral, for example.[47] Origen believed that every letter of the text of Scripture was directly
inspired by the Spirit and that the reader – if also inspired by the Spirit
– could draw something of spiritual worth out of every aspect of the text.
In places where the apparent meaning of the biblical text was immoral or
nonsense, Origen thought that the reader should seek for a deeper meaning.
Usually this meant moving from a literal reading of the passage in question
to a figurative or allegorical meaning. But it is worth noting that Origen
thought that *most* parts of Scripture had a useful obvious meaning, and that

in many places the text had *both* an obvious 'surface' *and* deeper allegorical meanings. Often he seems to have thought that the obvious meaning pointed to a real event in the past (e.g. the Passover), and that two further levels of meaning pointed to the moral application of that event (its meaning to the believer in the present) and to the eschatological perfection of the believer in the future.

Origen believed that not only learning about Christianity from a teacher, but indeed the very reading of Scripture, should be a life-changing experience.[48] His whole approach to Christian education assumed not only a dynamic progression from basic to more profound knowledge, but the idea that knowledge was transformatory. This is partly because knowledge, for Origen, was only one side of the coin, the other being love. The role of love in the spiritual journey is indicated with particular vividness and subtlety in his *Commentary* and his *Homilies* on the Song of Songs, in which the groom's relationship with his wife is taken to symbolize the relationship of Christ with the soul (or, with human souls collectively as the Church). This approach to the Song of Songs, not to mention many of Origen's interpretations of individual verses, became enormously influential in later Church Fathers and the medieval Church.[49]

Although he is usually portrayed as a deeply intellectual and spiritual man, Origen was always also clearly alive to the practical consequences of Christian faith: besides frequently bringing out the ethical implications of Bible passages, he wrote treatises on martyrdom and on prayer, for example. The latter gives us some fascinating information about the practical aspects of Christian prayer in this period, for example the way in which Christians prayed with 'hands outstretched and eyes lifted up', except when asking for forgiveness, when they knelt.[50] Although he suggests that these outward physical attitudes represent inner spiritual attitudes (stretching one's soul and lifting one's mind to God), one should not think that Origen was unconcerned with physical posture. Like modern spiritual guides or liturgists, he seems to be suggesting that the physical posture aids and leads to a particular inner disposition. This is exactly parallel to the way in which he thought that the 'body' or historical meaning of the biblical text led one to the inner 'spiritual' meaning.

The origins of Christianity in Carthage are even more hazy than those of Christianity in Alexandria. There was a Jewish community in Carthage, as can be seen, for example, from the evidence of a Jewish cemetery to the north of the city.[51] Some scholars have suggested that Christianity came to Carthage with Jews from the eastern Mediterranean who worshipped Christ as their Messiah and spread their belief among other Jews in the city.

Another theory is that Christianity in Carthage came from Rome and was dominated, like the Roman congregations in the second century, by converts from paganism. The most likely conclusion is that North African Christianity rose from a number of different sources.[52] Certainly in Tertullian's writing one finds no obvious sense of descent from communities in Rome or elsewhere, and he treated Christianity as if it had been in Carthage for a good while. The best guess is that there were Christians in Carthage at least by the mid-second century. Apuleius' *The Golden Ass* contains an ambiguous (and very scathing) description of a woman who 'sacrilegiously feigned bold awareness of a deity whom she proclaimed to be the only God'; if this referred to Christianity, it would confirm this date.[53]

The earliest secure evidence of Christianity in North Africa is the account of seven men and five women who were arrested in 180CE in the town of Scilli and brought to trial in neighbouring Carthage, where they were executed. Interestingly, one of them is described as carrying *Latin* copies of 'books and letters of Paul', which suggests that at least some of the leaders of the North African Christian community could not read Greek – setting them apart from nearly all other Christians leaders in this period, including those in Rome.[54] In 203CE another outbreak of persecution led to a small group of Carthaginian Christians being put to death in the arena. This event was recorded in the dramatic *Martyrdom of Felicity and Perpetua* (a text discussed in Chapter 2). Although Tertullian may not have actually been the editor of the latter text, it is unthinkable that these two groups of martyrs would not have made an impression on him: if he was born around 160CE, he would have been in his late teens or 20s when the Scillitan martyrs were killed and in middle age when Perpetua died. That the martyrs were revered by their contemporaries is shown by evidence that basilicas outside the city walls were built in their honour – possibly to contain their relics.[55]

Tertullian's description of the character and ceremonies of the Church in Carthage echoes Justin's account of the community in Rome: he mentioned, for example, a common meal, the reading of Scripture, the sharing of goods ('all things are common among us but our wives'), and voluntary collections for the support of the sick, the poor, orphans, the elderly, those who have suffered shipwreck and those Christians who have been imprisoned for their faith.[56] He put particular emphasis on the importance of common prayer:

> We meet together as an assembly and congregation, that, offering up prayer to God as with united force, we may wrestle with him in our supplications. … We pray, too, for the emperors, for their ministers and for all in authority, for the welfare of the world, for the prevalence of peace, for the delay of the final consummation.[57]

Two elements stand out slightly from Justin's account. First, Tertullian indicated that the meeting for prayer and reading Scripture was also the context in which the elders 'exhorted', 'rebuked' and 'censured' members of the congregation. Whether this was general ethical instruction in the form of a homily or the censure of particular members of the congregation is not clear, although the emphasis on discipline fits Tertullian's rigorous approach to ethics. Secondly, while Justin's meal was called a Eucharist and he focused on the sharing of bread and wine, Tertullian described an *agape*, which seems to have been a full meal: 'as much is eaten as satisfies the cravings of hunger; as much is drunk as befits the chaste'; 'with the good things of the feast we benefit the needy'.[58] The way Tertullian described the meal demonstrates nicely the difficult line which the apologists took in addressing their pagan contemporaries. On the one hand, he contrasted the drunken excess of pagan banquets with the modesty and moderation of the Christian *agape* (Christianity is better than paganism); on the other hand he implied that Christianity was no threat to the order of society because the *agape* was a normal Roman meal. The Christians first prayed, then reclined at the tables, eating a modest amount and talking as if God were overhearing them.

> After washing their hands, and the bringing in of lights, each is asked to stand forth and sing, as he can, a hymn to God, either one from the holy Scriptures or one of his own composing – a proof of the measure of our drinking.[59]

The invocation of gods, reclining whilst eating and talking, the washing of hands and music were all common features of Greek and Roman banquets (and of many Jewish celebratory meals as well). Although one might suspect Tertullian of working too hard to disabuse his audience of the fear that Christians were celebrating orgies, the description fits very well with the community meal celebrated by the Jewish *therapeutae* described by Philo.[60] It seems very likely that both Christians and Jews were adapting the practices of late antique culture, and that the order of their meals followed that of a Roman feast translated into a Christian or Jewish mode.

We have a large number of Tertullian's writings, and his literary character leaps off the page: erudite, witty, satirical, caustic, by turns elegantly persuasive and fiercely stern. But we know little of the man himself and – as with Origen – recent research has tended to challenge what used to be accepted fact.[61] We know from his own testimony that he lived and wrote in Carthage, was married and converted from paganism (probably in the late 190s, to judge from the date of his earliest extant works). He wrote in both Latin and Greek. His works are full of references to pagan philosophy and classical literature; they use the sophisticated techniques of contemporary rhetoric. Tertullian, we can conclude, had an excellent education; but although he may have received some legal training, he was probably not a lawyer by profession as once thought.[62] He was extremely well versed in the Scriptures, both Old and New, and had read Justin and Irenaeus (at least, their works against heresy).[63] Despite later assumptions to the contrary, Tertullian's own words imply that he was not a priest.[64] His education and cultural context affected not just his style but the kind of works he wrote. He appears to have written no commentaries or homilies (which again might suggest he was not a priest);[65] he did not write philosophical treatises, far less anything that might resemble systematic theology. Rather, his works are well understood as individual arguments, each defending the Christian position in a specific context or on a particular matter. In this sense *all* his works are 'apologetic' – they all argue a case for Christianity (although it has been traditional to divide his writings into 'apologetic', 'doctrinal' and 'ethical' works).[66] In a period when Latin prose was somewhat in the doldrums, Tertullian rejuvenated it, using rhetoric not for mere display but 'to achieve its original objective, persuasion. ... He did not describe, he advocated.'[67] Such argument and advocacy set a true case against a false one – either that of paganism (Tertullian's 'apologetic' works), or of unorthodox Christians ('doctrinal' works), or of Christians in danger of lapsing ('ethical' works). Underlying them all was a profound conviction of a fundamental choice which the Christian had to make: for one God against the gods; for truth against falsity; for modest and plain living against show and excess. Another way of putting this is that throughout his work Tertullian was concerned with the question of Christian identity: what did it mean to be a Christian? In an era where this very question was made urgent by the threat of death and real choices had to be made, Tertullian sought to articulate the answer and to encourage his fellow believers to carry out its consequences.

The question of identity is perhaps most explicit in Tertullian's *Apology* and in his ethical works, although the emphases are different. In the *Apology* he was keen to show the Roman authorities that Christians can be decent citizens – we have seen a typical strategy above in his description of Christian customs. In other works, Tertullian stressed the ways in which Christians were (or should be) a race apart from their contemporaries: their women should dress modestly and leave the house only when necessary; their men should pay no vain attention to the grooming of their hair or beards.[68] His ban on Christians attending gladiatorial shows was due not to a puritanical dislike of entertainment, nor even just to an abhorrence of the shows' endorsement of sexual immorality and violence. Rather Tertullian's main objection was to the pagan context: if shows were dedicated to the gods, anyone attending was guilty of idolatry.[69] A similar argument was used by Tertullian against many aspects of Carthaginian life, from an easily understandable ban on Christians assisting in the manufacture or selling of idols to the less obvious advice against borrowing money (which conventionally required swearing an oath).[70] Most striking perhaps were Tertullian's arguments against military service. As with the gladiatorial shows, although he was concerned about violence – the 'chain, and the prison, and the torture, and the punishment' – his fundamental objection was to the explicit or implicit demand for the soldier to be loyal to the Empire, the emperor and, therefore, their gods: 'the line is crossed in transferring one's name from the camp of light to the camp of darkness'.[71] Even the wearing of a wreath in some military parades could signify an implicit dedication to the pagan gods, for the wreath 'belongs to idols, both from the history of its origin and from its use by false religion ... the very doors, the very victims and altars, the very servants and priests are crowned'.[72] Tertullian's solution was hard: a Christian cannot serve as a soldier; a soldier cannot become a Christian and not renounce his military service. As leaving the army was difficult and might lead to persecution and death,[73] this was no easy creed to follow. For Tertullian it was an unambiguous choice: 'no one can serve two masters'.[74]

Some of Tertullian's ethical works seem to have been concerned in particular with arguments among the Christian community between those who took more and less rigorous lines. Tertullian was attracted by the movement he called the 'new prophecy', now commonly known as Montanism after its early leader Montanus. The movement emerged from Asia Minor and was characterized by an eager expectation of the end of the world, a belief in the continued prophetic inspiration of the Holy Spirit (which led to many claims of ecstatic and visionary experiences) and an extremely rigorous ascetic approach to Christianity. A version of the movement seems to have been very popular in North Africa in Tertullian's day and the influence of Montanism does seem to have become increasingly prominent in Tertullian's later writings – those on ethics became more rigorous on certain matters like remarriage and the question of whether the Church should forgive those who commit serious sin after baptism. Even in his earlier writings Tertullian argued that post-baptismal sin demanded deep penitence, demonstrated by such acts as prolonged prayer, weeping and fasting. Later, apparently riled by the claims of some clerics to have the authority to remit sin, Tertullian warned that God alone can forgive sin. While the Church could choose to admit sinners back into communion, there were some sins so serious that they should bar a Christian from church for the rest of his or her life (but no action from the Church predicted or foreclosed God's divine judgement).[75] Although it has often been claimed that Tertullian left the Church under the influence of Montanism, the current consensus is that Montanism coincided with and encouraged/deepened views which Tertullian already held, and that Tertullian remained within the Church.[76]

The question of identity emerged in two ways from Tertullian's arguments about Christian doctrine: he was concerned with the true identity of the Christian believer, eager to refute Marcionite, Valentinian and other opponents. But his sharp mind also analysed and probed deep into the question of the identity of Christ: what did it mean to say that Christ was 'man, of the flesh, of the spirit God'?[77] What did it mean to say that 'The Father, Son and the Spirit are one and the same'?[78] In pressing both the simplicity and the paradoxes of Christian faith, Tertullian developed some of the most memorable formulations of doctrine and a subtle theological vocabulary.[79]

As Irenaeus had done, Tertullian argued firmly against Marcion and Valentinus that the Word (Logos), the Son of God, had to have become truly human to save humanity.[80] He also seems to have shared the idea that Christ in some sense took on *the whole* of human nature in order to heal it: 'for in putting on our flesh he made it his own; in making it his own, he made it sinless'.[81] Furthermore, Christ had a human soul, so that he 'could save the soul'.[82] Indeed, Tertullian argued that through the Incarnation, all human souls could come to know Christ, and he set this true knowledge against the classical philosophical instruction to 'know yourself': 'For it was through ignorance, not of itself but of the Word of God, that it was in peril of its salvation.'[83]

Tertullian forcefully argued that in order to save human nature, body and soul, Christ's humanity had to be of the same substance as all humanity: Christ did not evade a human birth (as Marcion supposedly taught); his body was not composed of some ethereal or astral substance (as Valentinus' follower Apelles taught); he did not have a body composed of 'soul'. For this reason, Tertullian put a great deal of emphasis on the virgin birth: although Christ's *conception* by the Holy Spirit was unique, he had a normal human *birth* and his mother suffered the indignities, discomforts and pain of pregnancy and childbirth.[84] Although Tertullian did stress that Mary's virginity both confirmed the divine parentage of Christ and explained the purity of his human nature, he explicitly rejected the idea that Mary was a perpetual virgin. This is because he thought that her miraculous intactness in labour would have denied Christ a normal human birth.[85] The implications of this for Tertullian's view of women were quite startling: Christ received his *entire* humanity (both body and soul) from Mary, a woman – thus challenging a prevailing late antique pagan view that in human conception the woman provided the material and the man the rationality or soul, a view which could reinforce cultural stereotypes about the inferior 'bodily' nature of women.[86] Furthermore, Tertullian assumed that the genealogy in Matthew traced the descent from Adam to Mary (not Joseph): thus it was *through Mary* that Jesus summed up all of human nature from Adam and eradicated the sin which spread through humanity from Adam and Eve. Thus although Tertullian is notorious among feminists for announcing that Eve is the 'gateway to sin', he also asserted that Mary's womb, in its normal, fully human fleshliness which gave rise to Christ's human body and soul, was the gateway to salvation.[87] Furthermore, although Mary was chaste and virtuous, her giving birth to Christ was not presented as some kind of impossible ideal, entirely distant from any other experience of motherhood; rather, she bore in her own childbearing the labour and pain announced to Eve and all women as the result of the Fall.

Besides emphasizing Christ's real human birth, Tertullian also stressed that Christ truly died and that his risen body was flesh in the normal human sense and would be preserved in heaven.[88] His work *On the Resurrection of Christ* was an impassioned defence of the resurrection of the body against pagan philosophy, Valentinians and others, and the linch-pin of his argument was that Christ's true resurrection was the guarantee of the resurrection of all Christians. One needs to view the work in context in order to imagine the power of his argument to comfort and encourage his fellow Christians: it was written perhaps only two or three years after the martyrdoms of Perpetua and her companions in 203CE.[89] It is notable that he accuses the Valentinians not only of doubting the resurrection but of doubting the relevance of martyrdom.[90]

While Tertullian argued at length for the reality of Christ's human nature, he clearly felt less need to assert Christ's true divinity, which was accepted by all who called themselves Christians.[91] The questions at stake here were: how were Christ's divinity and humanity related? and how was Christ related to the Father and Spirit?

Tertullian's answer to the first question was expressed with typical economy and elegance: 'the two substances acted distinctly, each in its own character. ... Neither the flesh becomes Spirit nor the Spirit flesh. In one person they no doubt are well able to be co-existent. Of them Jesus consists – Man of the flesh; of the Spirit God.'[92] Tertullian argues that the Gospels provide evidence of this in their witness to the different aspects of his earthly ministry:

> Thus the nature of the two substances displayed him as man and God –in one respect born, in the other unborn; in one respect fleshly, in the other spiritual; in one sense weak, in the other exceeding strong; in one sense dying, in the

other living. This property of the two states – the divine and the human – is distinctly asserted with equal truth of both natures alike. … The powers of the Spirit, proved him to be God, his sufferings attested the flesh of man. … If his flesh with its sufferings was fictitious, for the same reason was the Spirit false with all its powers. Wherefore halve Christ with a lie? he was wholly the truth.[93]

This language of one person (*persona* in Latin) with two substances (*substantiae*) has been too easily associated with the later Chalcedonian formula of one person (*prosōpon* or *hypostasis*) and two natures (*physeis*). What is more important than the question of whether Tertullian's Christology can meaningfully be said to be 'Chalcedonian' is that he represented an important stage in attempts to explain the paradox of the Incarnation – in this case by explaining that each substance had its own properties which remained distinct and evident in the unity of the one person. Tertullian was clear that neither substance was changed into (*transfiguratus*) or blended with (*confusus*) the other. He was more reticent in asserting what *did* happen at the Incarnation – did Christ 'put on' human nature, or was he conjoined with it? – which suggests that he was aware of the difficulty of grappling with these matters in any human language.[94]

On the question of how Christ the Son or Word was related to Father and Spirit, Tertullian was arguing against not Marcion or the Valentinians but against the proponents of a view known as monarchianism or modalism, whom Tertullian addresses through an attack on a certain Praxeas.[95] This group called themselves 'monarchians' because they stressed the unity or single rule (*monarchia*) of God and were reluctant to admit any distinctions within God. They believed that Christ was worthy to be worshipped as God, and thus seemed to have concluded that Christ was to such a degree one with the Father that Father, Son and Spirit were merely successive aspects or modes of the one God – hence the modern term 'modalism'. (The belief is also commonly known as Sabellianism, after a later teacher.[96]) Tertullian pithily summed up his objection to the monarchians' ideas: they 'put to flight the Paraclete [the Holy Spirit] and crucified the Father'.[97] In other words, if one acknowledged no real distinction between Father and Son, it was the Father who died on the Cross (hence yet another term for the heresy – 'patripassianism', meaning 'the-Father-suffered'). Furthermore, it denied a real distinct existence to the Holy Spirit who inspired the authors of Scripture, and, according to Tertullian, still continued to inspire prophets and prophetesses in his day. Tertullian's insistence on the distinctive character and operation of the Spirit is surely connected with his interest in Montanism.

Tertullian's response to the problem of expressing the reality of the

Trinitarian God was not so much to offer a firm solution but to restate the paradox in a variety of persuasive ways, relying on a series of metaphors. Developing the language of Logos found in Justin and Irenaeus, he suggested that Reason (Logos) and Wisdom (the Spirit) are *eternal* (i.e. not successive) powers of the divine.[98] Tertullian here appealed to the presence of the Word and Wisdom in the Hebrew Scriptures. For example, he suggested that the way in which human monarchy is shared through various agents might explain how the divine power and nature is shared between the Father, Son and Spirit. He even used the very material metaphors of roots-tree-fruit and fountain-river-stream to suggest ways in which the three could be one. The latter metaphors in particular have been used to argue that Tertullian had a doctrine of the Trinity in which the Son and Spirit were subordinate to the Father. Tertullian also wrote the that Trinity flows down from the Father 'in intertwined and connected steps'.[99] He seems to have asserted that the three were one in quality, substance and power, but three in sequence, aspect and manifestation.[100] As with Origen, the question of subordination is complex: both writers assert a basic unity within which there is a kind of distinction and order (*taxis* or *gradus*).

Tertullian summed up his faith in a 'rule of faith'. The content of this seems familiar from the theology of Irenaeus and Origen, but its formulation seems more like one of the later creeds:

> We ... believe that there is one only God, but ... that this one only God has also a Son, His Word, who proceeded from Himself, by whom all things were made, and without whom nothing was made. Him we believe to have been sent by the Father into the Virgin, and to have been born of her – being both Man and God, the Son of Man and the Son of God, and to have been called by the name of Jesus Christ; we believe Him to have suffered, died, and been buried, according to the Scriptures, and, after He had been raised again by the Father and taken back to heaven, to be sitting at the right hand of the Father, and that He will come to judge the quick and the dead; who sent also from heaven from the Father, according to His own promise, the Holy Ghost, the Paraclete, the sanctifier of the faith of those who believe in the Father, and in the Son, and in the Holy Ghost. ... This rule of faith has come down to us from the beginning of the gospel.

But clearly for Tertullian Christian identity was not just about common belief: 'we are a body knit together as such by a common religious profession, by unity of discipline, and by the bond of a common hope'.[101] In this he is very similar to Origen: although each has a deeply intellectual side, both are certain that the basics of the Christian faith can be grasped by all, and their teaching about what it means to be a Christian was profoundly concerned with the ethical and spiritual as well as the doctrinal implications of the faith.

Sometimes Tertullian is contrasted with Origen on the grounds that Origen's theology was very 'Platonic', while Tertullian purports to eschew philosophy (famously in the words 'what of Athens and Jerusalem? What of the academy and the Church?'[102]). Yet the account of Origen's use of Platonism has in recent years become much more nuanced and there was much more to Origen's theology than a philosophical restatement of Christian belief. Both Origen and Tertullian were essentially interested in the same questions: what did it mean to be a Christian? What lifestyle did Christianity entail? What did Christians hope for? Both articulated their answers against a background of persecution, and the idea of martyrdom deeply affects their writings. Both were extremely intelligent, well-educated professionals with a deep understanding of their contemporary culture. Each was a man not only of his time but of his particular place. Finally, both seem to have shared a passion for writing and their outputs mark the beginnings – in the Greek East and in the Latin West – of a really substantial literary culture within Christianity.

CHAPTER 5

Church and Empire: Diocletian, Constantine and the Controversy over Arius
(THIRD TO FOURTH CENTURIES)

Tertullian died around 225CE. The next 100 years were crucial for the Church and they saw dramatic and wide-reaching changes in the way that Christians lived and worshipped as communities. When the emperors were minded to persecute Christians, their efforts became more systematic: this came to a head in the so-called 'Great Persecution' at the beginning of the fourth century, when Diocletian attempted an empire-wide policy. But at the same time, Christianity grew markedly in influence even among the ruling classes. Some pagan emperors pursued policies of religious toleration (albeit limited and often temporary) which gave Christians some liberties. One of Diocletian's co-rulers, Constantius, was sympathetic to Christianity and had a Christian wife. The child of this marriage was Constantine, who came to be not only the first Christian emperor but the first man who wanted to Christianize the Empire. In 325CE he summoned a council of bishops which adjudicated on controversial matters of Christian doctrine and practice – an event which Tertullian would have found hard to comprehend.

In order to appreciate these dramatic changes, it is necessary to understand a little about their political context – although attempting to summarize these years is a bit like trying to knit with spaghetti, so complex is the tangle of events and so slippery is our grasp of them. Any generalization is bound to distort but the unstable history of imperial rule in the third century can often be made to look like the inevitable decline of a weak pagan system, before the foundation of a stable Christian empire. This warps the account of the pagan empire as much as it warps the account of what came after, which was certainly not an era of total stability either for the Empire or for the Church – as the next chapter will show. Whilst acknowledging the huge difference made by Constantine, this account will try not to obscure some of the continuities between his rule and what went before and after.[1]

The century after Tertullian's death saw great instability on the Empire's borders. The Empire was vulnerable to attack from the Sassanid rulers of Persia in the east and from tribes attacking the Romans in the regions of the Rhine and Danube in the north.[2] Changes of rule in the east were particularly bewildering: in about 213 the Romans captured King Abgar IX of Osrhoene (the eastern area of Syria around Edessa) and sent him in chains to Rome; by the mid-third century Osrhoene had been captured by the Sassanids; by 256 the Sassanids had advanced into the Roman province of Syria and even attacked Antioch. The emperor Valerian retrieved the Roman province, but when he advanced further to Edessa in 260 he was captured and the Sassanids attacked Antioch again, taking away many captives. Earlier the Sassanids had captured Armenia, but they were far from invulnerable themselves: Queen Zenobia resisted them and gained territory in Egypt, Syria, Palestine, Asia Minor and Lebanon for a short-lived empire based in Palmyra (267–72). In the third century, every emperor from Caracalla (212-17) onwards died a violent death; this instability of the Empire's governance was intimately connected with the instability of the Empire's borders, for while emperors were expected to be military men leading expeditions to guard the frontiers they were especially vulnerable not only to enemy attack but also to the treachery of their own generals.[3] Between 235 and 284 there were over 50 men to whom one can refer as 'Emperor'. It was partly because of this political instability that those men who were emperors for a reasonable length of time were particularly concerned to put forward policies to promote the unity of the Empire. Inevitably, such policies had an adverse effect on those who were perceived not to fit in.

Not only did Christian communities not fit in, but during this period of instability they continued to grow and become more publicly visible. It is in this period – in other words *before* the accession of Constantine – that there is the first secure evidence of dwellings being adapted for use specifically for Christian worship. Most famously, a house which was converted to include a baptistry has been discovered at Dura Europos; it must pre-date 256 when the Sassanids attacked the town and it was abandoned.[4] By this date, Christians already owned substantial catacombs in Rome and it was probably in the second half of the third century that Christians began to construct buildings specifically for their own liturgies.[5] The first examples of securely identifiable Christian art date from this period: paintings in the catacombs (*c.*200CE) and Christian sarcophagi (*c.*270CE). Both use a combination of classical images (no doubt given a Christian interpretation) like the shepherd, or the philosopher and pupil(s) with biblical scenes, such as Noah's ark, Daniel in the lion's den and the three young men in the fiery furnace.[6] Christianity already had a well-organized network of paid clergy[7] and in some areas Christianity had become a major provider of poor relief, especially in times of famine or plague.[8] In this period, Christianity also seems to have spread into the countryside, whilst previously it had been mainly an urban phenomenon.[9] Expansion was sometimes due to the actions of a charismatic individual and companions – for example, Antony of Egypt who encouraged individuals to take up a celibate ascetic life in the desert regions of Egypt, or Gregory the Wonderworker who, according to his biographer Gregory of Nyssa, converted large numbers of people in the towns and villages of Pontus and Cappadocia in Asia Minor.[10]

In late 249 or very early 250 the emperor Decius ordered that everyone in the Empire should sacrifice to its gods. It seems to have been a measure designed with a combined religious and political purpose: to gain the gods' favour towards the Empire and its new ruler and to bind the Empire together in this act of propitiation.[11] The policy in itself was probably not aimed directly at Christians (although it has often been presented like that). Nevertheless, the way in which the policy was enacted inevitably affected Christians more than most others. Although it did not ban Christian worship, it did rule out the worship of the Christian God *alone*, and thus the policy collided with the religious exclusivism for which Christians were well known. The process was invigilated carefully and everyone who agreed was given a *libellus*, or a certificate, to prove that 'in accordance with the edict's decree I have made sacrifice and poured a libation, and partaken of the sacred victims'.[12]

The policy appears to have had a dramatic initial success: there were reports from both Alexandria and Carthage, for example, that many Christians gave in.[13] It is unclear what the sanction for refusal was: it may have been up to the discretion of local governors. Certainly they seemed to focus on punishing Church leaders – presumably because the priests and bishops refused to encourage their congregations to comply with the imperial edict. Consequently, the Church was in effect decapitated: in 250 the bishops of all the major cities in the Empire either died (Fabian of Rome, Alexander of Jerusalem, Babylas of Antioch) or were forced to flee (Dionysius of Alexandria, Cyprian of Carthage).[14] Many other Christians were imprisoned and were given the honorific title *confessor* for their willingness to declare their Christian faith and their readiness to become martyrs, even if death did not in fact become their final fate. As we shall see, their high status in the Church caused considerable problems for the ordained clergy. On the other hand, many Christians agreed to sacrifice, or gained *libelli* fraudulently. Furthermore, the administrative difficulty of rigorous enforcement may have meant that many of the less prominent members of the churches simply avoided confrontation. In any case the energetic pursuit of the policy did not last long: it was decreasing even by the time Decius died in 251.[15] Under his successor Gallus, and initially under the next emperor Valerian, Christianity seems to have recovered rapidly and large numbers of those who had lapsed sought readmission to the Church.

In 257–58, however, Valerian issued an edict against all Christians that they should recognize pagan ceremonies; they were also banned from public Christian worship (as opposed to worship in private houses) and from entering Christian burial places. There is little evidence for the overall implementation of the decree.[16] However, perhaps in the face of defiance from Christians, imperial policy seems to have hardened towards those with the most influence in the Church: bishops, priests and deacons from various regions of the Empire were executed.[17] Furthermore, those Christians with the highest standing in Roman society had their property confiscated and were threatened with execution or slavery.[18] In this period the bishops of Rome and Carthage (Sixtus and Cyprian) were killed, and Bishop Dionysius was deported again from Alexandria, having in vain argued that he did not need to recognize pagan ceremonies in order to pray for the Empire and its ruler:

> Not all men worship all gods; each worships some – those he believes in. We believe in the one God and creator of all things, who entrusted the throne to his most beloved emperors, Valerian and Gallienus; him we both worship and adore, and to him we continually pray that their throne may remain unshaken.[19]

When Gallienus succeeded his father Valerian, he reversed his father's policy against the Christians, allowing a certain amount of religious tolerance and the recovery of Church property. He perhaps recognized the difficulty of pursuing a policy of persecution when it lacked general popular support[20] in a period when the Empire faced more urgent, external threats. For 40 years Christians enjoyed peace from imperial persecution.

In 284 Diocletian came to power and ruled for 21 years, first on his own, then with a co-emperor, then finally in a rule of four – the 'tetrarchy'. Within the tetrarchy there were two senior emperors (the Augusti) and two junior emperors (the Caesars). The east was ruled by one Augustus and his Caesar and the west likewise; each half of the Empire was further divided into two regions so that each of the imperial tetrarchs had responsibility for a particular area. Roughly speaking, the Empire was thus divided into the north-west (Gaul, Britain), the south-west (Italy, Africa, Spain), the north-east (the Balkans, Greece, Asia Minor) and the south-east (Syria, Palestine, Egypt).²¹ Although complex, the way the Empire was divided became crucial for differing Christian experiences of persecution and for the eventual spread of official toleration of Christianity from the north-west to the south and east.

Diocletian's longevity as an emperor had a stabilizing influence in itself and he was determined to set the administration of the Empire on a more effective footing, reorganizing, for example, the currency, the tax system, the army and the provinces' boundaries. His aim for the unity and stability of the Empire was also expressed religiously through his re-emphasis on the gods of Rome.²² Like Decius, he was clearly appealing to the traditional ground of imperial stability; in particular Diocletian also expressed a strong distaste for religious novelty, whether Christian or Manichaean.²³ Yet there was also a certain amount of reinvention taking place: Diocletian identified his rule particularly with Jupiter (himself) and Hercules (his co-Augustus), and encouraged the explicit attribution of divine qualities to the emperors, without going so far as actually claiming to be a god.

For a long time Christians remained undisturbed, and it is unclear why Diocletian finally turned his attention to the Christians – his co-Augustus Galerius has been blamed both by Christian writers from the era and by some later historians. In February 303, Diocletian issued an edict throughout the Empire which ordered that Christian churches should be destroyed, that the churches' Scriptures and valuables should be handed over to imperial authorities, and that Christians should cease meeting to worship. The church building in the eastern imperial capital Nicomedia was the first symbolic victim of the decree. In Nicomedia there were violent reprisals against Christians who objected to the decree (and who were also suspected of being responsible for two fires in the imperial palace).²⁴ Possibly because of this local reaction, Diocletian declared shortly afterwards that Christians would lose any civic honours and judicial privileges they previously held (for example, all Christians could now be tortured, and none could bring civil court actions without swearing a pagan oath). In the summer of 303, a further edict ordered the arrest of bishops, priests and deacons. As the prisons rapidly filled up, this was followed in the autumn with the order that these clergy should be forced to sacrifice (if necessary, compelled by physical violence) and then set free.²⁵ These further edicts seem only to have applied to the eastern Empire, however.

The penalties for disobedience against the first edict were left unspecified and to a certain extent depended on the judgement of individual governors, who in turn may have been influenced by the mood of local populations. In the east, Diocletian's two further decrees suggest that his aim was not the extermination of individual Christians but rather forced compliance to his religious programme: sacrifice became the major test of loyalty. In the west, Christians focused on the issue of handing over the Scriptures. Many did so – and still others handed over books which they passed off as Scripture.[26] Certainly some were executed for their failure to comply, but it is very difficult to judge how many. In particular, although both rulers of the west seem to have destroyed Christian churches, Constantius in the north-west appears not to have enforced the other aspects of Diocletian's first edict in the vigorous way that Maximian did in the south-west.

In early 304, Diocletian ordered all inhabitants of the Empire to sacrifice to the gods on pain of death. While Decius provided certificates for those who sacrificed but had no sure means of checking whether everyone had presented themselves, Diocletian's new census lists (initially prepared for efficient tax collection) must have encouraged a belief that a more rigorous enactment was possible. Nevertheless, even this edict was not uniformly enforced: either it was only intended for the east, or the western emperors did not carry it out effectively. Indeed, when Diocletian and Maximian retired in 305, and Constantius replaced Maximian as the senior emperor in the west, the persecution of Christians in the west ceased. There was, however, still some unevenness of policy. When Constantius died in 306, Constantine claimed his father's emperorship and allowed Christians not only to worship but also to claim their property back. Meanwhile Maxentius, Constantine's co-emperor – and increasingly his rival – in the west, did not take this step until 311.

In the east the situation was rather different. In the same year that Constantine freed Christians in the north-west, the Caesar Maximinus launched an enthusiastic pursuit of the final edict in his region of Palestine and Syria and Egypt, using the new census data.[27] The senior tetrarch in the east was the Augustus Galerius. It is unclear what his policy was until 311 when, close to death, he issued an edict of toleration of Christians. In this he claimed superiority for himself as the senior emperor of all the Empire and issued the edict in the name of all his imperial colleagues; but Maximinus held to the terms for only half a year before he restarted his persecution, targeting Church leaders and encouraging cities to petition him for permission to expel Christians.[28]

Meanwhile, Constantine had defeated his western rival Maxentius at the Battle of the Milvian Bridge (312CE), fighting, he claimed, under the banner of Christ. For years there had been three claimants to imperial power in the west: Constantine, Maxentius and Licinius. For a while Constantine and Licinius united and Constantine claimed for himself the role as senior Augustus of the Empire, requesting that Maximinus stop persecuting Christians in the east. Maximinus merely pretended to comply, only truly capitulating shortly before he was defeated by Licinius in 313. That year, Constantine and Licinius issued the edict of Milan, proclaiming tolerance for all religious worship and the restitution of Christian property. Licinius gained responsibility for the east and although persecution never returned, his harassment of Christians (for example, refusing them jobs in his palaces or civil service) allowed Constantine to paint his eventual defeat of Licinius as the final liberation of Christians in the Empire.[29]

What can we learn from this narrative about the nature of the final phase of Christian persecution, from Decius to Maximinus? Firstly, in contrast with the earlier persecutions, these actions against Christians constituted an imperial policy imposed from the top rather than a response to popular sentiment rising from below. Secondly, although the various edicts testify that imperial policies were *conceived*, it is also evident that they were not necessarily *carried out* in a systematic or effective way. The division of the Empire into different regions had a lot to do with this; imperial reliance on individual governors in far-away cities was another factor. Thirdly, it was not a period of continuous persecution. Lactantius and Eusebius of Caesarea both wrote impassioned works against the persecuting emperors which have indelibly influenced later perspectives on the period, yet they spent most of their lives in peace.[30] It is also notoriously difficult to estimate the number of Christian deaths in this period. The persecutions made their impact as much through fear as through actual violence – a fear that was intensified by the inconsistency of policy across the Empire and by the clear shock when persecution was renewed in 304 after over 40 years. Finally, when seeking a cause for the policy of persecution it is simplistic to force a choice between a motive of political contingency (seeing Christians as a destabilizing force) or of religious conviction. *All* the emperors in this period seem to have believed that the destiny of the Empire was vitally connected with the correct veneration of the divine – Constantine is no different from Diocletian in this respect. Where they differed was on the question of which god(s) should be venerated and how important it was that all took part in broadly the same kinds of acts of veneration.

Throughout this period Christianity struggled with the effects of persecution. For many, the threat of martyrdom defined their sense of Christian identity much more clearly; for others, the shifting imperial policy created ambiguity and complexity. In particular, many Christians became absorbed with arguments about how to deal with those who had lapsed – that is, those who had sacrificed or obtained their certificates (*libelli*) by deception – but who wanted to return to the Church. Our best evidence for these conflicts

comes from the writings of Cyprian, Bishop of Carthage. He came from a
wealthy family, was well educated and probably destined for a prominent
public career. In 248, only a few years after conversion to Christianity, he
was elected bishop. During the Decian persecutions he (and other presbyters) fled Carthage in order, he wrote, 'to ensure that everyone is left
undisturbed', lest 'my presence may provoke an outburst of violence and
resentment among the pagans'.[31] Clearly, however, this action caused resentment among his fellow Christians, and in a document written on his return
he somewhat defensively emphasized that 'the Lord commanded us in the
persecution to depart and to flee'. While his example might not have been
as brilliant as that of the confessors (on whom he lavished praise), at least
– he claimed – he outshone those who stayed, held on to their wealth and
denied their faith.[32]

Although this work *On the Lapsed* celebrates the 'peace' brought about
by the end of the Decian persecutions, the Christian community was clearly
dangerously divided. Many were begging to be allowed to rejoin the Church
and some priests were apparently readmitting them without the imposition
of the kind of penance which would usually be required by the Church
for post-baptismal sin. Other priests were reluctant to readmit them at all,
on account of the seriousness of their sin of denying Christ.[33] Readmission
seems to have been encouraged by the actions of confessors in prison who
– anticipating that they would soon be martyrs – issued documents prom-
ising to intercede for the lapsed when the martyrs reached heaven. These
'letters of peace' (*libelli pacis*) were thus perceived by many to outweigh or
counteract the *libelli* which they had fraudulently gained in order to avoid
capture. There a suggestion in Cyprian's letters that they were being traded
(as no doubt the original *libelli* had been).[34]

In *On the Lapsed* Cyprian was careful not to criticize the confessors
directly, but was scathing about those who were trying to avoid the discipline of penance. Persecution arose, he argued, as a result of a failure of
discipline in the Church: congregations had become obsessed with wealth
and its ostentatious and fashionable display; priests lacked faith, piety and
mercy.[35] When persecution began, most Christians gave in immediately:
they 'ran to the market-place of their own accord'; they risked spiritual
death in order to save their property, and, not content with endangering
their own lives, they involved their own children in their pagan sacrifices.[36]
Cyprian asserted that there were two possible remedies for such actions:

> He is an unskilful physician who handles the swelling edges of wounds with
> a tender hand, and, by retaining the poison shut up in the deep recesses of
> the body, increases it. The wound must be opened, and cut, and healed by the
> stronger remedy of cutting out the corrupting parts.[37]

For Cyprian the remedy did not mean 'cutting out' the lapsed for ever, as some like the Roman presbyter Novatian argued. Rather, it meant giving them the right treatment. Foolishly 'tender' priests were allowing people back 'before their sin [was] expiated, before confession [had] been made of their crime, before their conscience [had] been purged by sacrifice and by the hand of the priest'.[38] But, Cyprian asserted, God alone has the authority to forgive sin. This precipitate action did the believers more harm than good: it brought an apparent 'peace', which was in fact 'another persecution'; it seemed to cure, but in reality attacked them with 'a secret corruption'.[39] In order to press his point home, Cyprian gave some lurid examples of those who were punished by sudden fatal illnesses when they tried to take communion without being truly penitent.[40] These gruesome passages reveal that both Cyprian and the lapsed believed that they were physically as well as spiritually polluted by their consumption of pagan sacrifices and that the Eucharist was in some sense an antidote.[41] Cyprian warned that believers needed to be suitably prepared for its consumption or it would have only dangerous consequences. Instead of hasty reception back into communion, then, Cyprian recommended full confession of sins to a priest and the performance of appropriate acts of penance, such as prayer vigils, weeping, prostration on the ground, fasting and the wearing of the most simple of clothes, almsgiving and good works.[42] Only then could the priest offer absolution on God's behalf and the lapsed could be received back into communion.[43]

While Cyprian's emphasis on a rigorous regime of penitence echoed some of Tertullian's concerns, his was a much more church-focused and priest-focused notion of penance. Tertullian's concept seemed to rely on the righting of the direct relationship between the believer and his God; priests possessed an authority not because of their ecclesiastical position but because of their possession of certain spiritual gifts (*charismata*). But precisely because Cyprian felt that the confessors and their priest-supporters had abused that charismatic notion of authority in the Church, in letting the lapsed back too easily, he insisted that the process of penance had to be properly regulated by the Church – specifically by councils of bishops as indicators of the unified will of the Church. So besides the theological response offered in *On the Lapsed*, Cyprian's practical response to the crisis was to call a council in Carthage, which in 251CE decided on the appropriate treatment of the lapsed: those who had falsely obtained certificates could be readmitted to the Church, but those who had sacrificed would only be readmitted on their death-beds. In each case, readmission was dependent on doing appropriate penance.[44]

Around this time, Cyprian also wrote his treatise *On the Unity of the*

Church. Like Irenaeus, he claimed that bishops were successors to Christ's
Apostles, but went beyond this, however, in stressing the unified foundation of the Church on one Apostle: Peter.[45] He asserted that this unity was
also foretold in the Song of Songs' depiction of the Church as the one bride
of Christ.[46] Expanding on this image, Cyprian commended the Church as
the one mother of all believers: 'from her womb we are born, by her milk
we are nourished, by her spirit we are animated'.[47] Conversely, he pictured
those who leave the Church either as miscarried foetuses who cannot live
without their mother or as men who faithlessly consort with an adulteress.[48]
The language of disease and contagion which he once applied to the lapsed
was now directed to those who break the unity of the Church, who assume
priestly or episcopal office with no authority and who thus deceive their
congregations, 'vomiting forth deadly poisons from pestilential tongues'.[49]
He is forthright even about the confessors: 'confession is the beginning
of glory, not the full desert of the crown'; 'even if such men were slain in
confession of the Name [of Christ] … the inexplicable and grave fault of
discord is not even purged by suffering'.[50] One might find his rhetoric tasteless – Cyprian undoubtedly wielded his metaphors with a great deal less
precision and grace than his predecessor Tertullian – but Cyprian's anxieties were not at all unfounded: his policy had failed to convince the most
dedicated forgivers of the lapsed, who elected a rival bishop to Cyprian.
Their party was probably an alliance of lapsed clergy and laity, perhaps with
the support of some confessors released from captivity.

    Other Christian communities were also split by the question of the
lapsed. Around the time of Cyprian's council in 251, there was a contested
election to the bishopric of Rome, in which Cornelius and Novatian were
elected as rivals. Cornelius took a line broadly similar to that of Cyprian,
but Novatian took an even more rigorous approach: none of the lapsed
should be readmitted to the Church. After some delay Cyprian chose to
recognize Cornelius, but Novatian and his followers proved to be a thorn
in his side, provoking rigorists in Africa to hostility and recognizing the
second rival bishop to Cyprian in Carthage.[51] Thus these events in Rome
further destabilized the Carthaginian situation.

    The rival groupings in Carthage arose partly because Cyprian's policy
of 251CE failed to deal with a pressing question: what about *clergy* who had
lapsed? More specifically, did those who had been baptized by a lapsed
priest need to be rebaptized? Cyprian's own answer provocatively equated
lapsed clergy with heretics: whatever their doctrinal beliefs were, by taking
a lax line on the question of penance and subsequently setting up their own
rival bishops and priests they were guilty of splitting themselves off from
the one Church.[52] He clashed in particular with Stephen, one of Cornelius'

successors as Bishop of Rome.[53] Stephen was inclined to be tolerant, apparently arguing that if there was 'one Lord, one faith, one baptism' (Ephesians 4.5) then it was unnecessary to rebaptize those baptized by heretics or schismatics. In response, Cyprian presented the issue to him as a neat dilemma: if you say that the Church is one and has one baptism, *either* you must recognize the Church of the schismatics along with their baptism *or* you must reject their Church and their baptism together. It is self-contradictory to accept their baptism and reject their Church. In fact, Cyprian argued, one should say that those from heretical or schismatic sects were simply baptized in the true Church not *re*baptized.[54]

The argument between Stephen and Cyprian quickly accelerated, not least because problems surrounding the issue of rebaptism were not confined to Rome and Africa. Cyprian had been right to think that, for the most part, order within a region could be maintained by councils of its bishops.[55] Although consensus among them was important, ultimately order was often dependent on a tacit understanding that one bishop had particular authority over other bishops in the same region – the bishop of Carthage in North Africa, the bishop of Rome in Italy, the bishop of Alexandria in Egypt, and so on. But there were no established methods for adjudging disagreements between regions – between Rome and Carthage, or Carthage and Alexandria. Congregations or individual bishops tended to appeal to men they thought had special moral, intellectual or spiritual authority, or those they thought would support their case. Thus, when Stephen allowed some Spanish lapsed bishops to retain their sees, their congregations appealed in protest to Cyprian. Novatian (still in place as rival bishop in Rome until 258) garnered support for his rigorist line from bishops in Gaul and Antioch.[56] Cyprian successfully appealed for support to bishops as far afield as Cappadocia. Meanwhile, Dionysius of Alexandria tried to intervene with an ameliorating line: although he personally agreed with Stephen he urged him and his successor not to interfere in other regions if they had come to a peaceable agreement. Writing to a Roman presbyter he recognized that both parties claimed long-established tradition for their different practices and he advised: 'I would not think of upsetting their arrangements and involving them in strife and contention. "You shall not move your neighbour's boundaries, which were fixed by your ancestors" [Deuteronomy 19.14].'[57] In fact, Valerian's persecutions began before the churches had time to resolve their differences, but the episode illustrates how churches were uncertain as to how to resolve disputes between each other – an issue which was only to grow in importance. What also emerges from these debates is the huge importance attributed to baptism – particularly in the African Church where it was seen as a watershed moment, utterly dividing the believer's previous life from his or her new life of absolute loyalty to God, creator of the world and father of the Lord and Saviour Jesus Christ. It is also clear that denying one was a Christian was widely regarded not just as hypocrisy, treachery or a weakness of faith, but as causing pollution – both of individuals and those with whom they associated and worshipped. Again, this view was particularly strong in North Africa, where it resurfaced after the persecutions of 303–5.

The debate in Cyprian's day had been over the *libellatici* – those who had either sacrificed or obtained certificates (*libelli*) saying they had. In the early fourth century arguments centred on the treatment of the *traditors* – those who had handed over Scriptures to the imperial authorities, as bidden by Diocletian's first decree. An increasing atmosphere of suspicion against them became evident. It was most strong in the congregations in Numidia, who suspected the Bishop of Carthage and his staff of not being sufficiently supportive of Christian martyrs and imprisoned confessors during the persecutions. The suspicion erupted into open dissent over an election of a successor to the Bishop of Carthage, who died in 311. The Bishop's archdeacon, Caelician, was chosen, but the Numidian rigorists objected, alleging, amongst other things, that one of Caecilian's consecrations was invalid because it involved a bishop who was a *traditor* (following a similar line of argument to Cyprian's claim that baptism by a lapsed priest had no efficacy). The rigorists elected their own rival bishop, who was supported then succeeded by the most powerful champion of the movement – a priest called Donatus from Casae Nigrae in Numidia.

The following years saw increasing tension between the two factions and a series of appeals for imperial support. Constantine backed Caelician from the start, probably because he suspected the Donatists of disrupting the unity of the Church with schism. Yet he gave a hearing to both parties and called councils at Rome (313), then Arles (314) for that reason. In 317 he attempted a stricter line and ordered the confiscation of Donatist church property; but this policy proved ineffective at curbing Donatist popularity and was abandoned in 321. In all likelihood, both Donatist and Catholic churches possessed bishops who were *traditors*; but rapidly questions about the status of lapsed individuals and the election of individual bishops were subsumed by rival visions of the Church as a whole. The followers of Donatus denied they were schismatics and saw themselves as the true inheritors of the one Catholic, i.e. whole, Church.[58] Known as Donatists by their opponents, they have a good claim to be known as 'African Christians', so dominant were they in that region for so many years.[59] According to them, the Church had to be kept pure from all taint of pagan idolatry; for the Catholics, the important thing was to keep the Church united. Both appealed to Cyprian to support their visions of the Church, the Catholics appealing to his notion of unity in *On the Unity of the Church*, and the Donatists using such images as his notion of the Church as a pure mother, or a saving Ark.

Constantine did not resolve the Donatist controversy: the Donatists' influence in North Africa was still extremely vigorous when Augustine was writing two centuries later. Yet the fact that he was appealed to and agreed to intervene on a question of Church unity is very significant. It was not the first time that a Roman emperor had become involved in a Christian dispute – in 270 the church of Antioch had appealed to Emperor Aurelian – but Constantine took a more active role than his predecessor. No doubt both his personal faith in the Christian God as God of the Empire and the destabilizing effect of large-scale schism in the Christian Church impelled Constantine to make these moves. In his letter calling the council at Rome, he wrote: 'I feel it to be a very serious matter that in those provinces which divine providence has freely entrusted to [me], and where the population is very large, the general public should be found persisting in the wrong course as if it were splitting in two.'[60] Nevertheless it is interesting that both emperors, the pagan and the Christian, acted with respect for Church councils as an already established method of Church order. Aurelian was only appealed to when Paul of Samosata refused to give up church buildings in Antioch, despite having been deposed by three councils which had the support of influential bishops such as Dionysius of Alexandria. The charges were heresy and immoral conduct. Aurelian's judgement against Paul rested on the idea that a bishop must be recognized as such by the wider Church, particularly in its councils.[61] Constantine went one step further: he summoned and attended councils and tried to use his authority to ensure that the Church came to a consensus on an issue, rather than leaving it hanging. Although opinions differ as to his influence on the outcome of the councils, he does not appear to have imposed his will on them in a direct and autocratic manner. Ultimately, unity was his concern and this required achieving a genuine consensus rather than telling bishops what he thought they should think. This policy seems to have united his behaviour at both Arles and Nicaea, despite the fact that they dealt with very different theological questions.

Inevitably such actions raise the question of Constantine's personal faith. Three issues need to be dealt with: first, Constantine's conversion; secondly, the material effects of his imperial policies on Christians, and finally his dealings with disputes among Christians.

The most famous account of what has often been called 'Constantine's conversion' was given by Eusebius in his *Life of Constantine*:

About the time of the midday sun when the day was just turning, he said
he saw with his own eyes, up in the sky and rising over the sun, a cross-
shaped trophy formed from light, and a text attached to it which said, 'By this
conquer.' ... He was, he said, wondering to himself what the manifestation
might mean; then, while he meditated, and thought long and hard, night
overtook him. Thereupon, as he slept, the Christ of God appeared to him
with the sign which had appeared in the sky, and urged him to make a copy
of the sign which had appeared in the sky, and to use this as a protection
against the attacks of the enemy.[62]

Unfortunately there are divergent interpretations of the event. Eusebius
set it some time before Constantine's crucial battle against Maxentius
at the Milvian Bridge across the Tiber near Rome; Lactantius placed it
more dramatically on the eve of the battle. An earlier account suggested
that Constantine interpreted the vision as being from Apollo/the Sun, not
from the Christian God.[63] Some modern scholars have suggested that what
Constantine saw was not a vision but a solar halo.[64]

The truth about when and where Constantine was 'converted' will
probably never be known. What is reasonably certain is that by 310 he was
a committed monotheist and by the Battle of the Milvian Bridge in 312
he was interested enough in Christianity to have a retinue of Christian
advisors. Like most conversions, Constantine's conversion to Christianity
was most likely a journey rather than a life-changing event. He may have
first interpreted a vision as being from Apollo/Sol, then reinterpreted it in
Christian terms at or after his defeat of Maxentius.[65]

What was crucial for the history of Christianity was that something
caused Constantine to connect his victory over Maxentius with the God of
Jesus Christ and to express his faith with a specific symbol, the *labarum*.
This sign Eusebius explains as the 'monogram of Christ': the artful combination of the first two letters of the word *Christos* in Greek, χ (chi) and ρ
(rho). Already in Christian art, the iconography of Apollo or Sol Invictus
had been applied to Christ: a third-century mosaic in a Roman necropolis
depicted Christ with sun-like rays radiating from his head. The *labarum*
appears to further stylize these rays into a chi-rho monogram. A particularly
beautiful application of the symbol, in which the monogram still appears
behind Christ's head, can be seen in a mid-fourth-century mosaic from
Hinton St Mary in Britain.[66] From 312 onwards the chi-rho symbol was
used in a variety of ways, both by the imperial authorities and by individuals: it was incorporated into military armour (appearing on the emperor's
own helmet from 315); it was used on coins (from at least 327, if not earlier);
it was carved on monuments, both public and personal; it was used as a seal
on signet rings; it appeared on domestic cutlery.[67] Archaeological evidence

from the fourth century attests to the use of the symbol in a wide variety of locations throughout the Empire.

Other tangible evidence of the effect of Constantine's support for Christianity was his programme of rebuilding churches – many of which, of course, had been destroyed in the years after 303. In the eastern imperial capital, Nicomedia, he rebuilt the church which had been destroyed immediately after Diocletian's edict in 304. Constantine provided money for the first church of the Holy Wisdom (Hagia Sophia) in Constantinople, the new eastern capital which Constantine dedicated in 330. In Rome he provided for a basilica, St John Lateran, and for the construction of shrines to the Roman martyrs, including a church dedicated to Peter on the Vatican hill.[68] Eusebius describes in detail Constantine's desire that a 'house of prayer worthy of the worship of God should be erected near the Saviour's tomb on a scale of rich and royal greatness', in order that the place of Jesus' resurrection should be 'an object of attraction and veneration to all'.[69] The original plan appears to have been to build a church on the presumed site. When, however, a pagan temple was removed, Eusebius reports that 'immediately and contrary to all expectation' the cave in which Jesus was buried was discovered.[70] The tradition that Helena, mother of Constantine, found relics of the true Cross there goes back only to Bishop Ambrose in the 390s; however, she clearly played an important role in Constantine's building programme in the Holy Land, as Eusebius attributes both to her and to her son the founding of churches at Bethlehem and the Mount of Olives.[71]

Besides granting Christians their property back and actively funding the rebuilding of their churches, Constantine seems to have made some changes in law which benefited them. For example, he exempted clergy certainly from paying the civic dues expected from rich citizens and possibly from all forms of taxation and he recognized the use of the bishop as a judge in civil cases between Christians. His social legislation was later interpreted as encouraging Christian values (although whether it was drawn up with that direct purpose is unclear): he removed the tax penalties for celibate citizens or couples without children and made divorce harder, especially for women. He declared Sunday a holy day on which no business could be conducted except the release (manumission) of slaves – this exception is explained by the fact that manumissions by Christians seemed to have taken place in church before the congregation in the presence of bishops, that is, presumably at the Sunday services.[72] Constantine abolished crucifixion as a form of execution, and forbade criminals to be branded or tattooed on their forehead (as had previously been the practice).[73] He banned gladiatorial combat, but only in 325 (and in fact it outlived the official ban for years). Some pagan temples were destroyed to make way for Christian churches (particularly at Christian holy sites, such as Jerusalem, or the oak at Mamre where Abraham was said to have been visited by three angels, Genesis 18), but there was no systematic policy of destruction. In Rome in particular the ancient temples were left standing, and public divination was tolerated 'as a relic of the past', even though private use of the practice was forbidden.[74]

There is no reason to doubt Constantine's sincerity as a Christian. At some point in or before 312 his pagan monotheism was replaced by Christianity. Even if he did sometimes deliberately blend the symbolism of the two, this was in order to avoid imposing an exclusively Christian piety on every citizen: he had seen enough of persecution to know that it did not promote the unity of the Empire. Nevertheless, it is almost impossible to separate personal and political aspects of Constantine's support for Christianity. His personal conviction in the truth of Christianity was combined with his belief that he required not only the goodwill of Christian citizens but the goodwill of the Christian God for the Empire to flourish. When he presented himself as liberator of Christians within the Empire and a protector of those outside it, this was both an expression of his belief that Christians deserved to practise their religion in peace and a demonstration of his power and influence. Again, his building programme demonstrated not only his personal devotion but also his patronage of the decorative arts. It advertised imperial favour towards certain cities of the Empire as pagan emperors had done before in building temples. For this reason, it is not wise to attempt to ask whether it was personal piety or political expediency that led him to intervene in the Christian controversy which led up to the first ecumenical council of Nicaea.

Whereas the issues which divided Cyprian, Novatian and Stephen, or Donatus and his opponents, were the nature of the Church and its sacraments, the main question under discussion at Nicaea was a more fundamental one about the nature of God as Trinity. The debate highlighted a difficulty underlying even the most sophisticated Christian theology up to this time: how is it possible to say that God is one and that the Father and the Son are both God?[75] Although the writings of such theologians as Justin, Irenaeus and Tertullian had affirmed both these propositions, none had attempted to *explain* their coherence except in rather basic terms, often using analogies such as Justin's mind and word and Tertullian's roots-tree-fruit or fountain-river-stream. A further problem – which was to have very serious implications – was that Origen's theology of the Trinity could be developed in two different directions: one which stressed the co-equality of the three persons and another which stressed the apparently subordinate roles of the three persons.[76]

This underlying tension between two possible readings of Origen came out into the open in Alexandria in the early years of the fourth century with an argument between Arius, a presbyter, and his bishop, Alexander. It is uncertain why the controversy began or who provoked it.[77] One of the first documents we have is a declaration of Arius' faith, which he addressed to Bishop Alexander of Alexandria probably around 321. It is a highly self-conscious piece of writing: Arius stresses the points on which he and Alexander agree, staking his claim to the orthodox tradition of the Church while at the same time claiming that any other position but his should be classified as one of the various heresies which he outlines. It is, in other words, precisely the kind of text one would expect from someone who has just been – or who anticipates being – accused of heterodox and untraditional views. (The precise theological issues at stake will be discussed below.)

Arius and his followers were probably deposed by a synod in Alexandria in around 321. They appear to have left for Palestine, where they were permitted to practise as presbyters, and gained a considerable amount of support from, amongst others, the influential Bishop Eusebius of Caesarea in Palestine.[78] During this period Arius wrote to a supporter, Eusebius, bishop of the imperial capital Nicomedia, 'the bishop [Alexander] greatly injures and persecutes us and does all he can against us, trying to drive us out of the city as godless men, since we do not agree with him when he says publicly, "Always Father, always Son"'.[79] A further synod in Alexandria (but with signatories from beyond Egypt) condemned Arius, but his views were still attracting a great deal of support both in the eastern provinces and in Egypt where there seem to have been rival congregations sympathetic to Arius. The controversy came to the attention of Constantine in 324CE. Newly victorious over Licinius and now sole emperor, the unity of the Empire and the unity of the Church within the Empire was very much on his mind. He sent his bishop-advisor Ossius to Alexandria with a letter begging both sides to cease from their quarrel. Recalling his efforts to heal the Donatist schism in North Africa, he expressed distress that another church was divided into rival parties:

> The impulse of your quarrel did not arise over the chief point of the precepts of the Law, nor are you faced with the intrusion of a new doctrine concerning the worship of God, but you have one and the same mind, so that you should be able to come together in a compact of fellowship. That so many of God's people, who ought to be subject to the direction of your minds, are at variance because you are quarrelling with each other about small and quite minute points is deemed neither to be fitting not in any way legitimate.[80]

'These small and very insignificant questions' seriously divided Christianity for the next half-century. Even after this, 'Arianism' was still an issue until at least the seventh century and some would argue Arianism in some shape or form never totally left the Church.

Even by 325 Constantine had clearly become convinced of the necessity of a different kind of response: he summoned bishops from all over Europe to meet at Nicaea, near the eastern imperial capital of Nicomedia.[81] Although it is impossible to know who had the original idea for such a council, it is clear that Constantine sponsored it (both morally and financially), attended it and that his advisor Ossius chaired it.

What caused Constantine's change of mind? Some have suggested that Alexander, on receipt of Constantine's letter, persuaded Ossius that the issues were far more serious than the emperor thought. Another factor may have been a large council at Antioch in 325 which produced a very clear-cut condemnation of Arianism and excommunicated three bishops, including the very influential Eusebius of Caesarea.[82] Constantine must have realized the destabilizing force of such a move – despite the fact that the Antioch excommunications were provisional on further debate at a council planned for Ancyra later that year. Constantine may also have been aware that the bishop of his eastern capital Nicomedia was a prominent supporter of Arius. It is likely that it was Constantine who proposed that the council of Ancyra be moved to Nicaea and opened the invitation to all bishops.

In the end, although the council was attended by around 250–300 bishops, they were overwhelmingly from the east. As one might expect, there were many representatives from Asia Minor (around 100 bishops), the region of Oriens (Arabia, Syria, Phoenicia, Palestine: about 50) and Egypt (22 bishops). Bishops came from Greece and its islands and the rest of the Balkan region (including the remote area near the Black Sea). There were bishops from Edessa in the Roman province of Mesopotamia and from two Roman cities on the Persian frontier (Rhesina and Nisibis). Two came from the kingdom of Armenia, which had become the first Christian kingdom in 314. On the other hand, there was only one from Gaul and none from Germany and Britain (all of which had sent delegates to the Council of Arles in 314); more surprisingly, there were no delegates from Italy or Africa. The only representative from Spain seems to have been Ossius himself. Seemingly, then, the westerners 'did not know what all the fuss … was about' – an interesting indication that it was perhaps not Constantine's theological naivety that led to his initial reaction to Alexander and Arius but rather a more widespread western lack of comprehension.[83] Arius' prominent episcopal supporters were present, but it was not a trial and it is unclear whether he himself attended.

What was at issue between Arius and Alexander and what did the council resolve? Amid all the rhetoric of the 'Arian controversies' it is easy to forget that both sides were united on some key issues. (Just as with earlier debates with the Gnostics, it was the similarity of the deviant views that made the deviation so threatening.) Bishop Alexander of Alexandria and his presbyter apparently *agreed* that there was 'one God, alone unbegotten, alone everlasting, alone unbegun, alone true … alone wise, alone good … judge, governor … God of Law and Prophets and New Testament; who begat an only-begotten Son before eternal times, through whom he made both the ages and the universe'.[84] Arius was concerned that Christian theology might fall into three different kinds of error. First, he was worried about any suggestion that there might be two or more 'unbegottens' (*agenneta*) – that is, two independent but absolutely divine principles.[85] Consequently he stressed that God the Father was the only unbegotten one and emphasized the status of the Son as begotten from the Father ('one God, alone unbegotten, who begat an only-begotten Son'). Secondly, he wanted to avoid any suggestion that the begetting of the Son from the Father was like the division of one material substance into two: the Son was not 'as Valentinus pronounced … an issue, nor, as Mani innovated, a consubstantial part (*homoousios meros*) of the Father'. Finally, he did not want the Son to appear an automatic or random offspring of the Father; rather he stressed that the Son was begotten 'by [the Father's] own will'.

Alexander no doubt shared such concerns. His *disagreement* centred on the way in which Arius conceived of the begetting of the Son from the Father: to Alexander it suggested that Arius and his followers 'deny [Christ's] divinity, and proclaim him equal to all mankind'.[86] In fact, Arius' language for the generation of the Son was often paradoxical: the Son was 'a perfect creature of God, but not as one of the creatures – an offspring, but not as one of things begotten'. He was 'begotten timelessly before all things', but he 'was not, before he was begotten'.[87] It seems that Arius felt that the Son's begetting was an absolutely unique event, equivalent neither to the splitting of the divine substance into two parts nor with the creation of the universe. Again, this belief itself was not contentious; the problem was the conclusion Arius drew from it: that therefore the Son's *status* was absolutely unique, being the equal neither of God nor the rest of creation. In order to explain the Son's divine attributes, Arius seems to have claimed that God 'promoted him as his Son by adoption',[88] and that the Son did not possess divine qualities by nature, but as a gift by the Father's will: 'by [God's] own will and counsel he has subsisted before time and before age as God, only-begotten and unchangeable'.[89]

Alexander's objections thus centred on two interrelated issues. He was impatient with Arius' denial that the Father and Son were co-eternal ('the bishop makes great havoc of us and persecutes us severely … he has driven us out of the city as atheists because we do not concur in what he publicly preaches, namely that "God has always been, and the Son has always been: Father and Son exist together"'[90]). Thus Arius' heresy was often encapsulated by his enemies as the claim that 'there was, when he was not' (that is, 'there was a time when there was God the Father, but not God the Son'). But the denial that the Son had always existed was only a symptom of the fundamental issue: Arius denied that the Son was God in the same way that the Father was God. Indeed, to stress this point Arius was not afraid to use the language of 'created' for the Son, even to the extent of arguing that the Son was created 'from nothing'.[91]

In recent years, scholars have debated whether Arius was motivated primarily by logic or by more theological, even spiritual, motives. One view is that Arius' excessive reliance on logic forced him to erroneous conclusions. Arius accepted the premises that (i) to be God is to be unbegotten (i.e. uncaused, ontologically independent); (ii) there cannot be two unbegottens and (iii) that the Son was 'the only-begotten one of the Father' (John 1.14).[92] From these Arius concluded that the Father alone was unbegotten, and that therefore the Father alone was God. The other view is that Arius was motivated by a concern to explain the workings of salvation: according to this interpretation Arius thought Jesus Christ was in many ways a human like other humans, but as 'he rose in stature' he was taken up by God into a relationship of Sonship. All humans now can imitate the love and obedience of Christ and, like him, although to a lesser degree, share in divine qualities as the adopted sons of God.[93]

The problem with the first view is that it does not explain the popularity of Arius' views. It has also tended to be accompanied by a very simplistic and negative view of the use of philosophy in Christian theology – as if 'Greek philosophy' in itself were the cause of heresy. The problem with the second is that it exaggerates some features of Arius' theology and does not give enough weight to others (it emphasizes the role of the Son incarnate and downplays his cosmic role, e.g. the idea that all things were created through him). The current consensus rests on two important understandings. First, philosophy and theology, ontology and salvation are interconnected. Arius seems to have thought that the Son's role as saviour and mediator depended on his ontological position half-way between God and creation. The Son could, as nothing else could, bridge the gap between God and humanity. It was this position that Athanasius most forcefully denied in his writings against the Arians, insisting that the 'mediatorship' expressed in the New Testament was based on the Son's *incarnate* life, being *both* fully divine (so that he could save) *and* fully human (so that he could save humanity). Secondly, all scholars are in agreement that the interpretation of Scripture was a hugely important element of the controversy: he felt compelled to explain biblical verses such as 'the Father is greater than I' (John 14.28). He seized on other verses which suggested Jesus' growth or improvement (e.g. Luke 2.52) and the 'emptying' (Philippians 2.5–11). Particularly popular among Arius' followers was Proverbs 8.22: 'The Lord created me at the beginning of his work', which to them suggested the Son's beginning in time. Arius' popularity can at least partly be explained by the fact that he endeavoured to explain the profoundly ambiguous (if not contradictory) nature of the New Testament's pronouncements about Jesus' relationship to the Father and the various ways in which the Hebrew Bible could be read as referring to the Son.

The creed which emerged from Nicaea seems above all to have had the aim of ruling Arius' views out. Whether it did anything more positive in the way of defining the precise nature of the Son is more difficult to determine. The creed itself, together with its condemnations, ran:

> We believe in one God, Father all-sovereign,
> maker of all things, seen and unseen;
>
> And in one Lord Jesus Christ, the Son of God,
> begotten from the Father as only-begotten, that is, from the substance of the Father,
> God from God, light from light, true God from true God,
> begotten not made,
> *homoousios* with the Father,
> through whom all things came into existence, the things in heaven and the things on earth,
> who because of us and because of our salvation came down and was incarnated, made human, suffered, and arose on the third day, ascended into heaven, comes to judge the living and the dead;
>
> And in one Holy Spirit.
>
> And those who say 'there was once when he was not' or 'he was not before he was begotten' or 'he came into existence from nothing' or who affirm that the Son of God is of another hypostasis or substance, or a creature, or mutable or subject to change, such ones the catholic and apostolic church pronounces accursed and separated from the church.

The phrases 'from the being of the Father' and 'not made' seem expressly to contradict Arius' claim that the Son was 'out of things which were not'. 'God from God, light from light, true God from true God' reiterates this point.[94] Similarly, the anathemas (condemnations) at the end are deliberately aimed at Arius' view.

The most famous word in the creed, *homoousios*, was probably chosen precisely because Arius had criticized its use. Presumably the council did not mean that the Father and Son were composed of the same physical or corporeal stuff, but beyond that it is not at all clear what they did think it meant. It is even possible that this uncertainty was precisely what the word's proponents desired: it allowed the council to rule out a negative (that the Son was *not homoousios* with the Father), without needing to explain what the positive statement meant. Certainly it allowed even an Arian supporter like Eusebius of Caesarea to agree to the Creed, although he did feel the need to explain to his congregation how he understood the word: it did not imply that the Godhead was corporeal, nor that the Son existed through the division of or subtraction of something from the Father. He carefully avoided the conclusion that *homoousios* established the equality of the Son and the Father. It is unknown who proposed the word (suggestions have included Ossius, or Constantine himself). Whoever it was may well have been aware of the advantages of a term which had a range of broadly acceptable meanings but which clearly ruled Arius' views out. The disadvantage of the word's flexibility only became apparent in later years when the fundamental questions of the controversy resurfaced.

CHAPTER 6

God and Humankind in Eastern Theology: Alexandria, Cappadocia, Nisibis and Edessa
(FOURTH CENTURY)

For Christian theologians the Council of Nicaea has come to have an iconic status: this point in Christian history is regarded as decisively significant because of the precise way in which the Nicene definition described God. In particular, theologians point to the use of the word *homoousios* ('of the same being' or 'consubstantial') to indicate the relationship between the Son and the Father. Historians, on the other hand, complain that in fact the Council of Nicaea was singularly ineffective: it was followed by half a century of further argument about the Father–Son relationship. During this period other alternatives to *homoousios* looked likely to win the day, and even Athanasius, legendary defender of the Nicene definition, did not think it fit to defend the specific term *homoousios* until around the middle of the century. What explains the discrepancy between these theological and historical perspectives?

The answer lies in the progressive development of thinking on Christ and the Trinity in the fourth century. Athanasius' theology itself evolved and then set in train a further phase of Christian thinking on God as Father, Son and Holy Spirit. In this period even more than before, no part of theology was an isolated exercise: reflection on the relation of Father to Son was intimately connected to Christian reflection on the Holy Spirit, Christ's human nature, salvation and the time to come, the sacraments and the best way to lead a holy life.

The attempt to understand Athanasius is not helped by the facts that most of what we know about him comes from his own pen, that he had very clear reasons for presenting himself (and his enemies) in a particular way, and that even the most fair-minded of readers admits that he was 'never a fanatically accurate controversialist'.[1] Current myths about Athanasius thus often stem precisely from the impression he wanted to create about himself. The first myth is that he had a prominent position at the Council of Nicaea in 325CE. In fact, he attended merely as a youthful deacon accompanying Alexander and it is unlikely that he made a significant contribution to the debates.[2] Three years later, he succeeded Alexander as Bishop of Alexandria, but his election 'was definitely contested, may have been illegal and looks as though it was enforced'.[3] In Egypt he inherited a province which was divided by a serious schism precipitated by a Bishop Melitius. The origins of the schism are now obscure but probably went back to the Diocletianic persecutions. The Council of Nicaea suggested a resolution, but by the time Athanasius was Bishop of Alexandria about half of the Egyptian bishops were of the Melitian party. It seems that Athanasius tried to impose a solution on them, probably by force, for which action he was condemned by a council at Tyre in 335. After a failed appeal to Constantine, Athanasius was exiled to the north-western imperial capital Trier. The legacy of this stay may have been two of his finest writings (*Against the Greeks* and *On the Incarnation*)[4] and possibly the introduction of some ideas from the ascetic movement which was already strong in Egypt (see Chapter 7).

One key to understanding Athanasius' theology is *On the Incarnation*. This made evident the reason for Athanasius' passionate conviction that Son was fully God: salvation. The central message of *On the Incarnation* was that in order to save humankind from the deadly and corrupting effects of the Fall, Jesus Christ had to be truly human and truly God. If he were not God, he would not be able to save; if he were not human he would not be able to make this salvation effective in and for human beings. The work is perhaps the most powerful demonstration of the belief in the early Church that salvation was not just a matter of God declaring that a punishment had been paid, or even of God deciding to forgive; rather salvation was conceived as the *transformation* of the individual, of the community of believers and even of the whole of creation. Human repentance, Athanasius believed, was not enough, for it could not 'call men back from what is their nature'.[5] In this theology, Athanasius was taking on and developing themes found especially in Irenaeus, but expressing them with new vigour and more attention to their systematic exposition.

Athanasius' theology pointed to three closely interrelated aspects of God's salvation: the defeat of death, cleansing from corruption and revelation of the truth. For Athanasius, God's actions were fundamentally all one; therefore the three aspects were not three things which the Saviour did; rather they were three perspectives from which the limited human mind viewed the divine work. First, Athanasius asserted that Jesus Christ defeated death by taking on a real, mortal nature and truly dying (which is only possible for a human) and then rising again to new life (which is only possible for God). This perspective was firmly centred on the Cross: for Athanasius, as for earlier Christian writers, the Cross was the literal, historical location of Christ's defeat of death and of his willing sacrifice on behalf of humanity:

> But since it was necessary also that the debt owing from all [because of the Fall] should be repaid ... he ... offered up his sacrifice also on behalf of all, yielding his temple [i.e. his body] to death in the stead of all, in order firstly to make men rid and free of their old sin, and further to show himself more powerful even than death, displaying his own body incorruptible, as first-fruits of the resurrection.[6]

The second perspective focused on the idea of salvation reversing the effects of the Fall, which included death, but also other symptoms of corruption.[7] Again, Athanasius stressed that this re-creation or new creation of human nature was only possible through the one who created it becoming incarnate in his creation: 'He, the incorruptible Son of God, being conjoined with all by a like nature, naturally clothed all with incorruption, by the promise of the resurrection.'[8] Finally, Athanasius stressed that Christ came to reveal God to humans (again, ignorance of God was often seen as one of the corrupting effects of the Fall). Christ did not, however, come 'to make a display, but to heal and teach those who were suffering'; he took a human body so as not to 'dazzle' people, but acted 'like a kind teacher who cares for his disciples ... [who] comes down to their level and teaches them ... by simpler courses'.[9] In sum, for Athanasius:

> it was in the power of none other to turn the corruptible to incorruption, except the Saviour himself, that had at the beginning also made all things out of nothing; and that none other could create anew that likeness of the God's image for men, save the image of the Father; and that none other could render the mortal immortal, save our Lord Jesus Christ, who is the very life; and that none other could teach men of the Father, and destroy the worship of idols, save the Word that orders all things and is alone the true Only-begotten Son of the Father.[10]

More epigrammatic is Athanasius' famous summary of the mystery of salvation: 'For he was made human that we might be made God.'[11]

Athanasius' foundational belief, then, was that in order to give God's salvation Christ must be *God*, rather than simply a conduit of divine grace. This theme is found again in his specifically anti-Arian writings,[12] and Athanasius also applied a similar argument to the Holy Spirit (in his *Letters to Serapion*, written around 259–61CE). Athanasius argued that the

Spirit has divine *characteristics* (that is, that the Spirit is uncreated, eternal, immutable, omnipresent and unique) and that the Spirit *acts* as God (the Spirit is bestower of life, holiness, illumination and divinizing perfection).[13] Therefore, Athanasius asserted, the Spirit must be truly divine and must be *homoousios* with the Father and Son.

The argument that the Son and Spirit must be God to impart divine grace was partnered in Athanasius' theology with an argument about the nature of transcendence. While both he and Arius agreed that God was transcendent they expressed this in very different ways. Arius assumed that God's transcendence separated God from the world – as if God needed to be protected from its taint. This separation of God and world necessitated a mediator, the Logos, who was between the two. Athanasius, on the other hand, taught that God acted in the world, not *despite* his transcendence but *because* of it. God's transcendent nature as the source of all that is was expressed in his creation of the world; his transcendent power was expressed by the ability to act in the world without being limited by it. Athanasius powerfully challenged the idea that transcendence meant separation, arguing that a God who was by necessity separated from the world would in fact be limited by it. Because God constantly acted in the world, even the Incarnation itself was not the arrival of God in the world but rather the Word's choosing to act through one person in one specific location in space and time. Against Arius' apparent view that the divine Son was adopted or raised by the Father to become God, Athanasius stressed that the movement was the other way round: following Philippians 2.5–11 he asserted that 'he was not from a lower state promoted; but rather, existing as God, he took the form of a servant, and in taking it, was not promoted, but humbled himself'.[14] This idea was sometimes known as 'divine condescension'.[15]

Athanasius returned to Alexandria in 337. In the next 30 years he was exiled four more times – although during the last two periods he never left Egypt, being sheltered by his supporters, especially the Egyptian monks. During his 'absences' alternative bishops were appointed. These changes of ecclesiastical power often reflected changes at an imperial level. Constantine left three sons who vied for power throughout this period. Unfortunately for Athanasius, Constantius II, who had responsibility for the eastern Empire, had sympathy with the opponents of the Nicene definition. These opponents have often been called 'Arians' and were so labelled by Athanasius for polemical reasons. (In his later writings they often appear as 'Ariomaniacs', described as raving mad, or as dangerous in their deviations – so Athanasius asserts – as Valentinians, or pagans or Jews.[16]) In reality they were not very close to Arius' theology and had little loyalty to the man himself (who had negligible influence from the Council of Nicaea until his death in 336). Instead, opposition to the Nicene definition crystallized around Eusebius of Nicomedia who was bishop first of the old eastern imperial capital Nicomedia then of the new capital Constantinople.[17] As such, he was a man of some influence. In the meantime, Athanasius sought and received a certain amount of support in the western half of the Empire. For example, during his second exile he appealed to Julius, Bishop of Rome; a council in Rome in 341CE exonerated Athanasius and accused his opponents of 'Arianism'.[18] However, those who opposed his theology were in the ascendancy for much of the period and organized a series of councils to discuss alternative formulations to the Nicene concept of *homoousios*.

In this period, through the maze of councils, creeds and counter-creeds, one can identify several important points. First, there was increasing suspicion between east and west: the west seemingly being anxious that eastern theology over-emphasized the distinctness of Father, Son and Spirit, and the east being concerned that this distinctness was not being sufficiently protected. This anxiety was heightened by Athanasius' known association, while he was in Rome, with Marcellus of Ancyra. Marcellus' interpretation of the Nicene term *homoousios* radically de-emphasized the distinctness of the three divine persons: against Arius' idea of three *hypostases* he thought that there was only one *ousia* in the Godhead and only one *hypostasis*.[19] In particular, Marcellus' theology appeared to suggest that the Son and the Spirit were only *temporary* manifestations of the Godhead which emerged in the course of salvation-history. His theology thus seemed alarmingly similar to the modalism combated by writers such as Tertullian.[20] His reading of I Corinthians 15.24–8 implied that the Son, in submitting all things to the Father, would himself be absorbed back in the Godhead: it was against this reading that the later Constantinopolitan rendering of the Nicene Creed insisted that Christ's kingdom 'would have no end'.[21]

Secondly, there were shifts in terminology. Nicaea had asserted that the Son was *homoousios*, 'of the same being/substance' as the Father. In its anathemas against Arius it declared that the view that 'the Son of God is of another *hypostasis* or *ousia*' was to be rejected. Literally translated one can indicate a slight difference between the two words: in Greek, *hypostasis* means an instantiation of something, an individual x, an actual thing; *ousia* can mean 'a being' or 'being as such' or it can refer to a particular kind of being. But one can see that it would be easy to read Nicaea as implying that the Greek words *hypostasis* and *ousia* were roughly equivalent – at least as used for Christian theology. Marcellus and some of his followers in the west clearly continued with this assumption, asserting that Father, Son and Spirit were one *ousia* and one *hypostasis*. On the other hand, the easterners were usually keen to maintain that Father, Son and Spirit were three *hypostases*,

following a strong tradition which they had inherited from Origen. They
were therefore, on this very narrow point, in agreement with Arius. The
question was: did the declaration that Father, Son and Spirit were three
hypostases also mean that they were three beings, three *ousiai*? To say so, of
course, would be directly to contradict Nicaea, which had declared with the
word *homoousios* that Father and Son were of the same *ousia*. The easterners
seemed to be keen not to go this far, and in fact the 340s and 350s saw a
marked reluctance to use any language referring to the divine *ousia*. For
example, the Council of Antioch in 341 declared that Father, Son and Spirit
were three *hypostases*, but avoided mention of *ousia*. The Council of Ancyra
in 358 suggested that the Son was 'like' (*homoios*) the Father but not 'of the
same substance' (*homoousios*) as the Father.[22] For a while it looked as if the
term *homoios* would win the day, particularly as it had backing from the
Emperor Constans. The advantage with *homoios* was that it could appeal to
a broad constituency. A prominent party of bishops led by Basil of Ancyra
seems to have been willing to accept the word *homoios* provided it was used
to indicate that the Son was like *in essence* to the Father. They apparently
also suggested the wording 'the Son is of similar substance (*homoiousios*) to
the Father'. (They are sometimes thus known as homoiousians, or homoeou-
sians).[23]

The third point to note is the way in which the tensions between east
and west, the councils and their use of theological terminology related to
Athanasius' own theological development. During his second exile, when
Eusebius of Nicomedia and his party were gaining influence and when
tensions between east and west were mounting, Athanasius wrote his three
Discourses against the Arians. Athanasius' work on the Nicene definition[24]
was written around 356–57. During his third exile, the idea that the Son
was 'like' (*homoios*) the Father was proposed at Ancyra (358); around this
time, Athanasius had begun to defend the specific term *homoousios*. During
a brief period of return to Alexandria in 362 Athanasius called a synod,
affirming the Nicene definition and accepting that God could be seen as
one *ousia* and three *hypostases*. The declaration was circulated in a document
known as the *Tome to the Antiochenes*.

As Athanasius wrote on these themes, he became increasingly convinced
of the need to express the relationship of the Son and the Father in more
precise terms. All his works quoted many Scriptural verses. For example,
he quoted phrases such as 'I and the Father are one' (John 10.30) and 'He
that hath seen me hath seen the Father' (John 14.9) against Arius' favourite
verses.[25] Athanasius also used individual biblical words: 'He is the image
and radiance of the Father and Expression and Truth.'[26] He developed
metaphors which had their origin in Scriptural language of light and water.

There are not 'three suns', he wrote, but sun, radiance and light: 'one is the light, from the sun, in the radiance'.[27] Athanasius also developed the image of God as 'fountain of living waters' (Jeremiah 2.13 and 17.12) or 'fountain of wisdom' (Baruch 3.12) with particular relation to the question of whether the Father existed before the Son:

> Is it then not irreligious to say, 'Once the Son was not?' for it is all one with saying, 'Once the Fountain was dry, destitute of Life and Wisdom.' But a fountain would then cease to be; for that which does not produce from itself, is not a fountain. … God is the eternal Fountain of His proper Wisdom; and if the Fountain be eternal, the Wisdom also must needs be eternal.[28]

In this work, Athanasius also began to use the terms *homoios* ('like': the Son is 'in the Father and *like the Father in all things*'[29]) or *idios* ('same': the Son possesses 'sameness of being' with the Father[30]). The Son is *like* God but, as creator, is *unlike* creation.[31] Interestingly, Athanasius was happy to affirm with Nicaea that the Son was 'an offspring of the being of the Father', but was seemingly still reluctant to use the term *homoousios*.[32]

This reluctance ceased in the 350s in his work *On the Council of Nicaea*. Athanasius asserted that although the term *homoousios* was not in the Bible, it did express a biblical idea, when properly understood. In essence he argued that *homoousios* protected the Father–Son analogy against misunderstanding by explaining what was truly at the heart of it. Thus, to say that the Son was begotten by the Father did not mean that the Father existed before the Son (as human fathers exist before their sons) or that the Son's begetting involved materiality or change (as human generation does). Rather, to say that the Son was begotten by the Father is to say that they *share* the same essence or being (*ousia*) *and* that the Son *derives* his essence from the Father. A human son too shares his father's essence and derives it from him; a human son too is *homoousios* with his father: this, not ideas of change or time, is what forms the root of the analogy between divine and human fatherhood. This clarification of the point that some concepts could be truthful and biblical, yet also be metaphors or analogies which need to be understood correctly, clearly has its roots in Origen's exegesis of Scripture. Athanasius' particular application of it to Trinitarian theology was to have enormous influence on the Cappadocian theologians of the next generation.

Around two years after the Council of Nicaea, a baby girl called Macrina was born to a wealthy Christian family in the province of Pontus on the north coast of Asia Minor. In the next 15 years or so she was followed by nine more children. The family were Christian and revered the memory of Macrina's maternal grandmother, Macrina the elder, who had been supposedly converted by Gregory the Wonderworker, pupil of Origen and missionary to the inner eastern regions of Asia Minor. By the late 350s (around the time when Athanasius was beginning to defend the Nicene term *homoousios*) Macrina persuaded her widowed mother Emmelia to turn their family home and country estate at Annesi into a monastery, with separate dwellings for men and women. Furthermore, the legend goes, she persuaded several of her brothers to join her in following 'the goal of philosophy' – that is a life of Christian asceticism.[33]

Whatever the truth concerning their reasons for joining the Church, what is certain is that the eldest boy, Basil, and his younger brother, Gregory of Nyssa, became two of the most influential theologians of the fourth century. They are usually grouped together with Gregory of Nazianzus, who was also from a wealthy family. His father was a pagan monotheist who was converted to Christianity by his wife. Gregory of Nazianzus became a close friend of Basil in their youth, probably while they both studied in Athens. Basil and Gregory of Nazianzus were ordained presbyters in around 362 (the year of Julian the Apostate's accession as emperor, and the year of Athanasius' council in Alexandria). Gregory of Nyssa – who unlike the other two was married – followed several years later. Although they never lost touch with the monastic life, these three men became increasingly involved in ecclesiastical politics, particularly the defence of the Nicene definition. Basil became Bishop of Caesarea in Cappadocia in about 370CE: he promptly elected his brother Gregory to one bishopric (in Nyssa) and his friend Gregory to another (in Sasima).[34]

The very considerable social and practical aspects of the Cappadocians' theology will be treated in the next chapter, but it is important to bear in mind that the theology of all three was profoundly influenced by the community at Annesi and by the values of the ascetic life. Their theology took up the great themes of Athanasius' theology – the equality of Father, Son and Spirit; the condescension of God in the Incarnation leading to the recovery of the image of God in humanity. In developing these themes further the Cappadocians integrated them with a deeper understanding of other aspects of Christian theology, such as the union of divine and human in Jesus Christ, the perfection of human nature at the eschaton, the nature of theological language and more formal thinking about the tasks and challenges of human life.

Although it is now standard to complain that textbook histories of the early Church have too easily lumped three rather distinct theologians together under the term 'the Cappadocians', nevertheless one must not go too far in the opposite direction. They did share common themes and approaches, and although they disagreed on some issues, these disagreements were not in the same category as the polemical arguments which they all addressed to Eunomius or Apollinarius, for example. Indeed, the fact that there were three highly educated and like-minded individuals in close correspondence with one another generated a sophisticated level of debate and mutual intellectual development which lies in between outright disagreement and total agreement. Both Gregories, for example, simultaneously praise Basil for his influence on their ideas and then subject his theology to a subtle critique.

The same kind of consideration applies to the relation all three Cappadocians had to Origen. Their exegesis was profoundly shaped by his, both in its general method and in their readings of individual passages. By the late 350s Basil and Gregory of Nazianzus had read enough of Origen to have edited a collection of excerpts from his writings on the themes of exegesis and the nature of divine punishment. They and Gregory of Nyssa by no means agreed with all of Origen's views, and each was influenced by Origen in different ways. Nevertheless, aspects of their thought can be read as a sustained commentary on and (in the positive sense) a critique of the Alexandrian's theology.

There seem to have been two main factors which led the Cappadocians to rethink Trinitarian theology. The first was that they seem to have been more sensitive than Athanasius to the concerns of many eastern bishops about the language of Nicaea. Athanasius paints a picture of debate in this period as between the defenders of Nicaea and everyone else (with a specific focus on Nicaea's ontological language: 'from the *ousia* of the Father', '*homoousios* with the Father'). In fact, a careful examination reveals a spectrum of beliefs and different degrees of tolerance for different kinds of wording. Thus, on the far 'left' [35] one could place Aetius (and later his pupil Eunomius), who argued that the Son was *unlike* (*anomoios*) the essence of the Father – they have thus been termed *anomoians*.[36] On the far 'right', one could place Marcellus and others who so emphasized the likeness of Son and Father that they apparently failed to identify any eternal distinction between the two. In between, there were a variety of positions, not all of which were clearly linked to any particular phrase or slogan. Precisely the problem with the term *homoios* (like) was that it was open to different interpretations: Athanasius could use it to emphasize the equality of Father and Son, those following Eunomius of Nicomedia could use it to suggest the subordination of Son to the Father. Basil of Ancyra was most happy using the term if it was qualified with some *ousia* language, 'the Son is like the essence of the Father'; Aetius could only accept it without this.

Perhaps more acutely than Athanasius, the Cappadocians could see how Origen's theology had led to two broad and divergent Trinitarian traditions. Origen himself avoided *ousia* language,[37] but he was willing to write of Father, Son and Spirit being three *hypostases*. There were those, like Eusebius of Caesarea and Arius himself, who agreed with the language of three *hypostases*, but denied Origen's doctrine of the eternal generation of the Son in order to establish a more clearly subordinationist doctrine of the Trinity. There were others, like Alexander and Athanasius, who strongly asserted the eternal generation of the Son, in order to affirm that the Son shared the *ousia* of the Father. The difficulty was that Athanasius' known early association with Marcellus, and Marcellus' insistence on writing of Father, Son and Spirit being just one *hypostasis*, made it seem as if Athanasius' reluctance to use the term *hypostasis* allied him completely with Marcellus's concept of the Trinity – even if this was not the case. Responding to this kind of anxiety about modalism, the Council of Antioch in 341CE suggested a formula for the relation of the three persons: they were 'three in *hypostasis* and one in agreement'.[38] The Cappadocians' success lay in recognizing the seriousness of fears about modalism and declaring that Father, Son and Spirit were three *hypostases* to counter that anxiety. But they also realized that concepts such as 'one in agreement' or 'like' were so open to a range of interpretations that some kind of *ousia* language was necessary. Hence, they strongly asserted that the Trinity of Father, Son and Holy Spirit was both three *hypostases* and one *ousia* (in other words whilst being individuals, the Son and the Spirit were both *homoousios* with the Father). Of course, the question remained of how exactly the three were related – an issue to which we shall return.

The second factor which contributed to the Cappadocians' approach to the doctrine of the Trinity was their encounters with Eunomius. This presbyter was a pupil of Aetius, but was a native of Cappadocia. He wrote works strongly defending the view that although the Son was begotten of the Father and thus derived some characteristics from him, the Son was not of the same *ousia* as the Father. His views are often described as 'neo-Arian', although 'Anomoian' or 'heterousian' are probably better terms. His theology was based on a strict logic deriving from the use of the terms 'begotten' (*gennetos*) for the Son and 'unbegotten' (*agennetos*) for the Father. If the Son is begotten, Eunomius reasoned, then the Father is the unbegotten one. Associating 'begottenness' not only with the concept of derivation but also with the idea of having a beginning in time and being dependent (not transcendent), Eunomius found it impossible to understand how anything could be begotten and be God. Indeed, the Cappadocians accused him of thinking 'unbegotten' was in effect a definition of the divine nature.

The Cappadocian response to this theology was two-fold. Firstly, Basil and Gregory of Nyssa attacked his premise that any term *could* define the nature of God (indeed, their philosophy of language went even further to claim that *no* nature, whether of God or of a goat, could be adequately understood or described by humans).[39] They pointed out that *agennetos*, like many words for God, was a negative term: God is *un*begotten, *in*visible, *im*material and so on. According to Basil and Gregory these words indicated that humans could say what God is *not*, but no one could say what God *is*. When positive language was used about God – God is love, God is a consuming fire – it was not literally describing God's very nature but using analogies from the created realm to describe humans' experience of God's action in the world. If one realized this it would become possible to say of *both* the Son and the Father that they are immaterial, invisible, unending and so on, whilst also affirming that within the Trinity, the Son is begotten and the Father is unbegotten.

This still leaves a problem, however. For it was clear that theologians were habitually using the term *agennetos*, not simply to distinguish the Father's relation to the Son but also to contrast God with the world: it had become a one-word summary of divine transcendence. Surely, though, it was not possible to say simultaneously that the Son was both 'begotten' and 'unbegotten'? All three Cappadocians appear to have worked towards solving this problem, making more explicit and attempting to explain an assumption that underlay Athanasius' theology: that the Son is begotten *in one sense* and unbegotten *in another sense*. That is, the Son is begotten in the sense that he derives his being *from* the Father; but he is unbegotten in the sense that, like the Father, he is God (he is unbegotten in the sense that he is absolutely transcendent over creation, the one source of all, and dependent on no other for his eternal existence). Whereas Arius thought that 'begotten' was synonymous with 'having a beginning in time', the Cappadocians explicitly noted that through the doctrine of eternal generation one could express the idea that the Son and Spirit could derive from the Father but that as God all three were the one eternal source of time. Gregory of Nazianzus attacked his opponents' misunderstanding of the question (which is quoted here in italics):

> *But*, it may be said, *the ingenerate* (agenneton) *and the generate* (genneton) *are not the same. If that is the case, the Father and the Son cannot be the same thing …* what are your grounds for denying that ingenerate and generate are the same? If you had said uncreated and created, I should agree – what has no origin and what is created cannot be the same in nature. … If you mean ingenerate*ness* and generate*ness* – no these [properties] are not the same thing; but if you mean the things which have these properties in them, why should they not be the same?[40]

Gregory is dealing with two issues here: first, that one *being* can possess or

contain different *properties* (in this case God – divine being – can contain
the properties of ingenerateness and generateness); secondly, that ingener-
ate in this context does *not* mean 'uncreated', and generate does *not* mean
'created'. In a similar argument, Gregory of Nyssa states that the term
agennetos is similar to the word *anarchos*. The problem is that *anarchos* can
mean two things: without origin or without beginning. The Son, like the
Father, but unlike creation, is without beginning (Gregory here affirms the
doctrine of the eternal generation of the Son from the Father); however the
Son is *not* without origin, for because he is begotten by the Father he has
his origin in the Father.[41]

What the two Gregories are here approaching (but never seem quite to
articulate in so many words) is a clear sense that *gennetos* and *agennetos* can
mean two different things. In fact, it has become clear through investigating
the origins of the words that the debates about the doctrine of the Trinity
rested on a confusion of two different verbs – a confusion of which even the
Cappadocians were unaware. Strictly speaking, the word *gennetos* (double
'n') is the past participle of the Greek verb *gennaomai*, 'to be begotten'. In
other words, it explicitly refers to the act of a man fathering a child. The
word *genetos* (single 'n') is the past participle of the Greek verb *gignomai*,
which literally means 'to come into existence' or 'to become'; it is inextricably tied up with notions of change and temporality – in other words, with
createdness. From this, it is clear that Greek writers should have been able
to say that the Son was *gennetos* (begotten of the Father) but not *genetos* (he
did not come into being in the way that creation did).

The confusion of the terms arose, however, because of the similarity of
meaning of their negative forms: 'unbegotten' is very similar in meaning to
'never having come into existence'. Both words indicate a transcendence,
independence of any origin or source. The confusion was so acute that to all
intents and purposes *agennetos* and *agenetos* became the same word (spelled
with a double or a single 'n'). Because they were considered to be the same
word, it was harder for theologians to argue that the Son was both *gennetos*
(begotten) and *agen(n)etos* (without any origin).

Nevertheless, both Gregories do suggest that *as Son* the Son is begotten
of the Father and that *as God* the Son is without origin. Gregory of Nyssa
uses the language of *hypostasis* to express this: 'so he, who according to
his *hypostasis* is not unoriginate (*anarchon*), in every other respect is agreed
to be unoriginate (*anarchon*)'.[42] It was this kind of argument that led the
Cappadocians to affirm the proposition for which they are now most famed:
that God is one in *ousia*, but three in *hypostases*. For what they were in fact
asserting was that the divine *essence* is without origin (*agenetos*), but that the
Son as a *hypostasis* of the divine *essence* derives from the Father.

There has been a tendency in some accounts of the Cappadocians to think that their defence of the Nicene concept of *homoousios* by using the idea of one *ousia* and three *hypostases* was a separate development from their writings on the Holy Spirit. Once they had got the problem of the Trinity out of the way, they could move on to the third hypostasis. However, there is a strong argument to suggest that their Trinitarian writings and their writings on the Spirit in particular are closely interconnected. Basil's *On the Holy Spirit* argues that if something is equal in honour (*homotimos*) to God the Father, then it is of the same substance (*homoousios*) with them.[43] He first argues the case with regard to the Son, then applies it to the Spirit. This is not because he thinks the cases can be treated separately – quite the opposite. It is a clever rhetorical strategy designed to persuade his opponents, the followers of Macedonius, known as the 'Spirit fighters' (*Pneumatomachians*). They argued that while the Son was *homoousios*, the Spirit was not. Basil counters this with an accusation of inconsistency. He brings forward numerous examples from the Bible to show that the Spirit, like the Son, is equal in honour with the Father and therefore that the three persons must share one divine essence. His argument also refers to the use of baptismal formulae – such as 'in the name of the Father and of the Son and of the Holy Spirit' – which seemed to Basil to assume that each person was *homoousios* with the others and the belief that they worked together. If the arguments worked for the Son, they would work for the Spirit. It was not a case of experimenting to see whether they applied to the Spirit too, for if they failed for the Spirit, they would fail for the Son. Either something is divine, or it is not: there is no third way. Even so, Basil was famously shy of asserting that the Spirit can be called 'God'. This was possibly because he was less clear about the way in which the persons related to each other, because thought on this issue rapidly raised the tricky question: if the Spirit and the Son both derive from the Father, how do they differ from one another?

Gregory of Nazianzus, however, was much more forthright on how to name the Spirit: 'What then? Is the Spirit God? Most certainly. Well then, is he consubstantial? Yes, if he is God.'[44] It is perhaps this clear avowal that leads him to discuss a knotty question mentioned above: how is it possible to distinguish between the Son and the Spirit? Is it that the Father has two sons – twins? – or even a son and a grandson?[45] Gregory ridiculed such conclusions, reminding his audience that such language was not to be taken in human terms. Instead he argued that the Spirit was begotten *from* the Father *through* the Son. This distinguishes the Spirit from the Son who was simply begotten of the Father. The distinction between the three is purely in terms of how they are related to one another (specifically, as to how the Spirit and Son are caused in different ways by the Father), *not* in their essence, qualities or roles.

In some contexts the Cappadocians explained the relation of *ousia* and *hypostasis* in terms of the relation of the general and the particular. Thus *ousia* could be seen as the general category of 'being God', whereas the *hypostasis* Son is a *particular instance* of being God. The example they often used to illustrate this – notoriously – was that of 'three men': all humans are united by their common human nature – the *ousia* of 'being human'; Peter, Andrew, John and James are all individual *hypostases* of the one human *ousia*.[46] The usefulness of this analogy was that it clearly indicated the *equality* of Father, Son and Spirit: the Father is no more divine than the Son, just as a human father is no more human than his son. To hostile readers, however, the analogy could seem tantamount to suggesting tritheism, for human beings seem not to be united very closely. This was problematic not only because it suggested pagan polytheism but because it raised the old Arian ghoul of two – in this case three – *agenneta*. But the analogy could be defended. First, to the ancient mind (and to the Cappadocians in particular), human nature was one in a much more strong sense that it is to modern readers. Basil and Gregory of Nyssa, for example, stress the idea that *all human nature* was created in the image of God.[47] Secondly, Gregory of Nyssa argued that whereas humans were divided by space and time, this was not true of God, in whom there is no interval. Even when humans claim to act 'together', they are still divided, whereas God's actions are one in a much more profound and thorough-going way. (Hence Gregory is most insistent that Father, Son and Holy Spirit were *all* involved in the act of creation, and the act of salvation and the act of perfection of human nature, lest one should come up with the picture of three separate gods: a Father who creates, a Son who saves and a Spirit who perfects.[48]) Thirdly, Gregory stressed the causal connections between the three *hypostases*: the Son is begotten of the Father, and the Spirit proceeds from the Father through the Son. These causal connections are the *only* way in which the three can be distinguished. The three cannot possess different properties, because they all necessarily possess the properties proper to the divine nature. They cannot act in three different ways, or they would indeed be three gods. The only way they can be distinguished is by their relations to one another – the three ways in which they exist as the one God. The Father exists as the origin of the Son and the Spirit; the Son exists as eternally begotten of the Father; the Spirit exists as proceeding from the Father and the Son. Because of this emphasis on causal connections, Gregory's use of the 'three men' analogy was nearly always accompanied by the use of other analogies which stressed the causal connection of the three. Thus, for example, he described the divine nature as a chain in which the three *hypostases* are interlinked and can only work together to haul humanity heavenward.[49]

Gregory of Nazianzus adapted the three-men analogy in a way which stressed the different causal relations between the three: his three humans were Adam (who originated from no other human), Eve (who originated from Adam's rib) and Seth (who originated from Adam and Eve). Instead of the analogy of a chain, which might be taken by the simple to suggest that the Spirit was inferior to the Son and the Son to the Father, Gregory of Nazianzus tried to show the way in which relations can bind three persons together in a way that simultaneously unites them and distinguishes each from the other. Seth clearly was derived from Adam in a different way from the way in which Eve derived from Adam. Indeed, according to some late-antique biological notions, a baby properly originated *from* her father *through* the agency of the mother, which would make Gregory of Nazianzus' parallel with the Spirit's origin from the Father through the Son even tighter. But Adam, Eve and Seth were bound together by the birth of Seth. This was obviously not a perfect analogy, and Gregory did not press it as much as I have done here: like all the Cappadocians, Gregory of Nazianzus was very cautious about the use of analogy.

In a very similar way to Gregory of Nyssa, Gregory of Nazianzus felt the need to defend against accusations of tritheism by appealing to the idea of perfectly unified divine action. He did this by nuancing the concept of monotheism, with the notion of *monarchia*:

> Monotheism with its single governing principle is what we value – not monotheism defined as the sovereignty of a single person ... but the single rule produced by equality of nature, harmony of will, identity of action, and the convergence towards their source of what springs from unity – none of which is possible in the case of created nature. The result is that although there is numerical distinction, there is no division in the being.[50]

Basil of Caesarea raised the question of whether, strictly speaking, one could 'count' the three persons in the one God and answered it in rather technical terms: one can say there are three persons, but one cannot count them 'one, two, three', for any such act of counting would set them in a kind of order, suggesting the superiority of the first. Instead, one can affirm three persons and *name* them: Father, Son and Spirit. Gregory of Nazianzus, on the other hand, writing in a more popular context, used the idea of number, to rise to more poetic heights:

> I cannot think of the One without immediately being surrounded by the radiance of the Three; nor can I discern the Three without at once being carried back to the One. When I think of the Three I think of him as a whole. ... I cannot grasp the greatness of the One so as to attribute a greater

greatness to the rest. When I contemplate the Three together, I see but one luminary [i.e. source of light] and cannot divide or measure out the undivided light.[51]

In 379 – the year of Basil's death – a new emperor came into power. Theodosius' personal sympathies lay with the pro-Nicene camp and he was prepared to put his official weight behind them. In 380 he issued a decree that the Empire should be united in acceptance of the Nicene Creed and he planned a council for the next year. The Niceno-Constantinopolitan Creed was the result of that council, but no detailed minutes of the proceedings remain. The creed fitted with a Cappadocian reading of the faith of Nicaea: it emphasized the divinity of the Spirit, without directly naming the Spirit 'God'; it omitted the embarrassing anathemas which implied that *ousia* and *hypostasis* meant the same thing.[52] But neither it nor Theodosius' subsequent proclamation quote the supposed Cappadocian catchphrase, 'one *ousia*, three *hypostases*'. The only place where that was mentioned directly was in a letter sent from the council to the western bishops in 382:

> [The 318 Fathers of Nicaea] teach us to believe in the name of the Father, and of the Son, and of the Holy Spirit; clearly, to believe in the one divinity (*theotēs*) and power (*dunamis*) and substance (*ousia*) of the Father, Son and Holy Spirit; in their dignity of equal honour and in their coeternal reign, in three most perfect *hypostases* or three perfect persons (*prosopa*).[53]

It seems to be the case that the idea of God as one *ousia*, three *hypostases* guided the Council of Constantinople's new understanding of the Nicene Creed, but it was not added. This indicates a reluctance among those present to look as if they were adding anything substantial to it.

An important effect of the Cappadocians' defence of the Son's shared substance with the Father was a renewed look at the relation of the divine and human in the incarnate Jesus Christ. If Christ was fully and truly God, how could he also be fully human? One of the things at issue was the question of agency. Both Athanasius and the Cappadocians argued that Christ was divine because he was God acting in the world (not an agent of God in the world). But if *God* acted in Christ, what of that traditional site of human agency, the soul or human mind? The second problem was Athanasius' own theology of the Incarnation: although exceptionally clear in asserting that Christ was both human and divine, he was not clear in explaining how that might be, and in particular was very hazy on the question of whether Christ had a human soul. In his early works, the issue is not mentioned at all, and in the *Tome to the Antiochenes* it is merely acknowledged, and apparently accepted, as a view belonging to another group.

Two things made the question more urgent: first, the Cappadocians brought the issue of agency to the fore in their defence of the doctrine of the Trinity; second, Apollinarius, a noted Christian scholar, follower of Athanasius and defender of the Nicene *homoousios* formula, directly asserted that Christ had no human soul. His reasoning appeared to be, first, that the divinity and the humanity must be fully united in Christ, or else Christ would either be a prophet (a true human merely blessed by God) or God in a fake replica of a human body.[54] Second, Apollinarius seemed to assume that a fully unified person must have one centre or source from which his action proceeds: in God, it is God's own undivided self; in humans (who are composed of parts) it is the soul. Apollinarius seems to have suggested that in Christ, the human soul's place was taken by the divine nature: he was thus in a way merely exaggerating some of Athanasius' tendencies to write of Christ's body as a 'tool' or an 'instrument', or to envisage Christ as putting on humanity as a person puts on a cloak. In order to stress the idea that Christ's body was not disposable, Apollinarius stressed the unity of the whole and seemed to work from the analogy that Christ the God-man was composed of the divine nature (the Son, or Logos) and human flesh (*sarx*) in a way similar to other humans' composition of soul and body. Apollinarius' view has thus sometimes been described as an exaggerated version of a 'Logos-sarx' Christology.[55]

Both Gregory of Nyssa and Gregory of Nazianzus articulated responses to Apollinarius. In order to do this they returned to the inheritance from Athanasius which they shared with Apollinarius: the divinity of Christ, the humanity of Christ and the relevance of both for salvation. Christ took on, or 'assumed', not just one human nature in the Incarnation but mysteriously assumed all of human nature in order that he might die for all, heal all and reveal God to all. Specifically, in taking on human nature Christ cleansed it from the corruption caused by the Fall. But surely, they argued, corruption was not only in the body, but in human souls also? If Christ were to heal all human nature, physical and spiritual, he must, as an individual human, have had a human soul. Gregory of Nazianzus reminded his readers that it was in his soul that Adam sinned first (if not, one would be obliged, like the Gnostics, to suspect God of having created some evil part of the material creation that led him astray). Hence, 'The very thing [i.e. the soul] that transgressed stood in special need of salvation. The very thing that needed salvation was assumed [by Christ]. Therefore mind was assumed.'[56]

That did leave the question hanging of how Christ could have two potential centres of agency, divine and human. Gregory of Nazianzus ridiculed his Apollinarianist opponents for supposedly saying that there was not enough 'room' for a human soul alongside the Logos, but that did not really respond to the main problem, which was the potential of division:

could it have been possible for Christ to have had in effect a divided mind? Gregory of Nazianzus suggested that the human mind of Christ was in harmony with the divine nature, playing a mediating role 'between Godhead and the grossness of the flesh'.[57] Gregory of Nyssa suggested that Christ's human mind became infused with the Godhead, until it was perfected and the question of a divided self could not arise. In order to express this idea he used the term *mixis* – most easily translated 'mixture' in English, but capable of a range of meanings in Greek, from the blending of two things into a third new compound, to (more colloquially) a sexual union in which two things remain two despite the intensity of their union. The particular analogy Gregory used suggests a meaning lying somewhere between the two: he argued that Christ's human soul became one with the divine in the way that a drop of vinegar becomes mixed with the water of the sea into which it is dropped.[58] Although capable of various interpretations, Gregory's main point seems to be that the *properties* of the mixture become that of the sea (salty rather than tasting of vinegar), whilst the actual atoms of the vinegar remain, however much they are diluted into the vast waters of the sea.[59] The language of *mixis* was easily misread, however, as suggesting that the Logos and Christ's human mind blended to form a unique quasi-human, quasi-divine compound. This kind of idea outraged later theologians when the issue of Christ's human nature erupted again in the fifth century.

The Cappadocians' emphasis on the idea that the humanity of Christ is humans' own humanity – albeit in a perfected state – had important implications for the rest of their theology. The first was the idea of salvation as the following of Christ. For the most part, this was expressed in the ideas, familiar from previous Church Fathers, that Christ defeated death and that his resurrection was the first-fruits of a general resurrection of humanity. The Cappadocians followed Athanasius in referring to this as the restoration of humanity to its state before the Fall. They were also interested in the effects of Christ's salvation on humans *before* their eschatological perfection. Again like Athanasius they believed that salvation had more than a juridical effect – it did not just pronounce people absolved from their sin. Rather, they believed that humans would embark on a process of transformation, beginning from the very day of their baptism. This process was made possible by God's grace through Christ; however, the Cappadocians did believe that the believer could work with God in making real some of the effects of salvation in their life. This idea was most prominent in the thought of Gregory of Nyssa (who referred to it as *sunergia* 'working with' or 'cooperation with' God), but it is implicit in what the other Gregory and Basil wrote about asceticism. The concept has often been criticized as if it suggested that salvation itself could be earned through human effort, but this is a misunderstanding. Cooperation with God is only possible as a result of the salvation already worked through the life, death and resurrection of Jesus Christ. Gregory's idea in particular implied that 'working with' God hastened some of the effects of salvation in one's life – not that it caused them.

In Gregory of Nyssa the idea of cooperation was accompanied – and indeed clarified – by his idea that in the end all of humanity would be saved. In this he was following on from an Origenistic tradition, although he was careful always to distance himself from the more controversial aspects of Origen's universalism.[60] The idea of universal salvation stressed the power of God's grace in Christ: Christ won a complete victory over evil and death on the Cross. It also emphasized that when Christ took on all human nature in the Incarnation he really did make it possible for all individual humans to be cleansed of their sin. (Athanasius would have found it difficult to explain how it was that some humans failed to be cleansed.) No early Christian theologian suggested that Christ's resurrection instantly wiped the slate clean for humans in actuality: they spoke of it being the firstfruits, or paving the way for, humans' salvation. Universalism's distinctive idea was that in the end, the cleansing of corruption gradually working its way through human nature would eventually become complete. Gregory of Nyssa sometimes wrote of Christ's action in human nature being like the leaven in dough, an analogy which implicitly relies on the idea of a waiting time, as the yeast does its work. The way in which this would work is through a double-sided process which is experienced in some aspects as cleansing and in others as a purificatory punishment. Gregory suggested that if humans willingly allowed, or even participated in, their own cleansing on earth they would avoid some punishment in the life after. On the other hand, recalcitrant sinners on earth would be punished for long ages in hell before eventually being pure enough to attain to heaven.[61]

Gregory of Nazianzus seems to have been in agreement with the basic idea that in the end all would be saved, although it forms a much less central part of his theology and it is not entirely clear whether he held the idea throughout his life.[62] Perhaps because of the vital role he has played in eastern Orthodox theology, the idea has in any case tended not to be attributed to him. On the other hand, the rather more marginal role of Gregory of Nyssa may partly be attributed to the unavoidable centrality of the idea in his theology. Unlike the two Gregories, Basil seems never to have held the idea. His preaching in particular is full of stern warnings about the eternal consequences of refusing the salvation which God has offered to humans in Christ.[63]

This last example shows the complexity of the Cappadocians' relationship to Origen. They would all have agreed with his fundamental principles of Christian theology, but they were far from unanimous in accepting other of his theological ideas – and the circumstances made it necessary for them to develop his doctrine of the Trinity very considerably. His influence on them was thus apparent less in the detailed doctrinal conclusions they came to and more in the modes in which they did theology. That is, it was apparent in their method of exegesis, their apophatic theology and in the way they wrote theology.

First, the Cappadocians all broadly agreed with the principle that although most of the Bible was historically true, it also contained other truths which should be investigated by the keen reader. They were keen readers of Origen's commentaries and homilies on biblical texts. Many examples can be given where their individual readings of verses follow Origen's precedent. As whole works, Gregory of Nyssa's *Commentary on the Song of Songs* is much indebted to Origen's *Commentary* and *Homilies*, and Basil's work on the six days of creation (*On the Hexameron*) is similarly indebted to Origen's various reflections on Genesis. On the other hand, there are also examples of where the Cappadocians' theological development away from Origen meant that they interpreted verses rather differently, for example Gregory of Nyssa's interpretation of Paul's account of the resurrection in I Corinthians 15. But the fundamental idea of the inexhaustible depths of Scripture remained and – crucially – was given further significance by Basil's and Gregory of Nyssa's arguments against Eunomius. Besides arguing that no human word could fully describe God, they were also committed to the view that even the inspired words of Scripture were just human words, albeit ones with authority and more than the usual accuracy. Discrepancies and even contradictions in Scripture could be explained as the inevitable clash of metaphors, analogies and images produced when trying to talk about God. While no words were sufficient to describe God, human language had an enormous potential to 'aim towards' God in prayer and praise: the Bible was a perfect demonstration of that.

Secondly, the Cappadocians were very influenced by Origen's notion of spiritual progress. He took classical ideas of education and philosophical discipline (intellectual, moral and physical) and applied these to Christianity. Although even the simplest believer could grasp what was necessary for their salvation, there was an imperative for all to advance in their faith. This was made clear by the nature of Scripture itself which contained not only simple truths, but also unplumbable depths of wisdom. Origen's development of these ideas gave a new dimension to Christian life. No longer was it conceived primarily in terms of the believer's relation to God in the present moment (as in the intense spirituality of writers such as Ignatius of Antioch or Tertullian). Nor was it focused on the community's collective expectation of a millennial reign of God on earth (as in Justin Martyr or Irenaeus). Instead, Origen's theology encouraged each believer to think of their own individual spiritual life as being like a journey towards God: it kept the dynamic, future-oriented aspect of Irenaeus' theology, but applied it in a more individualistic way. It did not abandon the material or communal sides of Christian life (Origen was profoundly interested in questions about the body, about the Church, the sacraments, and so on), but it did have the effect of a more internal and intellectual approach to Christian faith. The dynamic, future-oriented aspect of the individual's spiritual journey was strengthened further by the theology of Gregory of Nyssa, who argued that since God was infinite, no one could ever fully know God – even in heaven. The forward movement of each person towards God, therefore, would never end, like an arrow endlessly propelled but never quite reaching its target. One might think this a rather negative idea. However, according to Gregory, the recognition of divine infinity merely caused an endless desire for the divine: the soul in its advance was paradoxically endlessly satisfied, yet endlessly driven on in its desire for more. This kind of idea became enormously influential in Christian mysticism, especially in monastic circles. Although the average ascetic did not receive such ideas in a very sophisticated form, it is clear that the patterns of ascetic living, both practical and spiritual, were profoundly affected by the ideas of life as a dynamic journey into God, and God as an infinite resource which can never be exhausted.

Thirdly, Origen's theology affected the way in which the Cappadocians wrote. In fact their literary styles are rather different – both from each other and from Origen's. Nevertheless, all four theologians were propelled by an intense love of erudition, the belief that it could serve the Gospel and, above all, the desire to teach people about the Gospel by using their own individual learning. In particular, the Cappadocians seem to have picked up on the Platonist-Origenist idea that teachers must adapt their address to the capabilities of those listening to or reading them. Thus we find marked contrasts of style in works addressed to their congregations and letters addressed to learned contemporaries. None of the Cappadocians were frightened to use literary allusions or scientific analogies in order to explain or emphasize a theological idea. Although it might seem pretentious or laboured – or even dangerous – to a modern reader used to certain modes of popular or academic theology, this kind of approach was normal for their day, both in Christian and pagan literature. Indeed, the Cappadocians like other of their contemporaries, were probably seeking to show that Christian literature could be as sophisticated, varied, colourful and persuasive as contemporary pagan examples. They were not writing, as the apologists were, to prove that Christianity was moral and not a threat to the Empire. They were of course writing to teach and correct other Christians. But they were also keen, one suspects, with an eye on their pagan contemporaries, to show that Christian literature had, one might say, grown up. The one sure thing that pagans had been able to claim against Christianity – that it had no body of literature which was as serious, as varied, as useful and as beautiful as the Greek classics – was now seriously being challenged by such Christian writers as these.

Athanasius and the Cappadocians had an enormous influence on later Christian theology. Particularly in relation to their doctrines of the Trinity, but also with regard to their concepts of salvation and asceticism, they had an impact that spread into the west beyond the Greek theological tradition. In the later disputes over the exact relation between Christ's humanity and his divinity, each side appealed to the authority of these figures to bolster their case. Contemporary with these four churchmen was another writer who was no less prolific, who was preoccupied with defending very similar theological ideas and who did so with no less profundity and subtlety. His name was Ephrem. He was born at the beginning of the fourth century (being about ten years younger than Athanasius and about 20 years older than Basil). Ephrem spent most of his life in Nisibis, in the province of Mesopotamia on the edge of the Roman Empire. When the town was handed over to the Persians in a treaty of 363, Ephrem and other Christians migrated further west to Edessa. Ephrem wrote in Syriac, which was the language of the Christian communities in Nisibis and Edessa. For this reason, and because many of the Syriac-speaking churches broke communion with most of the Greek- and Latin-speaking churches after the Council of Chalcedon, Ephrem's theology has not had the same influence in Europe as that of Athanasius and the Cappadocians. Nevertheless, it has been enormously influential among Syriac-speaking Christians in the Middle East and his writings are now becoming more widely read (not least because of the appearance of translations into modern European languages).[64]

Like the other theologians studied in this chapter, Ephrem wrote treatises refuting theological errors and commentaries on various books of the Bible. (The fact that Ephrem wrote a commentary on the *Diatessaron*, the four-fold Gospel synopsis composed by Tatian in the second century, reminds us that it was this, not the four separate Gospels, that was still in use by Syriac-speaking Christians.) But he also wrote much poetry, which was a less common theological genre in Greek – Gregory of Nazianzus' poetry was somewhat of an exception. Many of his poems were composed for congregational singing, and the sixth-century Syriac poet Jacob of

Serugh celebrated the fact that Ephrem trained choirs of women specially to sing them:

> The blessed Ephrem saw that the women were silent from praise,
> And in his wisdom he decided it was right that they should sing out;
> So just as Moses gave timbrels to the young girls,
> Thus did this discerning man compose hymns for virgins.[65]

Ephrem shared with Athanasius and the Cappadocians an emphasis on the central theological idea that God had become human, so that humans could become divine:

> Free will succeeded in making Adam's beauty ugly,
> for he, a man, sought to become a God.
>
> Grace, however, made beautiful his deformities
> and God came to become a man.
>
> Divinity flew down
> to draw humanity up.
>
> For the Son had made beautiful the deformities of the servant
> and so he has become a God, just as he desired.[66]

As this passage suggests, Ephrem too used the Philippians' hymn and Paul's idea of Christ as the second Adam in order to express this idea of the 'divine exchange'.[67] But while the idea of Christ 'putting on' human nature was just one way which Athanasius, for example, had for describing the Incarnation, in Ephrem it was a dominant theme. He shared an ancient tradition of reading Genesis 3.21 to refer to God clothing Adam and Eve with *good* garments, *before* the Fall – an interpretation which depended on a variant reading of the Hebrew text to mean 'garments of light', not 'garments of skin'.[68] Thus, for Ephrem (as for many Syriac theologians), the pattern of salvation could be symbolically described thus: Adam and Eve lost their garments of light after the Fall and had to clothe themselves in leaves; Christ came and stripped off the signs of his glorious divinity in order to put on the garment of human nature; in doing so he was 'able to reclothe them [Adam and Eve, i.e. humankind] in the glory they had stripped off, thus replacing the leaves'.[69] A little like Irenaeus, Ephrem's usual way of explaining salvation is to recount a *narrative* of salvation-history: creation, the Fall, the Incarnation, Christ's life, death and resurrection and then salvation seen as the return of humanity to the condition of paradise: 'everyone has entered it; for through the first Adam who left it everyone had left it'.[70] This last theme is just one of the many theological emphases which Ephrem shares with Gregory of Nyssa. Like Gregory, Ephrem stresses the universality of the Incarnation – God has taken on *all* human nature (hence the emphasis in both theologians of the first Adam/second Adam parallel). Ephrem uses the idea of the harrowing of hell to explain how the effects of the Incarnation could extend 'backwards' to those before Christ.[71] Unlike Gregory, however, Ephrem does seem to think that some people will refuse God's offer of salvation and remain in hell (although he does share with Gregory the desire to see punishment after death in terms of separation from God and the torture of coming to recognize the full extent of one's sins).[72]

Underlying the idea of the divine exchange – 'he gave us divinity, we gave him humanity'[73] – was the idea that Jesus Christ must have been *truly* divine and *truly* human for this exchange to be effective. The former was emphatically expressed in Ephrem, who was aware of the Arian heresy and the danger which it posed to the Christian idea of salvation. Throughout his theology ran the deep conviction in Christ's full divinity. Less explicit, but nonetheless present, was the idea that the Holy Spirit too was divine. It was implied in the Spirit's roles, especially divinizing the believer and sanctifying the rites of baptism and Eucharist.[74] For Ephrem, the Spirit also played a vital part in the Incarnation and in Christ's own baptism, the idea that the Spirit was 'with the Son' in his baptism, suggesting perhaps their equality.[75] In one passage Ephrem appears to assert this explicitly, although typically this is expressed with an analogy rather than philosophically: 'It is not said of Eve that she was Adam's sister or his daughter, but that she came from him; likewise it is not to be said that the Spirit is a daughter or sister, but that [she] is *from* God and consubstantial with him.'[76] Here the author was trying to avoid any suggestion of inferiority that the metaphor of 'being the child of' might imply; it also possibly betrayed the anxiety that we saw in the Cappadocians: could there be two sons (or two children) of the Father – and in which case, what would make them different? (The passage also reminds one of the way in which the Syrian tradition referred to the Spirit as female, because of the grammatical gender of the term for spirit in Syriac.)

Christ's baptism, in particular, was held by Ephrem to be an important revelation of the three-fold nature of God.[77] This nature was sometimes expressed with the symbolism of light, which was developed in a distinctive direction by Ephrem, so that the Son represented the light of the sun and the Spirit the heat.[78] Thus sanctification is expressed by Ephrem as warming; it is another way of expressing the idea that God deals with the nakedness of fallen human nature, and also usefully suggests the completion (or here, 'ripening') of God's saving work: 'By means of warmth all things ripen, as by the Spirit all are sanctified.'[79]

The idea that Christ was fully human was emphasized by Ephrem, often by stressing that the garment/body that the Word put on was truly a *human* garment/body ('our body was your clothing'), not least because it came from the body of Mary the virgin ('he put on his mother's robe').[80] Importantly, Christ's taking on a real, material human body was connected with Christ's real presence in the material bread and wine of the Eucharist.[81]

The final important aspect of Ephrem's theology to be highlighted here is his apophaticism. Again, there are tantalizing similarities with Gregory of Nyssa's theology – although there is absolutely no evidence of any historical connection between Ephrem and any of the Cappadocians (despite a legend that he met Basil). Like Gregory's, Ephrem's apophaticism is both a deeply spiritual attitude of awe towards the divine, and is developed within the context of the Arian controversy. Ephrem's *Hymn on Virginity* 52, for example, positively bristles with anger at the effrontery of the Arians who claim to know God:

> The source of the rays is that bringing forth of our Saviour.
> Our mind is much too weak to investigate it.
> If one hopes to investigate it,
> is revealed that he is not sufficient to the Source
> Whose streams push on him ...
> They eject him, cast him out and hurl him by their rushing.[82]

As Gregory suggested that humans cannot even understand the nature of animals, let alone themselves, so Ephrem produced the example of a gnat:

> Let us take the gnat, smallest of all creatures ...
> In his substance [i.e. his nature, essence] the gnat became a mountain:
> Although his body is quite small, his investigation is great.
> Therefore, let all the mighty creatures be left out
> and more than these, the splendid human being,
> and more than the human, the distant heavenly [beings].
> What is left then is
> for us to contemplate in silence how hidden is
> this offspring whom we despised but who sustained us.[83]

CHAPTER 7

Saints and the City
(FOURTH TO FIFTH CENTURIES)

> It has often been a matter of discussion among many people as to which monk
> was the first to inhabit the desert. Some, going back further into the past,
> have ascribed the beginning to the blessed Elijah and to John [the Baptist]. ...
> Others, whose opinion is commonly accepted, claim that Antony was the first
> to undertake this way of life. ... Amathas and Macarius, Antony's disciples
> ... affirm to this day that a certain Paul of Thebes was the originator of the
> practice ... of the solitary life.[1]

So Jerome began his life of Paul the Hermit. According to this, Paul went
into the desert during the persecutions of Decius and Valerian – i.e. at some
point in the 250s – but it is clear from Jerome's account that although Paul
was supposedly 'the originator of the practice ... of the *solitary* life', he was
adapting a routine of spiritual discipline and self-denial that had already
been current in Christian circles for many years. This kind of practice is
known as asceticism, from the Greek *askesis* (practice, training). The ascetics themselves traced their way of life back to Christ's disciples who, according to the Acts of the Apostles, sold their possessions in order to share the
proceeds with the poor and who then shared all their goods (Acts 4.32–5).[2]
A popular form of asceticism for women – living a life of prayer and self-
denial within the parental home – was popularly traced back to the early life
of Mary, the mother of Christ, and to various early Christian disciples.[3]

The popular stories about the beginnings of asceticism and their very
practical concerns – money, food and sex – may seem very distant from
the theological debates discussed in the previous chapters. But Athanasius, the Cappadocians and Ephrem were deeply involved with the development of asceticism in the fourth century and their concern is evident in
their writings. Athanasius, for example, is credited with the *Life of Antony
of Egypt* which became swiftly famous and was translated into several
languages, including Latin and Syriac. Even if he was not the author, he
certainly gained much of his support from Egyptian monks. Basil wrote

some guidelines for life in a monastic community.[4] Both Gregory of Nyssa
and Gregory of Nazianzus wrote pieces encouraging Christians to imitate
Christ and take up an ascetic lifestyle, and Nyssa's *Life of Macrina* is one of
the most engaging accounts of fourth-century Christian ascetic life. Interestingly, becoming an ascetic did not seem necessarily to involve joining
a monastery or becoming a solitary monk or nun: the Cappadocians and
Ephrem seem to have been concerned to encourage other forms of ascetic
discipline, including ones within the family and even within marriage.

It is this fact that points us towards the heart of the fourth-century
enthusiasm for the ascetic life: ultimately, asceticism was not about the
following of a certain set of rules; instead, it was the choice of a life devoted
to God and the pursuit of that life in a way which presented as few distractions as possible. Such a life might be more easy as a member of a monastic
community, or as a hermit, but it was also possible for the bishop busy
with ecclesiastical politics or the wealthy woman with a large household to
run (indeed there was a strand of writing on asceticism which treated such
people as more 'heroic' ascetics than those who lived in the desert endur-
ing amazing privations!). Similarly, an ascetic life might be made easier by
the following of some basic rules, but these were not necessary; they were
never intended to define ascetic life absolutely and there was often a sense
in ascetic writing that the most perfect ascetics – such as Paul and Antony
– were those who had an instinctive grasp of their vocation, which made
rules redundant. Indeed, there is evidence that ascetic rules were introduced
as a solution to problems within ascetic communities rather than coming
about as founding documents.

At the heart of Christian asceticism was a search for God in and through
the life of this world. This search was based firmly on the belief in the
Incarnation – that is, the belief that God came to live in the world in Jesus
Christ. The fourth-century theologians of the ascetic life believed that in
the Incarnation God lived as human in a way that resisted the ways of the
world but which was yet somehow truer to the way in which the world
ought to have been. They thus firmly connected asceticism with Christology: it comes as no surprise that Antony of Egypt supported Athanasius
in his arguments against Arius. In the next generation, the Cappadocians'
idea that Christ was both fully God (their arguments again Eunomius)
and fully human (their arguments against Apollinarius) was a vital background to their writing on asceticism. The ascetics reasoned that the incarnate Christ was the true image of God (Genesis 1.27); he thus revealed what
true humanity was and promised salvation as the restoration of the state of
human nature before the Fall. Christ's resurrection was the first-fruits, or
the guarantee, of this restoration for human nature in general. The full and

perfect restoration of human nature would not be until the end of time, but in the meantime humans could work towards it with God's grace, by imitating Christ.

So the ascetic life was a paradox: it was seen both as the withdrawal from 'worldly' or 'secular' forms of life, but also as an example of, or a pointer towards, a more perfect form of human living which had the potential to transform the world. This explains the often ambivalent language about materiality and embodiment: orthodox ascetics agreed that the body, as part of God's creation, was good; nevertheless, they viewed it as profoundly and negatively affected by the Fall. The same was of course true of the soul, but it was the body, as the means by which humans interacted with the world, which was the site of the battle to regain the body – and the world – for God.[5] Some ascetics did come to believe that their eventual perfection would consist in leaving materiality behind for ever, but usually ascetic language about subduing or fleeing from the flesh needs to be viewed as expressing a desire to leave behind the particular quality of materiality or the particular kind of world left behind by the Fall. Another way of expressing the ambivalence about 'the world' was to think in terms of its present and future condition. Thus, for example, Gregory of Nyssa sometimes described monastic life in terms which are reminiscent of his eschatology: the harmonious existence of humans in a life dedicated to the praise of God; communities in which the distinctions of men and women, between former slaves and their masters became irrelevant; communities which took in the destitute and which shared worldly goods in a way which recognized that the goods came ultimately from God.[6] These descriptions were no doubt highly idealized. Nevertheless, they give a clear indication of the thinking behind the ascetic life and in particular reveal the connection between the practical disciplines of asceticism and the core theological belief that in Jesus Christ God became human that humans might become divine: 'Having become what we were, he through himself again united humanity to God.'[7] The other strong theological current running through asceticism in this period was the idea of the possibility of spiritual progress. Because this already incorporated ideas of training and preparation it was an ideal accompaniment to the more practical aspects of training expected of the Christian ascetic.

Besides these theological ideas about God, Christ and human nature, there are several practical concerns that one can trace in the development of asceticism in the first four centuries of Christianity. The first was the sharing of wealth. We have seen evidence for this in Acts, in Justin Martyr's emphasis on the collection of money for the support of widows and orphans (Rome, mid-second century CE) and in Tertullian's laconic comment that 'we have everything in common except our wives'.[8] Well before the conversion of Constantine there is ample evidence of the discomfort caused by disparities of wealth within congregations, and evidence that teachers were being called on to advise rich converts on what to do with their wealth.[9] Both Paul and Antony, revered as the founders of Egyptian desert monasticism, were praised specifically as wealthy men who gave their riches away – both because that benefited the poor and because wealth was seen as a distraction from the pursuit of a Godly life.

The second concern was discipline concerning dress, drink and especially food. Because Christian ceremony focused (amongst other things) on a ritual meal, Christians were often accused of drunken feasting. But, as we have seen, early Christian apologists such as Tertullian took great care to defend themselves against such an attack and portrayed their meals as more sober and sedate versions of pagan banquets.[10] Others responded by deliberately avoiding certain kinds of food and drink, especially those associated with luxury: one of the martyrs of Lyons and Vienne (late second century CE) was described as a vegetarian, for example, and early Christians known as 'enkratites' seem to have rejected both meat and alcohol.[11] Of course, the diet of many if not most early Christians would have been restricted by financial means and supply (famine was a frequent occurrence); fasting only made sense either for those who had food to give up or for those ascetics whose diet was so spectacularly limited that it would have counted as fasting even for the poor. So, for example, Paul was said to have survived in the desert on water and half a loaf of bread a day. Jerome's account of Paul's life associates this simple diet not only with Paul's self-discipline but also with his concern to set aside plentiful time for prayer: miraculously, a raven brought Paul his daily ration of bread, thus freeing him from the labour of either growing his own food or earning wages to buy it. (When he was visited by Antony, the obliging raven brought a full loaf.[12]) Other hermits, including Antony himself, were said to have gained their daily bread from local villagers in exchange for baskets: the hermits' weaving of these baskets was a simple activity which was compatible with their long periods of prayer and contemplation. The choice of very simple clothing had a similar function. Some ascetics chose to wear rags or animal skins, which had taken little or no effort to make; others wore the simplest of garments which they had made themselves. Like basket weaving, the tasks of spinning and weaving were compatible with prayer and were often taken up in particular by women in monastic communities.

Ascetics' choice of simple dress and food also served another important purpose. As in modern culture, extravagant clothing and lavish hospitality was often used in late antiquity as an ostentatious display of high status or as a way in which social climbers tried to claim high status for themselves. By rejecting such display, Christian ascetics were championing modesty and simplicity, which were virtues many pagan Romans would have valued highly, but they were also challenging Roman society in a radical way. The Roman culture of patronage complemented family relationships with a complex system in which patrons protected and benefited a number of clients from whom in turn they expected loyalty and various services. Patrons could themselves be clients of a patron higher up the social ladder: the emperor was in a sense the senior patron of the Empire. The provision of banquets and even distinctive clothing for clients was a very well-established way of keeping this structure together. By replacing patron-feasts with the common table of the Eucharist (and other similar meals), Christians were replacing the particular relationships created by patronage with the much more general bond of baptism. By agreeing to dress simply, well-to-do Christians were rejecting one of the obvious ways of distinguishing themselves from those of lower status. Many wealthy patrons who converted to Christianity in effect became patrons of Christian communities, providing places for worship and catacombs for burial. Even so, the use of their wealth for ostentatious display, for extravagant garments, jewellery and hair-styles and for lavish banquets was generally much less socially acceptable among Christians than among pagans.

The final concern in early Christian asceticism was sex. This is the most difficult aspect of asceticism to analyse because of the extreme difficulty of disentangling late antique and modern western assumptions about sexuality. Furthermore, Christian attitudes to sex seem to have differed widely even in late antiquity. Consequently, while it is true to say that some early Christian sources demonstrated disgust at the sexual act, this was by no means a universal feature of ascetic writing on sex, nor even perhaps a majority view.

An early text, the *Protoevangelium of James*, demonstrated a marked suspicion of sexuality – especially of female sexuality. Mary, the mother of Christ, was described as being dedicated to God as a young woman: her mother first 'made her chamber a holy place, and allowed nothing uncommon or unclean to come near her'. At the age of three she was taken to dwell in the temple, where she 'continued in the temple as a dove educated there and received her food from the hand of an angel'.[13] This enclosure by external walls mirrored Mary's internal intactness: not only was she a virgin when she conceived Christ but she remained intact even in giving birth – a point reinforced by the famous story of the midwife who, on doubting Mary's intact state after birth, dared to inspect the mother of God and was punished with a withered hand.[14] This tradition of Mary's perpetual virginity was denied by some early Church Fathers, for example, by Tertullian.[15] However, the kind of tradition found in the *Protoevangelium of James* played an important part in the theology of such writers as Ambrose, Jerome and Augustine, and it was through their huge influence on the western medieval theological tradition that the view took hold that virginity was the ideal and indeed 'proper' state of humanity – especially of women.

Particularly in the east, however, the situation was more complicated. There were undoubtedly groups among which chastity was the ideal, even from a very early stage. Rejection of marriage and sex was a feature of enkratite Christianity. There is specific evidence from the thought of Syrian enkratite groups that the motivation for this was not so much a disgust with sex as a belief that all human relationships were disrupted by conversion to Christianity: after baptism, the believer's relationship with the Holy Spirit was so strong that it left no room for any *particular* human relationships.[16] A rather different motivation to celibacy was the imitation of St Thecla. According to the narrative of the apocryphal *Acts of Paul and Thecla*, this young woman is said to have been persuaded away from marrying her fiancé by Paul. For this, she was condemned to be burnt to death, but she miraculously escaped. Although Thecla may in fact never have existed, she was a hugely popular object of devotion, many making pilgrimages to her supposed burial place at Meriemlik near Seleucia. Thecla's story also inspired many young women to refuse marriage and take up an ascetic life, often, perhaps usually, in their own household. Gregory of Nyssa tells us his sister was given the name Thecla by her mother in the hope that she might eventually take up such a life. (It can safely be said that Macrina exceeded even the most optimistic of maternal expectations!) Women 'household ascetics' followed a rigid regime of prayer and fasting and rarely left the house, even to go to church. The rejection of marriage by women (especially those of means) was firmly against the social norms of the time, for it might have left a family without heirs. However, their choice of an enclosed life at home did at least ameliorate the situation for their family: besides proving their virtue to their fellow believers, it protected the female ascetics and their families from the allegation that their failure to marry was due to some sexual misdemeanour. This is another example of the way in which Christian practices could simultaneously defend some basic values of Greco-Roman culture (the importance of female sexual purity), whilst radically challenging established custom (which valued marriage very highly). In recent years, however, scholars have tended to highlight the way in which Christian rejection of marriage explicitly or implicitly challenged the prevailing social structures.[17] By choosing not to marry, ascetics were choosing not to procreate and thus choosing not to continue the family structures which passed wealth and power from one generation to another. By choosing not to marry, ascetics were therefore withdrawing from society – or rather, they were withdrawing from one kind of society and creating another one, in which ties were created by a common faith and purpose rather than by blood and marriage.

There were also clearly some practical considerations involved in the choice of celibacy. Just as the production of food and clothing demanded labour, so families created a great deal of work; the education of several young sons and finding them a career was an expensive business, and daughters required dowries. The decision to become a monk or nun was a way of opting out of these concerns in order to devote oneself single-mindedly to the service of God. The distractions of marriage were not just financial of course: celibacy was also a way to opt out of certain kinds of emotional bonds, as Gregory of Nyssa so touchingly suggests in his work on virginity.[18] Wealthy women, in particular, sometimes had much to gain from virginity. Instead of submitting to an arranged marriage in their mid-teens and carrying out the responsibilities of producing heirs, running a household and (often) managing substantial estates, an ascetic woman could choose a life of relative independence. She was free from the considerable burdens (not to say dangers) of childbearing; she might be free to manage her own time; she could choose how to dispose of her own wealth. Many women gained positions of leadership in their monastic communities, even sometimes over men.[19] Of course, such independence was relative: ascetic women, even more than ascetic men, were expected to conform to strict standards of behaviour. The question is, however, whether ascetic women who voluntarily took on a life of ascetic discipline – even with all its strictures – were more free through being able to make that choice than those who submitted to the usual expectations of late antique society.[20]

All of these reasons for choosing a life of celibacy, however, were more concerned with social outcomes (broadly defined) or positive theological goals rather than with negative attitudes to the sexual act itself. This is reflected in the fact that often what was being talked about was not a state of physical virginity, but the choice at some point to remain single and chaste. Thus formerly promiscuous men who converted could be said to have chosen a virgin life, and young widows who chose not to remarry were often treated as virgins. There were, however, plenty of other examples of extreme hostility to sexuality and many ascetics who regarded sex as contamination: the sayings of the desert fathers and mothers, for example.[21] This hostility often translated into an extreme suspicion of women, who were habitually blamed for men's temptation or lapses. Despite the vividness of these warnings, however, they must not be thought to tell the whole story of early Christian attitudes to sexuality.

Such were the ideas lying behind asceticism in early Christianity. But what were its historical origins? From where did it emerge? And – to return to Jerome's question – who were the key figures in its emergence? Individual Christian men and women made the choice to reject marriage and lead disciplined lives of prayer and self-denial ever since the time of Jesus Christ. Under a broad definition of asceticism, Paul himself was an ascetic. The present question, however, concerns ascetic *movements* – identifiable strands within Christianity which saw the ascetic lifestyle as the only valid response to Christ, or at least as the preferred option. Although the evidence is hazy and much disputed, there seems to have been a strong ascetic strand to Christianity in Asia Minor and Syria from at least the second century. Although the term 'enkratite' falsely gives the impression of a coherent group, there were certain views and practices which can be described as enkratite: the rejection of marriage, meat and alcohol. A tendency to these views can be found in the writings of the Syrian Tatian (fl. 160), in the *Acts of Thomas* (beginning of the third century) and the preaching of Mani (fl. mid-third century CE).[22] Too close an association with Syria alone is warned against, however, by the fact that similar views can be found in Marcion (mid-second century CE) and second-century Gnostics from Egypt.

In the mid-third century a distinctive and increasingly more organized form of Christian asceticism began to emerge in Egypt. The literary evidence for this movement is rather late – fourth-century biographies/ hagiographies of ascetics like Antony and Paul and collections of 'sayings' of the desert fathers – but both types of literature were probably based on earlier oral traditions. From such sources as these, the main aspects of early Egyptian monasticism are fairly clear. First, although both Antony and Paul were each claimed to be the first *solitary* ascetic in the Egyptian desert, there were already other ascetics in Egypt. The *Life of Antony*, for example, implies that Antony's sister joined a 'group' of virgins (the fact that they are grouped together apparently distinguishing them from the usual pattern of individual women in their own homes).[23] Similarly, although the *Life* credits Antony with being the first hermit to enter 'the distant desert', it specifically says that he learnt his way of life from hermits who 'practised the discipline in solitude near their own village'.[24] Antony probably began this period of ascetic training some time in the early 270s (about 20 years after Paul's retreat to the desert).

After learning from village hermits, Antony moved into the desert, to Pispir, 'the outer mountain'. But even there he was not utterly alone: he is said to have woven baskets to earn money both for his bread and to help feed the poor. Around 305 he began to organize a loose group of hermits like himself. They were a community in the sense of having a common way of life, a common purpose, not in the sense that they lived and worshipped together as later communities did. This is the second notable aspect of Egyptian desert asceticism: although some hermits lived utterly alone, most came to live relatively close to others (not least because of the system of older monks teaching the younger ones).

In about 310 Antony withdrew further away: his 'inner mountain' near the Red Sea was said to be three days' journey from any human dwelling. But even there, he could not hope to be completely isolated, still being consulted by monks, churchmen and lay people. This usefully illustrates a third point: the role of the desert ascetic as a 'holy man' who occupied a boundary position between civilization and the wilderness, between the city and the desert. Such men rarely withdrew so far as to be absolutely beyond the reach of those who sought their help, yet their followers had to seek them out. Their remoteness seemed to symbolize the way in which they were both in the world but not quite of it, and their occupation of the boundary between city and desert also symbolized their mediatorial role between God and the faithful. Whilst never usurping the role of Christ as mediator of salvation, they helped Christians to imitate Christ, providing a model and an inspiration, besides theological teaching and practical advice.

Fourthly, then, these desert ascetics performed a similar kind of role to that played by many Christian martyrs. The martyrs' brave and faithful example inspired others to follow them (and Christ) in dying as witnesses to God. Although they were not the agents of salvation there was a sense in which they were thought to mediate salvation through their example and through their prayers – even after their death. In popular belief, the martyrs' role sometimes threatened to put Christ's actions into the shade.[25] Local martyrs assumed a huge importance for Christian communities, and ceremonies often centred on their graves – even their relics – precisely because they were close and tangible witnesses to the power of Christian faith. Like later ascetics, the martyrs were both there (their bodies in their tombs) and not there (they were thought to have ascended directly to heaven). Some commentators have suggested that after the period of persecution asceticism became a new form of martyrdom: it is easy to misunderstand this as the wilful seeking out of pain, as if self-persecution had replaced pagan persecution. Rather, what is meant is that asceticism became the most potent way of witnessing to the dramatically transformative effects of belief in Christ. The privations were important – ascetics were sometimes described as undergoing a 'living death' – but more important was the pursuit of God which they made possible. Furthermore, just as Christians had approached confessors in prison, asking them to pray for their salvation in the belief that the confessors would soon be martyrs raised to heaven, so they approached ascetics asking them to intercede for them. A letter from fourth-century Egypt has been preserved on its original papyrus: the writer Justin asks the ascetic Paphnuthius 'to think of me in your holy prayers', for 'we believe in your citizenship in heaven'.[26]

At around the same time that groups of hermits were beginning to move into the Egyptian desert, various forms of asceticism were developing in Syria. The most distinctive of these was groups of men and women known as 'children of the covenant'.[27] These groups included 'virgins' – celibate men and women – and married couples who remained together whilst giving up sex. Both kinds of ascetic could be described by the Syriac term *ihidaya*. The basic sense of this word is 'single' or 'only': it seems to have indicated both a person's social state – single, unmarried or chaste within marriage – and his or her spiritual aim – a single-minded devotion to God. Both these senses were combined in the idea that the 'single' person was spiritually speaking wedded to Christ (or, in some texts, the Holy Spirit). Taking the traditional Christian language of Christ as bridegroom and the Church as bride, these groups envisaged that each individual in the Church as well as the Church collectively could be the bride of Christ. Eschatological perfection of human nature was described in terms of 'entering the bridal chamber'.[28] In some early Syrian traditions only those who were 'single' were thought to enter the eschatological bridal chamber. In other traditions, those who were 'single' were like the wise virgins in the parable waiting for the bridegroom: they were the wakeful ones in the community witnessing to and preparing for the future arrival of Christ. In their virgin state they foreshadowed the condition of the eschatological life in which it was thought that all people would be unmarried, like the angels.[29] The sons and daughters of the covenant seem to have made a vow to be 'single' when they were baptized as adults. Ephrem the Syrian was probably a son of the covenant and his writings beautifully demonstrate the theological ideas underlying this kind of ascetic spirituality.

Aphrahat's *Demonstrations* also provide evidence not only of this kind of Syriac ascetic theology but of the concern for discipline among the 'singles': in his day there seems to have been increasing anxiety about the dangers of male and female ascetics living together:

> Therefore, my brethren, if any man who is a monk or a saint, who loves the solitary life, yet desires that a woman, bound by monastic vow like himself, should dwell with him, it would be better for him in that case to take (as a wife) a woman openly and not be made wanton by lust. ... And also whatever man desires to continue in holiness, let not his spouse dwell with him, lest he

turn back to his former condition and be deemed an adulterer.³⁰

Later, as the influence of Egyptian asceticism began to filter into Syria in the final decades of the fourth century, the groups of 'singles' began to take on a closer similarity to Egyptian monastic communities (the above quotation from Aphrahat is evidence of a move in this direction). The asceticism described by Ephrem is best thought of as something distinct.

In Egypt itself many continued to be attracted by the semi-isolated forms of desert monasticism. As the fourth century progressed, however, several men made efforts to establish more organized and tightly knit forms of ascetic life. From this movement came a distinction between what is known in English as eremitic and cenobitic monasticism. 'Eremitic' describes the discipline of a hermit (from the Greek *eremos*, 'desert').³¹ The term 'cenobitic' describes a group living, working and worshipping together (from the Greek *koinos bios*, a 'common life'). As the practice developed, cenobitic communities were typically governed by a common rule.

To a certain extent, different traditions of asceticism grew up in different areas along the Nile. The hermit followers of Antony and Paul scattered themselves in various locations in middle Egypt. In lower Egypt, nearer the Nile delta, were found small communities of ascetics usually focused around an elder monk. From groups like these came the collections of pithy *Sayings of the Desert Fathers and Mothers*. One estimate suggests that by the 370s there were around 3,000 ascetics in the region of Nitria; by the end of the fourth century there were as many as 5,000. They gradually developed a more communal way of life, worshipping and sometimes eating together. Some monks from Nitria moved to a more remote location in Kellia, which was the community chosen by Evagrius Ponticus, one of the great theologians of the spiritual life. Another great ascetic, Macarius, settled in Scetis in lower Egypt. His form of asceticism more closely resembled a community life: there are still four monasteries to this day, one of which traces its origin directly back to him. A distinctive form of this kind of life was established in Palestine in the fourth century: each community, known as a Lavra, consisted of a number of hermits living in the same area and governed by a single abbot.

In upper Egypt, around 320, Pachomius (*c*.290–346) founded a community of monks at Tabennisi. He was said to have been inspired to convert to Christianity by the kindness of local Christians when he was stationed as a soldier in appalling conditions. He became convinced that Christian charity was best practised through the ascetic life, ideally in a community. Pachomius began by living as a hermit with his brother; by the time of his death, he was responsible for the order of nine monasteries for men and two for women – about 3,000 people in all, mostly Coptic-speaking peasants.

He devised a common rule for these communities, which survives in a Latin translation. Stricter than Pachomius' rule was that of Shenoute (died *c*.466), abbot of the 'White Monastery' in the same region. Although living conditions were harsh, Shenoute insisted on strict limits to self-denial: a letter survives in which he instructed women who under-ate that they must eat the one meal a day which was permitted to members of the community (a simple serving of bread, water and vegetables). Pachomius and Shenoute both organized communities for women: unlike Pachomius, Shenoute allowed women to lead their own monastery. Indeed, he was most insistent that women were capable of the ascetic life: 'Has the kingdom of heaven solely been prepared for men? ... The same battle has been assigned to men and women, and the same crown stands before those men and women who together will have persevered.'[32] Nevertheless, there is evidence from correspondence that the female ascetics resented Shenoute's insistence that he had ultimate authority over all the White Monastery communities.[33] In fact, the establishment of female monasteries by both Pachomius and Shenoute seems to have reflected contemporary views of women. Whereas a few women had tried a hermit existence, it was thought difficult for them to survive the rigours of the desert alone and they were constantly under scrutiny in case they caused male ascetics to fall from virtue (the accusations were nearly always that way round!). In organized communities, women could worship and pray in a disciplined life and they could be kept apart from men except in carefully supervised conditions. Shenoute was also extremely influential in Egyptian Christianity as an author, in Coptic, of works relating to the ascetic life.

Varieties of cenobitic monasticism spread from Egypt to the east and north. In Pontus, to the north-east of Asia Minor, a man called Eustathius (*c*.300–377) became a particularly influential encourager of asceticism. So enthusiastic were his followers that by 340 some of them had been condemned for extremism by a synod at Gangra in the same region. But this did not stall Eustathius' own efforts. He set up a hospice in Sebaste, the principal town of the Roman province of Armenia, where he had been ordained bishop in around 356. His influence spread as far as Constantinople, where a hospice and some monastic communities were established, apparently following his example.

As a young man in his mid-20s, Basil of Caesarea took a gap-year from his profession as rhetor, travelling to visit monasteries in Egypt, Palestine, Syria and perhaps Mesopotamia. Even if he did not travel with Eustathius as has sometimes been argued, it was almost certainly direct or indirect Eustathian influence that sparked his interest in asceticism. It was also around this time that Basil's family estate at Annesi was turned into an ascetic community. According to Basil's brother, Gregory of Nyssa, the main buildings of the family home were put to the use of a community of women, and a men's community set itself up on a remote part of the substantial family estate. Gregory reports that his eldest sister Macrina 'put herself on a level with her maids, making them her sisters and equals, rather than her slaves and underlings'.[34] They had a life of great simplicity, helping each other to provide for their basic needs and devoting most of their time to worship: 'there was constant prayer and an unceasing singing of hymns distributed throughout the entire day and night, so that this was for them both their work and their rest from work'.[35] The men's community was described as a group of old men cared for by Naucratios, a younger brother of Basil and Macrina. To begin with, it may well have been a more loose association of hermits (akin to those crystallizing around Antony) than a community worshipping together as the women did. After his tour of monasteries, Basil was baptized and probably joined the men's community in around 357. He was soon joined by Gregory of Nazianzus. Their life, although simple, must have included materials allowing them to study, for it was in this period that they produced the *Philokalia*, an edition of excerpts from Origen.

In the course of the next few years, Basil was ordained deacon and then presbyter in the congregation of Caesarea in Cappadocia, but he returned several times to Annesi, as if uncertain whether he wanted to be embroiled in the Church politics of Caesarea. A similarly uncertain vacillation characterized Gregory of Nazianzus' life in this period. In 368–69 there was a severe famine in the region. Macrina is said to have responded by taking orphans into her community. In Caesarea Basil began negotiating with rich merchants to release stockpiled grain so that he could distribute it; he was also said to have used his own wealth to provide for the starving and the sick. In 370 he was ordained Bishop of Caesarea and was soon engaged in his project of establishing the *ptochotropheion*, or 'place to feed the poor', an institution that lasted at least until the fifth century. Basil himself described the place as consisting of,

> a house of prayer built in magnificent fashion, and, grouped around it, a residence, one portion being a generous home reserved for the head of the community, and the rest subordinate quarters, all in order, for the servants of the divinity. ... Hospices for strangers, for those who visit us while on a journey, for those who require some care because of sickness ... we extend to the latter the necessary comforts, such as nurses, physicians, beasts for travelling and attendants.[36]

Gregory of Nazianzus poetically described it as 'a new city outside the city', a phrase which nicely captured the ambiguity of Basil's community: while

symbolically withdrawn from the heart of secular life by being built outside
the city walls, its inhabitants were nevertheless deeply involved with the
life of Caesarea.[37] From the descriptions, it seems clear that the institution was not only a hospital and hospice but also a community of monks.
Besides building the physical infrastructure, Basil was also involved in its
institutional organization. Two forms of his rules for a monastic community survive, dealing with all sorts of issues, ranging from the care which
an abbot owed his monks – he should tend them as a mother – to particular
questions of discipline.[38]

By this time, Basil had had a major disagreement with Eustathius over
the question of the status of the Holy Spirit (Eustathius being unwilling to
grant that it was *homoousios* with the Father and Son). The Cappadocians'
writings on asceticism were also showing a marked concern to discourage
any extremes of ascetic practice. These two factors might explain why they
never acknowledged the influence of Eustathius and why Basil's rules in
some places explicitly banned the practices which had been alleged against
the followers of Eustathius at Gangra. For example, while the Eustathians
had been accused of encouraging women to dress like men and even to shave
their heads, Basil's rule insisted that women and men should dress differently. While those at Gangra had alleged that the Eustathians encouraged
sin by allowing ascetic men and women to live together, Basil's rules forbade
this. Eustathian asceticism had a very negative view of marriage (it was
accused of claiming that married persons could not be saved). By contrast,
the Cappadocian theologians had a generally positive view of marriage:
Gregory of Nazianzus praised the ascetic lifestyle practised by his sister
Gorgonia within marriage; Gregory of Nyssa suggested that the married
ascetic was in some ways more to be praised than the celibate, and Basil's
rules forbade any married person to become an ascetic unless their partner
agreed that they could leave. The moderate tenor of Basil's rule came to
have enormous impact not only in the east, but also in the west through its
influence on the rule of Benedict.[39]

The achievements of Basil of Caesarea dominate the historical landscape
in this period and his importance both in theology and the history of monasticism cannot be denied. Yet it is clear that he – like Antony, Pachomius,
Shenoute and Eustathius – was developing and adapting forms of asceticism
which were already in existence. Basil's family was influenced by Eustathian monasticism, and it may well have been Basil's siblings, Macrina and
Naucratios, who were the first in their family to take active steps towards
asceticism. Gregory suggests that Macrina became a dedicated virgin at the
age when young girls would normally be expected to marry and he claims
that when Basil returned from Athens 'excessively puffed up by his rhetori-

cal abilities and disdainful of all great reputations', it was Macrina who 'took him over and lured him to the goal of philosophy' (*philosophia* was the term typically used to denote the ascetic life).[40] More important than the question of which individual was responsible for Cappadocian monasticism is what the history of this remarkable family teaches us. First, their adoption of asceticism came by incremental steps: Macrina dedicating herself a virgin; Naucratios living as a hermit and (perhaps after a while) caring for a small group of 'old men'; Macrina and Emmelia turning the house into a female community; Basil and Gregory of Nazianzus joining the men's community; Basil forming a further community or communities. This kind of development was presumably typical of the growth of ascetic movements throughout the Empire and beyond and it is artificial to ask when any of the groups 'became' a monastery.

Secondly, even if her brother Gregory exaggerated it, Macrina's influence was very strong. In being a woman in this role she was notable, but not unique. From the pen of Jerome, writing a generation later, we learn of other remarkable women, also well educated and wealthy, who became increasingly interested in asceticism and eventually founded their own monasteries. Melania the elder, a wealthy woman from Rome, was widowed at the age of 22; she left her home to visit the holy men of Egypt, later moved to Palestine and was the leader of a community of about 50 women on the Mount of Olives by 378 (that is, shortly before the time of Basil of Caesarea's death). In Egypt she met Rufinus (a friend of Jerome), who a few years later also founded a monastery in Jerusalem. Jerome himself had had a couple of attempts at dedicating himself to an ascetic life in different contexts, first, in an informal ascetic community established by a friend in Aquileia, north Italy, next living as a hermit in Syria. The latter period in the 370s was ultimately an unhappy experience for Jerome: despite his clearly sincere desire for a very austere regime, he found the life of a solitary ascetic very difficult to square with his passion for scholarship, in particular his study of the Bible. Although he claimed to have supported himself in the desert by his own labour, he also had with him the equipment for study – not just his library but also assistants to enable him to copy books! (As his modern biographer dryly comments, 'his cave must have been roomier than most'.)[41] He was in constant contact with his friend Evagrius, a priest in Antioch, but, although he learnt a little Syriac, he could communicate very little with his fellow hermits. When he did, it became clear they disagreed strongly on basic issues, such as the doctrine of the Trinity. These factors increasingly caused tensions between Jerome and his neighbours and he left. Jerome never lost his enthusiasm for asceticism in general, but the episode in Syria is a useful reminder that that particular kind of ascetic life did not suit everyone, however great their initial desire for it.

In the early 380s Jerome stayed in Rome, and he became sought out for his scholarship and views on the ascetic life, in particular by a group of wealthy Roman women. The widow Marcella had converted to a life of austere simplicity, apparently after reading the *Life of Antony*. She had turned her house into a meeting place in which she taught Christian women about asceticism, among them the young widow Paula and her daughter Eustochium. Jerome encouraged these women in a particularly austere form of ascetic life which they carried out in their own homes. In a famous letter to Eustochium he attacks the evils of marriage and advises a very rigorous regime of prayer and fasting. Furthermore, Eustochium was to keep to her own room, avoiding the company of non-ascetic women, lest they should awaken a concern with her own appearance or other frivolities.[42] Eventually, Jerome, Paula and Eustochium left Rome to visit first the Egyptian ascetic communities and then the pilgrimage sites in the Holy Land. In the late 380s, Jerome, Paula and her daughter settled in Bethlehem where the women used their considerable wealth to found institutions for both men and women, together with accommodation for pilgrims. All three remained there until they died.[43]

Although this account demonstrates some similarities between Basil's circle and that of Jerome – notably the influence of wealthy, well-educated women – it also points to important contrasts. The particularly harsh ascetic practices of the men and women from Rome, their desire to be almost completely separated from the rest of the Christian community, together with their travels abroad, indicate that their primary influence was the very austere, withdrawn pattern of Egyptian monasticism. Jerome's advice to his female correspondents had a very different tone to the advice to ascetics given by Basil or Gregory of Nyssa. In particular, Jerome's writing was characterized by a strong fear of human sexuality, which closely echoed the vivid accounts of the Egyptian desert fathers' temptations in the wilderness. This was very different from the Cappadocians, who, whilst advocating sexual restraint, even (under certain conditions) within marriage, never appear to have regarded sexual temptation with the horror that Jerome did.

A second interesting point of contrast with Cappadocian asceticism is the way in which the Latin ascetics chose to found monasteries in the Holy Land. Cappadocian (and indeed Eustathian) monasticism had founded ascetic communities locally, Basil's family probably being typical in initially using its own land and buildings to do so. In travelling to the Holy Land, the western ascetics were not only following the increasing contemporary interest in pilgrimage to the sites of Jesus' birth, life and death; they were also imitating the desert ascetics' desire to leave civilization in order to live on the boundaries of the wilderness. It was a very dramatic step for wealthy aristocratic widows like Melania and Paula to leave Rome, the great, historic, civilized imperial capital (albeit one which was now somewhat in decline) and use their wealth to establish ascetic communities in Palestine on the edge of the Roman Empire, a region for centuries considered by Romans a cultural backwater. In this move, and in the character of their asceticism as a whole, these men and women were not only witness to the way in which Christianity could lead – *should* lead – to a new and radical way of life, but they were also deliberately setting themselves in contrast with the rank and file of 'normal Christians', the non-ascetic women, for example, whom Jerome forbade Eustochium to meet. In the era after persecution, these ascetics seem to be protesting against the way in which Christianity had become socially acceptable. Asceticism was their way of demonstrating in a visible and tangible way what they thought truly lay at the heart of the Christian life.

While these Latin ascetics' actions were dramatic, their form of piety was not, however, so spectacular as that developing in a similar period further east. Out of the monasteries that had developed there under the influence of Egyptian monasticism emerged a habit of extreme mortification of the flesh. As if the standard regimes were not harsh enough, individual monks would challenge themselves with more and more bizarre trials. The most famous of these was Simeon, a native of north Syria.[44] At first thrown out of his own monastery for extremism, then travelling from monastery to monastery, Simeon later sought out more remote places for his ascetic practices. At one point he chose to live in a water cistern.[45] Despite their remote locations, his ascetic feats attracted attention: pilgrims apparently flocked to him, eager to gain a blessing from touching him. Eventually, he built himself a pillar which – according to his biographer Theodoret – was intended to remove him from the crowds. If that really was his motivation, Simeon had seriously miscalculated. Living on top of a pillar merely intensified his mystique and, despite raising his pillar three more times until it reached a height of about 30 feet, Simeon was bothered by increasing numbers of visitors. He attracted the rich and poor, emperors and beggars; according to Theodoret they travelled from all over the Empire and beyond: Persians, Medes, Ethiopians, Scythians, Arabs, Armenians, Iberians, Spaniards, Britons and Gauls. Simeon's impact echoed that of the first Egyptian desert fathers a century earlier. His visitors did not come simply to gawp; they came for advice on a surprisingly varied range of topics, not only about the ascetic life but also about childlessness, the appropriate rate of interest, and weights and measures. Like the Egyptian desert fathers, Simeon performed the role of the holy man on the edge of a community, who was sought out to solve problems which threatened the peace of families and the village – although admittedly in a rather more bizarre location. Like the desert fathers, he occupied a boundary place between civilization and the desert, a boundary place in his case symbolized dramatically by his eyrie between earth and heaven. He seemed to be raised up to heaven in a symbolic foreshadowing of his hoped-for destiny. How could he fail not to be sought out as a special mediator of the divine? Indeed, in his case, the parallel between holy men and the martyrs became particularly clear. During his lifetime, his pillar became an important pilgrimage site, and the visitors continued in vast numbers after his death. Pilgrims could buy badges to prove they had been there; statuettes of him and his pillar were sold both there and abroad.[46]

Simeon's story reminds us of several important aspects of Christian piety in the fourth century and beyond. The phenomenon of asceticism did not just involve the heroes themselves. The success of the ascetics lay not merely in their personal qualities – their strength of character, convictions, genuine piety, their intelligence and ability to communicate – it also lay in the eagerness of the general population to receive what they had to offer. Simeon and the other holy men and women often dealt with Christians' problems in a very personal, direct and down-to-earth way. Despite their geographic location outside the city, their advice and prayers bound them closely with the communities who sought them out.

Next, the lives of Simeon and the western ascetics highlight the increasing importance of pilgrimage in this period. Local communities had long venerated their own saints and martyrs, and often elaborate festivals were celebrated at their shrines.[47] Increasingly, however, Christians travelled as pilgrims to sites associated with saints with whom they felt a particular connection: the supposed burial place of Thecla at Meriemlik was a very popular destination, and not just among women and simpler Christians.[48] In a parallel movement, pilgrims also flocked to the Holy Land, reacting to the physical encounter with the places where Jesus had lived and died in a very similar way to how devotees venerated the relics of martyrs. Encouraged by the building projects of Constantine, but also fuelled by a huge popular fascination for seeing the sites with their own eyes, pilgrimage was undertaken even by those with no intention of becoming an ascetic, and increasingly required the provision of hostels and guides. A glimpse of this enthusiasm – and the distances some pilgrims travelled – can be grasped through reading the account of Egeria, a fourth-century pilgrim to Palestine, Egypt and Syria.[49] So popular did pilgrimage become, in fact, that some fathers felt compelled to warn against its dangers: Gregory of Nyssa wrote a famously grumpy letter complaining about the crowds, noise and crime of Jerusalem and warning of the dangers of allowing female and male ascetics to travel together.[50] However, this letter is no more to be taken as a ban on pilgrimage than Basil's warnings about certain monks' behaviour is to be taken as a ban on monasticism.

Despite its language of withdrawal from the world, the history of Christian asceticism in this period is in fact a story about the different ways in which Christians were grappling with living in the world. This is revealed on one level in varying practices to do with food, drink and sex; it is apparent at another level in the development of the role of the ascetic as bishop. While this position might seem to involve two incompatible roles – and indeed the bishops themselves were deeply aware of the tensions – this role became of increasing importance in cities throughout the Empire. This fact testifies not only to the characters of the men involved but to the way in which an ascetic vocation was seen to invest a bishop with a particular spiritual authority. Even if asceticism had been intended by some of its practitioners as a counter-cultural rebellion against compromise with the world, it was not long before ascetics were employed in the heart of the Church, actively engaged in politics, both ecclesiastical and imperial.

For example, Basil of Caesarea showed himself very adept at dealing with Emperor Valens, who was sympathetic to the homoian cause. Valens benefited from Basil's support of his strategy of strengthening the Empire's position in Armenia through the Christian Church, while in return Basil benefited from the re-division of the province of Cappadocia: since ecclesiastical boundaries typically followed Roman administrative ones, Basil filled the newly created vacancies with bishops sympathetic to his own theology.

In the west, around the same time, Ambrose was Bishop of Milan (from 374 to 397). Born in Trier, educated in Rome and with a good position as governor of Liguria and Aemilia in northern Italy, Ambrose found himself chosen bishop by popular consent, when he appeared on the scene to calm tensions over a disputed episcopal succession. One of the contentious issues was Arianism, a form of which was still strong in north Italy, not least owing to the presence of the imperial court in Milan – the Emperor Valentinian II in particular was an advocate of the term *homoios* to describe the Son's relationship to the Father (he was merely 'like' the Father). In this context, Ambrose showed himself a brave defender of pro-Nicene Christianity even against emperors. On one famous occasion the Emperor Valentinian II (probably encouraged by his even more enthusiastically Arian mother Justina) demanded from the Milanese Christians the use of one of their major churches as an imperial – and thus Arian – place of worship. Ambrose refused. The next year, 386, Valentinian issued a decree formally declaring that Arians had the right to worship freely and then attempted to take the church he had demanded use of the year before. Again Ambrose did not give way: the story as recounted by Augustine was that the pro-Nicene congregation kept up their spirits by chanting hymns.[51] (This was supposedly the beginning of the hymn tradition in the west.) In the end – after his mother died – Valentinian even asked to be baptized by Ambrose.

In the last few years of Valentinian's reign, Ambrose developed a role as negotiator with the emperors on behalf of the Christian communities. For example, he was implacably opposed to the renewal of state subsidies for paganism and he successfully negotiated with both Valentinian II and his co-emperor in the east, Theodosius, on the issue. Despite repeated pleas from the Roman senate for such subsidies, the emperors refused and in fact issued a joint decree in 391 banning pagan rites. Less admirably, Ambrose persuaded Emperor Theodosius to treat lightly a bishop of a town near the Euphrates whose congregation burnt down a local synagogue, and some Christians near Antioch who had destroyed a Valentinian place of worship. In 390, however, Ambrose exerted his authority as a Christian bishop further than this ambassadorial role. Emperor Theodosius provoked horror among many in the Empire when he punished a riot in Thessaloniki with the massacre of about 7,000 of the town's citizens. Ambrose's response to this was to excommunicate the emperor. Even though Theodosius was welcomed back into communion by Ambrose the next year, it was still a bold move.

Although Ambrose was not a member of an ascetic community, so not strictly speaking a monk, his sister had been a dedicated virgin since he was a young boy and Ambrose himself was a vociferous defender of Christian asceticism throughout his life. When he was chosen to be bishop of Milan, one reason for his reluctance to accept was, according to his biographer Paulinus, a desire 'to become a philosopher' – that is, to live a life of withdrawal, prayer and study. The implication is that he would have to give that up in order to become a bishop. Nevertheless Augustine later described him as taking the opportunity of a pause in his day to read (silently – a practice which astonished others) and thus to 'refresh his mind'.[52] In fact, Paulinus argued, in becoming a bishop Ambrose became 'Christ's true philosopher': a nice way of expressing the way in which the Christian 'philosophy' quickly adapted itself to the 'secular' life.

Different bishops reacted to the tensions between ascetic withdrawal and political engagement in different ways. After their initial struggles, both Basil and Ambrose seem to have come to terms with the dual role very well. Basil's close friend, Gregory of Nazianzus, however, seems to have been tormented all his life by the competing claims of responsibility to his role as priest, then bishop, and of ascetic retreat. The height of influence came with the preaching of his five Theological Orations to the pro-Nicene congregation in Constantinople and his election as bishop there in 380. Only a few months later he had been deposed – at the very Council of Constantinople that acknowledged the truth of his theology – and he retired in despair at the arguments of bishops who squabbled like jackdaws or angry teenagers.[53]

To some extent, these anxieties reflected the concerns of earlier pagan generations who had been forced to square the circle between a life of philosophical retreat and political engagement. Christian bishops were not slow to use the same language of *praxis* and *theoria* (action and contemplation) for their own dilemmas. But the Christian struggles were given a different colour because of the theology that lay behind them. Many classical Greek or Roman philosophers could have expressed their problems as a choice *between* philosophy and the world, or *between* the soul and the body, eventually hoping that they would be released both from the world and from materiality. Because of the doctrines of creation and incarnation, however, Christian theologians were committed to a belief in the goodness of the world and the possibility – through grace – of living in it well. Although they often expressed their troubles as a tension between the material and the immaterial, in fact what was at stake was not a choice between the two but a decision as to how to live with both healthily.

CHAPTER 8

God and Humankind in Western Theology: Ambrose and Augustine
(FOURTH TO FIFTH CENTURIES)

Ambrose was right at the centre of things in his bishopric in Milan and this was because Milan was right at the centre of the changes in the political geography of the Empire in the west. Rome had gradually lost importance as the hub of the Empire as, first, Constantinople assumed more and more influence and, second, the attention of emperors was drawn ever more insistently out to the borders of the Empire. Successive emperors used Milan as a base, so that by the time Ambrose became governor of Aemilia and Liguria around 372 there was a fairly well-established imperial court there.[1] Some time before 355 there had been constructed in Milan the 'new basilica', a huge structure with a wide central nave and two aisles on each side, which could hold a congregation of some 3,000. At 80 by 40 metres it is the largest known church in north Italy of that era and comes close in size to Constantine's Lateran Basilica in Rome.[2]

As the last chapter suggested, relations among Christians in Milan were complicated by different loyalties arising from the Arian controversies – a situation which was complicated by the influence of the court. In the 350s Constantius II presided over the whole Empire and, in the hope that he could unite the divided Christian communities under one creed, he actively promoted the cause of the *homoians* – those Christians who thought that one should describe the Son as like (*homoios*) the Father. Constantius had an active role in the removal in 355 of the pro-Nicene Bishop Dionysius of Milan, who was exiled to Armenia and replaced by the 'Arian' Bishop Auxentius. Auxentius held his post until his death in 374, during which time imperial policy had tended to be relatively even-handed towards both Christian parties, regardless of the personal persuasion of the emperors.

In particular, Auxentius enjoyed the support of Valentinian I, much to the annoyance of the pro-Nicene Damasus, Bishop of Rome.[3] Despite Auxentius' long tenure of office, however, there clearly was a significant community of pro-Nicene Christians in Milan which led to the disputed succession upon Auxentius' death. When Ambrose showed his concern to keep the peace in Milan, the crowd may have demanded him because they thought that he, like the Emperor Valentinian, would maintain a neutral position on the question of *homoios* vs *homoousios*.[4]

However, Bishop Ambrose quickly revealed his true colours, taking various steps to strengthen the pro-Nicene cause in Milan and the north of Italy. Although Hilary of Poitiers had argued tirelessly for the Nicene formula, he lacked widespread influence. By contrast, as Bishop of Milan, Ambrose was in a better position to make a difference. First, he was involved with a series of synods in Italy which endorsed the pro-Nicene viewpoint and those bishops which held it.[5] In particular, he attended a synod at Rome in 382 which was intended to be a western equivalent of the Council of Constantinople the year before (which had been attended by relatively few western bishops).

It is important to be clear about what one means by 'Arianism' in this context. Auxentius in fact denounced Arius himself,[6] and he certainly did not advocate the idea that the Son was unlike (*anomoios*) the Father (as Eunomius and his anomoian followers did). Nevertheless, history, with the lack of precise labelling that is usually the lot of heretics, has tended to label Hilary's and Ambrose's opponents in Italy as 'Arians'. This is due not least to the rhetoric of pro-Nicene writers of the time: Hilary, for example, has a clear tendency to label as 'Arian' anyone who disagreed with his formulation of the doctrine of the Trinity.[7]

It was in this theological and political context that, a couple of years after the Synod of Rome, a young man from North Africa arrived in Milan to take up a post as public orator. He was later to credit the experience of hearing Ambrose preach as one of the turning points in his road to conversion to Christianity. Aurelius Augustinus, known to us as Augustine of Hippo, had been born 30 years earlier to a pagan father and a Christian mother in the town of Thagaste in North Africa. After a thorough education, he had begun to teach rhetoric first in his home town and then in Carthage. Obviously a talented and ambitious young man, he had left Africa to teach in Rome, where he had impressed the pagan senator and prefect of Rome, Symmachus, who recommended him for the appointment in Milan.

While his career path had been relatively smooth, Augustine's spiritual travels had been much more complicated. He implied that his mother, Monica, had taught him the rudiments of the faith (as was common practice for the women in Christian families).[8] Yet he had not been baptized as an infant, and Augustine suggested that it was not a living faith for him in his youth. In his *Confessions*, he relates various tumultuous episodes of his early life:

> I came to Carthage and all around me hissed a cauldron of illicit loves. ... I was in love with love. ... I was captivated by theatrical shows. They were full of representations of my own miseries and fuelled my fire.[9]

He became involved with a group of youths, who, whilst proclaiming their urbane sophistication, took delight in vandalism. Augustine longed to be accepted by his peers, yet was appalled by their behaviour: 'I lived among them shamelessly ashamed of not being one of the gang. I kept company with them ... though I always held their actions in abhorrence.'[10]

Although these are perhaps not particularly remarkable exploits for any young man, the public exposure of his faults in a work written many years later when Augustine was a recently ordained bishop is at first sight more surprising. Yet a careful reading reveals the purpose of Augustine's self-exposure. The *Confessions* is one of the world's great works of literature: combining biography, theology and philosophy, Augustine leads his reader through an account of his life and way to faith in a way which is intended not just to persuade intellectually but also to turn (or 'convert') his reader towards God, through sharing in Augustine's two-fold confession: the confession of his former way of life and his confession of faith in and love of God.

The artful construction of the work might lead one to doubt it as a historical source, yet there is no reason fundamentally to doubt the basic narrative of Augustine's early life as he presents it. Particularly interesting for a study of this period are his reflections about the various influences on his intellectual and spiritual journey. An early influence was classical philosophy, especially various forms of Platonism. Augustine recounts reading Cicero's *Hortensius*, which asks what the sources of happiness are and recommends philosophy as a way of finding out. In the *Confessions*, Augustine quotes Cicero's words, 'do not study one particular sect but love and seek and pursue and hold fast and strongly embrace wisdom itself, wherever found' – words which set him on his search for wisdom over the next years.[11] The *Hortensius* (in standard Platonic fashion) warned that in such a search one should always choose what is really beautiful over that which merely seems so. Ironically, it was in this period that Augustine's reading of Scripture seems to have convinced him that the lack of beauty in the Bible's written style was an obstacle to Christian faith:

> [I found it] a text lowly to the beginner, but on further reading, of mountainous

difficulty and enveloped in mysteries. ... It seemed unworthy in comparison
with the dignity of Cicero. My inflated conceit shunned the Bible's restraint,
and my gaze never penetrated to its inwardness. Yet the Bible was composed
in such a way that as beginners mature, its meaning grows with them. I
disclaimed to be a little beginner. Puffed up with pride, I considered myself
a mature adult.[12]

Also around about this time, when he was aged about 18, Augustine
became involved with the Manichees. By the mid-fourth century, the influence of Mani's teachings had spread all around the Mediterranean. Augustine seems to have been attracted to them for several reasons: first, their
exposition of the Christian Bible matched Augustine's own judgement;
second, the faith's bookishness and regard for eloquence appealed to the
young Augustine's intellectual snobbery; third, their rigid moral code with
its strict vegetarian diet, teetotalism and rejection of sex (at least for the elite
ranks) seemed to give him the structure and discipline he craved after his
years of – as he saw it – excessive freedom.

The other enormous influence on Augustine's life was Latin literature.
Although he claims not to have learnt well at school (supposedly being
distracted by 'ball games'), in fact the beatings he mentions were normal
for any schoolboy in this period. A more honest confession, perhaps, is his
great love of the Latin classics, especially Virgil's *Aeneid*. Book IV of this
epic describes how its hero Aeneas spent some time in Carthage enamoured
of Queen Dido, before leaving again for Italy, driven on by the gods to fulfil
his – and Rome's – destiny. It is not too fanciful to imagine that Augustine
both felt a deep sympathy with Aeneas as a character – passionate, but driven
by a profound sense of vocation – and constructed the *Confessions* partly to
echo the themes and structures of the *Aeneid*. (For example, the passage in
Book V where Augustine leaves Africa having deceived his mother as to his
departure deliberately echoes Aeneas' leave-taking of Dido.)

By contrast, Augustine had an ambivalent attitude to Greek literature
all his life. At school, he wrote, he hated learning it; later on, he claimed
that he was hardly proficient in it. The scholarly consensus now is that
Augustine knew more Greek literature (of both pagan and Christian varieties) than he admitted to. Although he rarely mentions sources by name, he
seems to have been aware of the writings of Philo, Origen, Basil of Caesarea and Gregory of Nyssa.[13] Some if not all of these he would have read in
Latin translations or indirectly through their being quoted or adapted by
Latin theologians; nevertheless, it seems that he was aware at the very least
of Greek theological terminology and – probably – of some Greek texts.

Ambrose, of course, had had a similar literary and rhetorical training a
generation earlier, and his preaching was famed for its polished and elegant

style. By the time he arrived in Milan, Augustine had tired intellectually of the Manichees: he had continued to read the philosophers and considered their systems of cosmology and astronomy far more convincing than those of Mani. Furthermore, he thought that the Manichees' negative biblical criticism and their verbal eloquence were distractions which masked a basic vacuum in their thought. This realization is encapsulated in Augustine's encounter with Faustus, the leading thinker of the Manichees. By this time, Augustine asserts, 'I was interested not in the decoration of the vessel in which his discourse was served up, but in the knowledge put before me to eat. ... What could this most presentable waiter do for my thirst by offering precious cups?'[14] By contrast, he was deeply impressed with Ambrose's preaching:

> I used enthusiastically to listen to him [Ambrose] preaching to the people, not with the intention which I ought to have had, but as if testing out his oratorical skill to see whether it merited the reputation it enjoyed or whether his fluency was better or inferior than it was reported to be. I hung on his diction in rapt attention, but remained bored and contemptuous of the subject-matter. My pleasure was in the charm of his language. It was more learned than that of Faustus, but less witty and entertaining, as far as the manner of his speaking went. But in content there could be no comparison. Through Manichee deceits Faustus wandered astray. Ambrose taught the sound doctrine of salvation. From sinners such as I was at that time, salvation is far distant. Nevertheless, gradually, though I did not realise it, I was drawing closer.[15]

It was in this period that Augustine had returned to reading 'Platonic books'.[16] In the passage quoted above he is playing with the Platonic idea of true beauty and apparent beauty: while Faustus' words had only the latter, Ambrose's sermons were both externally beautiful and pointed Augustine to an inner beauty. Through their use of allegorical interpretation, Ambrose's sermons even helped Augustine on the way to discovering the beauty hidden in the rather plain or crude style of the Bible.

Within a short space of time Augustine had retreated to a villa outside Milan to read and discuss Christianity with his friends. Even in that retreat, however, his progress was not without a struggle: he presents himself as both willing and unwilling to take the final step towards a final conversion. Famously, in the *Confessions* he records his prayer:

> But I was an unhappy young man, wretched as at the beginning of my adolescence when I prayed to you for chastity and said: 'Grant me chastity and continence but not yet.'[17]

It is easy to respond to this on the human level with a knowing (or sarcastic) smile: the structure of Augustine's writing calculated on a sympath human response. But behind this prayer lies a very important point – that for Augustine conversion to Christianity in effect meant conversion to an *ascetic* Christian life. There was no logical reason why this should be so – Augustine could have converted, been baptized and carried on his life in rhetoric or another profession.[18] But for the Augustine who sat in the garden of Cassiacum reading Scripture, the choice was all or nothing: either become a Christian and commit to an ascetic life or do not become a Christian at all.

Augustine chose, and on being baptized in Milan left Italy in 388 with the intention of forming a small monastic community back in Thagaste, with the two friends who had been converted with him. He was successful in this intention for a few years – the monastic Rule attributed to him may date from the experience of this period; but by 391 his talents had been recognized and he was called to the priesthood at the town of Hippo, of which he later became bishop in 395. Like Ambrose, he appears to have been a not entirely willing agent in his ordination. And like Ambrose he proved himself to excel in the vocation.

It is impossible to give a fully rounded picture of a thinker who produced so many writings and whose thought is so complex. Here, it will suffice merely to approach his theology from five different perspectives: Scripture, the doctrine of the Trinity, his concept of the Church, his theology of grace and his idea of salvation-history. These themes will introduce some of Augustine's most important works and will contextualize his thought in the most pressing controversies and crises of the day.

As we have seen, Augustine structured his conversion narrative in the *Confessions* partly around the issue of biblical exegesis. As a young adult, he was put off by a text which was both unscholarly in tone (suggesting its simplicity) and at the same time profoundly puzzling (showing its complexity). How could a text be both childish and opaque? The Manichees interpreted the Old Testament in an over-literal way, mainly with the aim of dismissing it, much like Marcion had done. For a while this tactic attracted Augustine, but when he tired of the Manichees he still had no method of solving his problem with reading Scripture. Ambrose's preaching seemed to offer a solution. Ambrose's method of exegesis followed a broadly Origenistic method, in which some (but by no means all) passages in Scripture were read allegorically in order to prevent a fundamental misunderstanding of the main point of the text. The Manichees objected in particular to the creation account in Genesis, which seemed to them to imply that God had a material, anthropomorphic shape: he was said to walk in the garden and humans were said to be created in his image. Ambrose's sermons on

Genesis, on the other hand, rejected such interpretations.

The text of Genesis continued to fascinate Augustine throughout his life, and after his baptism in Milan he produced no fewer than three commentaries on it, which provide us with a unique insight into the development of his exegesis. In the first, *On Genesis against the Manichees*, he was obviously most keen to dismiss the Manichees' over-literal interpretation of the Bible. Thus he launched a vociferous attack on the idea that Christians believe that human beings are created in the image of God with respect to their physical make-up. He also complained that the Manichees used the first verse of Genesis, 'In the beginning [when] God created the heavens and the earth', to ask inappropriate questions about what God was doing 'before' he created – another example of anthropomorphism, which did not reckon with the fact that, as creator, God transcended time. This commentary is divided into interpretations which are labelled 'historical' (*secundum historiam*) and 'prophetic' (*secundum prophetiam*). These do *not* map neatly to the modern distinction between literal and non-literal interpretation. For example, one of the *historical* interpretations put forward by Augustine was that the first verse, which declared that God created the world 'in the beginning', meant that God created the world 'in Christ' – an interpretation reached by reading Genesis 1.1 alongside John 1.1 in a manner which most modern exegetes would not recognize as a 'literal' reading. The literal reading for Augustine seems to have meant the basic, true meaning of the text – in many cases, what really happened. In this commentary Augustine thought that 'in the beginning' truly meant 'in Christ', because a non-literal reading of 'in the beginning' would suggest that there was a pre-God. The 'prophetic' meaning, on the other hand, concerned the application either to the life of the believer or to salvation-history as a whole. Thus he interpreted the six days of creation as meaning the six ages of world history or the six stages in a believer's progress in faith. The first, for example, indicated the infancy of the human race (the period from Adam to Noah) or the initial stages of faith when Christians 'begin believing visible things'. Regarding the seventh day, the meaning for history and for the individual coincided, for it referred to the eschaton when the faithful will take their rest with Christ. This kind of exegesis in *On Genesis against the Manichees* used an allegorical technique which was derived from the writings of Ambrose, the Cappadocians and of Origen

In the two later commentaries on Genesis, Augustine was much more cautious about such allegorical interpretation – a point which is indicated by the fact that they are both entitled as commentaries 'according to the letter' (*ad litteram*). The first of these (which was left unfinished when Augustine got to Genesis 1.26) commented that the six days of creation were not days in the ordinary sense. But Augustine saw this as a clarification of the *historical* sense of the text (a warning against over-literal interpretation of the word 'day'), and he offered no additional prophetic meanings of the six days as in his work against the Manichees.[19] In the later *Literal Meaning of Genesis* Augustine explained that it was appropriate for the author to say that the world was created in six days, because six is a perfect number.[20] Again, there were no further meanings offered.

Thus there is a clear sense that in these two works Augustine was shying away from prophetic meanings or allegorical readings of the text of Genesis. However, this did not mean that every phrase or word (like 'day') should be read absolutely literally. Nor did it mean that Augustine rejected Christo- logical interpretation of the text. In his *Literal Meaning of Genesis*, Augus- tine offered multiple suggestions for what 'in the beginning' might mean, but he was *more* insistent than before that Genesis 1 should be interpreted as referring not only to Christ but to the Spirit. The words 'a wind from God swept over the face of the water' refer to the Holy Spirit and thus, Augus- tine asserted, readers 'recognize the complete indication of the Trinity'.[21] In such readings as these, Christological, pneumatological and Trinitarian readings of the Old Testament are affirmed throughout Augustine's theol- ogy and, crucially, are affirmed as *historical* readings of the biblical text.

In his work *On Christian Teaching* (which was begun shortly before the *Confessions*) Augustine aimed to provide the reader with certain guidelines on how to read the Bible.[22] In this, he wrote at the end of the preface, he hoped to be like a teacher: a good teacher does not just tell children about the content of a book but teaches them the alphabet so that they can read it for themselves.[23] This is an interesting variation on the theme expressed in the *Confessions* that to a certain extent one needs to be child-like to read Scripture − not in the sense that one should be naive or credulous but in the sense that one should be humble enough to accept that one needs to learn how to read it without impiety.[24] Having said that, however, Augus- tine was always quite clear that even the most simple believer could grasp enough from Scripture. Scripture, he wrote, was like a body of water, whose surface shines to attract the 'simple' person but whose depths attract the more thoughtful reader:

> What wonderful profundity there is in your utterances! The surface meaning lies open before us and charms beginners. Yet the depth is amazing, my God the depth is amazing.[25]

In order to explain *how* Scripture can have such depth, Augustine uses the notion of signs (or symbols). Words are signs, but objects can themselves be signs (as an engagement ring is a sign of a promise to marry). In spoken c written language, of course, it is often the case that words refer to objects which refer to other things. Thus a complex web of signs is built up. In *On Christian Teaching*, Augustine argued that Scripture was just such a web of signs and that the complexity of that web led to the profundity of the text.

As we have just seen, Augustine was increasingly cautious about the use of allegorical interpretation in his commentaries. His theory of signs seems to have been developed first as a challenge to Origen's (overly allegorical) way of reading the Bible, but also as a method which allowed readers to avoid an overly literal reading of the text. Origen, as argued in Chapter 4, attributed three different levels of meaning to Scripture. While he agreed with Augustine that even the most simple believer could learn enough for their salvation from reading (or, more likely, hearing) Scripture, his notion of levels of meaning tended to suggest that such readers only grasped one level of meaning and failed to grasp the rest. It is hard not to make this sound elitist. For Augustine, however, it was not really the case that a word or phrase had different levels of meaning: rather, a word (e.g. 'lamb') signified an object (a young sheep), and that object signified something else (Jesus Christ). There was a sense then that the word 'lamb' *contained* the other significations within it, and that the reader/hearer who understood that the word 'lamb' signified a young sheep *potentially* grasped the possibility that the animal signified something else, even though the reader/hearer might not have yet made that connection. To use a rather crude analogy: on one reading of his exegesis, the meanings of Scripture for Origen might be seen as related but separate objects that one is encouraged to 'collect'. For example, the levels of meaning could be compared to three chairs: the first is the bare essential, necessary but plain; the second is more comfortable, practically and elegantly constructed for its purpose; the third is a more luxurious designer chair, built of the best materials by a master craftsman, satisfying both in terms of comfort and beauty. Despite the fact that Origen consistently argued that one needed to keep all three levels of meaning together, there is the constant danger that his theology suggests that once one has the third level of meaning, the other two are unnecessary. For Augustine, on the other hand, the multiple meanings were like a series of Russian dolls packed one inside the other: one might possess one doll without realizing that others are inside, but in possessing the one, one in fact has all the others in one's hands without realizing it.[26]

This theory might seem rather strange until it is placed next to Augustine's notion of sacraments, which also relies on an understanding of signs. A sacrament is the outward, tangible sign of an inward spiritual gift, in the same way that the visible or audible word 'lamb' signifies an animal (even if the animal is not present). Augustine believed that the sacraments of baptism and Eucharist worked not because of some power of the person administering them, nor because of the virtues of the person receiving them. Instead they had their effect by virtue only of God choosing them to be signs of his saving grace. Furthermore, for Augustine, the bread and wine of the Eucharist did not just *point towards* or *remind one of* the body and blood of Jesus Christ; rather they *contained* the body and blood of Jesus Christ within them.[27]

This understanding of the sacraments was crucial in his debates with the Donatists. The Donatist Church had not just survived but thrived in Africa from the time of the schism in the bishopric of Cyprian of Carthage.[28] In Augustine's time, it still had a claim to be the major church in North Africa, even though it was repudiated as schismatic by Augustine's church – the Catholic ('whole', 'universal') church. Augustine wrote several treatises regarding the Donatists, but at the heart of them was his understanding that they and he understood 'Church' to mean two completely different things. The Donatists traced their origins back to the church of the martyrs in North Africa, and despite the Constantinian change, they still tended to see the Church as fundamentally opposed to the 'world': the Church was an ark rescuing the pure from the stormy and corrupt seas of the world. Augustine had an entirely more realistic notion of human nature and a very much more nuanced picture of the members of the Church: it contained both saints and sinners. One could not even say that the clergy were pure; but this did not threaten the efficacy of the sacraments, for they did not depend on the holiness of the one who administered them but on God's grace.

Shortly after writing the *Confessions*, Augustine began work on the huge treatise *On the Trinity*, which was completed after 20 years' work in 419. The work has two interlinked aims. The first, as Augustine puts it in his introduction, is to give *reasons*: 'to account for the one and only true God being a trinity, and for the rightness of saying, believing, understanding that the Father and Son and Holy Spirit are of one and the same substance or essence'.[29] Even after the affirmation of the Nicene formula at Constantinople in 381 and Rome in 382, it was no mere academic matter to give such an account. Ambrose's struggles with Arians at the Milanese court in the mid-380s were enough to show that Arianism (or, more precisely, support for the *homoios* formula) was not dead. But in the period in which Augustine was writing, the stakes had got even higher. The Empire was being threatened by various tribes who had previously been restricted to territories east of the Rhine and north of the Danube. Two of the most important of these, the Vandals and the Visigoths, were Arian. For centuries Romans had boasted of the contrast between, on the one hand, the civilized, strong

Empire under the rule of law and protected by its gods and, on the other, the wild barbarians, divided into many warring tribes, lawless adherents of mysterious and primitive religions. Such a clear contrast was of course largely fictional, but its language was imported by Catholic Christians as they contrasted themselves as citizens of a Christian empire with the Arian tribes who were threatening the stability of the Empire on several sides. The Vandals did not invade North Africa until 428, shortly before Augustine's death and a decade after *On the Trinity* had been completed. Nevertheless, signs of the future threat were present: in 406 there was a huge influx of Germanic tribes into the Empire over the Rhine. Over the next few years they gained power over substantial territory in Gaul and Spain. Famously, Alaric the Visigoth sacked Rome in 410; although his armies retreated with their plunder, the event sent shock-waves through the Empire.

A defence of the Trinity against Arianism was not, therefore, just an academic point. But there was a second purpose to *On the Trinity*: like the *Confessions* it is carefully constructed in a way which suggests that Augustine intended its reading to be a spiritual, not just an academic, exercise – although it undoubtedly contains much learned theology and complex philosophy. The spiritual intention can be detected from the way in which Augustine frames the question: it is not just a case of 'how can one *know* that God is three in one?', but 'how can one *love* the God who is three in one?' As we shall see, that answer is tied up with his method, which is to proceed through a series of psychological analogies which centre on a person's knowledge and love of him or herself. Finally, Augustine ties his question ('how to know and love God?') together with his method ('how do I know and love myself?'). He suggests not only that one can understand a little more about the three-in-oneness of God through reflection on one's knowledge and love of oneself, but that – paradoxically – the best love and knowledge of self springs from the love and knowledge of God.

Before he reaches the climax of his argument, however, Augustine spends a long time in preparation.[30] In Books I–IV, he systematically works through the classic texts which had been at the centre of Trinitarian debate since Arius and Athanasius: for example, the prologue to John's Gospel, which could be interpreted to indicate the Word's full divinity; various other passages from John (such as 14.28) which were used by Arius and others to suggest that the Son was less than the Father; and finally some passages which were used by Marcellus in connection with his radically unified doctrine of the Trinity. The originality and subsequent theological influence of the last books of *On the Trinity* can sometimes obscure the importance of these early books, but it is crucial to remember that for Augustine the main reason for believing that God is three in one is that it is a doctrine that lay at the heart of the Church's teaching in the Bible and in the baptism of its members. It is no coincidence that the work which began with intensive study of the biblical sources of the doctrine ends by reflecting – in a prayer – on 'the text which presents this Trinity to us most plainly':[31]

> O Lord our God, we believe in you, Father and Son and Holy Spirit. Truth would not have said 'Go and baptize the nations in the name of the Father and of the Son and of the Holy Spirit' unless you were a triad.[32]

In Books V–VII, Augustine laid out some groundwork of a more philosophical kind. In particular, he investigated the language used to speak of the Father, Son and Spirit: how should one reply when faced with the question 'Three whats?'[33] Famously, Augustine is cautious about the Greek solution, one *ousia* and three *hypostases*. This is because one natural way of translating this into Latin would be 'one *essentia*, three *substantiae*' (one being/essence, three substances) – a confusing formulation because, as Augustine puts it, 'in our language ... "being" and "substance" do not usually mean anything different'. The Greek answer to 'three whats?', then, is unsatisfactory, because it might suggest three substances – that is, three gods. Augustine asserted that the Latin alternative was 'one being (*essentia*) or substance (*substantia*) and three persons (*personae*)', but he is also extremely cautious about the use of the term 'person', lest it suggest too great a similarity between the kind of persons that the Father, Son and Spirit are, and the kind of persons that human beings are. In the end, Augustine accepted the term, but with the caveat that although Scripture did not ban it, it was not affirmed by Scripture either.

Augustine's hesitation here reflected a fluidity in Latin theological language. It has sometimes been assumed that the west uniformly used a 'one nature (*natura*) and three persons (*personae*)' formula because it is found in both Tertullian and Hilary. But in fact their terminology was more varied: Hilary himself sometimes wrote of God's one nature (*natura*), sometimes of one substance (*substantia*). At other times, confusingly, he wrote of the Father, Son and Spirit as three substances (*substantiae*).[34] Two important points emerge from this confusion. First, as a modern commentator has noted, in the doctrine of God, 'the logic of unity and distinction could be adopted before a consistent terminology for that distinction was used'.[35] Secondly, with his caution over the language used, Augustine was highlighting the fact that, as he himself wrote, people used these terms 'for the sake of talking about inexpressible matters, that we may somehow express what we are completely unable to express'.[36]

It is precisely this difficulty that led Augustine to frame the key question in Book VIII: humans are commanded to love God, but how can they love what they do not know?

For 'since we are walking by faith and not by sight' (II Corinthians 5.7) we do not yet see God … 'face to face' (I Corinthians 13.12). Yet unless we love him even now, we shall never see him. But who can love what he does not know?[37]

Augustine offered a solution to the problem by meditating on the nature of love – or rather the structure of loving:

> Love is of someone who loves, and something is loved with love. So then there are three: the lover, the beloved, and the love. What else is love, therefore, except a kind of love which binds or seeks to bind some two together?[38]

Augustine warned his readers that this was not yet a direct analogy for the Trinity. Nevertheless, it was an analogy for an activity with three aspects: loving. It could not express unity because it described love between two beings; so Augustine moved forward to consider the activity of love in one mind. What happens if one person loves herself? The triad (love, lover, beloved) collapses into a pair (love and lover). Yet, Augustine argued, 'the mind cannot love itself unless it also knows itself'.[39] So he moved to the idea of a mind loving and knowing itself – the second analogy:

> But just as there are two things, the mind and its love, when it loves itself, so there are two things, the mind and its knowledge, when it knows itself. Therefore, the mind itself, its love and its knowledge are a kind of trinity; these three are one, and when they are perfect then they are equal.[40]

With his second analogy Augustine did not just establish a triad in one mind but also attempted to convey three other points which are crucial for his argument. First, he argued that, although inseparable, love and knowledge are distinct to the consciousness and that therefore each exists substantially (*substantialiter*) in the mind. Secondly, by extension from the first analogy, the mind is introduced not as a neutral agent but as a lover and as a knower: these actions define what the mind is. This allowed Augustine to argue that it was impossible to conceive of a knower without its knowledge, nor a lover without its love. (The importance of this to the doctrine of the Trinity becomes clearer when one thinks of Athanasius' argument that it is impossible to think of a father without a son: begetting defines who the father is.) The action of loving not only links a mind with its love but also logically distinguishes a mind from its love. Thirdly, the action of loving is not just mutually defining (love defines what the lover is, the lover's loving defines what love is) but it is reflexive: the mind loves itself. It is that which, for Augustine, makes the three 'equal', for he assumes (along with many of his pagan contemporaries) that the only love which *completely* possesses its object is mind's love of itself and that the only knowledge that can *completely* possess its object is the mind's love and knowledge of itself.

Yet there remained a problem. Augustine had established that the mind was permanently related to but logically distinct from its love, and that the mind was permanently related to but logically distinct from its knowledge. But could not someone argue that the mind's knowledge is the same thing as its love? Could not the triad of mind, knowledge and love in fact collapse into a pair of mind and its loving, knowing reflection on itself? After all, Augustine had assumed in his own treatise that knowledge and love were very close to each other. This difficulty moved Augustine on to his third analogy. In this he moved from a model of a mind with two actions to the model of three interrelated actions of one mind. These actions were memory, understanding (or knowledge) and will (or love). To put it very simply, the second model had suggested one thing *doing* two actions: one noun and two verbs. The third model suggested three interrelated actions: three verbs. Augustine suggested that in the mind, memory, understanding and will were connected in such a way that their interrelations both defined each other and united each other: memory was always a memory of something, knowledge was always knowledge of something, will always willed something. As one could not conceive of a lover without love, so one could not conceive of will without that which it willed. Furthermore, they were totally equal because in memory, understanding and will the activity of the mind was completely reflexive: the removal of the mind as one of the three, the one which 'did' things, seemed to remove all trace of the idea that one was superior to the other two. This idea is perhaps easiest to express in terms of thinking of memory, understanding and will as verbs again: the interrelation occurs because all three can be both reflexive verbs (one can remember, understand and will/love oneself), but they are also all auxiliary verbs: it makes sense to say 'I remember that I have memory, understanding, and will', 'I understand that I understand, will and remember', 'I will that I will, remember and understand'. The equality of the three depends on the fact that I remember my whole understanding and will, I understand my whole memory and will, I will my whole memory and understanding. Their distinction depends on the fact that what I do not remember, I do not know nor will; what I do not understand I do not know nor will; what I do not will, I do not remember nor understand.[41]

Of course the crucial question remained of whether this model – even if it made sense with regard to the human mind – could appropriately apply to the Trinity. Augustine argued that it did because of several prior assumptions that he made throughout *On the Trinity*. Despite his anxiety about language, he did assume that *some* literal language of God was possible: relational language (father–son; lover–love) was a prime example. Crucially, as we saw in relation to his exposition of Genesis, he thought that humans were created in the image of God, with respect to their soul or mind. Thus for Augustine one should *expect* to find traces ('vestiges') of the Trinity in the human mind, however imperfectly. Furthermore, Augustine argued that these traces were found more perfectly in those minds which know God. For Augustine, it was only in knowing God that we fully and perfectly know and love ourselves – that is only in knowing God do people act in full and complete reflexivity.

So, all of a sudden, Augustine pulled the rug out from under his readers' feet: he first produced the analogy of the mind in order to understand more about God; he concluded by affirming that in fact that deeper aim of the work is to know and love God *so that* the image of God could be renewed in his readers' minds. Of course, the treatise is still 'about' a correct doctrine of the Trinity, otherwise the biblical quotations at the beginning would not make sense; nevertheless, for Augustine there is more to it than that. The aim of the treatise is to draw the reader into a close relationship with the divine, by a progression through various stages: a study of the psychological self (about which Augustine, like Descartes, thinks one cannot be mistaken); a move to God (based on the idea of humanity being created in the image of God and the assumption that the terms Father, Son and Spirit are relational in a similar way to the way memory, understanding and will are relational); a move back to the spiritual self in order to purify it by adding the 'vertical' axis of knowledge and love of God to the 'horizontal' axis of knowledge and love of self.[42]

Although on the surface very different, the *Confessions* and *On the Trinity* share a similar dynamic: although seeming to be about one thing (Augustine's own life, the doctrine of the Trinity), the way they are constructed is designed to draw the reader into the narrative. In this way, without ceasing to be about Augustine's life or the Trinity, they also become about the reader herself and her relationship to God in love. They show Augustine at the height of his theological and literary powers.

Augustine was not, however, immune from the controversies which demanded the time of so many of the Church Fathers. One of these involved Pelagius, a British man, who came to Rome around 380 and probably learnt his theology there.[43] By the turn of the century he was established in Rome as an advisor on asceticism to various, often wealthy, Roman Christians. He is said to have been scandalized by hearing an excerpt from Augustine's *Confessions* (an interesting comment, besides anything else, on the influence that Augustine's work was already having). The particular aspect of the *Confessions* that exercised Pelagius was not the revelations about Augustine's youth, but Augustine's description of his response to God. The *Confessions'* narrative described Augustine as thoroughly caught up in his sinful life: a captive who was at once willing ('I was in love with love') and struggling to escape. The famous episode in which Augustine described how he and some friends stole some pears from a garden, not because they wanted to eat them but because of the sheer naughtiness of the deed, exemplified for Augustine the way in which he – like all humans – was unable to resist sinning. A consequence of this for Augustine was that when conversion came, it could be seen in no way as a reward for good behaviour – it was entirely due to the generosity of God:

> Is not human life a trial in which there is no respite? My entire hope is exclusively in your very great mercy. Grant what you command and command what you will. You require continence. A certain writer has said, '... no one can be continent except God grants it ...' (Wisdom 8.21). O love (*amor*), you ever burn and are never extinguished. O charity (*caritas*), my God set me on fire. You command continence; grant what you command and command what you will.[44]

The final sentence is said to have provoked Pelagius. It may be that the initial provocation was the fact that the words were being quoted out of context by a bishop who appeared to be condoning the sexual behaviour of some of his congregation (that is, Augustine's words were taken to mean 'if God wants you to be continent, he will make it happen').[45] For Pelagius, whose life was bound up with encouraging tough physical and spiritual discipline on his followers, this laxity was outrageous. But whatever the original circumstances, it rapidly became clear that there was a huge gulf between Pelagius' and Augustine's understandings of the human response to God.

Pelagius probably heard those words in Rome around 405, a decade after Augustine's consecration as Bishop of Hippo. In 409 Alaric the Visigoth besieged Rome and, like many others, Pelagius and a friend Caelestius escaped. They travelled to North Africa, where they preached in various cities, including Hippo and Carthage. After a while Pelagius left to visit Palestine, leaving Caelestius behind to continue preaching. Clearly they caused a stir, as it was around this time that Caelestius was excommunicated by a council in Carthage in 411 and Augustine began to denounce Pelagius and his teachings.

The six complaints of the council at Carthage against Caelestius can be summarized under four headings: Adam's condition before the Fall, the rest of humanity's relation to Adam, the possibility of virtue and the means of salvation.

It is important to remember that Pelagius and Augustine were both enthusiastic about asceticism. Both thought that a disciplined life in obedience to God was an important part of the Christian faith. Both were profoundly interested in the realities of everyday existence in which humans were faced with sin and temptation. Their differences lay in how they conceived the possibilities of the present life – particularly in comparison with the life which was lived by Adam and Eve before the Fall. In brief, Pelagius saw a significant continuity between the pre-Fall Adam and himself, while Augustine saw a deep gulf.

Pelagius' whole strategy as a spiritual guru was based on the assumption that Christians had some kind of choice over the kind of life they led: 'Man can be without sin, and can keep the commandment of God if he so wishes.'[46] But keeping God's command required disciplined effort: it was for this reason that Pelagius was most appalled by Augustine's 'grant what you command', for it seemed to him to deny that effort. In fact, contrary to his enemies' accusations, Pelagius appears to have thought it doubtful, if not impossible, that anyone (apart from Jesus Christ) had actually been sinless throughout their life. He did, however, seem to suggest that a pure life after conversion and baptism might be logically possible, if unlikely.

Pelagius was keen to emphasize that it was God who helped humans in their pursuit of the good and indeed that it was God who had implanted in humans the possibility of choosing the good in the first place ('man's power to will the good and effect it, is of God alone'[47]). Furthermore he recognized that sin could become an ingrained habit, both for individuals and for humanity as a whole. Nevertheless, he thought that sin could not utterly corrupt or obstruct the will, and he asserted that subsequent humans were not so different from Adam. Specifically Pelagius argued that humans did *not* inherit from Adam some 'congenital evil': all humans beings were created with the same human nature with which Adam was created.[48] Thus even though humans were not born into the same *context* as Adam, since they were born into a *society* which has inherited a habit of sinning, Pelagius emphasized the importance of the fact that *as individuals* they had not inherited a predetermination to sin.

In this system Pelagius understood divine grace primarily as the gift of creating humans able to do good:

> God wished to bestow on his rational creation the privilege of doing good voluntarily, and the power of free choice, by implanting in man the possibility of choosing either side; and so he gave him ... the power of being what he wished to be; so that he should be naturally capable of good and evil, that both should be within his power, and that he should incline his will towards one or the other.[49]

He thought that each human must then actualize this possibility by *willing* something good and then *doing* it. A secondary sense of grace in his system, therefore, was the help God gave humans in their willing and doing, for example, God's gift of moral law (both natural law and that revealed in the New and Old Testaments). He also acknowledged the grace of forgiveness of sins and the grace which illuminated the mind to give it wisdom: these aspects of grace were most apparent in baptism, which he thought cleansed the soul of sins the believer had committed and regenerated it for a life of future virtue. It would not be correct, therefore, to think that Pelagius had no place for grace. But all these senses of grace viewed it as something external: some force which operated in the creation of human nature or in assisting human nature. Just as Pelagius denied that sin could become internal to human nature (through being inherited from Adam), so he denied that grace could operate directly on or in human nature. It seems as if either inherited sin or internal grace would, to Pelagius' mind, have biased human choice in a way contrary to humans' God-given freedom of will.

Central to Pelagius' arguments were his convictions first that God would not command what humans were unable to will or perform and, second, that God would punish those who disobeyed his laws.[50] Underlying his theology seems to be a clear expectation of divine rewards and punishments – rewards and punishments which in some cases seem to be directly proportional to the amount of sin or virtue. Thus, for example, Pelagius' interpretation of the 'many dwelling places' of John 14.2[51] was that there would be different ranks in heaven to reward those of varying degrees of virtue. As one of Augustine's modern biographers remarks, this concept of 'religious meritocracy' brings to Pelagius' theology an unattractive focus on 'superhuman morality' – however appealing his focus on the freedom of the will.[52]

Augustine's response to Pelagius was to deny neither human freedom nor divine grace, but rather to offer an alternative account of them – an account which Augustine felt fitted with both his experience and the Church's understanding of the Bible.[53] The only humans who truly had the freedom to choose between good and evil were Adam and Eve. After their disobedience, all humans inherited from them the consequences of their sin – death, guilt and the corruption of human nature – which meant that humans were henceforth biased towards the choice of sin. This was in addition to being born into a world which had become corrupted by the human habit of sinning. Thus, in Augustine's theology, humans shared the guilt of Adam's sin and they bore the guilt of their own sins. For this, Augustine argued, humanity *en masse* deserved the punishment ordained by God: not just biological death but the 'second death' of hell.

This might seem a pretty desperate situation for humankind, but the idea of all humans inheriting Adam's original sin (or rather his original *guilt*) reflected a strong strand of western (especially North African) theology and to Augustine seemed also to reflect his own personal experience. Similarly his feeling that his call back to God was completely undeserved seems to have informed his concept of election. Because of sin, he argued, all humans deserve the divine punishment; through Christ, however, God had chosen some to be saved:

> The individual members of this race would not have been subject to death, had not the first two ... merited it by their disobedience. So great was the sin of those two that human nature was changed by it for the worse; and so bondage to sin and the necessity of death were transmitted to their posterity. Now the sway of the kingdom of death over men was so complete that all would have been driven headlong, as their due punishment, into that second death to which there is no end, had not some of them been redeemed by the unmerited grace of God.[54]

This theory inevitably raises the question: why are some saved and not others? Augustine's main answer is that since all sinned in Adam, all deserve the consequences. One should praise God for those who are saved, instead of presumptuously criticizing his failure to save them all.[55] In particular, one should not believe that God chose a certain group because of their virtue. This is because God's choice (or election) is not dependent on human good actions. Augustine illustrated this point with reference to the story of Cain and Abel. Many exegetes before him had puzzled over the question of why God had rejected the offering from one and accepted that of the other. Augustine's answer was simply that one had been chosen and the other had not:

> Now Cain was the first son born to those two parents of the human race, and he belonged to the City of man; the second son, Abel, belonged to the City of God. ... Each man, because he derives his origin from a condemned stock, is at first necessarily evil and fleshly, because he comes from Adam; but if, being reborn, he advances in Christ, he will afterwards be good and spiritual. So it is also with the whole human race. When those two cities began to run through their course of birth and death, the first to be born was a citizen of this world, and the second was a pilgrim in this world, belonging to the City of God. The latter was predestined by grace and chosen by grace; by grace he was a pilgrim below and by grace he was a citizen above. So far as he himself is concerned, he arises from the same lump which was wholly condemned originally; but God like a potter ... made out of the same lump, one vessel unto honour, and the other unto dishonour.[56]

Thus, while for Pelagius there was a clear connection between humans' actions and their ultimate destiny, Augustine seemed to have cut that connection: God chose some 'unto honour' not because they deserved it, but simply because that was his eternal choice.

But this theology raises a further question: if Augustine believed that God predestined some for salvation, did he think that that meant those people could behave immorally without fear of punishment or, more specifically, without fear of losing their salvation? Here Augustine's answer is complex, and one needs to return to the idea of the moral connection between humans' actions and their salvation. Augustine *seemed* to have cut the connection between them; in fact though, it is better to say that he understood the connection in a different way. For Pelagius, moral behaviour merited a reward in heaven: one's salvation was *caused* by one's actions. For Augustine, too, one could not enter heaven unless one was pure of heart; *but* one's purity of heart was *dependent on* one's election to salvation. That is, Augustine believed that God had chosen him, had given him the grace of *faith* to receive the offer of salvation, the grace of the *remission of the guilt from Adam* in baptism and the grace to *do good*. Through Christ, the believer is freed from being completely enslaved to a corrupt will and is liberated to do good.[57]

Augustine did not mean that Christians always did good – such a claim would be ridiculous, flying in the face of all the evidence. Nor did he mean that they did good without an effort: the corrupt will was still present and Augustine wrote frequently of the necessity and the difficulty of resisting it. Nevertheless, he asserted that although people must make the effort to resist evil, any good they do is due to the grace of God working within them. This is a difficult concept to understand. This is partly because there was an asymmetry in Augustine's theology between sin (for which humans are responsible although they are enslaved to it) and virtue (which God enables humans to attain freely). But Augustine's theory is also difficult to grasp because he was introducing a radical notion of what freedom truly was: 'The choice of the will, then, is truly free only when it is not the slave of vice and sins.'[58] In the present life, the freedom promised in Christ was partial: it existed in believers but was mixed with the lack of freedom brought by the corruption of human nature in the Fall. Ultimately, however, Augustine thought that the grace of salvation would be perfected so that eventually those who were predestined for heaven would be no longer able to sin. Thus humans would not return to their original, natural state (as supposed by Origen and other Greek theologians) but would transcend even that good condition to a new graced state in which sin would be impossible. Augustine expressed this in terms of a movement from 'being able to sin', to 'not being able not to sin', to 'not being able to sin'.[59]

Augustine's theology of grace and freedom is difficult on more than one count. It is extremely difficult for many readers to reconcile themselves to the idea that God might freely choose to elect some and not others for a reason not connected to their moral desert. His concept of freedom is philosophically complex. These difficulties are exacerbated when Augustine's theology is simplified and summarized. A more sympathetic perspective comes, perhaps, from considering his views from a more personal perspective, when the complexity is more clearly a reflection of humans' morally complex lives. Augustine thought that, like Abel, all those chosen by God would be 'citizens above', but he was more eloquent about those who were in the meantime 'pilgrims below'. Some of this is evident in Augustine's prayer for his mother Monica, in the *Confessions* (IX.xiii.34–5):

> But, now, on behalf of your maidservant, I pour out to you, our God, ... tears [which] flow from a spirit struck hard considering the perils threatening every soul that 'dies in Adam' (I Corinthians 15.22). She, being 'made alive' in Christ', though not yet delivered from the flesh, so lived that your name is praised in her faith and behaviour. But I do not dare to say that, since the day when you regenerated her through baptism, no word came from her mouth contrary to your precept. It was said by the Truth, your Son: 'If anyone says to his brother, Fool, he will be liable to the gehenna of fire' (Matthew 5.22). Woe even to those of praiseworthy life if you put their life under scrutiny and remove mercy. But because you do not search our faults with rigour, we confidently hope for some place with you. If anyone lists his true merits to you, what is he enumerating before you but your gifts? ... Therefore, God of my heart, my praise and my life, I set aside for a moment her good actions for which I rejoice and give you thanks. I now petition you for my mother's sins. 'Hear me' (Psalms 142.1) through the remedy for our wounds who hung upon the wood and sits at your right hand to intercede for us (Romans 8.34).

Predestination to salvation, then, did not mean the predestination of individuals' particular actions. Monica still had to struggle after baptism. In his prayer, Augustine was following traditions of penance and prayers for the dead, which thought that sin after baptism had to be 'made good'. Although salvation is not a reward, good deeds and salvation *are* connected, because Augustine believes that the elect will be given the grace of perseverance in their lives as pilgrims, so that eventually they will reach the final grace of the perfection of their salvation in heaven, the final City of God.

So far Augustine's theology has been considered more from an individualistic perspective: an individual like Monica, according to Augustine, was a pilgrim in this life because her life had a 'mixed' quality in which she was not quite liberated from the slavery of sin. For Augustine, this mixed quality also affected the Church as a whole: although one *hoped* that all those within it would eventually reach the City of God in heaven, Augustine was quite clear that one could not completely identify the Church with heaven on earth, because it was almost bound to contain those who would not remain true to their baptism. Just as he feared that Monica's sins after baptism might have meant that she was 'liable to the gehenna of fire', so he believed that it was possible that in the Church there were those who had not been given the grace to persevere in their faith.[60] (The question 'why?' could only be answered, as before, by reference to humans' inability to understand the workings of God's grace, and the whole of humanity's inheritance of sin.) For this reason, although he did believe that Christ dwells in the Church on earth through the Holy Spirit,[61] Augustine never forgot that the Church was a human institution with all the failings which followed from that. He particularly warned against identifying God's kingdom with any human institution, whether the Church or the Empire or any future earthly realm. His subtle theory of human law and government follows from this caution.

In Augustine's theology, the 'City of man' was the mass of humanity who had deserved the second death because of sharing in the sin of Adam. The 'City of God' was the sum of those who, despite also sharing in Adam's sin, were chosen from that mass by God for his kingdom. In his monumental work *The City of God*, Augustine traced the course of the two cities through history from Adam to the eschaton – the end of all things. Although the present age since Adam was characterized by the conflict caused by the rule of sin and the mixing of the two cities,[62] the Last Judgement would be the point at which the two cities would be divided for ever. The 'lot of those who do not belong in the City of God will be everlasting misery' (the nature of this punishment Augustine detailed in Book XXI).[63] The just would see the vision of God in heaven (the subject of Book XXII). Only this division by divine judgement will bring everlasting peace.

Although the two cities were thus distinguished by their destinies, more profoundly they were characterized by the different objects of their love:

> Two cities, then, have been created by two loves: that is, the earthly by love of self extending even to contempt of God, and the heavenly by love of God extending to contempt of self.[64]

People in the earthly city put created things before the creator, and Augustine therefore thought that they would be punished by being eternally separated from the creator. In hell, they are not only separated from God, but they are finally aware of the impossibility of their earthly loves ever being satisfied: their punishment of eternal fire, although Augustine treats it as literal fire, is surely also symbolic of the unquenchable fires of their passions. In heaven, however, those in the City of God will be ever satisfied in their love, for God will be 'all in all'.[65]

CHAPTER 9

Christology: A Tale of Three Cities
(FIFTH CENTURY)

Yet this I can say of my native city – that it is the fairest thing in the fairest
land under heaven. We have ... experienced not merely the best of kings but
also the best of queens. ... Our council is the greatest and the finest in the
world ... in the expensive duties of state they are most lavish, and in their care
and provision they avoid poverty.[1]

When you wish to praise the city, don't tell me about its suburb, Daphne, nor
about the number and height of its cypress trees, nor the numerous people who
live in the city, nor that its marketplace is frequented with great freedom right
into the evening, nor of the abundance of market goods. ... But if you can call
on virtue, gentleness, almsgiving, vigils, prayers, common sense and wisdom of
spirit – adorn the city with these qualities. To those who live in the desert, the
presence of these qualities makes Antioch more splendid than any city.[2]

Antioch's finest orators, the pagan Libanius and the Christian Chrysostom,
were of course exaggerating for rhetorical effect when they praised their
city's physical and moral virtues. However, the citizens of Antioch had good
reason for native pride. Antioch had long been a hub of commerce, military
power and Hellenic culture in the eastern Mediterranean. It was placed in
a fertile valley on the Orontes river leading to the sea, which was so close
that 'a fit man setting off from the coast at sunrise [could] carry goods from
there and arrive [at Antioch] by noon'.[3] It was frequently used by emperors
as a base in the east during their campaigns on the Persian frontier and as
a result it boasted a fine imperial palace. In the fifth century Antioch had
a population to rival that of Alexandria and Constantinople, although its
influence in the region was threatened both by the power of the bishops of
Alexandria and by the steadily increasing growth of Constantinople as the
eastern imperial capital.[4]

Antioch had had a Christian community from the first century – as Chrysostom boasted, '"It was in Antioch that the disciples were first called Christians." None of the cities in the world has this claim, not even the city of Romulus itself.'⁵ Christians continued to grow in number until by the mid-fifth century they probably formed a majority of the population. But Antioch had always had a very mixed society. Literary evidence and archaeological remains reveal the presence, for example, of a large flourishing Jewish community: in Chrysostom's day it was common practice for townspeople, Jews, Christians or pagans, to seal business contracts by swearing an oath in the local synagogue.⁶ Although most of the city's population were Greek-speaking, the rural peasants spoke Syriac. Out of this population came many of the ascetics for which the region was famed. While the ascetic discipline of Chrysostom and his contemporaries was somewhat less strange than that of some of the Syrian desert saints, many of them (including Chrysostom himself) spent periods of retreat outside the city. Furthermore, the enormous popular devotion which the rural ascetics inspired undoubtedly influenced events in the city. Most famously, the monks descended on Antioch after the notorious occasion when the statues of the Emperor Theodosius were overturned during riots in 387, precipitated by the imposition of a new tax. Their intention was to protect the city and its inhabitants from the severe imperial reprisals which were being rumoured:

> Although they had been shut up for so many years in their [hermits'] cells, when they saw such a great cloud encompassing the city, at nobody's behest and on nobody's advice, they left their tents and their caves and flowed together from every direction, just like angels arriving from heaven.⁷

On the other hand, Jerome's experience of the harsh isolation of the desert and the lack of education of his fellow hermits must have seemed all the more hard to bear by contrast with the sophisticated atmosphere of Antioch, where his close friend and correspondent Evagrius lived. The city was famous for its dozens of elegant colonnades, it boasted an impressive hippodrome and theatre, numerous baths (some built for summer and others for winter use) and an elegant quarter, Daphne, where the rich built luxurious villas. Antioch enjoyed a fine cultural reputation, in particular boasting the rhetorical school of Libanius himself, where young men would learn the art of public speaking, preparing them for life either as a wealthy landowner and politician, or perhaps as a lawyer, civil servant or – increasingly – a priest.

Naturally it was not Libanius' intention to prepare priests for preaching, although he did in fact teach John Chrysostom, whose verbal elegance earned him his nickname 'Golden mouth' (*chrysostomos* in Greek). Libanius was a determined and vocal pagan, who perceived Christianity as a threat to civilized classical Hellenic values. Famously he ignored any Christian building or indeed any Christian influence in his eulogy of Antioch's charms. Despite this (or perhaps as a sign of his studied pursuit of civilized qualities) he remained on good terms with several prominent Christians, corresponding, for example, with Gregory of Nyssa and Basil of Caesarea. Libanius supported the brief but energetic campaign of Julian the Apostate to ban Christians as teachers of classical literature. Although this threatened the careers of many intelligent Christians (for example, that of Gregory of Nyssa), Julian's early death meant that its impact was not as dramatic as he intended or Christians feared.

Libanius' other Christian pupils included Basil, Chrysostom's closest friend, and Theodore, later Bishop of Mopsuestia. Initially, Chrysostom appears to have toyed with the idea of living together with Basil in a small monastic cell in the city; apparently his mother dissuaded him. He later chose, with Theodore and several others, to place himself under the instruction of a Christian teacher of asceticism, Diodore (later Bishop of Tarsus). Although sometimes described as a 'monastery', Diodore's *asketerion* was apparently not a residential community (Chrysostom probably continued to live at home with his mother). In its gathering of a group of pupils around a master it was analogous both to a pagan philosophical school and to various forms of Christian ascetic teaching. The young men in Antioch considered themselves part of a community which was defined both by formal registration on a membership list and by swearing an oath of allegiance to Christ, in which they 'joined [themselves] to the heavenly bridegroom': this language is reminiscent of the covenant made by the members of Syrian communities of 'sons and daughters of the covenant', described in the previous chapter.[8] Diodore's community is another example of how fluid and various were Christian experiments in asceticism at this stage.[9]

It is probably from associations like this that there emerged what has been described as the 'Antiochene school' of theology. (As with many Christian groupings in this period, 'school' indicates an intellectual and religious network rather than a formal institution.) Although attempts have been made to trace it back earlier, it is with Diodore and especially with Theodore of Mopsuestia that one finds a style of theology that can be identified as distinctively 'Antiochene'. One of its features was a reaction against the kind of allegorical interpretation used by many followers of Origen. Already in the Cappadocians there was a clear recognition that such interpretation was becoming controversial: Basil of Caesarea boldly asserted in his sermons on the six days of creation that 'for me, grass is grass' – despite the fact that his interpretation in fact contained not a few allegorical readings.[10] In Diodore and Theodore this anxiety was heightened into a systematic rejection of allegorical interpretation, even of the Old Testament. Unfortunately, partly because they were later suspected of having been 'on the wrong side' in the later Christological controversies, the full writings of these two men have not survived in anything like a representative quantity. We can, however, get an indication of their approach from Theodore's comments on the Lord's prayer. Where Origen puzzles over the meaning of 'our daily bread', and suggests that it might mean spiritual nourishment instead of plain human food, Theodore simply suggests, 'It is as if [Jesus] had said: "... As to the things of this world, I allow you to make use of such of them as are necessary; and you should not ask nor strive to have more than this use."' [11] A second feature is opposition to Apollinarius' Christology. [12]

In the past it has sometimes been claimed that the Antiochene tradition of theology was particularly influenced by Aristotelian philosophy, while in Alexandria Platonism was the dominant Hellenic influence. However, this analysis now hardly ever appears in scholarly accounts of the fifth-century controversies, it being recognized that theologians' use of pagan philosophical sources in this period was in fact very complex. In any case, the essence of the claim that Antiochene theologians used Aristotelian philosophy and Alexandrians used Platonism was linked to their supposed views of human nature (specifically the relation of body and soul and/or mind). Even if that view was correct it should not be broadened out to a more general claim about the philosophical direction of either 'school'. The main differences between the Antiochene and Alexandrian positions were created by a variety of rather complex factors and cannot be reduced to the influence of different Greek philosophical schools – or indeed merely to the use of different approaches to exegesis.

Despite the glowing picture of Antioch given by both Libanius and Chrysostom, it underwent several crises in the late fourth century. The city faced several periods of famine, and there were frequent earthquakes. After the incident of the overturning of the imperial statues, the population apparently feared the razing of their city. In the end – perhaps partly owing to the monks' intervention – they suffered a milder fate: the public facilities (baths, theatre, hippodrome) were closed for a period, and members of the town council exiled or sentenced to execution. For the Christians there were particular trials, not least during the period of Julian's emperorship. Even under Christian emperors, however, the situation of the church in Antioch was extremely complex owing to the presence of both 'Arian' and 'orthodox' Christian communities. At times there were as many as three clerics in Antioch simultaneously claiming to be the rightful bishop. [13]

Paulinus (ordained c.362) represented a long-established community known as the Eustathians, after Eustathius, Bishop of Antioch, who had been ejected from his see in 331 for his support for the Nicene *homoousios* formula. The ousted Eustathius was officially succeeded by a series of bishops who took the position that one should describe the Son as being 'like' (*homoios*) the Father. They generally had imperial support and in the meantime Eustathius' loyal followers worshipped apart. On one occasion, however, the appointment of an apparently homoian bishop seems to have been misjudged: a certain Meletius, who had appeared happy to use *homoios* language, emerged as a rather more enthusiastic supporter of the Nicene formula, especially when *homoousios* was qualified (as by the Cappadocians) with the concept of the Trinity being one *ousia* and three *hypostases*. When this became apparent, Meletius was exiled to Armenia and replaced with a genuinely homoian bishop, Euzoius.

As imperial support for the homoians waxed and waned, Meletius was exiled, returned, was exiled and returned again. It was cruelly ironic that he died at the Council of Constantinople in 381 – that is, the council which re-established the Nicene position and of which Meletius had been the short-lived president. In Antioch, his Nicene successor was Bishop Flavian. For some of this period, then, not only did the Christians of Antioch have three bishops to choose from – Euzoius, Meletius (later Flavian) and Paulinus – but pro-Nicene opposition to the homoian camp was divided between the latter two, thus weakening their influence.[14] The situation caused waves far outside Antioch: up to 381 the emperors and bishops of Constantinople tended to support the homoian bishop; the Eustathians enjoyed the support of the see of Alexandria and (sometimes) of Rome; Meletius and his successor Flavian were supported by the Cappadocians and eventually by Emperor Theodosius.

The importance of this episode is that it sheds light on the Church's political alliances underlying the theological controversies which were to follow. Diodore and his pupils Chrysostom and Theodore were firmly in the Meletian camp. In 398 Chrysostom was consecrated Bishop of Constantinople, but was exiled in 403 after an upsurge of mistrust against him in the capital. Partly responsible for his exile was the involvement of Theophilus, Bishop of Alexandria, whose see had been supporters of the Eustathian rather than the Meletian faction in Antioch, and whose hostility had been further provoked by Chrysostom's apparent involvement in a dispute between a party of Egyptian ascetics and their bishop.[15] The monks were accused, amongst other things, of a form of Origenism influenced by the ascetic and philosopher Evagrius of Pontus. When the Christological controversies broke out in the late 420s, precipitated by the preaching of Nestorius (Bishop of Constantinople and former Antiochene presbyter) and

by the reaction of Cyril (Bishop of Alexandria), there was already a long
history of tension between Antioch and Alexandria. Partly this tension was
due to different loyalties within the pro-Nicene camp; partly it was due
to sensitivities over how much influence any of the major sees had outside
their own region (accusations of meddling were rife) and over the relative
importance of each of the sees to the bishopric of Constantinople.

Nestorius was an inheritor of the Antiochene tradition stemming from
such men as Diodore, Theodore of Mopsuestia and Chrysostom. He was
probably taught by Theodore, although that claim has sometimes been
disputed in an effort to dissociate Theodore from his much more controversial pupil.[16] The difficulty of tracing the theological influence of one
on the other has been exacerbated by the fact that many of their works
were destroyed or simply not preserved by copying when Nestorius was
anathematized. However, there is a clear similarity between their teaching,
evident, for example, in the surviving extracts of Theodore's *On the Incarnation* and the works of Nestorius produced before the Council of Ephesus
(and even more so with Nestorius' somewhat more considered *Book of Heraclides*, which he wrote in exile).[17] Like Diodore, Theodore and Chrysostom,
Nestorius was an ascetic, being a member of a monastery near Antioch. He
was a long-standing friend of John of Antioch (who had been appointed
its bishop succeeding Flavian) and of another prominent theologian of the
Antiochene school, Theodoret, Bishop of the city of Cyrrhus.

In 428, Nestorius was consecrated Bishop of Constantinople; his appointment was probably partly due to the influence of John of Antioch. As in most
cities of the Empire, Constantinople was by no means a haven of uniform
belief; being the capital, it attracted an unusual number of immigrants and
visitors who not only added to the religious mix but provided instant publicity to any controversial expression or action of its bishop. Added to this were
the inevitable rivalries and ambitions caused by the presence of the imperial
court. Nestorius himself seems to have come to office with the intention of
sweeping out heresies, and he did so with apparently little sensitivity to the
limits of Constantinople's jurisdiction with regard to other sees. [18] In this
atmosphere, Nestorius' choice to preach on the use of the title of *Theotokos*
('God-bearer') for the Virgin Mary was provocative, to say the least. He
claimed – wrongly as it turned out – that the term had enjoyed no tradition
of theological use.[19] He appeared to regard it as a piece of misguided and
unbiblical terminology from popular piety, which blasphemously implied
that Mary had given birth to God and which denied Christ's full humanity:

> Does God have a mother? ... Is Paul then a liar when he says of the deity
> of Christ, 'without father, without mother, without genealogy' (Heb. 7.3)?

Mary, my friend, did not give birth to the Godhead (for 'what is born of the flesh is flesh', John 3.6). A creature did not produce the Creator, rather she gave birth to the human being, the instrument of the Godhead.[20]

The way Nestorius introduced the question suggested that the issue was a topic of current theological debate – they 'are always enquiring among us now this way and now that: "Is Mary *Theotokos*," they say, or is she on the contrary *anthropotokos*?"' (That is, is Mary the 'mother of God' or 'mother of a human being'?[21]) Theodore had raised the same question in his writings on the Incarnation. Theodore's even tone contrasted with Nestorius' emotional delivery:

> When they ask whether Mary is a man's mother or God's mother, we must say, 'Both', the one by the nature of the thing, the other in virtue of a relation. Mary was a man's mother by nature, since what was in her womb was a man, just as it was also a man who came forth from her womb. But she is God's mother, since God was in the man who was fashioned – not circumscribed in him by nature by existing in him according to the disposition of his will. Therefore it is right to say both, but not in the same sense.[22]

In contrast to this irenic response, Nestorius in his sermon asserted that the term *Theotokos* should not be used at all; in doing so he must have known that he would be seen as attacking important interests. The term was especially valued in Egypt, particularly among the monks.[23] Furthermore, the veneration of Mary as *Theotokos* was also popular with some powerful people in Constantinople, not least the emperor's sister Pulcheria, a dedicated virgin who regarded Mary as her patroness.[24]

It is not surprising then that Nestorius' sermon caused a stir, provoking various parties in Constantinople against him. The most significant response to Nestorius, however, came in a series of letters from Cyril, Bishop of Alexandria. Cyril had been ordained presbyter, and no doubt 'groomed for office',[25] by his uncle, Bishop Theophilus, the enemy of Chrysostom. When Cyril was consecrated in 412 he swiftly established himself as an influential manager of his Egyptian see, having to deal with a crisis caused by his own contested election and the continued presence of various heretical and schismatic groups he felt bound to oppose.[26] The city had a very large Christian population given to being swayed by popular forces and was threatened with deep tensions between Christians and other religious communities. For example, Cyril, like Chrysostom in Antioch, revealed in his sermons his anxieties about Christians apparently taking on Jewish traditional practices in a city with a prominent Jewish population.[27] As for pagans, while Theodosius II's anti-pagan legislation of 437 perhaps encouraged the local monks' enthusiasm for attacking Egyptian pagan shrines, it certainly did not lead to the immediate cessation of pagan practice, nor to the end of the long Alexandrian tradition of pagan philosophy. It did, however, raise tensions. Although Cyril was probably not directly involved in the notorious murder of the pagan philosopher Hypatia in 415, he certainly found himself dealing with the consequences of her death; these included increasingly difficult relations between the ecclesiastical and imperial authorities, the latter being always more preoccupied with preserving peace, despite the imperial policy of promoting Christianity. Nevertheless, Cyril emerged with his head above water, and by the time of the newly consecrated Nestorius' sermons on the *Theotokos*, he was an experienced Church politician. As his modern biographer remarks, 'the difference in political acumen between the two men is obvious from the outset'.[28]

In 429, in response to Nestorius' sermon, Cyril wrote to him demanding that he must calm the uproar he had caused and accept the title *Theotokos* for Mary. Nestorius' reply was uncooperative, objecting to Cyril's lack of 'brotherly love'.[29] Cyril replied early in 430 with a longer and carefully argued text, his famous *Second Letter to Nestorius*, which later was received as a canonical expression of orthodoxy by the Councils of Ephesus and Chalcedon. Although for the most part it focused on the theological issues, it did not shrink from accusing Nestorius of causing a scandal which was likely to trip up those in his congregations who had no understanding of the theological niceties in Nestorius' subtle arguments.[30] Cyril ostentatiously claimed to have the plain meaning of the Nicene Creed on his side. His high-handed tone is that of an older, more experienced, but somewhat tactless churchman giving advice to a younger, idealistic, but rather rash colleague. Cyril had also by this stage successfully appealed to Bishop Celestine of Rome for a theological judgement on Nestorius' position, and Nestorius' teachings were condemned at a synod in Rome. In response, fearing a serious breach between Rome and Constantinople, Theodosius II summoned a council to be held at Ephesus.

Later in 430 Nestorius replied to Cyril with a discussion of the key theological issues: it did recognize the points on which they were in agreement and made a small concession on the issue of the *Theotokos*, arguing that *Christotokos* ('bearer of Christ') was preferable to *Theotokos*, because it was more 'exact'.[31] This perhaps suggests that Nestorius thought that *Theotokos* was merely in danger of being misunderstood, rather than that it was heretical in itself. But Nestorius also accused Cyril of misunderstanding the Creed and insinuated that Cyril's supporters were Manichaean. This was probably not a good way to win Cyril over. Cyril issued a *Third Letter* in which his claims to authority were even more pronounced. First, he referred repeatedly to Celestine's support for the Alexandrian position and spoke in effect as Celestine's representative in the east, conveying the Bishop of Rome's bald request that Nestorius should 'dissociate [himself] from the utterly mischievous and distorted doctrines ... by the date appointed'.[32] Secondly, Cyril demanded that Nestorius should not only be able to declare the words of the Nicene Creed, but that he should agree to its correct (i.e. Cyril's) interpretation. Finally, to make his views quite clear, Cyril attached a list of 12 bluntly expressed anathemas (sometimes referred to as 'the 12 chapters').

This phase of their correspondence was important for three reasons. First, the debate broadened out beyond the term *Theotokos* and the exchange of accusations of heresies to a more close discussion of some underlying issues, especially the problem of unity in Christ. Secondly, by 431 there was a definite acknowledgement by both sides that a mere repetition of the formula of Nicaea was not enough: it needed to be interpreted and it needed to be interpreted authoritatively.[33] Thirdly, it seems to have been the anathemas in particular that provoked the ire of Nestorius and his supporters, including John of Antioch and the Antiochene theologian Theodoret. One scholar has suggested that Cyril's motive in issuing the anathemas was 'to force Nestorius to abandon the provisos and nuances he had expressed hitherto and either accept [Cyril's] Christological position ... and thus bring an end to the controversy or else reject it and prove himself a heretic'.[34] However, Nestorius refused to back down, there was by no means a consensus that his theology was heretical and the divisions between Antioch and Alexandria were only deepened.

At the council, convened at Ephesus in 431, Nestorius was condemned and deposed, but this was largely due to the late arrival of the delegation from Antioch. When Bishop John arrived, he met with those who supported Nestorius and they in turn declared Cyril to be deposed. After a short period of uncertainty, Cyril's party gained the upper hand, not least because Cyril wrote a more conciliatory document defending the 12 anathemas in terms which some of those who had previously supported Nestorius could accept. Nestorius lost the trust of the emperor, who until that point had been inclined to support him.

Ephesus was undoubtedly an important moment, both in the east and west. Crucially the council condemned the idea that Jesus Christ could be described as being 'two Sons' (an idea which was in fact an exaggeration of Nestorius' position, but which was one of Cyril's main concerns) and accepted the title *Theotokos*. It was partly in response to this council that Bishop Sixtus II of Rome ordered the refashioning of the Liberian basilica in Rome into the new church of Santa Maria Maggiore, including the commissioning of a series of mosaics commemorating Mary as *Theotokos*, the mother of God. From this point, depictions of the Virgin – especially those of the annunciation – assumed a particular importance in Christian art, because with the title *Theotokos* the council had agreed that Jesus Christ was fully God and fully human from the moment of his conception, that is from the moment of Gabriel's annunciation to Mary.

Another important consequence of Ephesus concerned the Creed. In expressing their judgement, the fathers at the Council of Ephesus claimed that the Nicene Creed was 'pious and sufficient for the whole world'. Nevertheless, they added:

> Since some pretend to confess and accept it, while at the same time distorting the force of its expressions to their own opinion and so evading the truth ... it has proved necessary to add testimonies from the holy and orthodox fathers that can fill out the meaning they have given to the words and their courage in proclaiming it. All those who have a clear and blameless faith will understand, interpret and proclaim it in this way.[35]

Besides receiving the second and third letters of Cyril (together with the 12 anathemas), the council also appended a collection of quotes from select Fathers to back up their judgement. This practice was followed in very many latter councils and was of enormous significance for the way in which the Church operated and for how Christians viewed their tradition: the Fathers cited in this way were given an official authority which went beyond any intellectual or charismatic authority they might previously have enjoyed.[36]

The removal of Nestorius greatly alleviated relations between Antioch and Alexandria. He stayed in his monastery near Antioch for a while, but was later exiled, first to Petra and then to the colony of the Great Oasis in Egypt, where those who presented a problem to imperial authority were sent to be isolated from the outside world by the vast tracts of desert.[37] With Nestorius out of the way, there was a period of relatively constructive diplomacy, and in 433 Cyril and John of Antioch agreed on the wording of a document known as the 'Formula of Union'.[38] In this, John acknowledged the use of *Theotokos* and the deposition of Nestorius; Cyril accepted that one could talk of 'two natures' in Christ, whereas previously his theology had seemed to assume that in Christ there was 'one incarnate nature of the Word'.[39]

The Formula of Union raises the question, however, of whether Cyril of Alexandria changed his mind, compromised or came to a recognition that part of the problem was that he and Nestorius were using some words (particularly 'nature' and 'person') in different ways. More acutely, it forces one to examine the question of what theological issues were really at stake.

Nestorius and Cyril were united in their rejection of Arianism (which denied Jesus Christ's full divinity) and their denial of Apollinarius' Christology (which rejected the idea that Jesus had a human mind). Thus they *both* thought that the Saviour was fully human and fully divine. However, each theologian alleged that the other did not give enough place to one or other of these aspects.

Nestorius suspected that Cyril's Christology so stressed the intense union of the human and the divine that it in effect implied that the human was changed into the divine. He felt that this jeopardized Jesus Christ's true humanity (thus some Antiochenes tried to accuse Cyril of Apollinarianism). Because Nestorius feared that 'the Word became flesh' (John 1.1) might be taken to imply that the divine nature changed into human nature, he understood the phrase 'became flesh' as if it were qualified by the next few words, 'and dwelt among us'. Antiochene theology before Nestorius had developed a particular interpretation of those words which tried to explain how that kind of indwelling was particular to Christ. For example, Theodore of Mopsuestia wrote that 'God's indwelling is not in everyone' and, furthermore, that God's indwelling in Christ was unique in that 'the indwelling took place in him *as a son*'.[40] In fact the theology of indwelling seems to have been expressed rather more subtly by Theodore than by Nestorius.

Cyril, however, chose to ignore the subtleties of the Antiochene notion of indwelling and asserted that Nestorius and his supporters thought that the Word of God dwelt in a human, like one of the saints.[41] He feared that, in asserting that Mary gave birth to 'the human being ... the instrument of Godhead' and that in describing Christ's human nature as God-receiver (*theodochos*), Nestorius was guilty of asserting adoptionism – the idea that God chose ('adopted') the human Jesus at some time after his birth and then imparted divinity to him. This idea had for long been regarded as heretical in Christian communities because it suggested that Christ's divinity was an afterthought and it was difficult to explain in what respect he differed from a prophet or other holy man. Cyril's reply was uncompromising:

> For the God of all things dwells in us through the Holy Spirit. ... But God does not dwell in Christ in the same way as he does in us. For Christ was God by nature, who became like us. He was the one and only Son even when he became flesh. They who have the temerity to say that he was a God-bearing (*theodochos*) man instead of saying that he was God made man inevitably incur this anathema.[42]

Cyril insisted that human and divine were united in Mary's womb right from the moment of the annunciation: *Theotokos* was thus not merely allowable but it expressed the full truth of the Incarnation.

Thus the controversy over the title *Theotokos* was fundamentally not about how to address Mary but about what could be properly said about Jesus Christ. In particular, Nestorius and Cyril disagreed about how Christians should describe the birth and death of Jesus Christ. As we saw above,

Nestorius insisted that Mary 'did not give birth to the Godhead ... [but] the instrument of the Godhead', a 'temple for God the Logos, a temple in which he dwelt'. Similarly, 'the incarnate God did not die, he raised up the one in whom he was incarnate'. Nestorius was insistent that Christians should be clear about the distinction between the divine and human natures in Christ, but he argued that 'since God is within the one who was assumed, the one who was assumed *is styled God* because of the one who assumed him'. Consequently he believed that, although God alone was the true object of worship, 'we confess both and adore [the two natures] as one, for the duality of the natures is one on account of the unity'. He turned this point into a slogan: 'I divide the natures but I unite the worship'.[43]

Cyril ridiculed Nestorius' suggestion that the Alexandrian view entailed that the Logos 'found the beginning of his existence inside the holy virgin' or needed a 'second birth'. He argued that 'since ... the Logos was born of a woman after he had ... united human reality hypostatically to himself, *he is said* on this ground to have had a fleshly birth'. Consequently, Mary could be said to have given birth to the Logos; in other words she was *Theotokos*.[44] Cyril's thought on the crucifixion followed a similar logic:

> It is not that the Logos of God suffered in his own nature ... for the divine, since it is incorporeal, is impassible. Since, however, the body that had become his own underwent suffering, *he is ... said* to have suffered these things for our sakes, for the impassible One was within the suffering body.[45]

Finally, while Nestorius was happy to worship 'this one together with the Godhead because he is a sharer in the divine authority ... I adore him as an instrument of the Lord's goodness', Cyril thought these phrases implied a dangerous duality, tantamount to asserting that there were 'two Sons' in Christ – Son of God, and Son of Man. Against this, he argued that 'we worship one and the same, because the body of the Logos is not alien to him but accompanies him even as he is enthroned with the Father'.[46]

Cyril argued, then, that the Logos *could be said* to have been born; Nestorius (rather reluctantly) admitted that the human whom God assumed *could be styled* God: the argument centred on what could appropriately or piously be said about Jesus Christ. Nestorius' problem was that for generations Christians had acknowledged the mystery of the God-man Jesus Christ, by asserting – usually in the context of the liturgy – that Mary was the 'mother of God', or that the Word 'died for all'. There was a recognition in most theologians that this was stretching the limits of language, but in Nestorius there seemed to be a strong reluctance to tolerate that stretching, because he thought such phrases were in danger of being taken to mean that God could suffer in God's own nature. Consequently, he read the Nicene Creed in a particular way. It began, he said, with four titles, 'Lord', 'Jesus', 'Christ',

'Only Begotten', which were 'common names for both the Godhead and the manhood' – titles which belonged to the one person.[47] He argued that the Creed then proceeded with a series of phrases which could be attributed to *either* the Godhead *or* the manhood in Christ. He had a similar way of reading the New Testament. One could say of Christ that he had been born (hence *Christotokos*), or that he died, or was God; one could not say, strictly speaking, that God had been born or died, or that Jesus was God. Cyril, on the other hand, was completely opposed to this way of proceeding: according to his reading of the Creed the one subject of *all* the phrases was the Word:

> We declare that *the only-begotten Word of God*, begotten from the very substance of the Father ... who came down for our salvation emptying himself, *he it is* who was incarnate and made man, and underwent our human birth and came forth as man from woman without abandoning what he was but remaining, even when he had assumed flesh and blood, what he was, God, that is, in nature and in truth.[48]

As Nestorius saw it, Cyril was seriously in danger of endangering both Christ's humanity and his impassible divinity by suggesting that the divine Word was the subject of all Christ's experiences. On the other hand, Nestorius needed to explain: if the human nature was properly the subject of human experiences and the divine nature the subject of divine experiences, what was the mysterious commonality that the term 'Christ' described? Thus the disagreement over what could appropriately be said about Jesus Christ pointed to a second, more fundamental disagreement over the nature of the relation of the human and the divine in Christ. Consequently, a lot of the debate became focused on the terminology of *union* (in what way and when were the divine and human united in Jesus Christ?), of *nature* (did he consist of one nature or of two?) and of *person* (in what sense was Jesus Christ one person?).

Nestorius wrote of two natures, human and divine, but he often expressed their coming together in terms which Cyril found unsatisfactory. He tended to speak of the 'joining' or 'conjunction' of the two natures rather than their union, for example.[49] Because the divine 'assumed' the human nature, the human was the 'instrument', 'temple' or 'receiver' of the divine. Most of this language was traditional: Athanasius had written of Christ's human body as an instrument; Gregory of Nazianzus' famous dictum 'the unassumed is the unhealed' stated that the divine had assumed the human nature. Furthermore, Christians were united in agreeing that Christ's human nature was his 'temple', because of their reading of Mark 14.58 ('I will destroy this temple that is made with hands and in three days I will build another, not made with hands') to refer to the resurrection.

However, Cyril rejected such expressions unless they were accompanied by some language which very strongly asserted the *union* of the human and divine: his second letter is scattered with the words 'union' and 'unity' – or, more pointedly, a *'true* unity'.[50] The Logos did not merely join human nature to himself, but he 'made it *his own*'.[51] Underlying this language seems to be the assumption that there was one nature in Christ – 'one incarnate nature of the Word'. In fact, Cyril used that exact phrase rarely, possibly because he realized that it was contentious. One of the few examples comes in a letter where he seeks to explain and qualify it.[52] It is possible that the Antiochenes used it as an over-simplified label for Cyril's theology because it echoed Apollinarian theology.

Certainly Nestorius thought the idea of one nature in Christ was a step too far, whether it was an implicit or explicit part of Alexandrian theology. Nestorius seems to have been driven by the anxiety that such a view would imply that the uncreated divine nature had changed into or become mixed with part of his creation. Thus Cyril was forced to reiterate that 'we unite the word of God the Father to the holy flesh endowed with a rational soul, in an ineffable way that transcends understanding, *without confusion, without change, and without alteration*'.[53] Indeed, he was willing to state that in the Incarnation, 'two natures [came] together with one another, without confusion or change' or that 'the union took place out of two natures'.[54] The Formula of Union acknowledges a 'union of the two natures'. What Cyril was unwilling to admit, however, was the concept of a union *in* two natures, which is what Antiochene theologians preferred, but which to Cyril was a contradiction in terms: for him, the continued existence of two natures entailed that no *true* union had taken place.[55] Consequently he developed his own way of expressing the nature of that true union: the hypostatic union, or a union at the level of the Word's *hypostasis*:

> We say that in an unspeakable and incomprehensible way, the Logos united to himself, according to his *hypostasis* (*kath' hypostasin*), flesh enlivened by a rational soul, and in this way became a human being (*anthrōpos*) and has been designated 'Son of man'. He did not become a human being simply by an act of will or 'good pleasure', any more than he did so by merely taking on a person (*prosōpon*).[56]

What did Cyril mean by a union at the level of the *hypostasis*? Very generally expressed, *hypostasis* meant 'individual reality'. Cyril's concept of hypostatic union understood this in two ways. Above all, hypostatic union stressed that Christ was '*individual* reality': it seems to have been an attempt to preserve the Word as the *single subject* of all the experiences attributed to Jesus Christ: 'for Cyril, the union of two distinct levels of reality, Godhead and manhood, takes place dynamically because there is only one individual subject presiding over both, the one person of the incarnate deity'.[57] The thing that made Jesus Christ one was the single active agency of the Word: divine and human natures were not united like water and wine passively subjected to being mixed in a cup; they were united as body and soul are united through the agency of one individual. However, Cyril also exploited the meaning of *hypostasis* in another way: for him it indicated that the union in Christ was 'individual *reality*' (as opposed to a fiction, or a mere appearance): he exploited this in his writings against Nestorius to drive home the point that in his Christology 'the union is a real and concrete event', whereas in Nestorius' thought it was allegedly 'a cosmetic exercise'.

In the passage quoted above, Cyril contrasted his concept of union 'according to the *hypostasis*' with his caricature of Nestorius' concept of union: 'by an act of will or "good pleasure" ... merely taking on a person (*prosōpon*)'. In order to preserve what he thought was a proper boundary between the two natures, Nestorius seems to have asserted that they were each bound to their own *hypostasis* – in Cyril's terms they were *two* 'individual actualities'. Nestorius meant that Christ's humanity and his divinity were real and that they were 'individual' insofar as they remained unmixed even when brought together. They were united in what Nestorius termed a *prosōpon* of union. The key question is what *prosōpon* means: often translated as 'person', it could also mean 'persona' (in the English sense), and originally derived from the word for a face or a mask. Nestorius thought that it was this single *prosōpon* to which the Creed referred with the titles 'Lord', Jesus', 'Christ' and 'Only Begotten'. Nestorius probably chose the word to suggest a single agent, in a sense that was basically very similar to Cyril's use of *hypostasis*. But because of the range of the word's meanings it was easy for Cyril to imply that Christ's unity in Nestorius' theology was only an *appearance* and thus that the mysterious *prosōpon* of union was not a very secure basis for the unity of the Saviour.

When one looks behind the emotional subject of the *Theotokos*, the accusations of heresy and the claims to be reading the Bible or the Creed 'properly', one basic question faced Nestorius and Cyril: 'Who is Jesus Christ?' Cyril's strongest and most valuable contribution to the debate was to argue that Nestorius had no clear answer to that question (despite all Nestorius' claims to precision, his final conclusions were fuzzy). On the other hand, Nestorius was able to show that although Cyril's answer was clear, it carried implications which were unwelcome, even dangerous. Although there is a danger in caricaturing their theological styles, there is some truth in the argument that Nestorius' talent for sharp analysis and criticism of other people's positions was not matched by skill in constructive theology.[58] Conversely, Cyril, while a much better creator of theological systems, somewhat lacked the intellectual imagination which would enable him to see the weaknesses of his own theology as they might appear from another perspective.

What can one learn from this controversy, which seems so technical and alien from a modern perspective? First, the argument over the nature of the unity of Christ revealed that Cyril and Nestorius understood words like *hypostasis* and *prosōpon* in significantly different ways. In the background of the debates about Christ were dimmer and more confused arguments over the meaning of such words. Often one side assumed that their meaning of a word was correct, without appearing to realize that it was precisely that meaning which was being contested. (The same had happened in debates over the Trinity over the correct meaning of *ousia* and *hypostasis*.) In the Christological controversy, however, there were not only contested words but more general contested ideas. For example, although Cyril used the terms 'union' and 'unity' and Nestorius tended to write of 'conjunction', they both used the analogy of body and soul in human beings to describe the coming together of human and divine in Christ. There was much argument in late antiquity over the basic question of anthropology: how material and immaterial aspects of human nature were related in each individual. There was, however, agreement that each human being was basically one individual reality. The problem of the relation of the human and divine in Jesus Christ was more complex and there was more at stake. Nevertheless, it was possible that Christology might have followed anthropology's pattern – a basic agreement *that* Christ was one underlying any disagreements as to *how* that was possible. However, with Nestorius' claim that Cyril's Christ was a mixed unity, and Cyril's counter-claim that Nestorius' Christ was two, it became very difficult to find any common ground. The significance of the body–soul analogy became contested along with everything else.

Secondly, both Cyril and Nestorius recognized the importance of being able to say that in becoming incarnate the Word was in some sense related to all of humanity. Discussions of Nestorius' theology often ignore the fact that much of his writing is taken up with basic doctrine of salvation, which assumes that the Incarnation allowed Christ to die for all humans and which repeatedly asserts that Christ shares human nature.[59] This is not the clichéd Nestorius for whom Christ's human nature is an isolated human individual.

Finally, both Nestorius and Cyril were concerned with the implications that Christology had for everyday piety, liturgy and human behaviour. They may have followed these implications in rather different ways, but neither thought that theology was an armchair profession. In particular Cyril was concerned, as we have seen, to maintain the traditional veneration of the

Virgin Mary as *Theotokos*. His insistence on the idea that the Logos was *the* subject in Jesus Christ tended to emphasize the traditional Alexandrian idea of the divinization of the human being in the Incarnation (but not in a way which jeopardized the continued existence of that human nature as fully human). Because of Christ and through participating in Christ, for example, in the Eucharist, Christians were enabled to participate in that divinization: 'they envisaged assimilation to the Logos as the proper destiny of a human being'.[60] Antiochene theologians agreed on the question of the goal of becoming more like Christ, but their emphasis on Jesus' real humanity meant more of a focus on Jesus' obedience, his moral struggle, his growth in virtue. This was not, however, dissociated from an emphasis on the sacraments, which are the means by which Christians are brought into their own conjunction with the divine.[61]

Cyril of Alexandria died in 444; Nestorius remained in permanent exile. But the controversies did not end there. As Cyril had succeeded his uncle, Theophilus, so he was succeeded by his nephew, Dioscoros. Unfortunately Dioscoros was not in favour of the Formula of Union, particularly its admission of 'two natures'. There was increasing tension between him and theologians of the Antiochene school, especially Theodoret of Cyrrhus (who had earlier objected forcefully to Cyril's 12 anathemas) and Domnus, who had succeeded his uncle, John, as Bishop of Antioch in 441. The situation became complicated by a controversy surrounding Ibas, Bishop of Edessa: his theology was broadly of the Antiochene school, although he appears to have accepted the deposition of Nestorius. Despite this, some in his congregations who were much more sympathetic to the Alexandrian position tried to engineer his deposition on the grounds that he was Nestorian. The episode is a useful reminder of the high emotions still being roused by the controversy and that fact that a Syrian see (which might on the face of it be expected to have followed the Antiochene or 'Oriental' Christology) was split into 'Antiochene' and 'Alexandrian' camps.

In Constantinople, Nestorius had been succeeded by Proclus and then by Flavian, who was a supporter of the Formula of Union. Flavian's authority, however, was considerably undermined by the influence of Eutyches, who was a fierce opponent of the Formula of Union and a proponent of the view that Christ was of one nature. Despite being an 'aged and muddle-headed archimandrite',[62] he had considerable capacity to rock the ecclesiastical boat: it seems to have been he who inflamed the situation. In 448, Flavian summoned a council at Constantinople which condemned Eutyches, but, side-stepping that authority, Eutyches wrote to Dioscoros of Alexandria and Bishop Leo of Rome in order to explain his case and plead for help. In the meantime, Flavian had also written to Leo to defend his course of action.

As archdeacon to Bishop Celestine of Rome, Leo had been involved in the first phase of the Christological controversies. In June 449 Leo sent his reply to Flavian: as might be expected, it upheld the Formula of Union and its deposition of Nestorius, but it also condemned Eutyches and the extreme Alexandrian position that he and Dioscoros held. This might have been the end of the matter were it not for the fact that the Emperor Theodosius II had more sympathy for the Alexandrians and had already called a council to be held at Ephesus in 449. Dioscoros presided over the council, which restored Eutyches, canonized Cyril's 12 anathemas and deposed Flavian, along with Theodoret, Domnus and Ibas. He and his party either ignored or were completely unaware of Leo's letter to Flavian.

After the council both Flavian and Theodoret wrote to Leo, begging him to intervene and claiming that Dioscorus had achieved victory only by fraud and violence. Indeed the exiled Flavian was said to have died of injuries sustained at the council. The Bishop of Rome took up the challenge but the emperor's support for what Leo called the 'Robber Council' was a seemingly insuperable obstacle.[63]

Matters were resolved in a matter completely unrelated to theology and Church politics, when in July 450 the emperor fell off his horse and died. His sister Pulcheria, always of great influence in Constantinople, renounced her status as a dedicated virgin and married a senior soldier, Marcian, who became emperor. Marcian showed where his loyalties lay by exiling Eutyches and bringing Flavian's relics to Constantinople, where he was venerated as a martyr. He called a council at Chalcedon for the following year.

With the backing of the new emperor and leaning on the theology of Leo's letter, the Council of Chalcedon followed the kind of line aimed at by the Formula of Union, clearly ruling out extreme versions of both Alexandrian and Antiochene theologies and seeking to mark out some common ground on which all could agree. (Whether this amounted to a Christological 'definition' is a moot point.) The council reaffirmed the Creed of Nicaea, and officially accepted the texts of Cyril's *Second Letter to Nestorius* and Leo's *Letter to Flavian* (commonly known as the *Tome of Leo*). It did not, however, receive as canonical Cyril's *Third Letter* and its 12 anathemas. It condemned an exaggerated version of Nestorius' views – the doctrine of 'two sons' – and an equally exaggerated version of Cyril's: that 'the deity of the Only-Begotten is passible', that there is 'a confusion or mixture of the two natures of Christ'. It explicitly condemned Eutyches and his followers who have 'made up' the belief that 'before the union there are two natures of the Lord, but imagine that after the union there is one'.[64]

Despite claiming throughout to be adding nothing to the Nicene formula, the final few phrases of the Chalcedonian statement came to have lasting influence:

> Following, therefore, the holy fathers, we confess one and the same Son, who
> is our Lord Jesus Christ, and we all agree in teaching that this very same
> Son is complete in his deity and complete – the very same – in his humanity,
> truly God and truly as human being, this very same one being composed of a
> rational soul and a body, coessential [*homoousios*] with the Father as to his deity
> and coessential [*homoousios*] with us – the very same one – as to his humanity,
> being like us in every respect apart from sin. As to his deity, he was born from
> the Father before the ages, but as to his humanity, the very same one was born
> in the last days from the Virgin Mary, the Mother of God [*Theotokos*], for
> our sake and the sake of our salvation: one and the same Christ, Son, Lord,
> Only Begotten, acknowledged to be unconfusedly, unalterably, undividedly,
> inseparably in two natures [*physesin*], since the difference of the natures is not
> destroyed because of the union, but comes together in one person [*prosōpon*]
> and one *hypostasis*, not divided or torn into two persons [*prosōpa*] but one and
> the same Son and only-begotten God, Logos, Lord Jesus Christ.[65]

Clearly some of this language is aimed at earlier heresies – the views which
were not representative of either Cyril's or Nestorius' position, but which
they attempted to tar each other with. So Arianism is dismissed with the
assertion that the Son was 'complete in his deity', 'truly God', 'coessential
[*homoousios*] with the Father as to his deity', 'born from the Father before the
ages'. The views of Apollinarius or his more extreme followers were ruled
out with the affirmation that the Son was 'complete in his humanity', 'truly
a human being ... being composed of a rational soul and a body', 'coessential [*homoousios*] with us ... as to his humanity, being like us in every respect
apart from sin'. Against Nestorius, the title *Theotokos* was affirmed. The
acknowledgement of two natures is taken by some to be a vindication of the
Antiochene position, by others the further following through of the implications of the Formula of Union. The way in which the statement seems to
speak of Christ in one way 'as to his deity' and another 'as to his humanity'
might seem to follow the Antiochene method of reading the Creed, but
this is constantly qualified by the repeated emphasis on the Son's unity:
'we confess one and the same Son', 'this very same Son', 'the very same',
'this very same one', 'one and the same Christ, Son, Lord, Only Begotten'.
Although numerous scholars have debated whether the Antiochene or the
Alexandrian position was most vindicated by the Council of Chalcedon, in
effect the council's main aim seems to have been to rule out the negative
implications of a rigid adherence to either theory: the Son is 'unconfusedly,
unalterably' but also 'undividedly, inseparably' one; he is 'two natures' in
one *prosōpon* and one *hypostasis*.

Although Leo's letter was received with suspicion by some at Chalcedon, it seems to have played a useful role in presenting a theology which clearly acknowledged one agent in Christ whilst also arguing – with considerably more skill than Nestorius had done – for the necessity of distinguishing between the two natures after the Incarnation. The letter cleverly developed its theme, moving from sources which all Christians would acknowledge (the Scriptures, the Creed[66]) to the heart of Christian theology (the doctrine of salvation) and thence to confess Jesus Christ 'a unity of person, which must be understood to exist in a two-fold nature'.[67] It reminded the reader that the best of Nestorius' and Cyril's theology was also soteriological, but that it was precisely soteriology which often got lost in the heat of the debate. It was said that Nestorius read Leo's *Letter* and not only agreed with it but rejoiced; at the council itself, Nestorius' old ally Theodoret worked to show that it was consonant not with just Nestorius' but with Cyril's theology.[68]

For these reasons, it has sometimes been argued that Leo's letter was, as it were, more Antiochene than Alexandrian, but this would be to misunderstand both the letter and the context out of which it developed. First, it seems that one of Leo's primary concerns with Nestorius' theology was that it might tend to Pelagianism: it might, in other words, lead to the idea that Jesus was a perfectly virtuous man who was fore-chosen and adopted by God. Consequently, Leo was most concerned to stress Christ's true divinity and the truth of the Virgin as Mother of God. He was less concerned to oppose any perceived duality in Nestorius' thought, which became Cyril's main anxiety. Secondly, despite its acknowledgement of two natures, the letter's Christology clearly emphasized one person, which in key passages it identified with the Word: 'it is this very same being, this only and eternal Child of the eternal Begetter, who was born of the Holy Spirit and Mary the Virgin'.[69]

The theology of the letter centred on the key faith in the divine loving desire for the 'restoration of humanity'. The Incarnation came about because 'we would not be able to overcome the author of sin (the devil) and of death unless he whom sin could not stain nor death hold took on our nature and made it his own'.[70] Further on, Leo explained:

> In this way, as our salvation requires, one and the same mediator between God and human beings, the human being who is Jesus Christ, can at one and the same time die in virtue of the one nature and, in virtue of the other, be incapable of death. That is why true God was born in the integral and complete nature of a true human being, entire in what belongs to him and entire in what belongs to us.[71]

The emphasis that the Word 'took on our nature and made it his own' would satisfy a Cyril; the careful qualification of 'in virtue of one nature ...

in virtue of the other' would please a Nestorius. To avoid the accusation of blending the natures, Leo carefully and consistently argues that 'the *characteristic properties* of both natures ... are kept intact and come together in one person'.[72] This nicely reminded the reader that it was not two *agents* that are being kept apart. Consequently Leo was able to say, much more precisely than Nestorius, that although 'the Word does what belongs to it and the flesh carries out what belongs to it', strictly there is only one agent: 'the one whom the devil's cunning tempted as a human being is the same one to whom the angel's services were rendered as God'.[73] Leo tries to express how this might be so by using the language of two 'forms': 'each "form" carries on its proper activities in communion with the other'; the two forms have 'reciprocal spheres'.[74]

It is easy to be carried away with the elegance and fluid style of Leo's letter after the angry and somewhat staccato character of the correspondence between Cyril and Nestorius. Leo's theology was not the only factor which allowed for a settlement at Chalcedon, nor was it without its own weaknesses. Nevertheless its clear articulation of the way in which a theology of one person and two natures could make sense within the mainstream of Christian theological tradition had a significant – and lasting – impact.

CHAPTER 10

Epilogue
(FIFTH TO SIXTH CENTURIES)

In 451 the Council of Chalcedon defined the way in which Jesus Christ was believed to be 'truly God and truly a human being'; one person existing 'unconfusedly, unalterably, undividedly, inseparably in two natures'. Their pronouncement incorporated Bishop Leo of Rome's *Tome* on the doctrines of salvation and Christ, thus acknowledging it as an authoritative text. The following year, according to a sixth-century chronicle, 'for the sake of the Roman name [Leo] undertook an embassy and travelled to the king of the Huns, Attila by name, and he delivered the whole of Italy from the peril of the enemy'.[1]

Does the history of the early Church thus come to a neat end with Leo securing the theological unity of Christianity within the Empire and demonstrating his political power in defending Rome against the Huns? As with the Council of Nicaea, theological and historical accounts have tended to differ on this question. Theologians have invested the Christological definition of 451 with the same kind of conceptual finality as the 325 declaration that the Son is consubstantial (*homoousios*) with the Father. Catholic accounts of the rise of the papacy have also often seen Leo's tenure as a crucial period. Historians, however, have pointed out that the 'fall' of the Roman Empire came only 25 years after Chalcedon. Furthermore, the development of the Church in both west and east grew very complex and was not clearly marked by the rise of centralizing authorities like the Roman papacy. This was not least because the Chalcedon council, which was aimed at unity, only succeeded in precipitating the most serious schism the Church had yet seen. What, then, was the state of the Church in the following century?

It is now a commonplace to agree that in fact there was no sudden, cataclysmic 'fall' of the Roman Empire – even in the west. It is true that, although Attila was dissuaded in 452, Rome was sacked three years later by the Vandals, who attacked from their secure base in North Africa. For the next quarter of a century various interest groups vied with each other for power in Italy and southern Gaul, until the German Odoacer proclaimed himself 'King of Italy'. It is to this event in 476 that the 'fall' has traditionally been dated. But the picture of this 'fall' of Rome to the barbarians is complicated by various factors. First, Roman power in the west had for decades alternately been threatened by, and reliant on, varying combinations of 'barbarian' forces. For example, the Huns had been defeated in Gaul in 451 by an alliance between the Roman general Aetius and the Germanic groups who already had territory in Gaul – including the Arian Visigoths. After the fall of Rome, the eastern Emperor Zeno dispatched Theoderic to depose Odoacer: the Ostrogoth Theoderic defeated the 'barbarian' King Odoacer with a coalition of Ostrogoths and the Visigoths of Gaul. (From Zeno's perspective, the tactic backfired when Theoderic assumed an increasingly independent role in Italy, but the point remains that he gained power while acting on behalf of the emperor in Constantinople.) Secondly, the new kings of Italy brought a comparative stability: Odoacer ruled for ten years, and Theoderic for over 40. The fact that both chose Ravenna for their capital did not signify a change in itself, for the capital of the western part of the Empire had been officially moved from Rome to Ravenna a century earlier and in fact the imperial court had spent much time in Milan prior to that. Thirdly, the term 'barbarian' masks the similarities between 'Romans' and their neighbours.[2] There were differences, of course, but these were complex. A nomadic culture, combined with intermarriage and the hire of soldiers between tribes and across imperial borders had meant a great deal of blurring of ethnic boundaries. Some 'barbarians' who wanted influence assumed un-barbarian habits: Theoderic, for example, apparently dressed in a manner reminiscent of a classical client-king, and the beautiful and opulent mosaics which he commissioned for the Arian Baptistry and the Basilica of Sant' Apollinare Nuovo in Ravenna unmistakably follow the style of late antique Roman art.[3] Indeed, although some of the supposedly more 'Arian' mosaics in these churches were later destroyed, their depiction of the baptism of Christ, for example, shows no easily discernible difference from 'orthodox' Christian art of the time. So even the religious boundaries were blurred: not all barbarians were pagans; those who were Christian were not all Arian, and even Arian Christianity was not so different as one might expect. Nevertheless, the term 'Arian', which had been more or less invented by Athanasius to demonize his opponents, continued to be used to reinforce the otherness of the Goths and Vandals – much as the term 'barbarian' was used.

Given these complexities, various narratives have been proposed as an alternative to the story of the fall of Rome.[4] One has suggested that the fall of the Empire was compensated for by the rise of the Church, and in particular the rise of the papacy in Rome. But not only does this deal merely with the fall of the western Empire and the development of the western Church, it does not even seem to do justice to the situation in the west. In Gaul, Spain and North Africa, for example, churches had long showed themselves to have a strong sense of local identity; while they might have appealed to the Bishop of Rome for adjudication on difficult issues, this was not tantamount to recognizing his authority as a bishop above all (western) bishops. Although particular bishops of Rome, such as Leo and Gregory the Great, were successful in expanding their influence and in undertaking certain institutional reforms, their success depended on whether they were accepted as an authority by their fellows. Much as the authority of an umpire in sport depends on a combination of the players' acceptance of the rules of the game and the personal qualities of the umpire himself, so the Bishop of Rome's authority depended on a mixture of the common recognition of the traditional claims of Rome and each pope's personal and charismatic qualities.[5] It is not even clear that Catholic Christianity was growing in influence. Admittedly, Clovis I, King of the Franks, was baptized a Catholic Christian at the end of the fifth century, but the conversion of the Visigoths and the Lombards to Catholic Christianity did not occur until the end of the sixth.[6]

An alternative thesis is that the fall of Rome was compensated for by the continued importance of the Mediterranean as a centre of trade.[7] But archaeological evidence strongly suggests the weakening of the cities of the western Mediterranean coast: the population of Rome, for example decreased from 500,000 to 50,000 in the century after 450.[8] All the evidence points to a period of de-urbanization in the west.

Still another interpretation is to stress that as Rome sank so Constantinople rose in importance.[9] This was particularly so under a strong emperor like Justinian (ruled 527–65), who in the first 15 years of his reign was successful in recapturing North Africa and Italy for the Empire.[10] However, even here, the story is not quite so simple as 'the fall of the western Empire, the rise of the eastern Empire'. Justinian's reign was marked by various events which were destabilizing. In Constantinople there was an horrific echo of the riots of Thessaloniki in 390 when Theodosius' murder of 7,000 people earned him Ambrose's sharp disapproval. The grievances and the purpose of the Constantinople rioters is not clear. Popular riots were not uncommon in this period, but in 532 the crowd's fury led to more than usual destruction and a large part of central Constantinople, including Constantine's Hagia Sophia, was burnt to the ground. Justinian's response was violent, killing between 30,000 and 35,000 people (out of a city population of about 750,000).[11] In the latter half of Justinian's reign the threat on the Persian borders grew stronger and the region was shaken by a series of natural disasters: a virulent outbreak of the bubonic plague in 541–42 which may have killed as many as a quarter of a million people in Constantinople; a widespread famine in 535–36; and earthquakes in Constantinople in 542 and 557. (The second earthquake caused the collapse of the dome of the newly rebuilt Hagia Sophia: Justinian and his architects set to work again and the result still stands today.)[12] The eastern Roman Empire was shaken by these awe-inspiring occurrences, and they probably contributed to a certain amount of de-urbanization in the east as well as the west; but the events were probably not so cataclysmic as they have sometimes been portrayed.[13]

The depopulation of many towns across the Empire, east and west, did not mean the end of civilization, but rather a reconfiguring of communications and relations. In the west in particular, instead of imagining an empire with a clear centre, it is perhaps best to think of a network of towns, monasteries and small settlements. Throughout the Empire, the Christian Church continued, much as it had always done, to rely on networks established through personal friendship, education, family ties or recommendation. Trade did not cease (Alexandria was still sending goods as far afield as Cornwall), but Rome was no longer so obviously at the centre. Commodities, both physical and intellectual or spiritual, passed along the networks of contacts across the Middle East, the Mediterranean, Africa and Northern Europe.[14]

One of these commodities, one might say, was the Gospel. There had been Christians in Britain at least since the fourth century; Christianity presumably arrived both with the Roman legions and through trade links. Britain sent at least three delegates to the Council of Arles in 314 (the bishops of York, Lincoln and London) and Pelagius the theologian came from Britain.[15] But British Christian communities were very small and probably suffered when the Romans gradually withdrew from Britain over the course of the late fourth century. In the fifth and sixth centuries there seems to have been a new period of mission. Celestine, the Bishop of Rome during the Pelagian controversy, probably sent a certain Palladius to rid Britain of Pelagianism. Palladius settled in Wicklow in Ireland and may also have travelled to Scotland.

Great emphasis has been placed on the traditional 'fathers' of Celtic Christianity, who – in contrast to Palladius – came from the British Isles. However, much less is known about them than the legends would seem to convey. Patrick did not convert Ireland single-handedly: he arrived from Scotland after Palladius' arrival in Ireland, but settled a long way north, in Armagh, and seems to have had little contact with the Christian communities in the south. He encouraged monasticism in the region, although it is not clear whether he was a monk himself. Roughly a century later, an Irish monk, Columba, made the opposite journey: having founded some monasteries in Ireland,[16] he founded another on the island of Iona off the south-west coast of Scotland. Even more scarce is information on Ninian, the supposed missionary to the Picts and (by mythical extension) to the whole of Scotland. Although his story became widely known and the church he was believed to have founded at Whithorn became an important pilgrimage centre, scholars now disagree even about which century he was active in.[17]

One very striking aspect of the spread of Christianity was the influence of Christian asceticism and specifically of monastic communities, both eremitic and cenobitic.[18] Celtic Christianity was often noted for the very harsh disciplines practised by its monks – although from what is known of Columba's community on Iona, for example, he seems to have followed in the tradition of those monastic organizers who sought to curb excessive mortification.[19] Indeed, Columba's biographers said that he was influenced by Basil of Caesarea's moderating rule and also by that of John Cassian. Cassian himself is a useful illustration of the possibilities of movement around the Empire, along church and especially monastic networks. He was born in Dacia (roughly equivalent to modern Romania), but joined a monastery in Bethlehem in the 380s, at around the same time as Rufinus and Jerome began their Palestinian communities.[20] The interest in Palestine in various other monastic traditions is illustrated by the fact that Rufinus translated Basil's Rule into Latin at the end of the fourth century; Jerome followed a few years later with a translation of Pachomius' Rule.[21] After making two trips to Egypt (to experience the ascetic life there), to Constantinople and Rome, Cassian settled in Marseilles at the beginning of the fifth century, where he founded two monasteries and wrote the *Institutes* – a guide to monastic life. Another very influential work on the ascetic life was the Rule which emerged from Augustine's formation of a small community on his return to North Africa, also in the 380s. Some 250 years later, a man called Benedict and his sister, Scholastica, founded some ascetic communities in central Italy. Benedict's Rule was dependent on Basil's, Cassian's and Augustine's reflections on the monastic life. His Rule became the most influential set of guidelines for ascetic living in western Europe, not least because of its moderate attitude to discipline and its flexibility, which allowed for its application in multiple contexts. In 1203 the influence of Cassian and Basil returned to Iona, when the monastery was reformed according to the Benedictine Rule.

Although often described as Rules, the texts by Basil, Augustine and Cassian take different forms: Basil's is a series of questions and answers;

Augustine describes his as a 'pamphlet' rather than a formal rule, and Cassian's appears to have been codified into a more rule-like form only in the sixth century.[22] Another form, which became significant in the eastern Church, were letters written to those asking for spiritual guidance. A very influential collection was attributed to Barsanuphius and John, a pair of ascetics living near Gaza in Palestine in the first half of the sixth century, who were much influenced by Evagrius of Pontus. A Syriac set of rules was attributed to Bishop Rabbula of Edessa (bishop 412–35).[23] Notably, there are rules both for male monks and for the 'sons and daughters of the covenant', the distinctively Syrian community of ascetics which was discussed in Chapter 7. Whereas in the days of Ephrem of Edessa, this type of ascetic or hermit was the norm, by the mid-fifth century monasteries were more prominent and there was a great deal of interchange between Syrian and Egyptian monasteries.[24] The ascetic communities played a particularly important role in Syria, preserving the religious texts of the famous school of Edessa when it was closed down in 489. They also proved to be the source of most of the theological writing in the sixth century, although Boethius is one important exception to this rule.

The most fundamental theological problem overshadowing the Christian Church in the fifth and sixth centuries was that of the continuing disruption following the Council of Chalcedon. The Church in Egypt never accepted the council, because of its condemnation of Eutyches and Dioscoros – despite the fact that it also validated Cyril of Alexandria's theology through the inclusion of his *Second Letter to Nestorius* as an authoritative document. The council's approval of certain terminology which had been used by Nestorius and other Antiochene theologians and, perhaps, its use of Leo's *Tome* which was capable of being misunderstood in a Nestorian direction, was taken by many to be an unorthodox departure. Opposition to Chalcedon often crystallized around the use of Cyril's formula 'one incarnate nature of the Word' (one nature – *mia physis*). They became known by their opponents as 'monophysites', a somewhat perjorative term which implicitly criticizes their acknowledgment of *only* one nature (*monē physis*) in Christ, as opposed to the Chalcedonian formula's recognition of two. For this reason, many scholars today prefer to refer to them as 'miaphysites', which reflects Cyril's formula more accurately.[25] Even miaphysite, however, does not do justice to the variety of views which came to fall under the umbrella of opposition to Chalcedon. Because of a long history of tension with, and often oppression by, Chalcedonian churches, modern churches in the broadly Cyrilline tradition do not refer to themselves as either monophysite or miaphysite.

Opposition to Chalcedon was not just apparent in Egypt: it grew throughout the fifth and sixth centuries and was particularly strong in monastic communities in Palestine and Syria. Emperors in Constantinople, who had the stability of the Empire in mind, became increasingly anxious to heal the rift. In 482 Emperor Zeno issued a document known as the *Henotikon* ('the unifying act') which side-stepped the question of Chalcedon and instead invited acceptance of: the Nicene Creed, the councils of Constantinople and Ephesus and Cyril of Alexandria's 12 anathemas.[26] It condemned Nestorius and Eutyches. The statement was probably the work of the Chalcedonian Bishop Acacius of Constantinople and may also have been influenced by the miaphysite Bishop Peter Mongos of Alexandria. With this pedigree it gained some degree of acceptance in the east. The immediate problem, however, was Rome. Simplicius, Bishop of Rome, had not been consulted and he and his successor, Felix, refused to accept the *Henotikon*, which they felt undermined Chalcedon – a council in which Rome felt it had an important stake because of its inclusion of Leo's *Tome*. Shortly afterwards, Bishop Acacius was excommunicated by a Roman synod. The resulting 'Acacian' schism between east and west lasted until 518.

The most important theological exponent of miaphysite theology at the time was Severus, Bishop of Antioch. He had great influence and had enjoyed a certain degree of support from Emperor Anastasius who succeeded Zeno in 491.[27] Anastasius' own successor, however, was Justin I, who turned out to be an unwavering supporter of the Chalcedonian formula. In 518, with Justin's accession, the Romans were appeased and Severus' fortunes changed. He and other notable miaphysite bishops were deposed and several subsequent bishops of Antioch became involved in the persecution of miaphysite Christians.

When Justinian came to the throne, there was a period of comparative calm. He was essentially in favour of the settlement at Chalcedon, whilst seeming to retain a particular personal admiration for the writings of Cyril of Alexandria. His wife Theodora was even more sympathetic to Cyrilline theology and became a kind of patron to miaphysite exiles, providing support for them in Constantinople, a tactic which, of course, kept them conveniently away from their home congregations.[28] In 534 even Severus was invited to the capital, but the tide of favour soon retreated from him again and he returned to Alexandria where he had been sheltering.

Essentially, Justininian did not waver from his basic aim, which was to try to bring miaphysites back into the orthodox fold. In the latter part of his reign his chosen tactic was to appease those who felt aggrieved that Chalcedon, whilst endorsing Cyril's theology and upholding the condemnation of Nestorius, illogically also seemed to stop short of ruling out other

Antiochene theology. In particular, the Alexandrian miaphysites were implacably opposed to three writers – Theodore of Mopsuestia, Theodoret of Cyrrhus and Ibas of Edessa – not least because of these men's personal opposition to Cyril and his theology. Justin's hope was that a condemnation of the writings of these three (known as the 'three chapters') would reconcile them and convince them that Chalcedon was not letting Nestorianism back in through the back door. Thus in 544 Justinian issued his condemnation of the three chapters, and 553 this condemnation was approved by the second Council of Constantinople.

There were possibilities for a rapprochement in Justinian's reign, but neither the condemnation of the three chapters, nor a subsequent effort by his successor, succeeded. The west was very much divided about Justinian's policy and the east was perhaps already too fractured to come to agreement. (One of the problems from the fifth century onwards was the variety of opinions and depth of disagreements between different groups of miaphysites.) The practical results of this failure were painful and permanent. A Chalcedonian bishop was forced on Alexandria by Constantinople, but was never really accepted. The local church remained fundamentally miaphysite and loyal to the tradition of Cyril and after a while established their own parallel clergy and bishop. It was this, but not the Chalcedonian Church in Alexandria, that survived the Arab invasions in 641–42 and became what is now known as the Coptic Church.

A similar pattern of parallel lines of clergy emerged throughout the eastern Empire, greatly helped by the efforts of Jacob Baradeus – another one of Empress Theodora's former protégés, who, with her contrivance, had been consecrated bishop. Strictly, he was Bishop of Edessa, but he had a roving brief to help the miaphysite communities of the east. Legend in the miaphysite churches attributes thousands of priestly ordinations and many episcopal ordinations to him (and for this reason, some miaphysite communities became known as 'Jacobite').

The school of Edessa had traditionally been very influenced by Antiochene theology, particularly that of Theodore of Mopsuestia. Gradually, however, the dominant loyalty in Edessa was miaphysitism: two noted miaphysite theologians, Jacob of Serugh and Philoxenus of Mabbug, were educated at the school and in the late 470s several successive bishops were miaphysite. In 489 Philoxenus persuaded Zeno to close the school at Edessa because of its supposed Nestorianism. Many clergy from the Christian communities in the Persian Empire had trained in Edessa and as a result Christianity in that region was strongly Antiochene. When the school of Edessa closed, a school in Persian Nisibis carried on theological training in that tradition.

From these roots emerged another church, which has been described in the west as the 'Nestorian' Church, but is more correctly known as the (Assyrian) Church of the East. As mentioned, its theology is more properly Theodore's than Nestorius' and it supported Chalcedon; nevertheless it has remained out of communion with other churches, both the Chalcedonian churches further west and with the miaphysite churches.[29] It was however, extremely influential in the region and was involved in far-reaching missionary activity. It had, for example, strong links with several communities of Christians in south India: the sixth-century Christian traveller Cosmas Indicopleustes stated in his chronicles that the churches in Ceylon and Malabar had clergy trained in Persia.[30] In 638 the Church of the East established a monastery in the capital of imperial China.[31] It is worth reflecting on Cosmas' list of the people and places to which Christianity had spread by the mid-sixth century: India, Bactrians, Huns, Persians (of various groups), Ethiopia, Arabia, Palestine, Phoenicia, Syria, Nubia, across a large swathe of North Africa from Egypt in the east to Mauretania in the west, Cilicia, Asia, Cappadocia, Lazica and Pontus, and the countries occupied by the Scythians, Hyrcanians, Heruli (the people of Odoacer), Bulgarians, Greeks and Illyrians, Dalmatians, Goths, Spaniards, Romans and Franks. The areas with which Cosmas was familiar were all on trade routes: Christianity continued to spread, as it had done from the beginning, with trade. Moreover, the Middle East looked east as much as it looked west, and the peoples of north-west Europe are added almost as an after-thought.

If this chapter reads like the verbal equivalent of a kaleidoscope, it is because that is very much what Christianity at the end of the sixth century was – a kaleidoscopic variety of beliefs, practices, languages, traditions, texts and locations which, despite the bewildering succession of shifting patterns and alliances, nevertheless can be viewed through the same lens. Christianity right from the start was structured around a fascinating series of apparent paradoxes. It focused on the life of one who was both human and divine – indeed, fully human and fully divine – whose birth and death were at the same time both unique and normal. It strove for a kingdom 'not of this world' (John 8.23), while always being acutely and actively occupied with the conditions of this world, whether they concerned the poverty of widows and orphans, the feeding of the starving, the discipline of the body and soul in ascetic community, or the realm of politics (both ecclesiastical and secular). It disciplined the body, even to the point of death, while fervently arguing against those who dismissed the body as evil or a hindrance. It valued marriage and depended on the children of converts for the continuation of the Church, while being increasingly more favourable to the celibate life. It depended on men with a good pagan education to propagate, defend and explain the Gospel. From the beginning, it seems to have had the sense of being one, although divided by geography, different interpretations of the Scriptures and different regional loyalties.

It is clear from the preceding chapters what divided the Church. What, then, kept it together? One suggestion is that once the followers of Jesus believed that they had a mission to the Gentiles, once Christianity became a (potentially) universal religion, rather than an ethnic or local group, then it was possible for it not only to spread but to become diverse. (Indeed, diversity might be thought of as necessary for growth.) Once Christians realized that their transcendent God was above all geography, that God could be worshipped wherever and by whomever willed to worship, then Christianity became universal – but not uniform.[32] The crucial point seems to have been that although there were real, painful and destructive divisions between Christian groups, each of them thought that Christianity could and should be above that kind of division. It was precisely the mutually contradictory claims to be the 'universal' or Catholic Church that lay behind many of the most violent disputes.

A second, connected idea is Christianity's belief that through the Incarnation God took on and died for *all* humanity. God, for early Christians, was the transcendent ruler of all; but God had also, in a mysterious way, assumed not the body and soul of one individual but the human soul and human bodilyness *as a whole*. Thus from the beginning, Jesus Christ became a kind of figure to whom all could relate, regardless of their language, culture or ethnicity. The catacomb paintings which portrayed Jesus beardless in the toga of a philosopher, or as an Italian shepherd, were not naive misrepresentations of a Palestinian teacher but rather attempts to convey how Jesus was God for *them* in that particular place and time.

Thirdly, the fundamental rites of the Church had proved themselves remarkably steady focal points of community worship. Despite the frequent arguments about precisely what the rites meant and (even more often) who was permitted to administer or receive them, baptism and Eucharist were in one form or another central to all the Christian communities studied in this book. Furthermore, these rites were nearly always understood in a broadly Trinitarian way: baptism was nearly always in the names of Father, Son and Spirit; Eucharist was an offering to the Father of the bread and wine, which were the body and blood of Christ, through the action of the Holy Spirit whose presence was invited in prayer by the priest and congregation.

Fourthly, the Scriptures were another equally important focus for the Christians in this period. The earliest writers regard the Hebrew writings alone as 'Scripture' (and cite mainly the Pentateuch and the Prophets); later writers like Irenaeus argued with those who wanted to add or subtract from a rather larger canon of both Hebrew Bible and New Testament texts. Other arguments focused around the legitimacy of literal and or allegorical interpretation. Yet there was no Christian who suggested that none of these texts mattered and, in fact, few who rejected the basic set of Law, Prophets, Gospels and Pauline epistles.[33] In the theology of Origen, the Scriptures themselves came to embody the same kind of potentially universal reach that Christ had achieved in the Incarnation: the four Gospels might contain apparent contradictions, but in their variety they allowed Christians (at least) four different approaches to the one Christ.

The main languages of Christianity in the fifth and sixth centuries continued to be Greek and Latin, simply because they had been the languages of imperial administration and Greco-Roman literary culture. Latin had been a *lingua franca* in Gaul for many years and continued to be a Christian *lingua franca* as far north as the British Isles. However, some language groups in this period developed their own writing systems and began to translate the Bible: for example, by 600 the Bible (or parts of it) had been translated into Armenian, Ethiopic, Gothic and Georgian. Syriac became an increasingly important ecclesiastical language, with its influence ranging through Syria, Palestine and Persia, to Christian communities in the Arab peninsula and India. From the fifth century onwards, there was a move away from the use of the traditional single Gospel, the Syriac *Diatessaron*, to the use of the four Gospels in Syriac. Although promoted vigorously by men such as Rabbula of Edessa and Theodoret of Cyrrhus, the transition was probably rather more gradual in some areas, as the *Diatessaron* had become such an important part of Syrian Christian culture.[34]

The example of Scripture shows with particular clarity that the very things which can be held to unite Christians in this period were in themselves diverse and capable of being interpreted in many different ways in different contexts. Precisely this adaptability is a feature of other aspects of Christian culture in this period. In addition to the different languages of the biblical text, Christianity invented a startling variety of literary forms in which to explain, defend, celebrate and remember its faith. In the Greco-Roman world it adapted forms from both scholarship and rhetoric. So from the schools of philosophy and medicine it adapted the treatise and the commentary;[35] from rhetoric it adapted various types of formal speech into sermons, Christian funeral orations and the hagiographies of saints. Like scholars, politicians and men of business around the Empire, early Christians relied hugely on communication by letter. Some of the earliest Christian writings (both in the New Testament and outside it) were letters, and increasingly collections of letters from authoritative writers began to be circulated (either by their authors or their followers), much as the letters of

Cicero and Pliny the Younger circulated.

The basic elements of Christian liturgy were similar across linguistic and cultural boundaries: water in baptism, bread and wine in the Eucharist, the imposition of hands for ordination. There were, however, a great number of regional variations. By the fifth century different communities had developed their own distinctive liturgies in different languages, including many forms and prayers which are still in use today. The study of the development and variations in these has become an important field of inquiry within the study of the early Church. From an early stage it seems that Christian communities used sung or chanted psalms in their worship. Young children were taught psalms as part of their Christian formation, usually, it seems, by their mothers or a female relative or guardian. The singing of other songs or hymns, however, took longer to become widely established. In the fourth century Ephrem of Edessa composed hymns in Syriac which were designed to explain and defend the Christian faith in a vivid and memorable form. They were specifically designed to be sung by choirs of women.[36] Clearly, however, this practice was not regarded well elsewhere: in 270 Paul of Samosata, the then Bishop of Antioch, was accused (besides the more usual complaints of embezzlement, vanity and womanizing) of banning the 'traditional' hymns to Christ but arranging 'for women to sing hymns to himself in the middle of the church on the feast day of the Easter Festival'.[37] Indeed, there seems to have been a common suspicion of the hymn or religious song in the Greek-speaking churches for much of the period covered by this book. Arius, for example, was satirized for expressing his theology in a popular song and he was not the only alleged heretic who was accused of dumbing-down precisely by using music. The west was seemingly more tolerant. Ambrose of Milan was an enthusiastic and skilful composer of hymns, and Augustine credits him with bringing the practice to the west:

> It was then that the practice of singing hymns and psalms was introduced, in keeping with the usage of the Eastern churches, to revive the flagging spirits of the people during their long and cheerless watch. Ever since then the custom has been retained, and the example of Milan has been followed in many other places, in fact in almost every church throughout the world.[38]

In an interesting echo of the anti-Arian context of Ambrose's hymns, the historian Sozomen claims that John Chrysostom introduced hymn singing to Constantinople in order to counter the antiphonal hymns sung by Arians. Chrysostom was worried that his flock would be led astray by the Arians' words, but afterwards, as Sozomen comments, 'having commenced the custom of singing hymns … the members of the Catholic Church did not discontinue the practice, but have retained it to the present day'.[39] Another ancient historian gives a similar account, but traces the origin of the hymns back to Ignatius of Antioch:

> Ignatius third bishop of Antioch in Syria from the apostle Peter, who also had held intercourse with the apostles themselves, saw a vision of angels hymning in alternate chants the Holy Trinity. Accordingly he introduced the mode of singing he had observed in the vision into the Antiochian church; whence it was transmitted by tradition to all the other churches.[40]

Both this tradition, then, and the Ambrose story connect hymn singing with Syria (assuming that by 'eastern churches' Augustine meant those in the Syriac, not Greek-speaking east). It is notable that one of the earliest and most influential hymnodists in Greek was Romanos the Melodist, who was from Emesa in Syria and that his chosen form of hymn, the *kontakion*, was related to a Syriac form.[41]

Christian poetry was another form of literature used widely but in many different ways across the Empire. Gregory of Nazianzus wrote various kinds, ranging from the long, autobiographical and, on occasions, bitterly scathing *On My Own Life*, to beautiful poetic expressions of the theology of the Trinity[42] and brief lyrical reflections on the poignancy of life:

A morning prayer
At dawn, I raise my hand in oath to God:
I shall not do or praise the deeds of darkness.
Rather, this day shall be my sacrifice;
I shall remain unshaken, rule my passions.
My age would shame me, if I were to sin,
As would this altar over which I stand.
Thus my desire, my Christ: you bring it home!

A prayer to Christ the next morning
Yesterday, Christ, turned out a total loss!
Rage came upon me, all at once and took me.
Let me live *this* day as a day of light.
Gregory, look – be mindful, think of God!
You swore you would; remember your salvation![43]

Throughout the Empire and beyond poets seized on the traditional metres, forms and images of their language and culture and adapted them to Christian themes: so Ephrem used (amongst other things) the Middle East tradition of dialogue poems, and Latin poets experimented with epic, epigrammatic or bucolic verse. Prudentius even adapted elements of the classical drinking song:

> Give me my plectrum, boy, that I may sing in faithful verse
> A sweet and melodious song, of the glorious deeds of Christ.
> Him alone may my Muse sing of, Him alone may my lyre praise.[44]

A similar process of adaptation and creativity occurred in the visual arts. Very early Christian art is notoriously hard to interpret or even sometimes to identify, precisely because it used the techniques, genres and themes of contemporary pagan art. As we have mentioned, in the earliest wall paintings in the catacombs, Jesus Christ is portrayed as a toga-clad philosopher and an Italian shepherd; in an early Roman mosaic he is depicted as Apollo; even in Ravenna in a much later mosaic he appears as a classical hero, Cross over one shoulder almost like a lance.[45]

The example of art and literature also allows one to understand a deeply contested aspect of early Christianity in the Roman Empire, which is its use of 'pagan philosophy'. This volume has focused on the *results* of Christian use of earlier philosophy, in order to explain what it was that Christians believed and why. An account of which philosophers or philosophical texts and traditions were being employed to express those doctrines would have become very technical – precisely because it was so complex. It is not enough to say that Alexandrian theologians, or even Origenistic theologians, were 'Platonic', for example, because a closer examination reveals that the theologians in question were often using Stoic and Aristotelian ideas as well, *and* that they were clearly opposing various other Platonic, Stoic and Aristotelian ideas. Just as a Christian artist or writer who depicted Christ in ways reminiscent of a Greek hero was not implying that Jesus fought monsters or was a demi-god, but was trying to say something about his defeat of evil and his divine status, so Christian theologians' use of Greek philosophy was subtle and complicated. Christians regarded Greco-Roman art, literature and philosophy alike as a rich source of ideas which they then adapted to their own distinctive forms.

The conclusions that should be drawn from this brief survey of Christian culture are both theological and historical. The theological idea of the divine 'condescension' – that God came down to earth in human form – could have bound Christianity to one particular place and time. Remarkably, it had exactly the opposite effect, as Christians expressed their belief that the God who was God for them, in their particular context, was the same God incarnate in Palestine and could also be God for others in very different circumstances. Historically the immense flexibility of Christianity with regard to art and literature is a useful illustration of its adaptability in more general ways. Many individual groups were of course extremely conservative and rigid about their own particular customs and had deep-seated objections to other Christians' practice. Nevertheless, when early Christianity is viewed as a whole across five centuries and across Asia, the Middle East, Africa, the Mediterranean and Northern Europe, what strikes one is its immense variety and adaptability.

Notes

Preface

1. This became a semi-technical theological term, which is explained in Chapter 9. The argument was not about whether Mary was the mother of Jesus of Nazareth.
2. There were of course some borderline cases about which historians argue whether they had any reasonable claim to be Christian, for example, some Gnostic groups who used some Christian terminology or names, but otherwise had no distinctive Christian practices or beliefs.
3. Ludwig Wittgenstein, *Philosophical Investigations*, trans G.E.M. Anscombe, 2nd ed (Oxford: Blackwell, 1997), §66–7.

Chapter 1. From Jesus Christ to the Church

1. For a brief outline of this character see David Horrell, *An Introduction to the Study of Paul* (London and New York: Continuum, 2000), pp 12–13. I have omitted from the quotation from Acts any references to the rapid expansion of the community and the Apostles' miracles, which of course are much more contentious from a historical perspective.
2. Christopher Tuckett, *Christology and the New Testament: Jesus and His Earliest Followers* (Edinburgh: Edinburgh University Press, 2001), p 14.
3. Another highly contested issue. For an introduction to the debate see Horrell, *An Introduction to the Study of Paul*, pp 26–7. See Paul's own words: Philippians 3.4–14 and Galatians 1.12–16, especially v.15, 'called'.
4. *1 Clement* 13.2.
5. For the collections of sayings and the spread of the Gospels see Helmut Koester, 'Gospels and Gospel traditions', in Andrew Gregory and Christopher Tuckett (eds), *Trajectories through the New Testament and the Apostolic Fathers* (Oxford: Oxford University Press, 2007), especially pp 30ff.
6. Polycarp *c.*69–*c.*155; Ignatius *c.*35–107.
7. Arthur J. Bellinzoni, *The Sayings of Jesus in the Writings of Justin Martyr*, Novum Testamentum Supplements 17 (Leiden: Brill, 1967), pp 25, 108–11; a view shared by Koester, 'Gospels and Gospel traditions'.
8. By 'choice' here I do not mean the deliberate decision of a council or similar

body; nevertheless, it was not an undeliberated matter of chance for it was vigorously discussed, for example, in Irenaeus' and Origen's arguments for a four-fold Gospel.

9. On the question of Mark's ending see C.M. Tuckett, OBC, p 922.

10. For this argument in relation to Paul's letters see especially the work of Richard B. Hays, for example *Echoes of Scripture in the Letters of Paul* and *The Conversion of the Imagination*.

11. James D.G. Dunn, *Christology in the Making: A New Testament Inquiry into the Origins of the Doctrine of the Incarnation* (London: SCM, 1980), p 265.

12. The seven undisputed letters of Paul, I Thessalonians, I Corinthians, II Corinthians, Galatians, Romans, Philemon and Philippians, were probably written in the 50s CE.

13. Tuckett, *Christology*, p 45.

14. *Ibid.*, pp 43, 45; Donald Guthrie, *New Testament Theology* (Leicester: Inter-Varsity, 1981), p 225.

15. *1 Clement* 16; *Epistle to Diognetus* 10.4.

16. Polycarp's *Letter to the Philippians*, 8.2.

17. On this theme, see David M. Reis, 'Following in Paul's footsteps', in Gregory and Tuckett (eds), *Trajectories through the New Testament*, pp 287–305, especially p 294.

18. For an assessment of what Jesus thought about himself and his understanding of his role see Tuckett, *Christology*, chapter 13.

19. *Didache* 16.

20. This is described as a realized eschatology.

21. I Corinthians 13.12.

22. An example of an exception is the *Didache*, but that is a collection of moral and liturgical instructions.

23. For a full and easily accessible discussion of these titles see Tuckett, *Christology*.

24. *Ibid.*, pp 218–19.

25. John 20.16; 'Rabbouni' meant 'teacher' in Aramaic.

26. Tuckett, *Christology*, p 46.

27. For example, Mark 14.36; 'Abba' is the Aramaic form of address for a father.

28. Tuckett, *Christology*, p 220.

29. I Corinthians 15.22; cf. Romans 5.12–14.

30. Colossians 1.15–20. This passage seems to contain material which predates the composition of the letters themselves. Although they seem to have a liturgical tone, it is disputed whether they were in fact formal hymns as such.

31. For a discussion of this, with references, see Tuckett, *Christology*, p 163.

32. *1 Clement* 42.1; *Epistle to Diognetus* 7; *Letter of Barnabas* 5.

33. *Magnesians* 9.

34. On these two strands in Paul's thought see Horrell, *Introduction to the Study*

of Paul, pp 56–9.

35. *Barnabas* 5.1; see also *1 Clement* 12.7: 'redemption through the blood of the Lord'.

36. Ignatius, *Smyrnaeans* 6.1: 'even angels are condemned if they do not believe in the blood of Christ'.

37. Ignatius, *Philadelphians*, preface.

38. See Luke 24.49–51; John 14.26, 15.26, 16.13.

39. On Peter see Acts 2.33, 10.38, 44, 47; on Paul see Romans 8.9–17, I Corinthians 12.3–14, Galatians 3.26, 4.4–7, 5.22–3; see also Horrell, *Introduction to the Study of Paul*, p 64.

40. For example, Hebrews 8.6, 9.15, 12.24; see also I Timothy 2.5.

41. *1 Clement* 59.

42. *Didache*, opening of the eucharistic prayer, 9.

43. See the closing section of the *Didache*.

44. John 6.35, 6.48.

45. See also Carsten Claussen, 'The Eucharist in the Gospel of John and in the *Didache*', in Gregory and Tuckett (eds), *Trajectories through the New Testament*, for evidence of eucharistic prayers without words of institution.

46. On this much debated question see, for example, R.T. Beckwith, 'The Jewish Background to Christian Worship', in Cheslyn Jones, Geoffrey Wainwright, Edward Yarnold SJ and Paul Bradshaw (eds), *The Study of Liturgy* (London: SPCK, 1992), p 77.

47. Making present by remembering seems to have been a distinctively Christian development of the purpose of commemoration. See Beckwith, 'The Jewish Background', p 77.

48. In later texts there is evidence of a (rather fluid) distinction between a large community meal (the *agape*) and a meal-like ritual (the 'Eucharist'). That distinction did not exist in the first century.

49. This seems to be the implication of Galatians 3.23–9; see Beckwith, 'The Jewish Background', p 73, on the baptism of converts to Judaism.

50. K.W. Noakes, 'Initiation: From New Testament Times to St Cyprian', in Jones et al (eds), *The Study of Liturgy*, p 119.

51. Beckwith, 'The Jewish Background', p 73.

52. *The Shepherd of Hermas*, III.3; cf. I Peter 3.20.

53. Noakes, 'Initiation', p 117.

54. For the three-fold formula see *Didache* 9; Matthew 28.19; 'in the name of Jesus', Acts 2.38, 8.16, 10.48, 19.5; I Corinthians 6.11. See also Noakes, 'Initiation', p 117.

55. Romans 10.9; Philippians 2.11.

56. Galatians 3.27; Ephesians 4.22. There is a danger of reading later practice back into the texts here, however.

57. Noakes, 'Initiation', p 118.

58. David F. Wright 'The Apostolic Fathers and Infant Baptism', in Gregory and Tuckett (eds), *Trajectories through the New Testament*.

59. Thomas K. Carroll and Thomas Halton (eds), *Liturgical Practice in the Fathers*, Message of the Fathers of the Church, vol. 21 (Wilmington, Delaware: Michael Glazier, 1988), pp 36–7, referring to the *Epistle of Barnabas*.

60. This seems to be reflected in Ignatius' *Letter to the Magnesians*, for example.

61. Noakes, 'Initiation', p 117.

62. For example, the pastoral epistles (I Timothy, II Timothy, Titus), *1 Clement*.

63. *1 Clement* 42.

64. By finding the term *episkopous* in the Greek translation of Isaiah 60.17.

65. Philippians 1.1; Polycarp, *Letter* 5–6; *1 Clement* 42.

66. On bishops see I Timothy 3.1–2, Titus 1.7; on presbyters see I Timothy 4.14, 5.1.

67. The evidence for women's ministry in these texts and others from the early Church is assessed in great detail and with even handedness by Kevin Madigan and Carolyn Osiek (eds and trans), *Ordained Women in the Early Church: A Documentary History* (Baltimore and London: Johns Hopkins University Press, 2005).

68. *Ibid.*, p 11.

69. Possibly because of the designation 'Apostle', Junia's name has often been assumed to be a male one: Junias. But the arguments for this are weak. See C.H. Hill, OBC, p 1107: 'In short "Junias" is a scandalous mistranslation.'

70. See Tertullian, *The Prescription against Heretics* 41.5, discussed by Madigan and Osiek (eds), *Ordained Women*, pp 174–5.

71. *1 Clement* 38.

72. *1 Clement* 55.2.

73. On widows see I Timothy 5.3–16; Madigan and Osiek (eds), *Ordained Women*, p 5: as they note: 'liturgical' does not entail 'sacramental', and in this period 'among the clergy' does not imply ordination.

74. A concern for food customs can also be seen in Mark 7.1–23 and Matthew 15.1–20.

75. See Romans 14.14.

76. See Ephesians 2.19; I Timothy 3.15; I Peter 4.17.

77. See Ephesians 4.12. As Christ is the head of the Christian household, he is also the head of the Christian Church as body: Ephesians 5.23.

78. Ephesians 1.22; Colossians 1.24. See also Daniel N. Schowalter, 'Church', in Bruce M. Metzger and Michael D. Coogan (eds), *The Oxford Companion to the Bible* (Oxford University Press Inc., 1993), accessed via *Oxford Reference Online*, Oxford University Press, http://www.oxfordreference.com/views/ENTRY.html?subview=Main&entry=t120.e0144.

79. See, for example, Ignatius, *Letter to the Ephesians*, preface.

80. On the feast (linking with the idea of Eucharist) see Matthew 8.11; Revelation 19.9; on the new Jerusalem see Revelation 21–2.

81. See the discussion of Marcion and Gnostic groups in Chapter 3.

82. See, for example, Matthew's Gospel and the introduction to the commentary

on Matthew by Dale C. Allison Jr. in OBC.

83. The concept here is similar to, although not the same as, that used in Stephen Sykes, *The Identity of Christianity: Theologians and the Essence of Christianity from Scheiermacher to Barth* (London: SPCK, 1984).

Chapter 2. Hopes and Fears

1. See, for example, Pliny the Younger, *Letter to the Emperor Trajan* X.96, in which he commented that Christianity in Bithynia (Asia Minor) had spread beyond the cities into the countryside.
2. Eusebius, *Ecclesiastical History* IV.7.1. Eusebius was a fourth-century historian commenting here on the reign of Trajan (98–117).
3. Irenaeus, *Against Heresies* I.10.1–2.
4. *Against the Jews* (formerly thought to be a work of Tertullian) I.7.
5. David G.K. Taylor, 'The Syriac Tradition', in Gillian Evans, *The First Christian Theologians* (Oxford: Blackwell, 2004), p 201.
6. See Chapter 5.
7. *Acts of the Martyrs of Lyons and Vienne* 1.63.
8. See Tacitus, *Annals* XV.44.2–8.
9. Tertullian, *Apology* 40; see also the spurious letter of Antoninus Pius at the end of Justin Martyr *1 Apology*, where it is implied that the local populace are persecuting Christians because their atheism is connected to earthquakes. Even if the letter does not accurately present the emperor's stance, it is further evidence that Christians at least connected their persecutions to such local issues.
10. See *Martyrs of Lyons and Vienne* 1.9.
11. *Ibid.*, 1.14, 26, 52.
12. For these see Chapter 3.
13. Pliny the Younger, *Letters* X.96.
14. *The Passion of Saints Perpetua and Felicity* 5.4.
15. *Martyrs of Lyons and Vienne* 1.13–14.
16. In his letter to Trajan, Pliny thinks it worthy of mention that there had come to his notice Christians of every age and class, both men and women. *Letters* X.96.
17. *Martyrs of Lyons and Vienne* 1.7–8.
18. Pliny the Younger, *Letters* X.96.
19. This question of whether Christians were in fact formally charged with bearing the name 'Christian' is very controversial: the spurious letters which Justin Martyr attaches to the end of his *1 Apology* addressed to Antoninus Pius and his adopted sons, Marcus Aurelius and Lucius Verus, flatteringly present his addressees as rejecting the practice of condemning Christians merely for bearing that name. Whether the letters reflect their practice is very questionable.
20. Since Augustus, the Roman emperor was traditionally given the title and office of Pontifex Maximus – head of the college of priests in Rome, and

so was implicated in Roman religion, even if no personal divine status was imputed to him. The increasing identification of local deities with the Roman pantheon also meant that local loyalties became implicated with loyalties to the Empire. See Stephen Mitchell, *A History of the Later Roman Empire, AD 284–641: The Transformation of the Ancient World* (Malden, MA, and Oxford: Blackwell, 2007), p 229.

21. *The Passion of Saints Perpetua and Felicity* 16.3.

22. *The Martyrdom of Polycarp* 11; see also *The Passion of Saints Perpetua and Felicity* 11.9; in the *Martyrs of Lyons and Vienne* citizens were beheaded (1.47), with the exception of Attalus, who particularly enraged the crowds whom the governor wanted to please (1.50).

23. Ignatius, *Letter to the Romans* 5; cf. I Peter 5.8.

24. *Martyrdom of Polycarp* 5: 'the most admirable Polycarp, when he first heard [that he was sought for], was in no measure disturbed, but resolved to continue in the city. However, in deference to the wish of many, he was persuaded to leave it.'

25. *Martyrdom of Polycarp* 4, alluding to Matthew 10.23.

26. Justin Martyr, *2 Apology* 3–4.

27. *Ibid.*, 4.

28. Tertullian, *On Idolatry* 16: 'One soul cannot serve two masters – God and Caesar.' cf. *On the Military Crown* 12.

29. For example, *Martyrs of Lyons and Vienne* 2.3–4.

30. Ignatius, *Letter to the Romans* 4.

31. *The Martyrdom of Ignatius* 2. Note, we have no secure historical account of the circumstances of Ignatius' arrest. Saturus of Carthage is said to have 'voluntarily handed himself over for our sake' (*The Passion of Saints Perpetua and Felicity* 4.5).

32. *The Passion of Saints Perpetua and Felicity* 21.9–10. The *Martyrdom of Carpas* was rewritten in order to counter accusations of suicide: the original Greek described a female spectator, Agathonice, voluntarily joining a fellow Christian as he was burnt at the stake. The later Latin version had her being arrested, tried and condemned to death.

33. The word *martyria* in Greek means 'witness'.

34. *The Passion of Saints Perpetua and Felicity* 17.3; see also *Martyrs of Lyons and Vienne* 1.45–6 on martyrs strengthening those who were tempted to deny the name of Christ.

35. Revelation 3.14; see also Revelation 1.5. For this reason the martyrs of Lyons and Vienne eschewed the title 'witnesses' (*martyres*) for themselves, claiming Christ alone as the true martyr.

36. See the *Martyrdom of Polycarp*, especially 6–8, where Polycarp is betrayed by a member of his own household (who is compared to Judas); one of the local governors is named Herod; his pursuers are armed as if going out against a robber (cf. Matthew 26.55), and Polycarp is taken into the city on an ass.

37. Ignatius, *Letter to the Romans* 4, 6. See I Corinthians 7.22: 'For whoever was

called in the Lord as a slave is a freed person belonging to the Lord, just as whoever was free when called is a slave of Christ.'

38. John 6.33–5.

39. A similar bread symbol is found also in *Martyrdom of Polycarp* 15, where his body at the stake is alleged to smell like bread baking.

40. See the extraordinary range of images in *Martyrs of Lyons and Vienne* 1.45–6, 1.49–50.

41. *Martyrs of Lyons and Vienne* 1.6, 1.18 and 1.58; *The Passion of Saints Perpetua and Felicity* 4.7, 4.14.

42. *Martyrdom of Polycarp* 17–18; *Martyrs of Lyons and Vienne* 1.19, 1.36, 1.38, 1.42. The image of the victorious athlete echoes Pauline language, e.g. I Corinthians 9.24–7; Philippians 3.14; Colossians 2.18.

43. *Martyrs of Lyons and Vienne* 1.17, 1.23.

44. *The Passion of Saints Perpetua and Felicity* 18.8; alternatively the martyrs' destiny is contrasted with that of those who recanted: *Martyrs of Lyons and Vienne* 1.25.

45. As Eric Osborn succinctly put it in *Justin Martyr* (Tübingen: Möhr, 1973), p 14.

46. The Latin writer Tertullian, who is often regarded as an apologist but whose writings stretch far beyond this designation, will be treated in Chapter 4.

47. For example, the biographer, historian and moral philosopher Plutarch studied in Athens in the late 60s CE under a Platonist philosopher; the famous polymath Longinus (*c.*213–73) taught in Athens for 30 years before spending the last few years of his life in the employ of Queen Zenobia of Palmyra. One of Longinus' pupils in grammar and rhetoric in Athens in the 250s and early 260s was the Neoplatonist Porphyry. Porphyry then travelled to Rome to study under the Neoplatonist Plotinus (*c.*205–70), who spent most of his adult life teaching there. The Emperor Hadrian particularly favoured the city of Athens and its culture, endowing it with, amongst many other works, a library. Athens was a centre of the oratorical school known as the second sophistic, but two of its most famous practitioners, Favorinus of Arelata and Herodes Atticus, gained prominence both there and in Rome (the latter being brought to Rome by Emperor Antoninus Pius to teach his adoptive sons, Marcus Aurelius and Lucius Verus).

48. By which he means an area which is certainly beyond the Euphrates, possibly beyond the Tigris: Tatian, *Discourse to the Greeks* 42.

49. A contemporary Syriac work, Bar Daisan's dialogue *Book of the Laws of the Lands*, was supposedly addressed to an Antonine emperor, but this is much disputed and it shares little in common with the apologies discussed here.

50. Athenagoras, *Supplication* 31: 'But they have further also made up stories against us of impious feasts and forbidden intercourse between the sexes, both that they may appear to themselves to have rational grounds of hatred, and because they think either by fear to lead us away from our way of life, or to render the rulers harsh and inexorable by the magnitude of the charges

they bring.' See also Theophilus, *To Autolycus* III.4.

51. Justin, *1 Apology* 14; see also Theophilus, *To Autolycus* III.1–15.

52. Theophilus, *To Autolycus* III.15.

53. *Discourse to the Greeks* 23 (note how he cleverly turns back on the pagans their accusations of cannibalism).

54. Justin, *Dialogue with Trypho* 2; Tatian, *Discourse to the Greeks* 3.

55. Athenagoras, *Supplication* 11.

56. Luke 6.27, 28; Matthew 5.44, 45; Athenagoras, *Supplication* 11.

57. On myths about pagan gods see Justin, *1 Apology* 64; Theophilus, *To Autolycus* I.9, III.8, Tatian, *Discourse to the Greeks* 10. On idolatry see Justin, *1 Apology* 9; *To Autolycus* I.10. On demon worship see Tatian, *Discourse to the Greeks* 19.

58. Athenagoras, *Supplication* 4.

59. Justin, *1 Apology* 5.

60. For example, Theophilus complains that in the *Theogony* 'Hesiod himself also declared the origin, not only of the gods, but also of the world itself. And though he said that the world was created, he showed no inclination to tell us by whom it was created. Besides, he said that Saturn, and his sons Jupiter, Neptune, and Pluto, were gods, though we find that they are later born than the world' (Theophilus, *To Autolycus* II.5; see also II.13). Against the philosophers he complains that some deny the existence of any god; others deny divine involvement in the world; others 'say that all things are produced without external agency, and that the world is uncreated, and that nature is eternal', and still others 'maintain that the spirit which pervades all things is God'. The Platonists he accuses of contradiction, for they simultaneously assert that 'God is uncreated, and the Father and Maker of all things' and that 'matter as well as God is uncreated, and aver that it is coeval with God' (Theophilus, *To Autolycus* II.5).

61. For example, Athenagoras, *Supplication* 15.

62. Theophilus, *To Autolycus* II.10, 13 ('But the power of God is shown in this, that, first of all, He creates out of nothing, according to His will, the things that are made'); Tatian, *Address to the Greeks* 5 ('For matter is not, like God, without beginning, nor, as having no beginning, is of equal power with God; it is begotten, and not produced by any other being, but brought into existence by the Framer of all things alone'). See Gerhard May, *Creatio ex nihilo: The Doctrine of 'Creation out of nothing' in Early Christian Thought* (Edinburgh: T. & T. Clark, 1994), chapters 4 and 5. May's book asserts that Justin did not teach creation *ex nihilo*, but more recent research disagrees.

63. See Chapter 5.

64. Justin, *Dialogue with Trypho* 61, quoting a Septuagint version of Proverbs 8.21ff.

65. *Ibid.*, 45.

66. 'He is the first-born (*monogenes*) of the unbegotten (*agennetos*) God', *1 Apology* 53.

67. *1 Apology* 53.

68. *Dialogue* 56, 58–9.
69. *2 Apology* 10.
70. *2 Apology* 10; see also 13.
71. The Stoic concept of the *logos spermatikos* and the Platonic notion of different levels of participation in an ideal form.
72. The Word immanent in God (*Logos endiathetos*) and the Word expressed by God (*Logos prophorikos*).
73. On this see especially Mark Edwards, 'Justin's Logos and the Word of God', *Journal of Early Christian Studies* 3.3 (1995), pp 261–80.
74. *2 Apology* 13; see also *Dialogue* 17, 111.
75. This kind of question must have been deliberately offensive given the veneration of the martyrs' graves and the fact that some of them died from being mauled by beasts in the arena.
76. Athenagoras, *Resurrection* 3. The authorship of this text has been disputed; the current consensus attributes it to Athenagoras.
77. Athenagoras, *Supplication* 31; Theophilus, *To Autolycus* I.14; Justin, *1 Apology* 43; *2 Apology* 9; *Dialogue with Trypho* 45.
78. Brian E. Daley, *The Hope of the Early Church: A Handbook of Patristic Eschatology* (Cambridge: Cambridge University Press, 1991), p 21, citing Justin, *Dialogue* 28, 32, 40.
79. *1 Apology* 11.
80. Daley, *The Hope of the Early Church*, p 21, citing Justin, *Dialogue* 113, 139.
81. Richard A. Norris, in CHECL, p 36.
82. In other words, knowledge is lost as soon is it is gained, draining away like water through the sieve the Danaïds were forced to fill in Hades.
83. Tatian, *Discourse to the Greeks* 26.
84. Eusebius, EH IV.16; Norris in CHECL, p 43.

Chapter 3. Negotiating Boundaries

1. Justin Martyr, *1 Apology* 65.
2. Peter Lampe, *From Paul to Valentinus: The Christians of Rome in the First Two Centuries* (Minneapolis: Augsberg Fortress, 1999), p 362.
3. It is not clear, however, when the Eucharist and the *agape* became clearly separate; see below.
4. Tertullian, *Apology* (*c.*197); see James Stevenson, *The Catacombs: Rediscovered Monuments of Early Christianity* (London: Thames and Hudson, 1978), p 9.
5. Scholars now also reject the once common view that they were hiding places for Christians.
6. Lampe, *From Paul to Valentinus*, p 127.
7. On *Graptē* (teacher of orphans and widows) see Lampe, *From Paul to Valentinus*, p 354 (*The Shepherd of Hermas* II.4.3); on Marcellina, leader of the Carpocratians, see *ibid.*, p 319. According to Irenaeus women presided at the Eucharist of the Marcosian Gnostics (Irenaeus, *Against Heresies* 1.13.2f).
8. Lampe, *From Paul to Valentinus*, pp 352–3. A similar pattern existed in

Carthage: evidence around 200 suggests that there were women who taught and even baptized. The author Tertullian is scandalized by this, but on the other hand shows great respect for widows, who are given a privileged role in the congregation. See Tertullian, *The Prescription against Heretics* 41.5, discussed by Madigan and Osiek (eds), *Ordained Women in the Early Church*, pp 174–5.

9. Justin Martyr, *1 Apology* 53.3; Lampe, *From Paul to Valentinus*, p 102.

10. Justin Martyr, *1 Apology* 67.1 (trans Ludlow). Justin explains that those who are better off give what each thinks appropriate at the Sunday service and it is then distributed by the presiding member of the congregation.

11. On Marcion's gift see Lampe, *From Paul to Valentinus*, p 245.

12. Lampe, *From Paul to Valentinus*, pp 298–312.

13. *The Shepherd of Hermas*, Commandments 43–5.

14. Peter Brown, *The Rise of Western Christendom: Triumph and Diversity, AD 200–1000* (Oxford: Blackwell, 1996), p 54.

15. See the quotation from Irenaeus at the beginning of Chapter 2.

16. On baptism and Eucharist for Marcionites see Adolf von Harnack, *Marcion: The Gospel of the Alien God* (Durham, NC: Labyrinth Press, 1990), pp 93–4. Initially Valentinian reading groups may well have appealed most to the social and intellectual elites, but once they formed their own congregations they probably had a similar social mix to other congregations.

17. See Harnack, *Marcion*, p 97; Clarke in CAH, p 617; on the more difficult question of Valentinian attitudes to martyrdom see Elaine Pagels, *The Gnostic Gospels* (London: Penguin, 1982), pp 109–11.

18. Harnack, *Marcion*, p 96.

19. Although little is known about Celsus' life, it is likely that he wrote in Rome or Alexandria. See Henry Chadwick, 'Introduction', to Origen, *Contra Celsum* (Cambridge: Cambridge University Press, 1953), pp xxiii–xxix.

20. Lampe, *From Paul to Valentinus*, pp 245–6.

21. Justin Martyr, *1 Apology* 26.4. Lampe assesses this claim, *From Paul to Valentinus*, pp 250–1.

22. Tertullian, *Against Marcion* IV.5.

23. See the background to the term *Christos*/messiah, the anointed one, in Chapter 1.

24. Tertullian, *Against Marcion* I.14; Harnack, *Marcion*, p 155, n.13: underlying Marcion's thought 'there seems to have been a certain overwrought irritation on Marcion's part concerning life's vexatious troubles'.

25. Tertullian, *On the Flesh of Christ* 4.

26. Translated by Han Drijvers, quoted in Drijvers, 'Syrian Christianity and Judaism', in Judith Lieu, John North and Tessa Rajak (eds), *The Jews among Pagans and Christians in the Roman Empire* (London: Routledge, 1994); Eusebius (EH, IV.30.3) says that Bar Daisan wrote dialogues against Marcionites.

27. For Marcion's theology see Harnack, *Marcion*, chapter VI; Christoph

Markschies, *Gnosis: An Introduction* (London and New York: T. & T. Clark, 2003), pp 86–9.

28. The Greek *demiourgos* means craftsman; the word does *not* denote a half-way state between god and world.
29. As Harnack memorably put it, *Marcion*, p 69.
30. Tertullian, *Against Marcion* IV.7.
31. Harnack, *Marcion*, p 96.
32. I Corinthians 7.29, 31. Tertullian, *Against Marcion* I.29, implies Marcion used this verse.
33. Irenaeus, *Against Heresies* III.11.7–8.
34. Harnack, *Marcion*, p 98.
35. Fragment F. This and subsequent fragments come from Bentley Layton (ed), *The Gnostic Scriptures* (New York: Doubleday, 1987), pp 229–45.
36. Fragment D.
37. Fragment D.
38. Fragment F.
39. Fragment H.
40. Tertullian, *On the Flesh of Christ* 15.
41. Fragments F and C.
42. Irenaeus, *Against Heresies* I.11.1.
43. Mark Edwards, 'Gnostics and Valentinians in the Church Fathers', *The Journal of Theological Studies* (April 1989) NS 40:1, p 40, referring to II Corinthians 4.4.
44. Irenaeus, *Against Heresies* I.11.4.
45. See Markschies, *Gnosis*, p 92.
46. For example, I Thessalonians 5.23: 'May your whole spirit, soul and body be kept blameless at the coming of our Lord Jesus Christ.'
47. Irenaeus, *Against Heresies* I.25.6; '[they] say that the world and what is in it was created by angels much inferior to the ungenerated Father. Jesus was the son of Joseph and was like all other men ...' (I.25.1); he deals with the other groups in *Against Heresies* I.29–30 (see especially I.29.1). On this issue see Edwards, 'Gnostics and Valentinians'.
48. Irenaeus, *Against Heresies* I.11.1.
49. The system is 'monistic' (Greek *monos*, 'single').
50. That is, a dualist system.
51. See the opening paragraphs of Chapter 2.
52. Eusebius, EH V.20.4–8; Irenaeus, *Against Heresies* III.3.4: when he was 'still a boy' he saw the aged Polycarp.
53. Robert M. Grant, *Irenaeus of Lyons* (London: Routledge, 1997), p 39.
54. Eusebius, EH V.24.
55. Irenaeus, *Against Heresies* I.22.1; see also II.28.1.
56. Irenaeus, *On the Apostolic Preaching* 1.6 (sometimes also known as *Demonstration of the Apostolic Preaching*).
57. *Ibid.*, 15.

58. *Ibid.*, 12.

59. *Ibid.*

60. See Irenaeus, *Against Heresies* IV.38.3.

61. That is, all the things reversed by Jesus Christ, *Against Heresies* II.20.3.

62. Irenaeus, *Against Heresies* IV.35.4, III.8.3, III.9.1.

63. Remember that *Logos* in Greek can mean both 'word' and 'reason': to capture the emphatic play on words here, Irenaeus' words could also be translated: 'And as God is logical, therefore he made created things by the Logos.'

64. Irenaeus, *Against Heresies* IV.20.3.

65. *Ibid.*, V.1.3, V.6.1.

66. *Ibid.*, II.28.2.

67. On Christ's flesh see *ibid.* IV.24.1; *On the Apostolic Preaching* 6; see also *Against Heresies* I.9.3.

68. Irenaeus, *Against Heresies* II.22.4. Irenaeus rejected the idea that Jesus was about 30 when he died (the Valentinians conveniently associated the number with their 30 aeons), arguing that Jesus the wise teacher must have been old or full in years when he died – perhaps around 40 or 50.

69. My italics; cf. Romans 5.12, 19.

70. Irenaeus, *Against Heresies* III.5.1.

71. Irenaeus, *On the Apostolic Preaching* 38.

72. Irenaeus, *Against Heresies* III.9.1, III.9.3, III.16.6.

73. Irenaeus, *Against Heresies* IV.20.2; *On the Apostolic Preaching* 40.

74. Irenaeus, *Against Heresies* III.4.2. His concern was the lack of Bibles in barbarian languages. He does not appear to have considered the possibility of those who have not even had the opportunity to hear the Gospel.

75. On judgement see *Against Heresies* IV.4.1, IV.33.1, IV.33.13, IV.36.3 (see also Daley, *The Hope of the Early Church*, p 30). On punishment of spiritual death see V.27.2, V.22.2, V.11.1.

76. Irenaeus, *Against Heresies* V.27.2; trans ANF, vol. 1 (translation adapted by Ludlow).

77. *Ibid.*, V.29.2.

78. For a brief discussion of this see Daley, *The Hope of the Early Church*, p 231, n.8.

79. Irenaeus, *Against Heresies* V.31.2.

80. Polycarp is revered because he was 'taught by the Apostles' and established by them in Smyrna to teach others the same truth: Irenaeus, *Against Heresies* III.3.4.

81. For example, Justin Martyr, *Dialogue* 11.

82. *Ibid.*, 19.

83. Justin Martyr, *1 Apology* 103.

84. In the early Church, *Pascha* meant both Passover and Easter. Melito plays on this ambiguity in his claim that Easter fulfils and overrides the celebration of the Passover. Following Hall, I have left the Greek term untranslated.

85. Melito of Sardis, *On the Pascha* 72, 81. Melito is using a tradition that

'Israel' means 'I see God', which was used by Philo (and probably earlier Jewish writers) and which passed into Christian usage. On this see Philo of Alexandria, *The Contemplative Life, The Giants, and Selections*, ed and trans David Winston, pp 143, 351.

86. Mark 12.30–1 and parallels (referring back to Deuteronomy 6.4–5; Leviticus 19.18).

87. Justin Martyr, *Dialogue* 93. My emphasis.

88. Palestinian Talmud, *c*.400; Babylonian Talmud, *c*.500. For an introduction to Jewish literature of this period see Everett Ferguson, *Backgrounds of Early Christianity*, 3rd ed (Grand Rapids, Michigan: Eerdmans, 2003), pp 431–513.

89. Grant, *Irenaeus of Lyons*, p 31.

90. Hall, introduction to Melito, *On the Pascha*, pp xxvi–xxvii; Alistair Stewart-Sykes, *The Lamb's High Feast: Melito, Peri Pascha, and the Quartodeciman Paschal Liturgy at Sardis*, Vigiliae Christianae Supplements XLII (Leiden: Brill, 1998), p 64.

91. Stewart-Sykes, *The Lamb's High Feast*, pp 97–9, reporting in particular the views of Jean Daniélou.

92. There had been Jews in Sardis from at least the second century BCE. The synagogue in Sardis is the largest so far to be discovered. See Stewart-Sykes, *The Lamb's High Feast*, pp 8–9.

93. For all these aspects of Justin's knowledge of Jews see Judith Lieu, *Image and Reality: Jews in the World of the Christians in the Second Century* (Edinburgh: T. & T. Clark, 1996), pp 141–2.

94. Usually dated between the first and third centuries CE, but some estimates place it much later.

95. For a discussion of this issue see David G.K. Taylor, 'The Syriac Tradition', in Gillian Evans, *The First Christian Theologians*, pp 202–6.

96. This is a highly contested question. See, for example, the chapters (presenting different views) by Han Drijvers and Michael P. Weitzman, in Lieu et al (eds), *The Jews among Pagans and Christians*; see also Taylor's conclusions, 'The Syriac Tradition', p 205.

97. Neither of these methods denied the historicity of the events depicted in the Old Testament: Moses was a type of (prefigured) Christ *in his actual historical self*, not merely as a character in a literary narrative.

98. On prophecy see *1 Apology* 31–53, see also *Dialogue* 50–3; on typology see *Dialogue* 40–3.

99. Lynn H. Cohick, *The Peri Pascha Attributed to Melito of Sardis: Setting, Purpose, and Sources* (Providence: Brown Judaic Studies, *c*.2000), p 150.

100. Drijvers, in Lieu et al (eds), *The Jews among Pagans and Christians*.

101. For example, Justin Martyr, *Dialogue* 9, 12, 38, 110.

Chapter 4. Alexandria and Carthage

1. For the history of the library see R. Barnes, 'Cloistered bookworms in the

chicken-coop of the Muses: The ancient library of Alexandria', in Roy MacLeod (ed), *The Library of Alexandria: Centre of Learning in the Ancient World* (London: I.B.Tauris, 2004); Mostafa El-Abbadi, *The Life and Fate of the Ancient Library of Alexandria* (Paris: Unesco/UNDP, 1990).

2. El-Abbadi, *The Ancient Library of Alexandria*, p 49.
3. *Ibid.*, pp 50–4.
4. Susan Raven, *Rome in Africa*, 3rd ed (London and New York: Routledge, 1993), chapter 8, pp 122–31.
5. Quoted in *ibid.*, p 124.
6. Barnes, 'Cloistered bookworms', p 87.
7. Eusebius, EH II.16.
8. *Ibid.*, II.17.
9. Philo, *The Contemplative Life*, passim.
10. David T. Runia, *Philo and the Church Fathers: A Collection of Papers* (Leiden and New York: E.J. Brill, 1995), p 189.
11. See Harry Austryn Wolfson, *Philo: Foundations of Religious Philosophy in Judaism, Christianity, and Islam* (Cambridge, Mass.: Harvard University Press, 1968), 4th printing revised, vol. 1, p 141.
12. See Mark Edwards, *Origen against Plato* (Aldershot: Ashgate, 2002), p 54, for example, his comment that 'the majority of surviving commentaries on Aristotle were composed by scholars resident in the city'.
13. ODCC, p 364; see especially the relation of this concept to Clement's writings.
14. For an account of Origen's life and background see Eusebius, EH VI.1– 39. Scholars are divided about the degree to which this can be trusted: for judicious assessments see especially J.W. Trigg, *Origen* (London: Routledge, 1998); *Origen: The Bible and Philosophy in the Third-Century Church* (London: SCM Press, 1985); Edwards, *Origen against Plato*.
15. His father was a Christian, but it is not clear when he converted.
16. Eusebius, EH VI.23.
17. *Panegyric [Letter of Praise] to Origen*, traditionally attributed to Gregory the Wonderworker, 7 and 13.
18. *Ibid.*
19. Origen, *Against Celsus* IV.15.
20. *Ibid.*, IV.16; Michel Fédou, *La sagesse et le monde: essai sur la christologie d'Origène* (Paris: Desclée, 1995), pp 177–9, on Origen's *Commentary on Matthew*.
21. *Commentary on John* X.2–4.
22. *Commentary on John* XXXII.116. On Jesus' words, 'If I, your teacher and Lord, have washed your feet …' (John 13.14): 'It is by teaching that the dust that comes from the earth and from worldly affairs … is wiped off.'
23. Origen, *Homily 19 on Luke* 6.
24. Origen, *On First Principles*, preface 2–3, translation adapted very slightly.
25. See previous chapter, pp 60–1.

26. Origen, *On First Principles*, preface 4–8.
27. *Ibid.*, preface 10.
28. *Ibid.*, II.11.4.
29. *Ibid.*
30. *Ibid.*, II.11.6.
31. See previous chapter, p 58.
32. Origen, *On First Principles* I.6.4.
33. *Ibid.*, I.1.2.
34. For example, Hebrews 1.5.5: 'For to which of the angels did God ever say, "You are my Son; today I have begotten you?"' (citing Psalms 2.7); for other references to Psalms 2.7 see Hebrews 5.5 and Acts 13.33.
35. Origen, *On First Principles* I.2.2.
36. Colossians 1.15: 'He is the image of the invisible God, first-born over all creation'; Hebrews 1.3: 'the brightness of God's glory and the express image of his substance'; Wisdom 7.25: Wisdom is 'breath of the power of God'; 'pure effluence of the glory of the almighty'; 'the brightness of the eternal light and an unspotted mirror of the working of God and an image of his goodness' (Christ is the 'Wisdom of God', I Corinthians 1.24).
37. Origen, *On First Principles* I.2.6.
38. Trigg, *Origen: The Bible and Philosophy*, pp 251–3.
39. Origen, *On Prayer* X.2 (trans p 100); see also XV and XVI.
40. For example, I Timothy 2.5; Hebrews 2.17, 3.1.
41. Origen, *On First Principles* I.6.2.
42. Most recently by Mark Edwards, *Origen against Plato*, pp 111–14.
43. I Corinthians 15.44: 'It is sown a physical body, it is raised a spiritual body. If there is a physical body, there is also a spiritual body.'
44. Origen, *On First Principles* II.11.2.
45. See especially *On First Principles* I.6.2–3; II.10.4–8.
46. A further controversy surrounds the question of whether, after this universal restoration of creation back to God, there could be further falls. I think Origen did *not* think this, but the matter is not certain.
47. Trigg, *Origen*, pp 5–7.
48. Edwards, *Origen against Plato*, pp 136–42.
49. The Preface to the *Commentary on the Song of Songs* is an excellent introduction to Origen's method of reading Scripture.
50. Origen, *On Prayer*, pp 164–5.
51. See Geoffrey Dunn, *Tertullian* (London: Routledge, 2004), p 67.
52. For a very useful summary of the evidence and the rival interpretations, see *ibid.*, pp 13–18.
53. Apuleius, *The Golden Ass* 9.14 (trans Walsh), p 170.
54. *Acts of the Scillitan Martyrs* 12.
55. Dunn, *Tertullian*, pp 15, 17.
56. Tertullian, *Apology* 39.
57. *Ibid.* This passage echoes I Timothy 2.2, but since it was aimed at persuading

pagans that Christianity was moral and not a threat to Rome, Tertullian may of course have exaggerated Christian concern for their rulers!

58. *Ibid.*

59. *Ibid.*

60. Philo, *The Contemplative Life* 8–10.

61. The classic work on the subject is Timothy Barnes, *Tertullian: A Historical and Literary Study* (Oxford: Clarendon Press, 1971); again Dunn provides a useful summary of the main issues in *Tertullian*, pp 3–11.

62. Barnes, *Tertullian*, pp 187–210, 22–9.

63. *Ibid.*, pp 209–10.

64. Dunn, *Tertullian*, p 5.

65. The preaching of homilies was part of a presbyter's responsibility; the writing of commentaries complemented and aided this task. Origen's homilies were written after his ordination as presbyter.

66. Eric Francis Osborn, *Tertullian: First Theologian of the West* (Cambridge: Cambridge University Press, 1997), p 9; Dunn, *Tertullian*, p 29.

67. Dunn, *Tertullian*, pp 28, 29.

68. Tertullian, *On the Apparel of Women* II.8.

69. Tertullian, *On the Shows*; Dunn, *Tertullian*, p 41.

70. Tertullian, *On Idolatry*; see also Dunn, *Tertullian*, p 42.

71. Tertullian, *On the Military Crown* 11.

72. *Ibid.*, 10.

73. As implied by *On the Military Crown* 1.

74. Tertullian, *On the Shows* 26, referring to Matthew 6.24.

75. J.B. Rives, *Religion and Authority in Roman Carthage from Augustus to Constantine* (Oxford: Clarendon Press, 1995), pp 278–81.

76. As Rives points out, Cyprian, the great scourge of schismatics, was a devoted reader of Tertullian; he would surely have known if Tertullian had left the Church. See Rives, *Religion and Authority*, p 275.

77. Tertullian, *Against Praxeas* 27.

78. *Ibid.*, 2.

79. On the idea of simplicity and paradox in Tertullian see Osborn, *Tertullian*, especially pp 1–26, 48–64.

80. For example, Tertullian, *On the Flesh of Christ* 14.

81. *Ibid.*, 16.

82. *Ibid.*, 13.

83. *Ibid.*, 12.

84. *Ibid.*, 4.

85. Uniquely, Mary's womb was 'opened' not by a man entering but by a man leaving it (*On the Flesh of Christ* 23). Tertullian does not mean that Mary had a sexual relationship.

86. This view fits with Tertullian's idea that all human souls were composed of a quasi-material substance and did not pre-exist nor were created by God individually at each conception or birth but were generated along

with bodies (in all cases but Jesus') through sexual intercourse. Technically speaking Tertullian was a traducianist. For a brief summary of this position see J.N.D. Kelly, *Early Christian Doctrines* (London: Black, 1965), p 175.

87. Tertullian, *On the Apparel of Women* 1.1. I do not think that the feminist case against Tertullian is empty; it is, however, much more complex than usually presented.

88. Tertullian, *On the Flesh of Christ* 5, 15–16; *On the Resurrection* 51.

89. According to Barnes's chronology, *Tertullian*, p 55.

90. Tertullian, *Antidote for the Scorpion's Sting* 1.11; see also Dunn, *Tertullian*, p 44.

91. Tertullian, *On the Flesh of Christ* 1: 'let us examine our Lord's bodily substance, for about his spiritual nature all are agreed' (presumably meaning 'all *Christians*').

92. Tertullian, *Against Praxeas* 27.

93. Tertullian, *On the Flesh of Christ* 5, see also *Against Praxeas* 27.

94. Tertullian, *Against Praxeas* 27.

95. Evans's introduction to his edition of Tertullian's *Against Praxeas* is most helpful on the complex terminology here, especially pp 8–11: Ernest Evans (trans), *Tertullian Adversus Praxean liber: Tertullian's Treatise against Praxeas* (London: SPCK, 1948).

96. Noetus appears to have been the first to propose this idea. Praxeas may have been a pseudonym for an opponent whom Tertullian preferred not to name. 'Modalism' and 'Sabellianism' are now used to distinguish Praxeas' 'monarchians' from another group of 'monarchians' who secured the unity of God by denying the real divinity of the Son. The latter are sometimes called 'dynamic' or 'adoptionist' monarchians, because they held that the power (*dynamis*) of God rested on Jesus, thus 'adopting' him as the Son of God.

97. Tertullian, *Against Praxeas* 1.

98. Osborn, *Tertullian*, p 129.

99. Tertullian, *Against Praxeas* 8.

100. *Ibid.*, 2.

101. Tertullian, *Apology* 39.

102. Sometimes translated 'What has Athens to do with Jerusalem?' This translation from *On the Prescriptions of Heretics* 7.9 is in Dunn, *Tertullian*, p 31. For good assessments of Tertullian's use of philosophy see Osborn, *Tertullian*, chapter 2, and Dunn, *Tertullian*, chapter 5.

Chapter 5. Church and Empire

1. For a very nuanced account see Stephen Mitchell, *A History of the Later Roman Empire, AD 284–641: The Transformation of the Ancient World* (Malden, MA, and Oxford: Blackwell, 2007), chapter 7.

2. F. Millar, *The Roman Empire and Its Neighbours*, p 240: threats over the Danube from the Sarmatians, over the Rhine from the Franks, over the Apennines from the Alamanni.

3. *Ibid.*, p 240.
4. See Harry D. Maier, 'Heresy, households, and the disciplining of diversity', in Virginia Burrus (ed), *Late Ancient Christianity* (Minneapolis: Fortress Press, 2005), pp 224–6 (with illustrations).
5. Millar, *The Roman Empire*, p 247; Graeme Clarke, 'Third-century Christianity', in CAH, vol. 12, p 591.
6. Janet Huskinson, 'Art and architecture, 193–337', in CAH, vol. 12, p 694.
7. W.H.C. Frend, *The Early Church* (London: Hodder & Stoughton, 1965), p 104.
8. *Ibid.*, pp 102, 104.
9. Millar, *The Roman Empire*, pp 247–8; W.H.C. Frend, 'The Winning of the Countryside', *Journal of Ecclesiastical History* 18:1 (April 1967), p 5.
10. Frend, 'The Winning of the Countryside', pp 4–5.
11. See Mitchell, *The Later Roman Empire*, p 240.
12. That is, eaten some of the flesh of a sacrificed animal. Wording found in papyrus *libelli* found in Egypt, quoted in J. Patout Burns Jr., *Cyprian the Bishop* (London: Routledge, 2002), pp 177–8, n.4.
13. Frend, *The Early Church*, p 98.
14. Although they are regarded as martyrs, it is not clear whether these bishops were executed or died in prison (perhaps as the result of torture); contrast e.g. Frend, *The Early Church*, p 97 and Clarke, in CAH, vol. 12, p 634, on Fabian of Rome.
15. Clarke, in CAH, vol. 12, p 628.
16. *Ibid.*, p 641.
17. *Ibid.*, pp 644–5.
18. Frend, *The Early Church*, p 105.
19. Eusebius, EH VII.11.
20. G.E.M. de Ste Croix, 'Why were the early Christians persecuted?', *Past and Present* 26 (November 1963), pp 26–7.
21. As later tetrarchs vied for power, some areas (e.g. Spain and the Balkans) passed from one sphere of influence to another.
22. Mitchell, *The Later Roman Empire*, p 241: 'Diocletian's restoration of the Roman state was based on a systematic reinvention of Roman religion.'
23. For example, Clarke, in CAH, vol. 12, p 648.
24. *Ibid.*, p 653.
25. *Ibid.*
26. *Ibid.*, p 652.
27. *Ibid.*, p 655. Possibly Galerius followed suit, but there is no firm evidence.
28. *Ibid.*, p 660. Peter, Bishop of Alexandria, was executed in this period.
29. Averil Cameron, 'Constantius and Constantine: An exercise in publicity', in Elizabeth Hartley, Jane Hawkes, Martin Henig with Frances Mee (eds), *Constantine the Great: York's Roman Emperor* (York: York Museums and Galleries Trust in association with Lund Humphries, 2006), p 28; and *ibid.*, p 96.

30. Lactantius, *c*.250–325; Eusebius of Caesarea, *c*.260–*c*.240.
31. *Letter* 7.1.1, cited in Rives, *Religion and Authority in Roman Carthage*, p 294.
32. Cyprian, *On the Lapsed* 10.
33. See previous chapter on Tertullian's views on the seriousness of post-baptismal sin.
34. Patout Burns Jr., *Cyprian the Bishop*, pp 2–3.
35. Cyprian, *On the Lapsed* 6.
36. *Ibid.*, 8, 9, 10.
37. *Ibid.*, 14.
38. *Ibid.*, 16.
39. *Ibid.*, 16–18.
40. *Ibid.*, 23–6.
41. See also a similar and contemporary story recounted by Dionysius of Alexandria: Eusebius, EH VI.44.
42. Cyprian, *On the Lapsed* 35.
43. *Ibid.*, 29.
44. Patout Burns Jr., *Cyprian the Bishop*, p 5.
45. Cyprian, *On the Unity of the Church* 4: 'Assuredly, the rest of the apostles were also the same as was Peter, endowed with a like partnership both of honour and power; but the beginning proceeds from unity.'
46. *Ibid.*, 4.
47. *Ibid.*, 5.
48. *Ibid.*, 23, 6.
49. *Ibid.*, 10; on other language of poison, disease etc. see 16, 22.
50. *Ibid.*, 21, 14.
51. Patout Burns Jr., *Cyprian the Bishop*, pp 6–7.
52. Cyprian, *On the Unity of the Church* 3, 5.
53. Bishop, 245–47CE.
54. *Letters* 71.1, 74.1–2.
55. There is thus good evidence for the systematic use of Church councils before Constantine.
56. Eusebius reports that Fabius 'inclined a little' to Novatian's views, EH VI.44.
57. Letter from Dionysius preserved by Eusebius, EH VII.7.
58. 'Catholic' comes from the Greek word *katholos*, meaning whole.
59. Thus Stephen Mitchell, following Brent Shaw: Mitchell, *The Later Roman Empire*, p 280.
60. Letter recorded in Eusebius, EH X.5.
61. Eusebius, EH VII.30.
62. Eusebius, *Life of Constantine* I.28, cited in Mitchell, *The Later Roman Empire*, pp 257–8.
63. Mitchell, *The Later Roman Empire*, pp 257–8.
64. Mitchell, following M. Weiss: Mitchell, *The Later Roman Empire*, p 258.
65. Mitchell, *The Later Roman Empire*, pp 257–9.

66. Now in the British Museum. For useful illustrations of the Rome and Hinton St Mary mosaics see Elizabeth Hartley et al (eds), *Constantine the Great*, pp 86, 205.
67. For examples see *ibid.*, pp 206, 208, 210, 214, 217, 219, 222.
68. Barnes, *Constantine and Eusebius*, p 49.
69. Eusebius, *Life of Constantine* IV.28.
70. *Ibid.*, IV.25.
71. Modern scholars, however, reject the story of the finding of the true Cross. See, for example, Averil Cameron, 'Constantine and Christianity', in Elizabeth Hartley et al (eds), *Constantine the Great*, p 100.
72. Barnes, *Constantine and Eusebius*, pp 52–3.
73. The idea of the seal of God on the foreheads of the faithful in the Book of Revelation (e.g. 7.3 and 9.4 etc.) seems to be both picking up on the idea of wearing the words of the Lord on one's forehead (e.g. Deuteronomy 6.8 and 11.8) and reversing the Roman symbol of slavery and oppression.
74. Barnes, *Constantine and Eusebius*, p 52.
75. In the initial phases of the controversy, the debate focused on this relationship, and the Holy Spirit did not become a focus for Trinitarian theology until the 360s–70s.
76. See my discussion of Origen's theology in Chapter 4.
77. The dating of the surviving documents is problematic. This account follows the reconstruction of Rowan Williams, *Arius: Heresy and Tradition* (London: Darton, Longman and Todd, 1987), pp 48–66.
78. The same Eusebius who wrote the *Ecclesiastical History* and *The Life of Constantine*, but *not* the same man as Eusebius of Nicomedia.
79. Arius, *Letter to Eusebius*.
80. Eusebius, *Life of Constantine* II.70–1.
81. See Constantine's letter summoning the council, NE document 299, p 358.
82. This council had probably been called for another reason (to debate a disputed succession), but the fact that it felt the need to pronounce an opinion on Arianism showed the growing tensions.
83. R.P.C. Hanson, *The Search for the Christian Doctrine of God: The Arian Controversy, 318–381* (Edinburgh: T. & T. Clark, 1988), p 156. Only one bishop from Gaul (Die) attended Nicaea, in contrast with the 16 bishops at Arles; from Germany, none attended Nicaea and two (Trier and Cologne) attended Arles; from Britain, none attended Nicaea and three (York, London and Lincoln) attended Arles (see Clarke, in CAH, vol. 12, pp 590–2).
84. Arius *Letter to Alexander of Alexandria* (= Arius' *Confession of Faith*), NE, p 346. All quotations from Arius in this paragraph are from that document (some altered in minor respects). Cf. the letter from the Council of Antioch, which says it agreed with what Alexander declared against Arius: it declares belief in 'One God, Father almighty, incomprehensible, immutable and unchangeable, providential ruler and guide of the universe, just, good, maker of heaven and earth and of all the things in them, Lord of the Law and of the

prophets and of the new covenant', NE, p 355.

85. Arius, *Letter to Eusebius*, criticizes those who see the Son as 'also unbegotten', NE, p 344.

86. Alexander, *Letter to Alexander*, NE, p 348.

87. Williams, *Arius*, p 160: 'Arius' language is under strain here, and it is not surprising that this led to misunderstanding.'

88. Arius, extract from *Thalia*, in Athanasius, *On the Councils of Ariminium and Seleucia* (*De synodis*) 15.

89. Arius, *Letter to Eusebius*, NE, p 345.

90. *Ibid.*, p 344.

91. *Ibid.*, p 345.

92. The epithet 'only-begotten' (*monogenes*) appears also in John 1.18, 3.16; I John 4.9. The NT and the Fathers read Psalm 2.7 christologically ('You are my son, today I have begotten you'): Acts 13.33; Hebrews 1.5.

93. This is a much simplified version of the argument made famous by Robert C. Gregg and Dennis E. Groh, *Early Arianism: A View of Salvation* (London: SCM Press, 1981).

94. The phrases allude to Hebrews 1.3, Wisdom 7.26, John 17.3, I John 5.20.

Chapter 6. God and Humankind in Eastern Theology

1. Williams, *Arius: Heresy and Tradition*, p 36; cf. Hanson, *The Search*, p 244: 'It is difficult to acquit Athanasius from the charge of having on occasion used equivocation, not to say mendacity.'

2. He was born *c.*297.

3. Frances M. Young, *From Nicaea to Chalcedon: A Guide to the Literature and its Background* (London: SCM Press, 1983), p 67.

4. The former, *Contra Gentes*, is sometimes known as *Against the Heathen*; the two works are closely related, possibly should even be regarded as two parts of a whole.

5. Athanasius, *On the Incarnation* 7.

6. *Ibid.*, 20.

7. Corruption is a very important theme in *On the Incarnation* 4–10 etc.

8. Athanasius, *On the Incarnation* 9.

9. *Ibid.*, 43, 15.

10. *Ibid.*, 20.

11. *Ibid.*, 54.3.

12. For example, Athanasius, *Against the Arians* I.38, II.19ff, III.25, cited in Rowan Williams, 'Athanasius and the Arian crisis', in Gillian Evans, *The First Christian Theologians*, p 164.

13. On characteristics see *To Serapion* I.22–7; on actions see *ibid.* I.9, I.19–20, I.24; II.4, II.7.

14. Athanasius, *Against the Arians* I.40.

15. Modern 'kenotic' theology develops the idea in a rather different direction from Athanasius' theology.

16. For example, *Against the Arians* II.70, III.15, III.27.
17. Eusebius of Nicomedia had been in correspondence with Arius in the earliest phase of the controversy.
18. Joseph T. Lienhard, '*Ousia* and *hypostasis*: The Cappadocian settlement and the theology of "one *hypostasis*"', in Stephen Davis, Daniel Kendall SJ, and Gerard O'Collins SJ (eds), *The Trinity: An Interdisciplinary Symposium* (Oxford: Oxford University Press, 1999), pp 112–13.
19. Hanson, *The Search*, pp 224ff, for an account of Marcellus' theology.
20. See Chapter 4.
21. For the complex relationship between Athanasius and Marcellus see Lewis Ayres, *Nicaea and its Legacy: An Approach to Fourth-Century Trinitarian Theology* (Oxford: Oxford University Press, 2004), pp 96–7, 106–7.
22. A crucial point here is the difference between the Greek prefixes *homo-* ('same') and *homoi-* ('like' or 'similar'). These have entered English in words such as homosexual (sexual attraction to someone of the *same* sex) and homoeopathy (treatment of a disease by inducing *similar* symptoms to those produced by the disease, in the hope of stimulating the body's own immune system).
23. But see Ayres on Basil of Ancyra: the word *homoiousios* is not found in Basil of Ancyra's extant writings: Ayres, *Nicaea and its Legacy*, p 150.
24. *On the Council of Nicaea* (= *On the Nicene Definition*), Latin title *De decretis*.
25. Athanasius, *Against the Arians* I.4, I.16, I.9, I.34, III.5.
26. On image see Colossians 1.15; on radiance and expression see Hebrews 1.3; on truth see John 14.6.
27. Athanasius, *Against the Arians* III.15–16.
28. *Ibid.*, I.19.
29. *Ibid.*, I.21, I.40.
30. *Ibid.*, I.58.
31. For example, *ibid.*, I.13.
32. *Ibid.*, I.58.
33. Gregory of Nyssa, *Life of Macrina*, trans Callahan, p 167.
34. Gregory of Nazianzus is so-called after his birth-place, Nazianzus, which was also the place where he first served as priest, helping his father who was bishop there.
35. The terminology of 'left' for the 'Arian' (extreme subordinationist) position is long standing, but is not to be given any modern political connotations.
36. Ayres prefers the term *heterousians*: see Ayres, *Nicaea and its Legacy*, pp 139ff.
37. Hanson, *The Search*, p 183.
38. I am not here suggesting that this formula from Antioch was the direct cause of the Cappadocians' concept, but merely using it as an example of the possibilities of the use of *hypostasis* before their writings.
39. For an introduction to this aspect of Cappadocian theology see Anthony Meredith, *Gregory of Nyssa* (London: Routledge, 1999), pp 11–15.

40. Gregory of Nazianzus, *Oration* 29 (*Third Theological Oration*), 10.
41. Gregory of Nyssa, *Against Eunomius* (GNO I.466–9), trans NPNF I.33, p 78.
42. *Ibid.*
43. Basil of Caesarea, *On the Holy Spirit* VI–VIII.
44. Gregory of Nazianzus, *Oration* 31.10.
45. *Ibid.*, 31.7.
46. Gregory of Nyssa, *On* ousia *and* hypostasis (= 'Basil' *Letter* 38), trans Wiles and Santer, pp 31–5.
47. Gregory of Nyssa, *On the Making of Humanity* 22.3, NPNF 2, vol. 5.
48. Gregory of Nyssa, *To Ablabius*, NPNF 2, p 334.
49. Gregory of Nyssa, *On* ousia *and* hypostasis, previously thought to be Basil's *Letter* 38, in *Collected Letters of St Basil*, trans R. Deferrari, Loeb Classical Library (Cambridge, Massachusetts, and London: Harvard University Press, 2003), p 211.
50. Gregory of Nazianzus, *Oration* 29.2.
51. *Ibid.*, 40.31.
52. Hanson, *The Search*, pp 816–17.
53. Quoted in Lienhard, '*Ousia* and *hypostasis*', p 100.
54. The first concern seems to have been developed in response to Diodore of Tarsus' theology, which informed later Antichene Christology.
55. The 'Logos-Sarx' / 'Logos-Anthropos' terminology was used especially by Aloys Grillmeier, *Christ in Christian Tradition. Vol. 1: From the Apostolic Age to Chalcedon (451)* (London: Mowbray, 1965).
56. Gregory of Nazianzus, *Letter to Cledonius* 9; cf. 5 for the more famous quote, 'the unassumed is the unhealed'.
57. *Ibid.*, 8.
58. 'As a result, these [natures] no longer [i.e. after his resurrection] seem to exist separately on their own, according to some kind of distinction, but the mortal nature, mingled with the divine in a way that overwhelms it, it made new, and shares in the divine nature – just as if, let us say, the process of mixture were to make a drop of vinegar, mingled in the, into sea itself, simply by the fact that the natural quality of that liquid no longer remained perceptible within the infinite mass that overwhelmed it.' *Against Eunomius* (GNO II, 132.26–133.4), trans NPNF vol. V, III.3.68–9 (this translation, Brian Daley, '"Heavenly Man" and "Eternal Christ": Apollinarius and Gregory of Nyssa on the personal identity of the Saviour', *Journal of Early Christian Studies*, 10:4 (2002), pp 481–2).
59. For a discussion of the debate, see Morwenna Ludlow, *Gregory of Nyssa, Ancient and (Post)modern* (Oxford: Oxford University Press, 2007), chapter 5.
60. For example, in *On the Soul and the Resurrection* he is careful to deny the idea of pre-existent souls.
61. Morwenna Ludlow, *Universal Salvation: Eschatology in the Thought of Gregory*

of Nyssa and Karl Rahner (Oxford: Oxford University Press, 2000), pp 82–5.

62. *Ibid.*, p 36.

63. *Ibid.*

64. The best introduction to Ephrem is Sebastian P. Brock, *The Luminous Eye: The Spiritual World Vision of Saint Ephrem* (Kalamazoo, Michigan: Cistercian Publications, 1992); see also his 'Introduction' to *Saint Ephrem. Hymns on Paradise*, trans Brock (Crestwood, NY: St Vladimir's Seminary Press, 1990); for a good brief summary see also David G.K. Taylor, 'The Syriac tradition', in Gillian Evans, *The First Christian Theologians*.

65. Quoted in Brock, *The Luminous Eye*, p 168.

66. Ephrem, *Hymns on Virginity*, quoted in Brock, *The Luminous Eye*, pp 152–3.

67. Philippians 2.6–11; I Corinthians 15.22; see also Brock, *The Luminous Eye*, p 31, 154.

68. Brock, *The Luminous Eye*, p 86.

69. Ephrem, *Hymns on the Nativity* 1.43, quoted in Brock, *The Luminous Eye*, p 88; cf. pp 42–3.

70. Ephrem, *Unleavened Bread* 17.10, quoted in Brock, *The Luminous Eye*, p 89.

71. See Brock, *The Luminous Eye*, p 30.

72. *Ibid.*, pp 77, 147.

73. Ephrem, *Hymns on Faith*, 5.17, quoted in Brock, *The Luminous Eye*, p 154.

74. For the sacraments, see Robert Murray, *Symbols of Church and Kingdom: A Study in Early Syriac Tradition* (Cambridge: Cambridge University Press, 1975), p 21.

75. For the quotation see Brock, *The Luminous Eye*, p 92. The interpretation is my own.

76. Ephrem, quoted in Murray, *Symbols of Church and Kingdom*, p 318.

77. Brock, *The Luminous Eye*, p 90.

78. *Ibid.*, p 94.

79. Murray, *Symbols of Church and Kingdom*, pp 80–1, quoting Ephrem, *Hymns on Faith* 74.

80. Ephrem, *Hymn on the Nativity* 22.39, quoted in Brock, *The Luminous Eye*, p 93; *Hymn on the Nativity* 16.11, quoted in Brock, *The Luminous Eye*, p 89; see also pp 85, 88, 91.

81. Brock, *The Luminous Eye*, p 37.

82. Ephrem, *Hymn on the Nativity*, 52.4, trans Kathleen E. McVey.

83. *Ibid.*, 52.9.

Chapter 7. Saints and the City

1. Jerome, *The Life of Paul the Hermit*, in Carolinne White (ed and trans), *Early Christian Lives* (London: Penguin, 1998), p 75.

2. Athanasius (attributed to Athanasius), *Life of Antony* 2.

3. See, for example, the *Protoevangelium of James*.

4. The *Long Rules* and *Short Rules* are presented in a question-and-answer form.

5. This is one of the overarching themes in Peter Brown, *The Body and Society: Men, Women and Sexual Renunciation in Early Christianity* (London: Faber and Faber, 1989).
6. See, for example, Gregory's *Life of Macrina*, trans Callahan, pp 167–73.
7. Gregory of Nyssa, *Against Eunomius* III.10.12 (GNO II, 294.3–4); cf. Gregory of Nyssa, *Antirrheticus against Apollinarius*: '[the Logos] mingled with what is human and received our entire nature within himself, so that the human might mingle with what is divine and be divinized with it, and that the whole mass of our nature might be made holy through that first-fruit' (GNO III:1, 151:16–20, trans Daley in his article '"Heavenly Man" and "Eternal Christ"', p 479).
8. Tertullian, *Apology* 39.
9. See, for example, Clement of Alexandria's *Who Is the Rich Man Who Will Be Saved?*
10. See Tertullian in Chapter 4, p 88.
11. Enkratite comes from the Greek *enkrateia*, 'self-control'.
12. Athanasius, *Life of Antony* 10; presumably the story is also a reference back to the story of Elijah: I Kings 17.1–11.
13. *Protoevangelium of James* 6.3, 8.2.
14. *Ibid.*, 14.14–21.
15. See the discussion of this in Chapter 4.
16. Brown, *The Body and Society*, p 92.
17. See especially Brown, *The Body and Society*, passim.
18. Gregory of Nyssa, *On Virginity* 3.
19. Women were not priests, but there is evidence of double monasteries where men and women lived in separate quarters but were part of the same worshipping community; women were sometimes sole leaders of such double monasteries. See Daniel F. Stramara, 'Double monasticism in the Greek East, fourth through eighth centuries', *Journal of Early Christian Studies* 6:2 (1998), p 276.
20. For a discussion of this kind of question see, for example, Rosemary Radford Ruether, 'Misogynism and virginal feminism in the fathers of the Church', in Ruether (ed), *Religion and Sexism: Images of Women in the Jewish and Christian Tradition* (New York: Simon and Schuster, 1974), pp 150–83; and Elizabeth A. Clark, 'Devil's gateway and bride of Christ: Women in the early Christian world', in Elizabeth A. Clark, *Ascetic Piety and Women's Faith: Essays on Late Ancient Christianity* (Lewiston, NY: Edwin Mellen Press, 1986), pp 23–60.
21. See, for example, Benedicta Ward (ed and trans), *The Sayings of the Desert Fathers* (London: Penguin, 2003), chapter 5.
22. Although Mani was not strictly speaking a Christian, he was strongly influenced by Christian asceticism.
23. Athanasius, *Life of Antony* 3.
24. *Ibid.*

25. Some of Cyprian's problems, for example, stemmed from the view that martyrs could intercede with God on behalf of sinners on earth. Thus confessors in prison were being plied with prayer requests in the expectation that they would soon die. See Chapter 5.
26. Cited by Christoph Markschies, *Between Two Worlds: Structures of Early Christianity* (London: SCM, 1999), p 152.
27. For this account I am indebted to Sebastian Brock, 'Introduction' to *Saint Ephrem. Hymns on Paradise* (Crestwood, NY: St Vladimir's Seminary Press, 1990), pp 25–33. See also his *The Luminous Eye*, pp 131–41.
28. Brock, *The Luminous Eye*, chapter 7.
29. Brock, 'Introduction' to *Saint Ephrem. Hymns on Paradise*, p 30; Luke 20.35–6. This idea of asceticism mirroring the angelic life is also found in Cappadocian writing on monasticism: Gregory of Nyssa, *Life of Macrina*, trans Callahan, p 171.
30. Aphrahat, *Demonstrations* VI.4.
31. The term 'anchorite' (someone who withdraws) is usually applied to this kind of ascetic, although strictly it can also apply to a member of a cenobitic community.
32. Quoted by Susanna Elm, *'Virgins of God': The Making of Asceticism in Late Antiquity* (Oxford: Clarendon Press, c.1994), p 303.
33. *Ibid.*, pp 304-5.
34. Gregory of Nyssa, *Life of Macrina*, p 168.
35. *Ibid.*, p 171.
36. Basil of Caesarea, *Letter* 94.
37. Gregory of Nazianzus, *Funeral Oration on His Brother Basil*, Oration 43.63.
38. Basil of Caesarea, *Long Rules* and *Short Rules*.
39. See Chapter 10.
40. Gregory of Nyssa, *Life of Macrina*, pp 165–7.
41. Kelly, *Jerome*, p 48.
42. Jerome, *Letter* 22.
43. See Kelly, *Jerome*, chapters XII and XIII.
44. See Theodoret's *Life of Simeon Stylites* and, for an introduction, Markschies, *Between Two Worlds*, pp 107–10.
45. Theodoret, *Life of Simeon Stylites* 6.
46. Markschies, *Between Two Worlds*, p 109 and also fig. 2 for picture of a badge.
47. See John Chrysostom's sermons, e.g. *On Saint Phocas* and *On the Holy Martyr Ignatius*.
48. Possibly Gregory of Nazianzus visited it. See John McGuckin, *St. Gregory of Nazianzus: An Intellectual Biography* (New York: St Vladimir's Seminary Press, 2001), pp 229–30.
49. Egeria, *Travels*.
50. Gregory of Nyssa, *Letter* 2.
51. Augustine, *Confessions* IX.vii.14–15.

52. *Ibid.*, VI.iii.3.
53. Gregory of Nazianzus' poem *On His Own Life*, ll.1680ff, trans White, p 133.

Chapter 8. God and Humankind in Western Theology

1. By this period, emperors no longer had permanent capitals. Valentian I was in Milan for a whole year in 364.
2. Neil B. McLynn, *Ambrose of Milan: Church and Court in a Christian Capital* (Berkeley and London: University of California Press, 1994), p 28; Boniface Ramsey, *Ambrose* (London: Routledge, 1997), p 21. Both books are excellent guides to Ambrose's career.
3. McLynn, *Ambrose of Milan*, pp 40–1.
4. So suggests Ramsey, *Ambrose*, p 16.
5. 375 or 378 synod in Sirmium; 381 council at Aquileia.
6. McLynn, *Ambrose*, pp 24, 26.
7. Ayres, *Nicaea and its Legacy*, p 182.
8. Augustine, *Confessions* I.xi.17.
9. *Ibid.*, III.i.1–III.ii.2.
10. *Ibid.*, III.iii.6.
11. *Ibid.*, III.iv.8.
12. *Ibid.*, III.v.9.
13. Goulven Madec, 'Christian Influences on Augustine', ATA, pp 151–6.
14. Augustine, *Confessions* V.iii.3, V.vi.10.
15. *Ibid.*, V.xiii.23.
16. *Ibid.*, VII.x.16.
17. *Ibid.*, VIII.vii.17.
18. See Mitchell on Augustine's conversion: Stephen Mitchell, *A History of the Later Roman Empire*, pp 268–9.
19. *Unfinished Literal Commentary on Genesis* 50.
20. *Literal Meaning of Genesis* IV (2) 6.
21. *Ibid.*, I (6) 12.
22. Most of *On Christian Teaching* was written around the same time as Augustine's *Confessions*; however, Augustine seems to have put it down approximately three-quarters of the way through and completed it only in 426/27, a couple of years before his death.
23. Preface, trans Green, p 7.
24. See Augustine, *Confessions* III.v.9.
25. *Ibid.*, XII.xiv.1.
26. This explanation necessarily exaggerates the difference between Origen's and Augustine's exegesis even more than Augustine did himself; however, it does reflect some of Augustine's anxieties about the potential of Origen's theory to mislead.
27. Michael Cameron on 'Sign', in ATA, p 795.
28. See Chapter 5.
29. *On the Trinity* I.1.4.

30. In what follows, my reading of *On the Trinity* has been greatly aided by Gareth B. Matthews, 'Introduction', to Gareth B. Matthews and Stephen McKenna (eds and trans), *Augustine: On the Trinity Books 8–15* (Cambridge: Cambridge University Press, 2002); Michel René Barnes, 'Rereading Augustine's theology of the Trinity', in Stephen Davis, Daniel Kendall and Gerard O'Collins (eds), *The Trinity: An Interdisciplinary Symposium* (Oxford: Oxford University Press, 1999), pp 145–76; Ayres, *Nicaea and its Legacy*, pp 364–83; Cyril C. Richardson, 'The enigma of the Trinity', in R.W. Battenhouse (ed), *A Companion to the Study of St Augustine* (London: Oxford University Press, 1970), pp 235–55.

31. *On the Trinity* XV.46.

32. *Ibid.*, XV.51 (epilogue).

33. This and the following quotations in this paragraph are from *On the Trinity* VII.7.

34. Ayres, *Nicaea and its Legacy*, p 183.

35. *Ibid.*, p 184.

36. *On the Trinity* VII.7.

37. *Ibid.*, VIII.6.

38. *Ibid.*, VIII.14.

39. *Ibid.*, IX.3.

40. *Ibid.*, IX.4.

41. Augustine wrote, 'And whatever else they are called in respect to themselves, they are spoken of together, not in the plural but in the singular. But they are three in that they are mutually referred to each other. And if they were not equal, not only each one to each one, but each one to all, they would certainly not comprehend each other. For not only is each one comprehended by each one, but all are also comprehended by each one.' *On the Trinity* X.18.

42. See, for example, XIII.26, XIV.11, XIV.18.

43. Eugene TeSelle, in ATA, p 633.

44. Augustine, *Confessions* X.xxix.40.

45. See Chadwick's footnote, Augustine, *Confessions*, trans Chadwick, pp 202–3.

46. Augustine, quoting Pelagius, in Henry Bettenson (ed), *The Later Christian Fathers* (Oxford: Oxford University Press, 1970), p 194.

47. Bettenson (ed), *The Later Christian Fathers*, p 193.

48. *Ibid.*

49. Pelagius, *Letter to Demetrius*, in *ibid.*, p 194.

50. For Pelagius' views on divine judgement see Gerald Bonner, *St Augustine of Hippo: Life and Controversies*, rev ed (Norwich: Canterbury Press, 1986), pp 335–6.

51. Most commonly known as the 'many mansions' of the King James' version.

52. Serge Lancel, *Saint Augustine* (London: SCM Press, 2002), p 343.

53. Eugene TeSelle, in ATA, p 633.

54. Augustine, *City of God* XIV.1.

55. *Ibid.*, XXI.12.
56. *Ibid.*, XV.1, referring to Genesis 4.1–2, and quoting I Corinthians 15.46 and Romans 9.17.
57. *Ibid.*, XIV.11.
58. *Ibid.*
59. Expressed succinctly in Latin: *posse peccare, non posse non peccare, non posse peccare.*
60. 'Anyone, therefore, who desires to escape everlasting punishment requires not only to be baptized but also to be justified in Christ, and so to pass over to the devil to Christ'. *City of God* XXI.16.
61. Augustine, *City of God* XX.9.
62. For example, *ibid.*, XIX.27–8.
63. *Ibid.*, XIX.28.
64. *Ibid.*, XIV.28.
65. *Ibid.*, XIV.28, quoting I Corinthians 15.28.

Chapter 9. Christology: A Tale of Three Cities

1. Libanius, *Oration 11, On Antioch* 16, 128, 133–4.
2. John Chrysostom, *Homily 17, On the Statues*, trans Allen and Meyer, pp 115–16.
3. Libanius, *Oration 11, On Antioch* 41, translation slighted altered.
4. For an introduction to Antioch in the fourth to fifth centuries see J.N.D. Kelly, *Golden Mouth: The Story of John Chrysostom, Ascetic, Preacher, Bishop* (London: Duckworth, 1995), chapter 1.
5. John Chrysostom, *Homily 17, On the Statues*, p 112, quoting Acts 11.26.
6. John Chrysostom, *Against the Jews, Oration 1*, trans Allen and Meyer, p 154.
7. John Chrysostom, *Homily 17, On the Statues*, p 107.
8. For this interpretation of Chrysostom's *asketerion* see especially Kelly, *Golden Mouth*, pp 18–23.
9. Chrysostom's period of ascetic retreat into the hills around Antioch seems to have taken place after his membership of Diodore's community.
10. Basil of Caesarea, *Homilies on the Hexameron* XII.1.
11. Theodore of Mopsuestia, *On the Lord's Prayer.*
12. Diodore also had argued with Apollinarius. See Young, *From Nicaea to Chalcedon*, pp 194–9.
13. On this period see Kelly, *Golden Mouth*, chapter 1.
14. *Ibid.*, p 12.
15. While John Chrysostom never offered explicit support to the Egyptian monks (the 'Long brothers'), their presence in Constantinople for two years aroused suspicion. Theophilus was an important member of the 'Synod of the Oak' which deposed Chrysostom. On these episodes see Kelly, *Golden Mouth*, chapters 14–16.
16. The Assyrian Church of the East, which had commonly been described by Westerners as 'Nestorian', has always stressed its indebtedness to Theodore

of Mopsuestia and has tended to minimize the influence of Nestorius. One consequence of this is the occasional denial of a direct connection between Theodore's and Nestorius' theologies.

17. See R.A. Norris, *The Christological Controversy* (Philadelphia: Fortress Press, 1980) for easy access to some key texts. For the *Bazaar of Heraclides* see the translation of G.R. Driver and Leonard Hodgson (Oxford: Clarendon Press, 1925), available online at http://www.ccel.org/p/pearse/morefathers/nestorius_bazaar_o_intro.htm.

18. S.G. Hall, *Doctrine and Practice in the Early Church* (London: SPCK, 1991), pp 212–13.

19. Theologians who had previously used the term included Origen, Bishops Peter, Alexander and Athanasius of Alexandria, Eusebius of Caesarea, Gregory of Nazianzus and Gregory of Nyssa (the latter using *Theotokos* together with *anthropotokos* – 'man-bearer'). See John McGuckin, *Saint Cyril of Alexandria: The Christological Controversy: Its History, Theology, and Texts* (Leiden and New York: E.J. Brill, 1994), p 22.

20. Nestorius, *First Sermon on the Theotokos*, in Norris, *The Christological Controversy*, pp 124–5.

21. Literally 'God-bearer'/'human-bearer', but I follow the alternative translation because the English term 'bearer' is ambiguous: it can refer to a mother's bearing/carrying a child, or more generally to someone carrying something in a less intimate sense. The Greek word specifically refers to the act of giving birth.

22. Theodore, *On the Incarnation*, fragment 11, in Norris, *The Christological Controversy*, pp 121–2.

23. See Grillmeier, *Christ in Christian Tradition*, p 370, and the evidence of Cyril's *Letter to the Monks of Egypt*, in McGuckin, *Saint Cyril of Alexandria*, pp 245–61.

24. McGuckin, *Saint Cyril of Alexandria*, pp 24–5.

25. *Ibid.*, p 6.

26. For this early period of Cyril's life see *ibid.*, chapter 1.

27. *Ibid.*, p 10.

28. *Ibid.*, p 5.

29. Norman Russell, *Cyril of Alexandria* (London: Routledge, 2000), p 130.

30. Cyril of Alexandria, *Second Letter to Nestorius*, in Norris, *The Christological Controversy*, p 132.

31. Nestorius, *Second Letter to Cyril* 6–7.

32. Cyril, *Third Letter* 2.

33. Hall, *Doctrine and Practice in the Early Church*, p 217.

34. Russell, *Cyril of Alexandria*, p 175.

35. *Documents from the Council of Ephesus*.

36. Gillian Evans and Morwenna Ludlow, 'Patristics', in Gareth Jones (ed), *The Blackwell Companion to Modern Theology* (Oxford: Blackwell, 2004), p 114, citing M.F. Wiles, 'Patristic appeals to tradition', in M.F. Wiles, *Explorations*

in Theology 4 (London: SCM, 1979).

37. McGuckin, *Saint Cyril of Alexandria*, pp 117–18.

38. Found in Cyril's *Letter to John of Antioch*, in Norris, *The Christological Controversy*, pp 140–5.

39. Cyril of Alexandria, *Letter to Succensus*. This precise phrase came from a text by a follower of Apollinarius which was falsely circulating under the name of Athanasius. It expressed for Cyril a crucial emphasis on the incarnate unity of Jesus Christ, but although Cyril's theology shows some general similarities to that of Apollinarius, the use of this phrase in itself of course does not mean that Cyril was 'an Apollinarian', any more than Nestorius was an Arian or adoptionist.

40. Theodore of Mopsuestia, fragment 2, in Norris, *The Christological Controversy*, pp 114–15.

41. See the *Third Letter* 4: 'we recognize that "being made flesh" is not to be defined by us as meaning a residence of the Word in him precisely comparable with his residence in the saints. No, he was actually united with flesh, without being changed into it, and brought about the sort of residence in it which a man's souls can be said to have in relation to its body.'

42. Cyril of Alexandria, *An Explanation of the Twelve Chapters*, trans Russell, in *Cyril of Alexandria*, pp 183–4. The ambiguity of the English verb to 'bear' is confusing here: 'God-bearing man' in this context means 'taking on' or 'carrying' God, not 'bearing God' in the sense that Mary was ' God-bearer', giving birth to God.

43. All quotations from Nestorius in this paragraph come from his *First Letter against Cyril*, in Norris, *The Christological Controversy*, pp 125ff.

44. Cyril of Alexandria, *Second Letter to Nestorius*, in *ibid.*, p 133.

45. *Ibid.*

46. *Ibid.*, p 134.

47. Nestorius, *Second Letter to Cyril*, trans McGuckin, p 365.

48. Cyril of Alexandria, *Third Letter to Nestorius* 3.

49. Grillmeier, *Christ in Christian Tradition*, p 383.

50. The Greek words *henōsis* and *henotēs* are more obviously close in sound to the word for 'one' (*hen*), than are the English words 'union' and 'unity', which are usually used to translate them.

51. All phrases from Cyril of Alexandria's *Second Letter to Nestorius*.

52. *Second Letter of Cyril to Succensus*, trans McGuckin. For the phrase see 2.

53. *Ibid.*, 6, p 354.

54. *Ibid.*

55. McGuckin, *Saint Cyril of Alexandria*, p 355, note.

56. Cyril of Alexandria, *Second Letter to Nestorius*, trans Norris, *The Christological Controversy*, p 133, slightly adapted.

57. In this interpretation, I am adapting the very helpful analysis of McGuckin, p 212, from which all quotations in this paragraph derive.

58. George Leonard Prestige, *Fathers and Heretics: Six Studies in Dogmatic Faith*

with Prologue and Epilogue (London: SPCK, 1963), p 125.

59. Nestorius extract, in Norris, *The Christological Controversy*, pp 127–8.
60. Norris, 'Introduction' to *The Christological Controversy*, p 24.
61. Grillmeier, *Christ in Christian Tradition*, p 340.
62. Kelly, *Early Christian Doctrines*, p 331.
63. Hall, *Doctrine and Practice in the Early Church*, p 230.
64. *The Council of Chalcedon's 'Definition of the Faith'*, in Norris, *The Christological Controversy*, p 158.
65. *Ibid.*, p 159.
66. Although, as Hall points out, it was a Roman version of the Creed, related to the Apostles' Creed, not Nicaea that Leo naturally turned to, in order to expound his theology. See Hall, *Doctrine and Practice in the Early Church*, p 227.
67. Leo, *Letter to Flavian*, in Norris, *The Christological Controversy*, p 151.
68. Hall, *Doctrine and Practice in the Early Church*, pp 227–8, 231.
69. Leo, *Letter to Flavian*, in Norris, *The Christological Controversy*, p 146. I am indebted to conversations with Dr Bernard Green on the subject of Leo's Christology; my final interpretation of the evidence is my own.
70. *Ibid.*, p 146.
71. *Ibid.*, p 148.
72. *Ibid.*, pp 148, 152. My emphasis.
73. *Ibid.*, p 150.
74. *Ibid.*, p 150, 149.

Chapter 10. Epilogue

1. From *The Book of Pontiffs* (*Liber Pontificalis*), ed Davis, p 39.
2. Of course the term 'barbarian' was used deliberately by Greeks and Romans to accentuate or create differences between them and those they considered 'other'. For the notion of 'barbarian' see Brown, *The Rise of Western Christendom*, pp 43-8, 99–106.
3. For the complex mix of 'Roman' and 'Gothic' culture exemplified by Theoderic see Stephen Mitchell, *A History of the Later Roman Empire*, pp 215–21.
4. For delineation of some of these see Brown, 'Introduction', in *The Rise of Western Christendom*.
5. Adapting Brown's metaphor of Leo as 'tie-breaker', *The Rise of Western Christendom*, p 115.
6. The date of Clovis' conversion is disputed; see Mitchell, *A History of the Later Roman Empire*, pp 212–13.
7. A thesis proposed by Pirenne, discussed by Brown, *The Rise of Western Christendom*, pp 9ff.
8. Brown, *The Rise of Western Christendom*, p 12 (on southern Gaul) and p 21 (on Rome, citing Horden and Purcell).
9. On the rise in population see Mitchell, *A History of the Later Roman Empire*, p 137.

10. North Africa fell in 534; Naples, Rome and Ravenna fell in 536–38.

11. Mitchell, *A History of the Later Roman Empire*, p 138.

12. For these events see Mitchell, *A History of the Later Roman Empire*, pp 372–7, on Hagia Sophia see *ibid.*, pp 139–40.

13. For a challenge to the 'cataclysmic' interpretation see Mitchell, *A History of the Later Roman Empire*, pp 327–8.

14. Brown, *The Rise of Western Christendom*, pp 15–16 (Brown uses the concept of 'symbolic goods').

15. Graeme Clarke, 'Third-century Christianity', in CAH, vol. 12, pp 590–2.

16. At Derry, Durrow and Kells.

17. That is, the fifth or the sixth. See Dauvit Broun, 'Ninian [St Ninian] (*supp. fl.* 5th–6th cent.)', *Oxford Dictionary of National Biography* (Oxford University Press, 2004), http://o-www.oxforddnb.com.lib.ex.ac.uk:80/view/article/20198 (accessed 27 February 2008). Whithorn lies on the south-west coast of Scotland, roughly due north of the Isle of Man.

18. For this distinction see Chapter 7, p 155.

19. Máire Herbert, 'Columba (*c.*521–597)', *Oxford Dictionary of National Biography* (Oxford University Press, 2004), http://o-www.oxforddnb.com.lib.ex.ac.uk:80/view/article/6001 (accessed 27 February 2008).

20. Boniface Ramsey, 'Cassian', in ATA, pp 133–5.

21. See George Lawless, 'Rules', in ATA, p 739.

22. Lawless, '*Regula*' and 'Rules', in ATA.

23. For a summary of their content see W. Stewart McCullough, *A Short History of Syriac Christianity to the Rise of Islam* (Chico, California: Scholars Press, 1982), p 73.

24. *Ibid.*, p 73.

25. The distinction here is between the Greek *mia* (the simple number 'one') and *monos* ('single' or '*only* one'). While, literally speaking, both accurately describe the anti-Chalcedonian position that Jesus Christ had one nature, they differ in tone. 'Monophysite' derives from the phrase *monē physis* ('*only* one nature', 'a single nature') which appears to imply that there could or should be two natures in Christ – just as the description of someone as 'single' can in some social circles pejoratively imply that adults are meant to live in couples. 'Miaphysite' derives from the neutral phrase 'one nature' (*mia physis*), which does not imply there are, ought to be or could be two natures.

26. See Chapter 9.

27. At least some of the disruption of this period can be traced to the varying imperial policies with regard to Chalcedon (a situation which echoes imperial vacillation in the fourth century over the doctrine of the Trinity): Zeno wanted to bring the miaphysites and Chalcedonians together; Anastasius was miaphysite; Justin I was Chalcedonian; Justinian was moderately Chalcedonian, but his influential wife had sympathies with the miaphysites.

28. A point made by Brown, *The Rise of Western Christendom*, p 185.
29. The Church of the East supported the theological settlement of Chalcedon, although they continued to object to its anathematization of Nestorius, which they believed went too far.
30. *Christian Topography*, Book III.
31. David G.K. Taylor, 'The Syriac tradition', in Gillian Evans, *The First Christian Theologians*, p 215.
32. Brown, *The Rise of Western Christendom*, pp 14–15.
33. Even Marcion read the Pentateuch and the Prophets (whilst rejecting them as part of the Christian canon), and even he included one Gospel.
34. McCullough, *A Short History of Syriac Christianity*, p 87.
35. This is not to say that this was the *only* source or model for Christian commentary on Scripture.
36. See Chapter 6.
37. Eusebius, EH VII.30.
38. Augustine, *Confessions* 7.7.15.
39. Sozomen, *Ecclesiastical History* VIII.8.
40. Socrates, *Ecclesiastical History* VI.8. My thanks to Dr Peter van Nuffelen for supplying me with these references to hymnody.
41. Brown, *The Rise of Western Christendom*, p 187.
42. The *Poemata arcana* ('Poems on the mysteries'). Very roughly speaking, these are the poem versions of his theological orations. For a selection in translation see Gregory of Nazianzus, *On God and Man*, trans Peter Gilbert (Crestwood, NY: St Vladimir's Seminary Press, 2001).
43. 'A morning prayer', 'A prayer the next morning' translated by Brian Daley in his *Gregory of Nazianzus* (London: Routledge, 2006), pp 170–1.
44. Prudentius, *Cathemerinon* 9, trans C. White. White's collection is a wonderful introduction to the fantastic variety and inventiveness of Christian Latin verse in this period.
45. See the mosaic from Ravenna on the cover of Brown, *The Rise of Western Christendom*.

Bibliography

Abbreviations

ANF = *The Ante-Nicene Fathers* series (Grand Rapids, MI: Eerdmans)
EH = Eusebius, *Ecclesiastical History*, trans G.A. Williamson; revised Andrew
    Louth (London: Penguin, 1989)
GNO = *Gregorii Nysseni Opera* (Leiden: Brill, 1960–)
NPNF = *The Post-Nicene Fathers* series (Grand Rapids, MI: Eerdmans) (NPNF
    2 = series 2)
Note: both ANF and NPNF are also available online at http://www.ccel.org/
    fathers.html.

Bible

All quotations are from the *New Revised Standard Version* (NRSV) (Oxford:
    Oxford University Press, 2001), including quotations from books of the
    Apocrypha (Wisdom, Baruch, etc)

General works of reference

Augustine through the Ages: An Encyclopedia (ATA), ed Allan D. Fitzgerald (Grand
    Rapids, MI: Eerdmans, 1999)
The Cambridge Ancient History (CAH), *Volume 12, The Crisis of Empire, AD 193–337*,
    eds Alan Bowman, Averil Cameron and Peter Garnsey, 2nd ed (Cambridge:
    Cambridge University Press, 2005)
Cambridge History of Early Christian Literature (CHECL), eds Frances Young,
    Lewis Ayres and Andrew Louth (Cambridge: Cambridge University Press,
    2004)
A New Eusebius: Documents Illustrating the History of the Church to AD 337 (NE),
    eds J. Stevenson and W.H.C. Frend, 2nd revised ed (London: SPCK, 1987)
Oxford Bible Commentary (OBC), eds John Barton and John Muddiman (Oxford:
    Oxford University Press, 2001)
Oxford Dictionary of the Christian Church (ODCC), ed E.A. Livingstone, 3rd ed
    (London: Oxford University Press, 1997)

Secondary works cited

Anatolios, Khaled, *Athanasius* (London: Routledge, 2004)

Ayres, Lewis, *Nicaea and its Legacy: An Approach to Fourth-Century Trinitarian Theology* (Oxford: Oxford University Press, 2004)

Barnes, Michel René, 'Rereading Augustine's theology of the Trinity', in Stephen Davis, Daniel Kendall and Gerard O'Collins (eds), *The Trinity: An Interdisciplinary Symposium* (Oxford: Oxford University Press, 1999), pp 145–76

Barnes, Timothy, *Tertullian: A Historical and Literary Study* (Oxford: Clarendon Press, 1971)

___, *Constantine and Eusebius* (Cambridge, Mass.: Harvard University Press, 1981)

Beckwith, R.T., 'The Jewish Background to Christian Worship', in Cheslyn Jones, Geoffrey Wainwright, Edward Yarnold SJ and Paul Bradshaw (eds), *The Study of Liturgy* (London: SPCK, 1992)

Behr, John, *The Way to Nicaea* (Crestwood, NY: St Vladimir's Seminary Press, 2001)

Brock, Sebastian, 'Introduction' to *Saint Ephrem. Hymns on Paradise*, trans Brock (Crestwood, NY: St Vladimir's Seminary Press, 1990)

___, *The Luminous Eye: The Spiritual World Vision of Saint Ephrem* (Kalamazoo, Michigan: Cistercian Publications, 1992)

Broun, Dauvit, 'Ninian [St Ninian] (*supp. fl.* 5th–6th cent.)', *Oxford Dictionary of National Biography* (Oxford University Press, 2004), http://o-www.oxforddnb.com.lib.ex.ac.uk:80/view/article/20198

Brown, Peter, *The Body and Society: Men, Women and Sexual Renunciation in Early Christianity* (London: Faber and Faber, 1989)

___, *The Rise of Western Christendom: Triumph and Diversity, AD 200–1000* (Oxford: Blackwell, 1996)

Burrus, Virginia (ed), *Late Ancient Christianity* (Minneapolis: Fortress Press, 2005)

Cameron, Averil, 'Constantius and Constantine: An exercise in publicity', in Elizabeth Hartley, Jane Hawkes, Martin Henig with Frances Mee (eds), *Constantine the Great: York's Roman Emperor* (York: York Museums and Galleries Trust in association with Lund Humphries, 2006)

Carroll, Thomas K. and Thomas Halton (eds), *Liturgical Practice in the Fathers*, Message of the Fathers of the Church, vol. 21 (Wilmington, Delaware: Michael Glazier, 1988)

Chadwick, Henry, 'Introduction', to Origen, *Contra Celsum* (Cambridge: Cambridge University Press, 1953)

Clark, Elizabeth A., 'Devil's gateway and bride of Christ: Women in the early Christian world', in Elizabeth A. Clark, *Ascetic Piety and Women's Faith: Essays on Late Ancient Christianity* (Lewiston, NY: Edwin Mellen Press, 1986), pp 23–60

Clarke, Graeme, 'Third-century Christianity', in Alan Bowman, Averil Cameron and Peter Garnsey (eds), *The Cambridge Ancient History. Volume 12, The Crisis of Empire, AD 193–337*, 2nd ed (Cambridge: Cambridge University Press, 2005)

Claussen, Carsten, 'The Eucharist in the Gospel of John and in the *Didache*', in Andrew Gregory and Christopher Tuckett (eds), *Trajectories through the New Testament and the Apostolic Fathers* (Oxford: Oxford University Press, 2007)

Cohick, Lynn H., *The Peri Pascha Attributed to Melito of Sardis: Setting, Purpose, and Sources* (Providence: Brown Judaic Studies, c.2000)

Daley, Brian E., *The Hope of the Early Church: A Handbook of Patristic Eschatology* (Cambridge: Cambridge University Press, 1991)

___, '"Heavenly Man" and "Eternal Christ": Apollinarius and Gregory of Nyssa on the personal identity of the Saviour', *Journal of Early Christian Studies*, 10:4 (2002)

De Ste Croix, G.E.M., 'Why were the early Christians persecuted?', *Past and Present* 26 (November 1963), pp 6–38

Dunn, Geoffrey D., *Tertullian* (London: Routledge, 2004)

Dunn, James D.G., *Christology in the Making: A New Testament Inquiry into the Origins of the Doctrine of the Incarnation* (London: SCM, 1980)

Edwards, Mark, 'Gnostics and Valentinians in the Church Fathers', *The Journal of Theological Studies*, NS 40:1 (April 1989), pp 26–47

Edwards, Mark, 'Justin's Logos and the Word of God', *Journal of Early Christian Studies* 3.3 (1995), pp 261–80

___, *Origen against Plato* (Aldershot: Ashgate, 2002)

El-Abbadi, Mostafa, *The Life and Fate of the Ancient Library of Alexandria* (Paris: Unesco/UNDP, 1990)

Elm, Susanna, *'Virgins of God': The Making of Asceticism in Late Antiquity* (Oxford: Clarendon Press, c.1994)

Evans, Gillian, *The First Christian Theologians* (Oxford: Blackwell, 2004)

Fédou, Michel, *La sagesse et le monde: essai sur la christologie d'Origène* (Paris: Desclée, 1995)

Frend, W.H.C., *The Early Church*, (London: Hodder & Stoughton, 1965)

___, 'The Winning of the Countryside', *Journal of Ecclesiastical History* 18:1 (April 1967)

Green, Bernard, *The Soteriology of Leo the Great* (Oxford University, D.Phil. thesis, 2004)

Gregg, Robert C. and Dennis E. Groh, *Early Arianism: A View of Salvation* (London: SCM Press, 1981)

Gregory, Andrew and Christopher Tuckett, *Trajectories through the New Testament and the Apostolic Fathers* (Oxford: Oxford University Press, 2007)

Grillmeier, Aloys, *Christ in Christian Tradition. Vol. 1: From the Apostolic Age to Chalcedon (451)* (London: Mowbray, 1965)

Guthrie, Donald, *New Testament Theology* (Leicester: Inter-Varsity, 1981)

Hall, Stuart George, *Doctrine and Practice in the Early Church* (London: SPCK, 1991)

Hanson, Richard P.C., *The Search for the Christian Doctrine of God: The Arian Controversy, 318–381* (Edinburgh: T. & T. Clark, 1988)

Harnack, Adolf von, *Marcion: The Gospel of the Alien God* (Durham, NC: Labyrinth Press, 1990)

Herbert, Máire, 'Columba (*c.*521–597)', *Oxford Dictionary of National Biography* (Oxford: Oxford University Press, 2004), http://0-www.oxforddnb.com.lib.ex.ac.uk:80/view/article/6001

Horrell, David, *An Introduction to the Study of Paul* (London and New York: Continuum, 2000)

Huskinson, Janet, 'Art and architecture, 193–337', in Alan Bowman, Averil Cameron and Peter Garnsey (eds), *The Cambridge Ancient History. Volume 12, The Crisis of Empire, AD 193–337*, 2nd ed (Cambridge: Cambridge University Press, 2005)

Kelly, John Norman Davidson, *Early Christian Doctrines*, 3rd ed (London: Black, 1965)

___, *Jerome: His Life, Writings, and Controversies* (London: Duckworth, 1975)

___, *Golden Mouth: The Story of John Chrysostom, Ascetic, Preacher, Bishop* (London: Duckworth, 1995)

Koester, Helmut, 'Gospels and Gospel traditions', in Andrew Gregory and Christopher Tuckett (eds), *Trajectories through the New Testament and the Apostolic Fathers* (Oxford: Oxford University Press, 2007)

Lampe, Peter, *From Paul to Valentinus: The Christians of Rome in the First Two Centuries* (Minneapolis: Augsberg Fortress, 1999)

Lancel, Serge, *Saint Augustine* (London: SCM Press, 2002)

Lienhard, Joseph T., '*Ousia* and *hypostasis*: The Cappadocian settlement and the theology of "one *hypostasis*"', in Stephen Davis, Daniel Kendall SJ and Gerard O'Collins SJ (eds), *The Trinity: An Interdisciplinary Symposium* (Oxford: Oxford University Press, 1999), pp 99–121

Lieu, Judith, *Image and Reality: Jews in the World of the Christians in the Second Century* (Edinburgh: T. & T. Clark, 1996)

Lieu, Judith, John North and Tessa Rajak, *The Jews among Pagans and Christians in the Roman Empire* (London: Routledge, 1994)

Ludlow, Morwenna, *Universal Salvation: Eschatology in the Thought of Gregory of Nyssa and Karl Rahner* (Oxford: Oxford University Press, 2000)

___, *Gregory of Nyssa, Ancient and (Post)modern* (Oxford: Oxford University Press, 2007)

McCullough, W. Stewart, *A Short History of Syriac Christianity to the Rise of Islam* (Chico, California: Scholars Press, 1982)

McGuckin, John, *Saint Cyril of Alexandria: The Christological Controversy: Its History, Theology, and Texts* (Leiden and New York: E.J. Brill, 1994)

___, *St. Gregory of Nazianzus: An Intellectual Biography* (New York: St Vladimir's Seminary Press, 2001)

MacLeod, Roy, *The Library of Alexandria: Centre of Learning in the Ancient World* (London: I.B.Tauris, 2004)

McLynn, Neil B., *Ambrose of Milan: Church and Court in a Christian Capital* (Berkeley and London: University of California Press, 1994)

Madigan, Kevin and Carolyn Osiek (eds and trans), *Ordained Women in the Early Church: A Documentary History* (Baltimore and London: Johns Hopkins University Press, 2005)

Maier, Harry D., 'Heresy, households, and the disciplining of diversity', in Virginia Burrus (ed), *Late Ancient Christianity* (Minneapolis: Fortress Press, 2005), pp 213–33

Markschies, Christoph, *Between Two Worlds: Structures of Early Christianity* (London: SCM, 1999)

___, *Gnosis: An Introduction* (London and New York: T. & T. Clark, 2003)

Matthews, Gareth B., 'Introduction', in Gareth B. Matthews and Stephen McKenna (eds and trans), *Augustine: On the Trinity Books 8–15* (Cambridge: Cambridge University Press, 2002)

May, Gerhard, *Creatio ex nihilo: The Doctrine of 'Creation out of nothing' in Early Christian Thought* (Edinburgh: T. & T. Clark, 1994)

Meredith Anthony, *Gregory of Nyssa* (London: Routledge, 1999)

Mitchell, Stephen, *A History of the Later Roman Empire, AD 284–641: The Transformation of the Ancient World* (Malden, MA, and Oxford: Blackwell, 2007)

Norris, Richard Alfred, *The Christological Controversy* (Philadelphia: Fortress Press, 1980)

Osborn, Eric, *Justin Martyr* (Tübingen: Mohr, 1973)

___, *Tertullian: First Theologian of the West* (Cambridge: Cambridge University Press, 1997)

Pagels, Elaine, *The Gnostic Gospels* (London: Penguin, 1982)

Patout Burns Jr., J., *Cyprian the Bishop* (London: Routledge, 2002)

Prestige, George Leonard, *Fathers and Heretics: Six Studies in Dogmatic Faith with Prologue and Epilogue* (London: SPCK, 1963)

Ramsey, Boniface, *Ambrose* (London: Routledge, 1997)

Raven, Susan, *Rome in Africa*, 3rd ed (London and New York: Routledge, 1993)

Reis, David M., 'Following in Paul's footsteps', in Tuckett, *Christology*, pp 287–305

Rives, J.B, *Religion and Authority in Roman Carthage from Augustus to Constantine* (Oxford: Clarendon Press, 1995)

Ruether, Rosemary Radford, 'Misogynism and virginal feminism in the fathers of the Church', in Ruether (ed), *Religion and Sexism: Images of Women in the Jewish and Christian Tradition* (New York: Simon and Schuster, 1974), pp 150–83

Runia, David T., *Philo and the Church Fathers: A Collection of Papers* (Leiden and New York: E.J. Brill, 1995)

Russell, Norman, *Cyril of Alexandria* (London: Routledge, 2000)

Stevenson, James, *The Catacombs: Rediscovered Monuments of Early Christianity* (London: Thames and Hudson, 1978)

Stewart-Sykes, Alistair, *The Lamb's High Feast: Melito, Peri Pascha, and the Quartodeciman Paschal Liturgy at Sardis* (Leiden: Brill, 1998)

Stramara, Daniel F., 'Double monasticism in the Greek East, fourth through eighth centuries', *Journal of Early Christian Studies* 6:2 (1998), pp 269–312

Sykes, Stephen, *The Identity of Christianity: Theologians and the Essence of Christianity from Scheiermacher to Barth* (London: SPCK, 1984)

Taylor, David G.K., 'The Syriac tradition', in Gillian Evans, *The First Christian Theologians* (Oxford: Blackwell, 2004)

Trigg, Joseph Wilson, *Origen: The Bible and Philosophy in the Third-Century Church* (London: SCM Press, 1985)

___, *Origen* (London: Routledge, 1998)

Tuckett, Christopher, *Christology and the New Testament. Jesus and His Earliest Followers* (Edinburgh: Edinburgh University Press, 2001)

Williams, Rowan, *Arius: Heresy and Tradition* (London: Darton, Longman and Todd, 1987)

___, 'Athanasius and the Arian crisis', in Gillian Evans, *The First Christian Theologians* (Oxford: Blackwell, 2004)

Wolfson, Harry Austryn, *Philo: Foundations of Religious Philosophy in Judaism, Christianity, and Islam*, 4th printing revised (Cambridge, Mass: Harvard University Press, 1968)

Wright, David F., 'The Apostolic Fathers and infant baptism', in Andrew Gregory and Christopher Tuckett, *Trajectories through the New Testament and the Apostolic Fathers* (Oxford: Oxford University Press, 2007)

Young, Frances M., *From Nicaea to Chalcedon: A Guide to the Literature and its Background* (London: SCM Press, 1983)

Primary texts in translation

Chapter 1

The Apostolic Fathers, trans Bart D. Ehrman, Loeb Classical Library (Cambridge, Massachusetts, and London: Harvard University Press, 2003)

Chapter 2

Acts of the Martyrs of Lyons and Vienne, trans Frederick Weidmann, in Richard Valantasis (ed), *Religions of Late Antiquity in Practice* (Princeton, NJ, and Oxford: Princeton University Press, 2000), pp 398–412

Athenagoras, *Supplication*; Athenagoras, *Resurrection*, ANF, vol. 2

Eusebius, *Ecclesiastical History* (EH): Eusebius, *The History of the Church from Christ to Constantine*, trans G.A. Williamson; revised Andrew Louth (London: Penguin, 1989)

Ignatius, *Letters*, in Bart D. Ehrman (trans), *The Apostolic Fathers*, Loeb Classical Library (Cambridge, Massachusetts, and London: Harvard University Press, 2003), vol. 1

Irenaeus, *Against Heresies*, substantial extracts translated by Robert M. Grant in

Irenaeus of Lyons (London: Routledge, 1997); remaining passages from ANF, vol. 1

Justin Martyr, *1 Apology*, *2 Apology*, *Dialogue with Trypho*, ANF, vol. 1

The Passion of Saints Felicity and Perpetua, trans Maureen Tilley, in Valantasis (ed), *Religions of Late Antiquity in Practice*, pp 387–97

Ps-Tertullian, *Against the Jews*, ANF, vol. 3

The Shepherd of Hermas, in Bart D. Ehrman (trans), *The Apostolic Fathers*, Loeb Classical Library (Cambridge, Massachusetts, and London: Harvard University Press, 2003), vol. 1

Tatian, *Discourse to the Greeks*, ANF, vol.2.

Tertullian, *Apology*, *On Idolatry*, *On the Military Crown*, ANF, vol. 3

Theophilus, *To Autolycus*, ANF, vol. 2

Chapter 3

Irenaeus, *Against Heresies*, substantial extracts translated by Robert M. Grant, *Irenaeus of Lyons* (London: Routledge, 1997); remaining passages from ANF, vol. 1

___, *On the Apostolic Preaching*, trans John Behr (Crestwood, NY: St Vladimir's Seminary Press, 1997)

Melito of Sardis, *On Pascha*, trans S.G. Hall (Oxford: Clarendon Press, 1979)

Philo of Alexandria, *The Contemplative Life, The Giants, and Selections*, ed and trans David Winston (Ramsey, NJ: Paulist Press, 1981)

The Shepherd of Hermas, trans Bart D. Ehrman, Loeb Classical Library (Cambridge, Massachusetts, and London: Harvard University Press, 2003), vol. 2

Tertullian, *Against Marcion*, *On the Flesh of Christ*, ANF, vol. 3

Valentinus, fragments in Bentley Layton (ed), *The Gnostic Scriptures* (New York: Doubleday, 1987), pp 229–45

Chapter 4

Acts of the Scillitan Martyrs, in Herbert Musurillo (ed and trans), *The Acts of the Christian Martyrs* (Oxford: Clarendon Press, 1972)

Apuleius, *The Golden Ass*, trans P.G. Walsh (Oxford: Oxford University Press, 1999)

Origen, *Against Celsus*, trans Henry Chadwick, Origen, *Contra Celsum* (Cambridge: Cambridge University Press, 1953)

___, *Commentary on John*, Books I and XXXII, trans Joseph Wilson Trigg in *Origen* (London: Routledge, 1998); other books in ANF, vol. 4

___, *Homily 19 on Luke*, trans Trigg in *Origen*

___, *On First Principles: Being Koetschau's Text of the De Principiis*, trans G.W. Butterworth (New York: Harper Torchbooks, 1966)

___, *On Prayer*, trans Rowan A. Greer in *Origen: An Exhortation to Martyrdom* etc. (New York: Paulist Press, c.1979)

___, Preface to the *Commentary on the Song of Songs*, trans Greer in *Origen: An*

Exhortation to Martyrdom

Philo of Alexandria, *The Contemplative Life, The Giants, and Selections*, ed and trans David Winston (Ramsey, NJ: Paulist Press, 1981)

Tertullian, *Against Praxeas*, trans Ernest Evans in *Tertullian Adversus Praxean liber: Tertullian's Treatise against Praxeas* (London: SPCK, 1948)

___, *Antidote for the Scorpion's Sting*, trans Geoffrey Dunn in *Tertullian* (London: Routledge, 2004)

___, *Apology, On the Shows, On Idolatry, On the Military Crown, On the Flesh of Christ*, ANF, vol. 3

___, *On the Apparel of Women*, ANF, vol. 4

Chapter 5

Alexander, *Letter to Alexander*, in NE

Arius, *Letter to Eusebius, Confession of Faith*, in J. Stevenson and W.H.C. Frend (eds), *A New Eusebius: Documents Illustrating the History of the Church to AD 337* (NE) 2nd ed (London: SPCK, 1987), pp 344–7

Athanasius, *On the Councils of Ariminium and Seleucia (De synodis)*, NPNF 2, vol. 4

Cyprian, *On the Lapsed, On the Unity of the Church, Letters*, ANF, vol. 5

Eusebius, *Ecclesiastical History* (EH): Eusebius, *The History of the Church from Christ to Constantine*, trans G.A. Williamson; revised Andrew Louth (London: Penguin, 1989)

___, *Life of Constantine*, trans Averil Cameron and Stuart G. Hall (Oxford: Oxford University Press, 1999)

Chapter 6

Athanasius, *Against the Arians* (selections), trans Khaled Anatolios, *Athanasius* (London: Routledge, 2004); the whole text is in NPNF 2, vol. 4

___, *Against the Greeks* [or *Heathen*], *On the Incarnation*, NPNF 2, vol. 4

___, *On the Council of Nicaea* (= *On the Nicene Definition*), Latin title *De decretis*, trans Khaled Anatolios, *Athanasius* (London: Routledge, 2004)

___, *To Serapion*, trans Khaled Anatolios, *Athanasius* (London: Routledge, 2004)

Ephrem, *Hymns*, trans Kathleen E. McVey (New York: Paulist Press, 1989)

Gregory of Nazianzus, *Orations*, 27–31 (= *First–Fifth Theological Orations*), trans Frederick Williams and Lionel Wickham, in *St Gregory of Nazianzus, On God and Christ* (Crestwood, NY: St Vladimir's Seminary Press, 2002)

___, *The Two Letters to Cledonius* (= *Letters* 101 and 102), trans Lionel Wickham, in *St Gregory of Nazianzus, On God and Christ* (Crestwood, NY: St Vladimir's Seminary Press, 2002)

Gregory of Nyssa, *Against Eunomius*, NPNF 2, vol. 5 (the parts of this work are numbered differently in the various editions; volume and page numbers of the Greek edition are also given for clarification: Gregory of Nyssa, *Contra Eunomium*, in GNO, vols. 1 and 2, ed W. Jaeger (Leiden: Brill, 1960))

___, *Against Eunomius II*, trans S.G. Hall, in *Gregory of Nyssa: Contra Eunomium II: An English Version with Supporting Studies: Proceedings of the 10th International Colloquium on Gregory of Nyssa (Olomouc, September 15–18, 2004)*, ed Lenka Karfíková, Scot Douglass and Johannes Zachhuber, with the assistance of Vít Hušek and Ladislav Chvátal (Leiden: Brill, 2007)

___, *Life of Macrina*, in Virginia Woods Callahan (trans), *Saint Gregory of Nyssa. Ascetical Works*, 2nd ed (Washington, DC: Catholic University of America Press, 1990)

___, *On ousia and hypostasis* (= 'Basil' *Letter* 38), in Maurice Wiles and Mark Santer (eds), *Documents in Early Christian Thought* (Cambridge: Cambridge University Press, 1975), pp 31–5

Chapter 7

Aphrahat, *Demonstrations*, NPNF 2, vol. 13

Athanasius (attributed to Athanasius), *The Life of Antony*, in Carolinne White (ed and trans), *Early Christian Lives* (London: Penguin, 1998)

Augustine, *Confessions*, trans Henry Chadwick (Oxford: Oxford University Press, 1991)

Basil, *Long Rules* and *Short Rules*, in W.K.L. Clarke (trans), *The Ascetic Works of Saint Basil* (London: SPCK; New York: Macmillan, 1925)

Clement of Alexandria, *Who is the Rich Man Who Will be Saved?* (= *The Rich Man's Salvation*), in Clement of Alexandria, *The Exhortation to the Greeks. The Rich Man's Salvation. To the Newly Baptized (fragment)*, trans G.W. Butterworth, Loeb Classical Library (Cambridge, Massachusetts, and London: Harvard University Press, 1919)

Egeria, *Travels*, in John Wilkinson (trans), *Egeria's Travels*, 3rd ed (Warminster: Aris and Phillips, 1999)

Gregory of Nazianzus, *Funeral Oration on His Brother Basil*, Oration 43, NPNF 2, vol. 7

___, poem *On His Own Life*, in Carolinne White (trans), *Gregory of Nazianzus: Autobiographical Poems* (Cambridge: Cambridge University Press, 1996)

Gregory of Nyssa, *Letters*, in Anna M. Silvas (trans), *Gregory of Nyssa: The Letters. Introduction, Translation, and Commentary* (Leiden: Brill, 2007)

___, *On Virginity*, in Virginia Woods Callahan (trans), *Saint Gregory of Nyssa. Ascetical Works*, 2nd ed (Washington, DC: Catholic University of America Press, 1990)

Jerome, *Letters*, NPNF 2, vol. 6

___, *The Life of Paul the Hermit*, in Carolinne White (ed and trans), *Early Christian Lives* (London: Penguin, 1998)

John Chrysostom, *On Saint Phocas* and *On the Holy Martyr Ignatius*, in Wendy Mayer (trans), *John Chrysostom, The Cult of the Saints: Select Homilies and Letters* (Crestwood, NY: St Vladimir's Seminary Press, 2006)

Theodoret, *Life of Symeon Stylites*, in *The Lives of Simeon Stylites*, trans Robert Doran (Kalamazoo, Michigan: Cistercian Publications, c.1992)

Chapter 8

Augustine, *On Christian Teaching*, trans R.P.H. Green (Oxford: Oxford University Press, 1999)

___, *Confessions*, trans Henry Chadwick (Oxford: Oxford University Press, 1991)

___, *Literal Meaning of Genesis* and *Unfinished Literal Commentary on Genesis*, in Roland J. Teske (trans), *Augustine: On Genesis* (Washington, DC: Catholic University of America Press, 1990)

___, *On the Trinity*, trans Edmund Hill (Brooklyn, NY: New City Press, c.1991)

Pelagius, as quoted by Augustine in *On the Grace of Christ and Original Sin* (*De gratia Christi et de peccato originali*), *On the Deeds of Pelagius* (= *De gestis Pelagii*); excerpts in Henry Bettenson (ed), *The Later Christian Fathers* (Oxford: Oxford University Press, 1970), pp 191–4

Chapter 9

The Council of Chalcedon's 'Definition of the Faith', in Richard Alfred Norris, *The Christological Controversy* (Philadelphia: Fortress Press, 1980)

Cyril of Alexandria, *An Explanation of the Twelve Chapters*, trans Norman Russell in *Cyril of Alexandria* (London: Routledge, 2000)

___, *Letters to Succensus*, trans John McGuckin in *St. Cyril of Alexandria: The Christological Controversy: Its History, Theology, and Texts* (Leiden and New York: E.J. Brill, 1994), pp 352–63

___, *Second Letter to Nestorius*, in Richard Alfred Norris, *The Christological Controversy* (Philadelphia: Fortress Press, 1980)

John Chrysostom, *Homily 17, On the Statues*, in Wendy Mayer and Pauline Allen (eds and trans), *John Chrysostom* (London: Routledge, 2000)

Leo of Rome, *Letter to Flavian* (= *The Tome of Leo*), in Richard Alfred Norris, *The Christological Controversy* (Philadelphia: Fortress Press, 1980)

Libanius, *Oration 11 On Antioch*, in A.F. Norman, *Antioch as a Centre of Hellenic Culture as Observed by Libanius* (Liverpool: Liverpool University Press, 2000)

Nestorius, extracts, in Richard Alfred Norris, *The Christological Controversy* (Philadelphia: Fortress Press, 1980)

Theodore of Mopsuestia, extracts, in Richard Alfred Norris, *The Christological Controversy* (Philadelphia: Fortress Press, 1980)

Chapter 10

The Book of Pontiffs (Liber pontificalis): The Ancient Biographies of the First Ninety Roman Bishops to AD 715, trans Raymond Davis (Liverpool: Liverpool University Press, 1989)

Gregory of Nazianzus, 'A morning prayer', 'A prayer the next morning', trans Brian Daley in *Gregory of Nazianzus* (Routledge, London, 2006), pp 170–1

___, *Poemata arcana* ('Poems on the Mysteries'), selection in translation in Gregory of Nazianzus, *On God and Man*, trans Peter Gilbert (Crestwood, NY: St Vladimir's Seminary Press, 2001)

Prudentius, *Cathemerinon*, in Carolinne White (trans), *Early Christian Latin Poets* (London: Routledge, 2000)

Socrates, *Ecclesiastical History*, NPNF 2, vol. 2

Sozomen, *Ecclesiastical History*, NPNF 2, vol. 2

Index

Abba, 9, 226 n.27
Abraham, 2, 14, 38, 60, 112
Acts of Paul and Thecla, 150
Acts of the Apostles, 1, 12, 19, 145, 147, 225
 n.1, 227 n.39, 227 n.54, 239 n.34, 245
 n.92, 253 n.5
Acts of the Martyrs of Lyons and Vienne,
 26, 229 n.7
Acts of the Scillitan Martyrs, 239 n.54
Acts of Thomas, 152
Adam, 10, 58, 61, 62, 63, 69, 92, 133,
 135, 141–2, 173, 182–8
Aetius, neo-Arian (d. *c.*366), 127–8
Africa *see* North Africa
agape, or love-feast, 27, 46, 88
agape-love *see* love
agenetos and *agennetos* (unoriginate,
 unbegotten), 115, 128–30, 132
Alexander of Alexandria (Bishop
 from 312; d. 328), 113–15, 120, 128
Alexander of Jerusalem, 99
Alexander the Great (356–323 BCE), 73
Alexandria, xvii, xviii, xix, 50–1, 53,
 66, 67, 73–8, 86, 99–100, 107, 113,
 120, 122, 124, 126, 189, 192–4, 196–8,
 200, 202, 205, 214, 217, 218, 234 n.19
Alexandrian Christology, 192, 196,
 200, 202, 205–8, 218, 224
allegory, allegorical, 71, 85–6, 171–5,
 191–2, 221
Ambrose (*c.*339–97), xviii, 111, 150,
 163–4, 167–8, 170–3, 176, 213, 222–3
analogy, 37, 58, 83, 112, 125, 129, 132–3,
 135–9, 142, 175, 177, 179–81, 191, 204

Anastasius I (Emperor 491–518), 217,
 257 n.27
Ancyra, 114
Ancyra, Council of (358), 124
Andronicus, 18
angel, archangel, 7, 62, 112, 149, 154,
 190, 223, 227 n.36, 235 n.47, 239 n.34,
 250 n.29
animals, animal nature, 19, 39, 82, 143,
 148, 175, 242 n.12
Annesi, 126, 156–7
anointing, 8, 15, 234 n.23
Antioch, xiv, xvii, xix, 4, 34, 73–4,
 98–9, 107, 109, 114, 124, 128, 159, 164,
 189–94, 197–8, 217, 253 n.4
Antioch, Council of (325), 114, 244
 n.84
Antioch, Council of (341), 124, 128,
 246 n.38
Antiochene school of theology/
 Christology, 191–4, 197, 199, 202,
 205–8, 216, 218
Antoninus Pius (Emperor 138–61), 34,
 229 n.9, 229 n.19, 231 n.47
Antony of Egypt (*c.*251–356), 99, 145–
 6, 148, 152–3, 155, 157–8, 160
Aphrahat (d. 345), 154–5, 250 n.30
Apollinarius of Laodicea (*c.*320–*c.*390),
 127, 135, 146, 192, 198, 199, 202, 207,
 247 n.58, 253 n.12, 255 n.39
Apollo, 36, 110, 224
apologists, 33–43, 75, 84, 88, 139, 148
apology, as literary form, xvii, 33–5,
 40–2